# Transforming from Consumer to Producer in 90 Days

## $aving Money, Energy, and Time Equals More Money to INVEST

### Darryl L. Wortham

authorHOUSE®

*AuthorHouse™*
*1663 Liberty Drive*
*Bloomington, IN 47403*
*www.authorhouse.com*
*Phone: 1-800-839-8640*

*First published by AuthorHouse    08/04/2011*

*ISBN: 978-1-4490-4523-4 (sc)*
*ISBN: 978-1-4490-4524-1 (hc)*
*ISBN: 978-1-4490-4525-8 (ebk)*

*Library of Congress Control Number: 2011910061*

*Printed in the United States of America*

# PART I – SETTING THE STAGE FOR SUCCESS AND FUN

*"Babe Ruth hit more home runs than almost everyone who played the game. He also struck out more often than anyone." ~ Anonymous*

## FOREWORD

The core concept is not just saving money, but saving time and energy as well. These savings are multiplied together, giving you more money to invest. To summarize, I created the equation: "**\$ET = M² to INVEST**", in which saving Money, Energy, and Time (\$ET) are multiplied to generate (=) More Money (M²) to INVEST. This equation is fundamental to your success!

You must be prepared to take action to start having enough money to accomplish your goals, to stop living paycheck to paycheck, and to retire early. If you are on course to make the same income as last year or, worse, facing declining take-home pay because of ever-increasing taxes, medical costs and declining economy, don't give up! Saving money, energy, and time will generate more money to invest—creating real income and wealth. Transforming you from consumer to producer!

You must expand yourself personally as well as enhance your inner and macro economics. Rather than growing a mega-company's revenue or the financial fortitude of millionaires' pockets, you are going to grow your own individual savings account, retirement plan, and children's college funds. This book is a guide to help you create a path and roadmap to a life of saving money, reducing debt, living efficiently, and creating wealth by investing within a reasonable timeframe.

Together we will examine several major building blocks that inspire and accelerate behavioral changes:

1. Why and how to change your behavior and lifestyle.
2. How to save money, energy, and time.

3. How to invest your money, energy, and time savings to improve your present situation and build for the future.
4. How to create and implement a transformation plan.

Progressive ideas and hilarious cheap strategies are also detailed. These are necessary to exceed your personal and financial goals. I want you to be thrilled about life, saving money for a brighter future, and early retirement, while having fun at the same time.

You may become frustrated when your dreams seem unattainable, but there are transformation plans that can be implemented within days, weeks, and years. In the pages that follow, you will find transformation plans with instructions on how to complete them. If you follow these guidelines, your transformation from consumer to producer will start or be accelerated today. You might find that the strategies and behavioral changes described herein require a paradigm shift—but change is a good thing!

**Expect to Win!** If we are to get anywhere beyond where we are today in any facet of life, we cannot stop dreaming; we cannot give up. Opportunities are everywhere! Live with thoughts of abundance and expect each day to be wonderful, perfect, and full of promise! Always start off thinking positively, with a smile. The plan is to take action, and "Better Sooner Than Later," so let's begin . . . .

**Where do you want to be in four weeks, three months, or five years?**

# THE TRANSFORMATION STRATEGY

*"It always seems impossible until it's done." ~ Nelson Mandela*

Now is the time to transform from a person consuming other people's products and services into that person from whom other people buy—going from *consumer* to *producer*. There are two critical definitions to understand:

- **Consumer:** someone who **trades money** for goods as an individual.[1]
- **Producer:** an individual or organization that **creates goods or services**.[2]

Your life goals will be challenging to accomplish if you insist on remaining a consumer, focused on daily wants and living paycheck to paycheck. It is better to choose to be a producer who invests in growing the economy and has the propensity to retire wealthy. The power to move forward comes from the shift to becoming a leader. This transformation will be explained in detail, along with illustrations and checklists you can use to create a personalized roadmap.

So, what constitutes an *investment*? Buying mutual funds, buying stocks, or paying off debt is investing. Investments also include starting a business and owning real estate. CDs and interest-bearing savings accounts are other examples of investments because the money is not spent on a want and will generate income. *Wants* can be dangerous, temporary temptations, because an unnecessary item will divert energy and time from a producer's more important activities, like living a greener, simpler life and donating to charities. Energy spent on physical fitness, mental health, and community volunteerism is a vital investment as well.

Your transformation may be subtle or dramatic. In many cases, little changes will happen quickly, but the overall result takes time. There will be positive changes within ninety days, but the main focus is on lifelong

---

[1]    Wiktionary at *en.wiktionary.org/wiki/consumer* (April 29, 2011)
[2]    Wiktionary at *en.wiktionary.org/wiki/producer* (April 29, 2011)

changes that enable you to achieve your goals. The long-term benefits will be substantial. To gauge the real progress of your accomplishments and transformation to a producer, action plan templates have been created.

They will be completed after **$ET = M^2$ to INVEST** strategies have been explained and checklists have been completed. Take a deep breath to relax, my friend! There is plenty to learn and enjoy before the planning session at the end.

**Present → Transforming → Future**

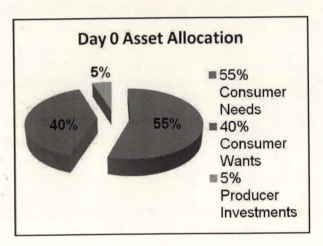

**to**

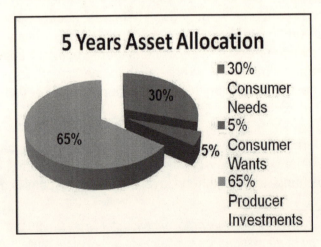

# HOW TO ENJOY THIS BOOK AND EFFECTIVELY APPLY THE LESSONS YOU LEARN

*"A pessimist sees the difficulty in every opportunity; an optimist sees the opportunity in every difficulty." ~ Winston Churchill*

## Wortham Logic

**N.W.A**: I was born in Da' Bronx and grew up in New Jersey. When somebody asks me where I'm from, I say, "I'm from the South . . . South Bronx." Yes, I still have a little bit of an accent and a lot of East Coast attitude to go along with it. What about it?!?!? My approach is in-your-face, and it is time to turn up the heat!

Growing up, I exhibited unique ideas, thoughts, and character. My friends called it "Wortham Logic." So if something in this book appears "out there," outspoken, or different, just call it "Wortham Logic." Consider starting your own local Wortham Logic Support Group; I would be honored.

I have had many life-changing experiences. My brothers and I are the

second generation to go to college. We are very proud of our parents for supporting us and impressed at what our grandparents sacrificed to put them through college. I am a bit of a ham (as you might notice in my photo below), so hopefully this book will be as entertaining as it is inspiring to you.

Brent, Darryl, and Kendall Wortham in 1973. Guess which one is me.

After attending college in Long Island, New York, my next stop was Colorado. It was there that I was encouraged to learn how special I was and to loosen up the East Coast attitude. I worked with some of the brightest and nicest people, which humbled me. Going to a country bar with a leopard-print hat and cowboy boots was one way to make a statement while still being respectful. Wearing a sari on a first date to a

Denver Grizzlies IHL minor league hockey game was very interesting. Guys, you try going to the bathroom during second period intermission in a sari without getting beat up and still have a fun date. Now that was an experience!

My journey continued to San Francisco, where I was pushed to gain my voice in a large urban city. Presently, I am a Senior Project Manager, implementing data networking services for Fortune 500 companies. I am also a successful real estate investor and mentor.

My amusing and embarrassing moments (we all have them) are shared to educate and make a point. I encourage you to have fun reading this book while you learn how to master being progressively "cheap" in order to move yourself closer to your dreams. I seek to continuously grow. You may be in a similar situation. I am here to empower you to be a change agent for yourself and others. Please allow me to coach and lead you through this transformation.

Live life with ample attitude to enable you to push yourself further than you've gone before while positively influencing others. My style is unique from what you may have seen in other financial and motivational books, but I urge you to stick with me. It is hard work swimming against the current, but once you get through the rapids, it will get much easier. The harder you work, the luckier you will be and the more opportunities you will be exposed to. You make your own luck!

## How to Read and Utilize the Book

The strategies and concepts introduced here are not just possible or probable but are also totally achievable and doable. Be creative and modify them to meet your needs. You are never too young or too old to learn to implement these techniques. Once you start identifying a few great strategies and ideas, implement them. Do not wait until you finish reading this book. Start hitting the base-hit singles that will soon be doubles, then triples, and eventually home runs! With teamwork from your friends and family, there will be multiple-scoring hits (RBIs). Grand slams will also be achieved!

Add your own ideas, notes, and to-do tasks in the margins. Feel free to take notes everywhere in the book. Highlight the important sections and sentences while you are reading. This will make it easier to reread the book and find the information that is most important to you.

For items that require a follow-up action, mark the page with a dog ear, sticky note, or paper clip. Then draw a line with an arrow ("→") pointing to it and write "**AI** _____" for action items. Once you complete an action item, check off the box, write what action was taken on the line, and unfold the dog ear on the page. Be sure to include specifics and completion date. Some examples are:

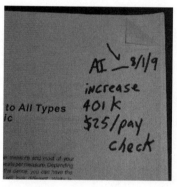

- Reduce premium cable/satellite TV package to basic and only one movie channel
- Increase 401(k) pre-tax contribution to 10 percent
- Volunteer monthly at favorite charity
- Take yoga class every Saturday

For items I think most readers will consider a personal action item, I took the liberty to add the note at the end of a paragraph that requires follow up:

❑ **AI:** _____

Here is an example of how to fill it in:

☑ **AI: <u>Set up S-Corp 6/10/12</u>**

There are also bulleted lists. If these items apply to you, check when completed and note the completion date. For example:

| | |
|---|---|
| ❑ Get Master's degree | __/__/__ |
| ❑ 6-Month Transformation Plan | __/__/__ |
| ☑ Pay off Credit Card A | *Chase* <u>10/01/11</u> |
| ☑ Add extra $100/month principal on home mortgage | *Wells Fargo* <u>12/15/11</u> |

If you have already completed an item or task, just check it off as finished, note the estimated completion date, and add "AC" for already completed:

> ☑ Home cleaning service every two weeks
> to once a month　　　　　　　　　**4/01/11** *AC*

Key tips and strategies are noted with "👍".

To assist you in remembering a strategy, tip, or idea, utilize a fun word association tactic called the "Phrase Game." The purpose of the Phrase Game is to help you remember a concept by correlating it to something unique and interesting. They will be shaded and can typically be found at the beginning of a paragraph. Some phrases will have pictures associated with them to drive the point into memory for those who are visual learners. Many phrases may be new to you, while some may appear out of place. Please be patient and remain open minded, because they should be apparent in the following paragraph. Play a game with the family or a friend to see how many you can associate correctly.

To eliminate any confusion because both footnotes and endnotes are numbered, footnotes are used for explanatory notes or references within the chapters. Endnotes are used for citied material at the end of each part. Endnotes content is in quotations, while footnotes are not.

To provide more guidance and instructions, a **tutorial workbook** has been created to compliment this book. There will be additional resources, supporting material, checklists, extra blank list sheets, and extra blank transformation plan sheets. The workbook format will be 8¼ by 11 inches so checklists, list sheets, and transformation plans will be a full page width. This allows extra space to write in more comfortably and extra lines to track more tasks. The Phrase Game answers are also included.

Be assured that all of the information you need to transform to a producer is in this book. Due to page count and size constrains, the supplemental workbook was created to consolidate all of the lists, sheets, and plans to be completed in a larger textbook format with more lines. This workbook will be available November 2011.

It's okay to laugh or shake your head at some ideas. Just push forward and enjoy. Keep this book readily available as a reference. For each issue, there will be an explanation and guidance provided. Opportunity knocks hardest in the face of problems! One should not lend out or borrow good "brain food" books. If it is worth reading, it is worth keeping!

## How the Book Is Organized

This book is designed to easily guide you through the transformation from consumer to producer and provides the necessary building blocks to make this complex process quite simple and efficient. There are ideas, strategies, and lessons learned, shared, and pulled together into lists and plans that you will personalize and execute.

This outline illustrates the major parts of this work:

I.  **Setting the Stage for Success and Fun:** Introduce the transformation strategy and how to effectively utilize this book.

II.  **You Are the Change Agent:** Why you should change, bold actions, benefits of being cheap, success principles, and gaining respect.

III.  **Generating Savings ($ET):** Define $ET=M^2 to INVEST and detail the techniques for saving your money, energy, and time.

IV.  **Your Investing Strategy:** Discover the power of money by investing in debt reduction, increasing savings, career or job, generating income, retirement plan, business, real estate, yourself, and the community.

    a.  Financial and Investment Strategies List
    b.  Passion List
    c.  Motivational Questions Lists
    d.  Behaviors, Habits, and Savings to Repeat List
    e.  Behaviors, Habits, and Expenses to Discontinue List
    f.  Smartphone Applications List
    g.  Delegation List
    h.  Educational and Knowledge Requirements List

    i.  Debts List
    j.  Specialties, Strengths, and Weaknesses List
    k.  Unemployment Course Correction Task List
    l.  Retirement Plans List

**V.  The Plan of Attack:** A producer's mindset puts your investment strategies into action by understanding the relationship between savings and investing, letting go, goal setting, creating a business plan, transforming to producer, and completing transformation plans.

    a.  Ten Steps to Start a Business
    b.  Financial Checklist for Starting a Business
    c.  Vices to Give Up List
    d.  Trading-Down Wants List
    e.  Living Paycheck to Paycheck
    f.  Needs List
    g.  Wants/Doodads List
    h.  Career and Financial Goals List
    i.  Life and Personal Goals List
    j.  90-Day, 6-Month, 1-Year, 3-Year, 5-Year, and 10-Year Transformation Plans

**VI. Beyond the Speed of Light:** Gives you the urgency and confidence to successfully execute your transformation plans while celebrating your success.

**VII. Your Support Structure and Resources:** Recommended readings, reference material, suggested training, websites, charitable organizations to volunteer at and donate to, and additional resources.

Read the chapters you are most interested in, as well as those that challenge you. Please take the time to read *Part II – You Are the Change Agent* because it lays the foundation for the rest of the book. You will find a plethora of information covering many diverse topics. The advice of many experts and various techniques has been consolidated here for you to learn from. Implement what you can apply to your life.

# ACKNOWLEDGEMENTS

*"Our background and circumstances may have influenced who we are, but we are responsible for who we become." ~ A. R. Bernard*

## Dedications

I believe there are several major influences that shape us, starting at a very young age and continuing throughout our lives for as long as we let them: 1) Parents and family, 2) Friends and peers, 3) Environment, 4) Genetics.[3] I truly cherish these relationships in my own life. A heartfelt "Thank You" goes out to these people and organizations that have deeply influenced me:

Barbara and Alonzo Wortham (Mom and Dad)

- All of my grandparents, aunts, and uncles
- My brothers, Brent and Kendall Wortham
- Best friends and their families in my neighborhood in Manalapan Township, New Jersey
- Pals and gals at the New York Institute of Technology
- Buffs classmates at University of Colorado
- Friends at AT&T Bell Laboratories and Lucent Technologies
- Friends and customers at Cisco Systems
- Hands-On Bay Area volunteers and staff
- Denver Young Democrats

---

[3]   There is not much we can do about genetics, but it can be a useful warning mechanism or planning tool.

The most influential people that have positively affected my growth are: Charles S., Claudia G., George M., Howard G., Jack R., James H., Jean N., Kelli F., Mark G., Marty G., Marty L., Mike F., Mike R., Richie B., Rick B., Rolf B., Roger Y., and Steve K. I am forever thankful for all of the wonderful relationships I've had with people who have had a deep, significant impact, encouraging me to learn more about myself so I could become a better stronger person.

## Special Recognitions

My life, knowledge, experiences, and successes are a strong driving force throughout this book. Like a thesis, many ideas have been consolidated to create a total picture and strategy with solutions for you. I have included poignant material from brilliant authors I have followed for years, those who have played a tangible, integral role in my success. All of these contributing authors, professionals, and organizations offer fantastic information. I highly recommend you add them to your collection of reference material:

➢ Adrian Flores at *www.AdrianFlorespresents.com*
➢ Dave Ramsey at *www.DaveRamsey.com*
➢ Dr. Christina Scott-Moncrieff, MB, ChB, MFHom
➢ Dr. Stephen R. Covey at *www.StephenCovey.com*
➢ His Holiness, the Dalai Lama and Howard C. Cutler, MD at *www.TheArtOfHappiness.com*
➢ Jeff Davidson at *www.JeffDavidson.net*
➢ John Dessauer at *www.theDessauerGroup.com*
➢ Mark J. Kohler, Attorney at Lawyer, CPA at *www.MarkjKohler.com*
➢ Pacific Power at *www.PacificPower.net*
➢ Timothy J. Mayclin, CPA at *www.TaxBizServices.com*
➢ Trent Hamm at *www.TheSimpleDollar.com*
➢ World Volunteer Web at *www.WorldVolunteerWeb.org*

There are many other authors and organizations that have provided excellent reference material. A complete list of authors, books, articles, and websites are compiled in *Part VII – Your Support Structure and Resources* at the back of the book.

Special thank you to these friends for suggesting I write this book:

- ➤ Claudia Gorham, "You are so cheap you should write a book about it."
- ➤ Erica Combs (*www.GoldenMastermind.com*), "You should write a book on your life experiences."

Finally, thanks to chief editor, Autumn J. Conley. Also warm thanks to contributing editors: Clarence Johnson, Claudia J. Gorham, Joanne Lamanna, Jean Nicolas, Rachel Lagunoff, Rick Bywater, Sharon R. Reaves, and Terri Williams.

*"Darryl Wortham applies street knowledge and personal wisdom to break habits and bring forth the producer and, perhaps more importantly, the saver in all of use. Darryl is concise and to the point. You won't be bothered with complex formulas or generalities found in some how-to books. Mr. Wortham takes you step-by-step through a series of habit breaking, thought provoking and frugal actions that can free you from being controlled by today's economic environment."*
*~ Rolf Behrsing (Silicon Valley Entrepreneur)*

# TABLE OF CONTENTS

# PART II – YOU ARE THE CHANGE AGENT

*"A leader has the vision and conviction that a dream can be achieved. He inspires the power and energy to get it done." ~ Ralph Lauren*

## CHAPTER 1: PREPARING YOUR MINDSET

This is a money management and investment book, but it is also a spiritual and wellness guide that may make you laugh, cry, or angry enough to take action. This is not a one-size-fits-all approach, but rather a blueprint to success. In other words, the implementation may need to be modified for your individual needs.

### Define and Prioritize Your Strategies

Take a moment to define your savings and investment strategies. This will assist you in deciding whether to proceed conservatively or with urgency. If you are playing catch-up, you may require major changes. For those nearing retirement, minor adjustments may be sufficient.

**Old Habits Die Easy:** This is the time to break old habits, routines, and rituals. Take educated and calculated chances. Restructure your schedule to meet the new priorities. Be at a constant high degree of alertness to find new areas to save money and the determination to find opportunities to invest. "[Dave Ramsey's] financial life began turning around when he took responsibility for it. Turning all your problems over to someone else treats the symptoms, not the problem."[1]

☝ Start the week on Sunday to get a jump start on your goals and competitors. Check e-mails, start reports, market to potential clients, update business plans, set out clothes, prepare lunches, etc.

## Implementing Multiple Investment Strategies Simultaneously

Attacking multiple fronts at once is the key strategy to quickly transforming to a producer while reducing consumer behavior. Investing while still reducing debt does drain some of your resources to pay off debt sooner. It may be difficult to prioritize the goals of competing needs among wants, needs, and investments. However, the benefit lies in investing in growth opportunities like stocks and mutual funds that may outperform loan interest rates. In most retirement plans, funds have the added advantage of growing tax deferred with a compounding effect. The other critical factor you must immediately address is the feeling of contributing to society by being a producer. This will help lift the weight off your shoulders and reduce stress while raising your confidence that it can be achieved—even if dramatic cuts in living expenses and taking on an extra job or two are necessary. Part-time and seasonal jobs are good too. Don't think about how it looks . . . just do it!

👍 There must be some positive reinforcement to saving, so I also suggest funding investments as well. Place some of your investments in the type of accounts or plans you know you will have access to with little or no early withdraw penalties. *Bad debt* is not an income or appreciating asset, while *good debt* is an income or appreciating asset. Bad debts includes credit cards, personal car loans, furniture store credit, and school loans. Good debt would include business loans and home mortgages. Borrowing for appreciating assets and for the opportunity to increase income may be a vital part of your plan to create wealth. The ultimate goal is to become financially free by having enough money and resources to retire without depending on anybody else. Position the transition to investing in good debt when most of the bad debt is paid off.

It is wise to start with a few strategies and begin implementing them immediately. You will begin to see results within one to six months. Continue evaluating your needs over the next year and implement many more strategies that pertain to you. Within three years, implement most strategies in your transformation plan.

A few **financial and investment strategies** include (all may not apply to you):

| | | |
|---|---|---|
| ❏ Good health and wellness program | _/_/_ |
| ❏ Short-term aggressive cost savings | _/_/_ |
| ❏ Long-term sustainable expensive reductions | _/_/_ |
| ❏ Bad debt reductions | _/_/_ |
| ❏ Good debt reductions | _/_/_ |
| ❏ Amassing an emergency fund | _/_/_ |
| ❏ Investing in increasing income | _/_/_ |
| ❏ Investing in retirement plan | _/_/_ |
| ❏ Investing in college fund | _/_/_ |
| ❏ Investing in home ownership | _/_/_ |
| ❏ Investing in real estate | _/_/_ |
| ❏ Investing in business(es) | _/_/_ |
| ❏ Volunteering regularly | _/_/_ |
| ❏ Giving to nonprofit charities | _/_/_ |
| ❏ _____ | _/_/_ |
| ❏ _____ | _/_/_ |

So this is a done deal, right? Focus on paying off debts, building an initial emergency fund, and starting a retirement plan before starting a college fund. Even after all this, you still need to be more aggressive. Accelerate your investing in businesses, real estate, and stocks. Do not hesitate. The time is NOW!

## Imagine the Possibilities

With an open mind and passionate heart, anything can be achieved, no matter how unbelievable or unobtainable it may seem at first. Move forward to fulfilling your desires and succeeding in achieving your life goals while becoming financially free. This is a starting point, not a stopping point. This may also be a transition point in your life. **Everything is possible and imaginable**, so don't limit your possibilities! Take a chance to experiment with new ideas. Imagine things that were thought of as impossible: VCRs, microwaves, laptop computers, small cell phones, iPods, landing on the moon, and even an African-American president.

John Lennon (1940-1980) Strawberry Fields Forever Memorial,[4] Wikimedia Commons, CMKillagb

👍 Think positively and act accordingly. Believe in yourself and your support system. Look at your present situation with optimism, not hopelessness. It is never too late! How many sporting events have you seen when the team that was far behind came up from nowhere to win the game in the last quarter, period, or inning? Comebacks happen every minute of every day. Why not make a comeback of your own?

On November 1, 2009, in the fourth game of World Series, the New York Yankees were playing the Phillies in Philadelphia. In the top of the ninth inning, the Yankees were ahead four to three. The Phillies scored a run to tie the game at four-four, leaving the Yankees one last inning to win the game without going into extra innings. The first two batters were struck out. The last hope, Johnny Damon, had a full count (three balls, two strikes). With two outs, Damon hit a single and then stole not one, but two bases. After a few more batters, the score was seven to four, Yanks! The Phillies had to score three runs to tie and four to win, but the Yankees retired all three batters to ultimately win the 2009 World Series over the 2008 champions, seven to four.[5] I joined the game late and all the excitement of that Series was at the tail end. I only had to watch the last twenty minutes of the game to enjoy it!

*"The only way things are going to change for you is when you change." ~ Jim Rohn and Chris Widener*

---

[4]   A must-hear song ("Imagine" by John Lennon): *www.youtube.com/watch?v=-b7qaSxuZUg* (April 29, 2011)

[5]   Congratulations to San Francisco Giants—the 2010 World Series Champions!!!

# CHAPTER 2: HOW TO CHANGE YOUR BEHAVIOR AND LIFESTYLE

*"Move out of your comfort zone. You can only grow if you are willing to feel awkward and uncomfortable when you try something new."*
~ Brian Tracy

## What Is Your Passion?

**"Kiss Me, and I'll Kiss You Back."** Kiss yourself. Yes, kiss yourself often. Do it now! Lift your arm and kiss your forearm or the back of your hand. It's not weird, although kissing your ankle is a little creepy and may require a bit more flexibility than you are used to. Kiss yourself at least twice a week, but more often is recommended. Who better to love you than you? I am always my first choice before I seek love from others.

❏  **AI:** _____

Besides yourself, there are other things worthy of your <u>love and support</u>: education, green initiatives, first responders, military troops, nature, God, spirituality, coaching and leading people, real estate, working out, running, climbing, gardening, teaching, traveling, volunteering, giving back, pushing the envelope, valuing other people's cultures, children, family, and life, just to name a few. Your passions need to be inclusive, not exclusive. The more the better. What falls on your list of loves? What are you most passionate about?

**I am passionate about** _____
_____
_____
_____

❏  **AI:** _____

Use your burning passions to make the appropriate changes. Show people what you are passionate about, and maybe you'll inspire them too! Always be friendly and positive. You never know where it will take you or what you will reap from it!

## Motivational Questions

Changes need to be made. These questions will be your ammunition if you still wonder why changing your behavior and lifestyle are necessary. If applicable, write your answers to the right of the questions.

High-level **life motivational questions** (all may not apply to you):

1. How can I help others?
2. How can I still have fun doing and having less?
3. How do I ask for help when I am overwhelmed?
4. How do I find the time to plan for my future?
5. How do I gain muscle strength while losing fifteen pounds?
6. How do I get control of my life back?
7. How do I live a happier life?
8. How do I say "No" to my family, friends, and myself?
9. What do I need to do differently to change my life?
10. When can I retire, or can I ever?

❑ **AI:** _____

Detailed **financial motivational questions** (all may not apply to you):

1. Can I fully fund my retirement plan?
2. How can I afford the increasing healthcare costs?
3. How do I convince my family to change our spending habits?
4. How do I pay for my children's college?
5. How do I pay off these credit cards quicker?
6. How do I tell my family we cannot afford that trip or event?
7. Is Social Security the biggest part of my retirement plan?
8. Should I answer the phone, or is it another debt collector?
9. Why do I have to wait until my kids are out of school to invest in my future and myself?
10. Why I am over my head in debt?

❑ **AI:** _____

What other questions do you need to answer?

_____

_____

_____

                                        ❑ **AI:** _____

Your changes will make you fiscally stable and help you move toward becoming financially free with a large investment portfolio.

## Taking Charge of Your Destiny

**Ask, and You Shall Receive:** If you do not want it or expect it, you will not get it. Now remove the word "not." If you do want it or expect it, you will get it.

Stop blaming the government, the Great Recession, and Wall Street for your situation. These are external forces that, in general, should not affect your day-to-day activities and core principles. Say, "I will *not* be affected by downturns in the global economy."

                                        ❑ **AI:** _____

Take charge of your unnecessary purchases, extravagant lifestyle, and lack of retirement fund. Wants are okay sometimes, but just keep shifting the percentage from wants to needs. The migration will be from consumer "wants" and "desires" to your "needs." Let's add in another factor called "**investments**." This will mean drawing resources from both needs and wants. Then transform "needs" to "investments" into the micro-economy as a producer. This is how you will invest your money, energy, and time as a true contributor to your "Inner Economy."[6] You will create an industry shift!

With your reenergized desire to reach your destiny, start moving forward toward it with confidence. "To begin with the end in mind means to start with a clear understanding of your destination."[2] Slow and steady wins

---

[6]     *"Inner Economy"* consists of your personal and household finances that drive your profit and loss balance sheet. These are all of the funds that you received weighed against your expenditures.

the race, but you need to be in the game to win. "Failing does not make anyone a failure, but quitting most certainly does . . . and quitting is a decision."[3]

*"Nothing will change in your life until you identify who is responsible for your behavior. YOU!" ~ A. R. Bernard*

# CHAPTER 3: CHALLENGING TIMES REQUIRE BOLD ACTIONS

*"Some people say I have attitude—maybe I do. But I think you have to. You have to believe in yourself when no one else does . . . that makes you a winner right there." ~ Venus Williams*

To exceed your expectations within an accelerated timeframe you must be bold and act with: <u>cheapness</u>, <u>attitude</u>, <u>urgency</u>, and <u>intensity</u>.

## The "C" Word

Cheap is <u>not</u> the "C word." Say it in public: "Cheap!" Do not censor yourself. Being cheap does not mean stealing, cheating, or using shenanigans. There is no free lunch. Sacrifice will be required. Good things do cost money, and you are worth it. I by no means subscribe to the philosophy of mooching all the time. You need to pay people for their valuable time with monetary rewards. I prefer not to piecemeal my way through life, always looking for freebies.

Cheap is getting the best value for your money and time. It also encompasses actions that best utilize your energy. Please do not view being cheap as penny pinching, cutting corners, or being thrifty just to save a few dollars and cents. If you call me a tightwad, cheapskate, or miser, you can expect a karate chop in the back of the neck (a soft one). If you encounter naysayers, just remember they are misdirecting their own inadequacies and projecting them onto you.

This is a strong, powerful movement to change our spending habits to create "millionaire" behavior. If you are having financial problems, it is most likely not because you are overspending, but because you are simply off balance. A sharp downward shift toward cheapness may be required to remain in equilibrium and make the shift to contributing more than taking.

**Cheap is chic!** Keep reminding yourself that you choose to be cheap. It is not necessarily that you cannot afford it; being cheap is a lifestyle. Being practical in how you spend your money is for no one to question.

Cheapness will supercharge you to spend way less than you earn. This may not be easy, but it can be simple if you allow it to be. Focus on your near-term goals with immediate returns. This will make it easier to formulate the economic decision to save and consume less.

Feel good about passing on something you really do not need. While nothing should be wasted, that does not mean you need to keep everything for yourself. Selling these wants and unused items will generate income for you and meet someone else's need in the process.

## More Attitude Required

**B.A.D. can be Good**: When running up a mountain, if you take the wrong trail, you can always run back to get on the correct path. However, if you hike slowly, by the time you get near the summit, you might get snowed out because it took too long. Then you have to turn around before reaching your goals. You want to reach the summit ahead of schedule . . . and without frostbite.

Longs Peak Mountain in Colorado. The north facing ascent is a two-day climb that requires climbers to sleep roped in on a small ridge.

👍 "Psychologists tell us you can actually change your attitude by changing your posture and speed of movement."[4] People that produce walk faster than the average person and maintain a long, cool stride with style and grace. There seems to be a slight spirit in the way we walk. "Throw your shoulders back, lift up your head, move ahead just a little faster, and feel the self-confidence grow."[5] People will notice you, so it is important that you notice and acknowledge them with a friendly smile and eye contact. Be prepared to make it a big smile to show off your pearly whites.

~~NO GRAY~~: My coming from the East Coast, people are more black and white in their opinions and are comfortable with their choices.

There is not much room for gray areas. What will enable you to make faster, more decisive decisions and immediately take action on them? Thrive to gather the knowledge and make quick, educated decisions by being decisive.

## Do It Now with Urgency

**Moving Forward to Your Dream in a New York Minute:** I am often very forward, logical, blunt, and tough. At other times, I am thoughtful, sensitive, savvy, and caring. My personality enables me to be productive in all aspects of my life, as I am able to adapt in different situations and connect with people of diverse backgrounds. Some of these traits can benefit you to expand your network and access opportunities while quickly advancing forward.

Now is the time to make rapid decisions without regret. Don't procrastinate or over-process everything; too much boiling turns the pasta to mush! But you need to move from procrastination and over-processing to production activities that generate results. You can make corrections as needed, but if you feel you have nothing to correct, then you have not started yet.

**"Move it, move it, move it!"** You need to pick up the pace or get run over. Since time is constant, we need to get more accomplished in the same time. Use your passion for success to compel you to fully implement these strategies and ideas faster. It is okay to fail. Please learn from your mistakes and setbacks. If at first you don't succeed, try, try again—but try faster. Apologize for your mistakes after crossing the finish line.

Moving fast may carry risks. "In our daily life, problems invariably arise. But problems themselves do not automatically cause suffering. If we can directly address our problem and focus our energies on finding a solution. For instance, the problem can be transformed into a challenge."[6] "Despite the universal unpleasantness, there is little doubt that our suffering can test, strengthen, and deepen the experience of life. Dr. Martin Luther King, Jr. once said, 'What does not destroy me makes me stronger.'"[7]

Resistance is often a response to change or challenge. This is a natural behavior, but it can be overcome. Use urgency as a driving force to quickly implement the required changes. Compulsive wants and non-productive habits must be stopped! Please try to have fun during this transformation! "Why is my health and marriage failing?" "Why did I not get that promotion at work?" "Why am I living paycheck to paycheck when I make over $100,000 a year?" The answers to these questions may reveal why you are not as happy and fulfilled as you would like. Use this as the fuel to take calculated risks at an accelerated pace.

## Live Life with Intensity

**INTENSE:** Be positive where you are today, for you are alive. Have a fire in your stomach. Think positive thoughts, have positive emotions, speak positive words, and take positive actions to create the positive results you deserve.

Stay <u>intense</u> and focused, like an arrow. Start small with completing tasks and objectives as you work toward accomplishing well-defined

goals. Follow a divide-and-conquer approach of breaking an objective into manageable tasks to accomplish each goal. Identify, isolate, and attack your problems to achieve positive results. Be intense with passion and dedication. Be enthusiastic and persistent with intensity!

John McGinley (Edgler Foreman Vess) and Molly Parker (Chyna Shepherd) in "Intensity"© 1997 CPT Holdings, Inc., Courtesy of Sony Pictures Television, All Rights Reserved

As stated by Well and Balanced Lifestyle, "For those of us with tighter purse strings, think outside the box. Look for the abundance of opportunities. Remember 'there were more millionaires created during the Great Depression than at any time in history.' Opportunities do not just come in an upward economy, there are many more in a downward economy. How do you recognize these opportunities? How can you capitalize on these opportunities and make them benefit you? Be open minded, think outside of your comfort zone. See how you are living now and what would you like to change if you could. Rethink how you are living. Dream your desires every day. Think positive. Many will rise above their financial situations in these times precisely because of these challenging times have caused them to think in a different way."[8]

**Pete and Repeat**: If you find something that works, continue to do it. Repeat good behavior. Then do it again and again. We gain confidence by repeating behaviors that become familiar and that lead to success, which will be repeated. Repeating this sequence will implant the habit of recurring positive results.

**List of behaviors, habits, and savings to <u>repeat</u>:**

_____     _____
_____     _____
_____     _____
                                      ❏ AI: _____

Discontinue behaviors, habits, and expenses that do not contribute to your goals and are instead holding you back.

**List of behaviors, habits, and expenses to <u>discontinue</u>:**

_____     _____
_____     _____
_____     _____
                                        ❏ AI: _____

*"There are risks and costs to action, but they are far less than the long-range risks of comfortable inaction."*
*~ President John F. Kennedy*

# CHAPTER 4: THE IMPORTANCE OF STRENGTH AND CHARACTER

*"A man can fail many times, but he isn't a failure until he begins to blame someone else." ~ John Burroughs*

## Honor with Principles

Your character is one of your best tools to drive necessary change. You must honor your obligations and commitments by paying all bills on time unless there are extreme unforeseen circumstances. This includes credit cards, mortgages, rent, utilities, college loans, personal loans, child support, parking tickets, and so on. If not yesterday, you will start today, not tomorrow. If you have debt, money issues, marital problems, bad credit, and lack of retirement funds, there is only one person to blame, and that person is you.

❑   **AI:** _____

Many people don't take responsibility for their situation. You must no longer blame it on your spouse, parents, employer, the recession, unexpected bills, high debt, or anything else. Most financial problems are due to poor decisions and the failure to plan in advance. If you refuse to own up to your past mistakes and failures, it's unlikely you'll change your behavior in the future. It's vital to openly confront past mistakes and shortcomings.

"Discipline is the basic set of tools we require to solve life's problem. Without discipline, we can solve nothing. With only some discipline, we can solve only some problems. With total discipline, we can solve all problems. Problems call forth our courage and our wisdom. It is through the pain of confronting and resolving problems that we learn."[9] "By bringing about a certain inner discipline, we can undergo a transformation of our attitude, our entire outlook and approach to living."[10]

## Success Breeds Success

If you keep doing the same things you've been doing, you should expect the same results. Your decisions create the life you want. Ask yourself, "How can I maximize this situation to improve my life and reach my desired goals?" Every idea and strategy you implement and master will strengthen your thinking and build confidence. Give this a 110 percent effort! "Success is often inconvenient. The more you are willing to be inconvenienced because you are committed to something, the more success you will experience in life. This is a contract you make with yourself."[11]

The more experience you have, the easier this will get. You will feel more comfortable and move faster. It will be like running downhill with long strides, gaining speed efficiently without falling. Continue to practice these strategies even if you are unemployed, retired, on disability, in a down economy, in an up economy, out of the "rat race," or recently won the lottery. In most of these situations, you should be intensifying more of these methods.

**"Play, and you got to pay."** Risky behavior may come at a price. Past poor judgments, decisions, and mistakes will need to be acknowledged and corrected. This will be tough. Are you up to the challenge?!?!?

When I was ten, I had a life-threatening accident, and my right arm was almost completely severed. I was teasing my brother in the house and running to go outside to avoid his clutches, but I was not paying attention. My arm went through a front door storm-glass window. Thank goodness my mom was on duty as a First Aider (a.k.a., EMS) and reacted quickly to save my life and the use of my arm. Also thanks to the local Manalapan First Aiders that arrived within minutes to administer emergency care.

Because of the excellent First Aiders, surgeons, nurses, and therapists, my arm was saved. Rehabilitation was long and challenging, but it worked out great, and I regained over 95 percent of the use of my arm. I was even able to play football in high school and currently work out with 75-pound-each dumbbell chest press, 150-pound lats pull down, and 155-pound seated rows!

Little Darryl in Atlantic City (AC) with vanilla fudge. "Turn your scars into stars," said Robert H. Schuller.

The accident was my fault. The lesson is that reckless behavior has consequences, but with hard work and determination, mistakes can be trumped with positive results and tremendous success.

## Top of the Food Chain

**"It's good to be the King/Queen."** Your strength and power to succeed are important in implementing these strategies. Be the aggressor to achieve your goals. We all have different sensitivities and personalities, but as intelligent human beings, we are at the top of the evolutionary chain and have goals. When I need motivation, I watch *Wild: Predators at War* on the National Geographic Channel just so I don't forget that I'm not prey! Which are you?

- Are you a lion or a hyena, killer or scavenger?
- Are you a shark or seal, predator or prey?
- Are you the chaser or being chased, cheetah or gazelle?

Wikimedia Commons, Robek

👍 Being at the top of the food chain comes with responsibilities to respectfully care for others by being socially conscience. People can hear your thoughts and read your mind. I use this technique to remove my negative thinking when walking amongst people. I do not know if this is true, but anything is possible. If nothing else, your posture, demeanor, and facial muscles will show your upbeat attitude toward people. Be positive to people, and they will reciprocate and open up new opportunities for you. You never know who you are talking or standing next to, so be careful.

Great White Sharks are at the top of the food chain, but Killer Whales (Orcas) have intelligence coupled with excellent communication capabilities, along with family structure. They have learned to turn sharks upside down to place the shark in a state of "tonic immobility" to drown them. As apex predators,[7] Orcas prey on sharks, whales, string rays, seals, and fish.

Wikimedia Commons, Mila Zinkova

NOAA's National Marine Mammal Laboratory, Holly Fearnbach

## "I'm Special and Deserve Respect"

**I rule!** Say it: "I am very important and matter!" and positive things will happen to you. Pro means good. We are pros, not cons. Mainly, "pro" is a positive prefix for something proactive or professional, so that is all I need to see to make a swift decision. Begin with a positive mindset. Act first and ask questions later.

One of my favorite sayings when I am wading through a crowd is **"Look out! Hot stuff, comin' through! Hot stuff! Look out!"** Say it

---

[7]   *"Apex predators* have virtually no predators of their own, residing at the top of their food chain. Apex predator species are often at the end of long food chains, where they have a crucial role in maintaining the health of ecosystems." (Wikipedia, *www.en.wikipedia.org/wiki/Talk%3AApex predator*, April 29, 2011)

[8]   View "!!Killer Whale vs Great White Shark!!" video, abcNEWS.com: *www. youtube.com/watch?v=SS6NjdGLVZs*

standing tall while watching where you are going. Do not say it too loud, but with confidence and a crisp smile. Let them know you're coming through whether they like it or not.

**"I am better than you all. I can outrun you. I can out-read you. I can outthink you. I can out-philosophize you. I'm going to outlast you."** Be proud of where you came from, where you are today, and where you are going. Use your uniqueness to build confidence and command respect.

*"There are two ways of exerting one's strength: one is pushing down, the other is pulling up." ~ Booker T. Washington*

# CHAPTER 5: BEING PROGRESSIVELY CHEAP IS FUN!!!

*"Enjoy the little things, for one day you may look back and realize they were the big things." ~ Robert Brault*

## The Benefits of Being Cheap

In order to enhance your current budget strategy and possibly grow to being financially independent, you have to change your perspective of money and needs. Cheapness is a tool that will shift the power to control your current budget strategy into your hands from your past spending habits. It will save you money, energy, and time that can be better directed toward achieving your dreams.

Summary of the <u>benefits of being progressively cheap</u>:

- You will have the drive to negotiate a better deal or just say "No."
- Save money on things and save time on events.
- Make life simpler and reduce clutter.
- Focus on value, not quantity.
- Shift the "wants" resources and energy to "needs."
- Shift the "needs" resources and energy to "investments."
- Shift from consuming to producing.

Being cheap is not taboo, but very cool, progressive, and acceptable. Really challenge yourself to get the maximum benefits and rewards of living a cheap lifestyle. "Kick butt!" For many of us in the analytical, process, and management professions, this is a great outlet to exercise the creative side of our brains while being logical. You only have to convince yourself, and others will follow your lead.

**Be at Peace with Being Cheap:** Enjoy your cheapness. Embrace it. Celebrate your newfound cheapness and what returns it will generate for you. This is your excuse to make drastic course corrections and behavior modifications.

Cheapness is a means to an end. After a while, you, your partner, and your family will not even notice it. Your friends will grow to accept your new way of life. Stand tall, and if your white socks show a little too much from your high-water pants or you are missing a shirt button, so what? Act like you just lost the button that morning and move to a more meaningful topic. If you are confident and moving faster to accomplish your dreams, that is all that matters.

There is a difference between being cheap and being frugal. For me, being cheap is more a frame of mind and an active way of life, while being frugal is a more passive approach. Cheapness is bolder, forward thinking, more extreme, and less compromising than frugality.

**"To be cheap or not to be cheap? That is the question."** Being cheap is an aggressive and abrasive means of cutting waste. There is a time and place for <u>not</u> being cheap. At times, tone down or hide your cheapness. Cutting corners does not always save money, and in the long run, it may cost you more. Being the King or Queen of Cheap is an art form. These progressively cheap strategies are vital for transforming you from a consumer to producer, so you are going to bend, not break to achieve your dreams.

It is understood that money will need to be spent to operate a business and to build a suitable retirement fund. Utilizing cheapness will generate the required savings to be invested. Some of these expenditures may be costly but necessary. This will be a judgment call, and with discipline, you will make the appropriate choice. Over time, these choices will become less stressful, and people will accept your guilt-free decision that fits your new producer lifestyle.

## Simplicity

Living simply and minimally are key factors of being cheap. Focus on the little things that bring you a tear of joy and make you really smile. What makes you laugh out loud? I bet they are not expensive items. Excessive or compulsive spending behaviors are keeping people in the rat race. Do you really need to buy that luxury car? Are all of those shoes necessary? Wouldn't that money be better spent growing your mind, retirement account, or business?

"Simplicity may mean the following to you: more time, less stress, more leisure, fewer bills to pay, less clutter, less to clean and maintain, great peace of mind, and spirituality."[12] Living a simpler life, which is good for Mother Earth, will produce long-term savings benefits that outweigh short-term gratifications. Reflect on the things you did not get: that house, car, shoes, date, or piece of artwork. Did it really matter? It is in the past, and there are infinite opportunities today and tomorrow.

**"Forget About It!"** Extravagant toys include cars, bikes, cycles, RVs, boats, airplanes, vacation homes, exotic pets, and high-maintenance people. Expensive habits include flying unnecessarily; extreme sports; collecting wine, artwork, or antiques with no intent to sell; hobbies; shopping; and hoarding. Let's say this together: "NO!" It may take time, but be persistent by letting pricey toys go.

There is no such thing as a vacation home. A second home is an investment. Your dream should be to first be happy where you live and then own one or more investment properties.

❏ **AI:** _____

Get the fever to save and invest. Sometimes you will go into survivor mode and be insanely cheap; use this to your advantage. This may be the extra attitude you need to leap ahead of others.

## Cheap Pride

Be proud to be cheap! Open up your window and scream, "I am cheap and am dang proud of it!" You may not love every aspect of cheapness, but change and sacrifice are not easy. Being the first is fun to implement a progressive idea. Saving five bucks at the store with a promotional coupon is fun, but saving fifty dollars by comparing online deals is a bigger thrill. Saying "No" to yourself on "wants" so those savings will be invested to build a better future is a rush, and it reinforces the benefits of being cheap.

# CHAPTER 5: BEING PROGRESSIVELY CHEAP IS FUN!!!

Create a fun game of being cheap with your family and friends. Make your own narrative blog of why you need to be cheap to become a producer. Start your own local cheap meet-up, mailing list, and/or wealth-building group.

❏ **AI:** _____

Acts of cheapness do not mean you are poor, and they are not reserved for people with lower incomes. You don't have to be rich to have fun or contribute to society. "What makes life interesting is not the things you own, but the sh*t that you do."[13]

**Take the Cheap Pledge:** "I will be cheap to reach my goals faster and achieve my dreams sooner as a producer."

❏ _____        _____
    **Signature**                                    **Date**

*"If your only goal is to become rich, you will never achieve it."*
*~ John D. Rockefeller*

# Part II: You Are the Change Agent Endnotes

1    Dave Ramsey, *The Total Money Makeover: A Proven Plan for Financial Fitness*, Thomas Nelson Publishing, 2003, pp. 8, 84.

2    Stephen R. Covey, *The 7 Habits of Highly Effective People*, Simon and Schuster, 1989, p. 98.

3    Chris J. Snook with Chet Snook, *Wealth Matters: Abundance is Your Birthright!*, LifeSuccess Publishing, 2007, p. 180.

4    David J. Schwartz, PhD, *The Magic of Thinking Big: Acquire the Secrets of Success…Achieve Everything You've Always Wanted*, Simon & Schuster, 1987, p. 62.

5    Ibid.

6    His Holiness, the Dalai Lama and Howard C. Cutler, MD, *The Art of Happiness: A Handbook, for Living,* permission of Riverhead Books, imprint of Penguin Group (USA) Inc., 1998, p. 154.

7    Ibid, p. 201.

8    Well and Balanced Lifestyle.

9    M. Scott Peck, MD, *The Road Less Traveled: A New Psychology of Love, Traditional Values and Spiritual Growth*, Simon and Schuster, 1978, pp. 15-16.

10   Dalai Lama and Cutler, p. 15.

11   Adrian Flores, *Transforming Your Community Through Dance: 13 Steps to a Great Dance Team*, Mitchell Levy, 2009, p. 58.

12   Jeff Davidson, *The Joy of Simple Living: Over 1,500 Simple Ways to Make Your Life Easy and Content*, Rodale Press, p. 3.

13   Stuart Schuffman, *Broke-Ass Stuart's Guide to Living Cheaply in New York*, Falls Media, 2008, p. 10.

# PART III – GENERATING SAVINGS ($ET)

*"Obstacles don't have to stop you. If you run into a wall, don't turn around and give up. Figure out how to climb it, go through it, or work around it." ~ Michael Jordan*

## CHAPTER 6: $ET = M² TO INVEST

This philosophy is all about multiplying savings: **Money, Energy, Time ($ET) that equals More Money (M²)** to **INVEST!** I am happy to provide details on how to manage your money, energy, and time to maximize your valuable resources, all while saving your money and reducing stress. There are millions of people who consider themselves rich, yet they do not have the energy, time, and knowledge to manage their investments to become wealthy. BUT WE WILL!

**$ET=M² to INVEST** is the formula to successfully generate enough

money not only to improve your current situation, but also invest in a brighter future. Say, *"I will be SET to have enough MONEY to INVEST!"* Constantly comparing yourself to others is a losing battle, and you have an inner war to win reaching your dreams! You must set your own goals.

## Saving Money, Energy, and Time

The first side of the equation is how to save money, energy, and time ($ET). This is the foundation to generating more money while your income remains the same. Enjoy this journey from being in the rat race and living paycheck to paycheck to a future on the "fast track." How? By investing in the stock market, commodities, businesses, real estate, community, and yourself. Move material items that do not help you accomplish your goals, those that do not directly affect $ET=M^2$ to INVEST, to the "Wants/Doodads List" to be sold.

Cheapness will be the primary tool to save money, while productivity will save energy and efficiency gets back time. Each element of the **$ET** equation will be discussed in detail:

- Saving your money strategies and ideas in *Chapter 7: $aving Your Money (Stretching the Dollar)*
- Saving your energy in *Chapter 8: Saving Your Energy (Increase Productivity)*
- Saving your time in *Chapter 9: Saving Your Time (Increase Efficiency)*

## More Money

You can spend your way out of a recession. True or false? The answer is BOTH: <u>false</u>, because spending on consumable items will leave you in a recession; <u>true</u>, because spending on producing items will grow you out of a recession. Yes, you need to spend money to make money. However, you need to spend it on producer investments such as education, marketing, new tools, updated systems, and professional services that will grow your business revenue as well as profitability. These are not expenses like consumable items, but tax write-offs like capital investments.

Apply cheap money-saving techniques and master the investment success-minded principles in your everyday activities. Most of these **money**-saving techniques and strategies will also save energy and time. **Energy** and **time** are the <u>great multipliers</u> part of the equation that generate **more money (M²)** from what was saved. Ideas and how-to instructions are documented throughout the book. Many activities and chores may be the most cost effective by employing an expert like legal services, maid services, sewing, repairing cars, washing cars, building decks, painting, etc.

## Invest

I encourage you <u>not</u> to **spend,** <u>but</u> to **INVEST!** Smart shopping means determining if items are an investment or not:

- Home improvement store cart: Does it add value or just beatification?
- Grocery cart: Is it healthy or junk food?
- Department store cart: Is this business attire or sportswear?
- Loan statement: Good or bad debt?
- Credit card statements: Needs or wants?

Have a plan in place to invest these savings immediately. Invest your time and energy in fulfilling a dream that makes you truly happy. Create a consistent pattern of expense reduction activities and steady rhythmic flow to funnel these savings into investments. Throughout this book, there are lists to be completed to help you achieve this. The list providing examples of how to document this move from "wants" to "needs" to "investment" is in *Part V – The Plan of Attack, Chapter 21: Setting Goals, Creating and Documenting Your Goals*. Investment strategies are detailed in *Part IV – Your Investing Strategy*. Consistency and efficiency will allow you to focus as a productive person. You will be effective in executing your action and business plans.

Income tax refunds, sale commissions, raises, bonuses, overtime pay, and royalties are not a free pass to spend. Do <u>not</u> spend these in advance. Have a plan for this money so that it will be instantly applied to reducing or eliminating debt, funding your retirement plan, and/or growing your business. Know when these funds are coming in and treat them like any other money that gets you closer to your dream. This will be your real long-term producer reward and not just an impulse consumer buy. Use this as an opportunity to make up lost ground and leapfrog ahead.

❑ **AI:** _____

*"Acting now generally beats waiting."* ~ *Charles Schwab*

# CHAPTER 7: $AVING YOUR MONEY (STRETCHING THE DOLLAR)

*"The very first step to building wealth is to spend less than you make." ~ Brian Koslow*

## The Value and Cost of Money

Value money and what joy plus comforts it provides to you and the ones you love. Your relationship with money is important. Do not focus on the negative aspects of money or the flashy people you see on TV. **Money** has value because it builds bridges, hospitals, schools, manufacturing plants, and windmills. Money also fixes your teeth, buys your kids' clothes, feeds the less fortunate, and will find the cure for cancer and other diseases over time. Make savings a habit and then a learned behavior.

**Treat Money with Respect:** In your wallet or purse, keep the dollars neat. Line them up from highest to lowest with the highest denominations toward the back so you are less likely to give them out by accident. Be sure the bills face the same direction, toward you and right side up so it is easier to read the denominations.

❑ **AI:** _____

👍 Search for banks that have no or low ATM fees. Also many banking institutions will provide a certain dollar amount that they will reimburse each month; even better, some institutions reimburse all ATM fees. Be informed as to any limits on the maximum free withdrawals per month. Investigate large national or regional banks as well as brokerage firms and credit unions.

👍 Always double-check the ATM dispenser to verify that you did not leave any bills behind. Count the number of bills by listening to the bills hitting the front dispenser wall. Then count them again before putting them in your purse or wallet. When getting money out of an ATM, many bills are new and will stick together. This can cause you to mistakenly give somebody two twenties when you mean to give them only one. How many times has this happened to you? As soon as the money is dispended from an ATM, crumple the crisp bills and then shuffle them like a deck of cards. Then crumple them one more time and shuffle again before putting them in your purse or wallet. Watch your back so you do not get robbed!

✋ If you get a "Dispensing Error" using an ATM, verify that you received the correct amount and compare the receipt withdraw amount with the cash received. I know from firsthand experience that this is very important because I once received only $60 instead of the $100 I requested. Even though the machine receipt stated it gave $100, there was an error. The next day, I called the vendor number on the ATM receipt and then my bank. They both verified that there was an error, and my $40 was immediately added back into my account. One final note: Do not check your cash balance on an ATM because there is usually a charge if you are not a member of that banking institution. Keep all of your ATM receipts because they will show your balance and any dispensing errors.

**Consider the Opportunity Cost:** "Before you make a purchase, give yourself some financial coaching. Think about your money as an investment. 'Should I take this money and invest in new clothes, give to a charitable cause, or even give to self in the form of a Roth IRA earning annual interest (so that I can give to charity while I'm retired)?' It's important to realize that 'money,' in and of itself, is of no value. The true value of money all depends on the value of what it purchases or the value we give to it. Considering the opportunity cost of a purchase gives you better discernment and puts your spending-habits into perspective."[1]

Calculate the interest rate charged for a desire. Is it a 5 percent, 10 percent, or 25 percent annualized interest rate? You need to consider this when charging a "want" item or service to a credit card or getting a loan. Ask yourself these types of questions:

- "Do I need to get that fully loaded SUV at 10 percent?" Probably not. Pay cash for add-ons and install them yourself.
- "Do I need to go to Disney World at 20 percent?" Probably not. Pay cash for vacations and make them a business trip.

- "Do I need that huge wedding at five-star hotel at 30 percent?" Probably not. Have the wedding in your back yard or at a park.
- "Do I need to buy that investment property with $200 monthly positive cash flow[9] in an appreciating market near good schools at 5 percent?" Possibly, but do your due diligence first.

👍 The best ways to save money when buying items are:

1. Get the full usefulness and life from the item before replacing it.
2. Retire the item to another use, sell it, barter with a neighbor, or get a tax write-off.
3. Buy only when you truly need things.
4. Purchase at the best value.

**Reset Existing Replacement Dates:** Eliminate any artificially set or preexisting dates to replace an item. Delay replacing the item by pushing back the replacement date one or several years. The goal is to break rituals that are more a habit than practical. For cleanliness, maintenance, and safety, do what is the best practice or recommended by the manufacturer, but look for creative ways to save money by prolonging its usefulness.

Organize your clothes so the most recently worn items are kept at the front of the closet and the tops of your drawers. The oldest worn clothes should be kept at the back or bottom. The 80/20 rule usually applies with what clothes you wear: 20 percent of clothes are worn 80 percent of the time. At least twice a week, to add flair and attitude to your outfits, grab from the back of the closet or bottom of the drawers rather than going to the store to buy something new. This is like wearing an artifact you are proud of.

❑ **AI:** _____

---

[9]    *Monthly positive cash flow* is when the rent collected is more than all of the expenses including mortgage(s), HOA dues, property management fee, utilities, etc. The vacancy rate, tenant placement fee, and maintenance cost also need to be factored in.

If you are fifty years or older, join the American Association of Retired Persons (AARP) to take advantage of their discounts and benefits at *www.aarp.org*.

❏ **AI:** _____

## Household

### Home Ownership and Renting

👍 "The U.S., which is home to only 4.5 percent of the world's population, consumes 25 percent of the world's energy."[2] Live a simple, meaningful lifestyle by managing a modest household. When you purchase or move into a new home, do not buy a lot of new furniture and extras for it. Bring over all of your furniture, appliances, and artwork from your previous residence. My current home still looks much like my first house. I still have the booming speakers and equalizer from my college days. My shoes and sneakers are still in plastic milk crates. There is no reason to ever get rid of them, and they will outlast me as family heirlooms.

👍 If you have a large sailboat and a small family or none at all, consider living on the boat where it is docked. Purchasing a house boat is another option. This is not for everybody, but in some areas of the country it is a terrific alternative. If you can get a permit to claim the boat as your residence, it will save a lot of money.

If you rent a house or apartment, renegotiate your current home lease to reduce the rent and maybe have the owner pay utilities. If you are happy there, do not push it. As a renter, you absolutely need renter's insurance!

❏ **AI:** _____

👍 If you or your child is in college, investigate if it is cheaper to live on or off campus. Take into account food and utilities, as well as a car (if they even need one) with maintenance and insurance costs.

## Home Improvements and Repairs

If you can pay cash or get a short-term, no-interest credit card or loan, it may be wise to remodel your existing home versus buying a bigger home. Verify that any remodeling will add value to the home. Keep the modifications or additions simple and modest. When you get ready to sell your home, others may not pay a premium for over-the-top taste. Be sure your home improvement would be viewed as an improvement by most potential buyers!

### Improvement Ideas

Some enhancements that add value include remodeling the kitchen and bathroom. You might also consider adding a deck, porch, skylight, ceiling fans, attic fan, walk-in closets, kitchen island, bathroom, and extra parking spaces. Easy improvements like painting the exterior and interior, converting the den to an office, and converting the basement to a bedroom (with closet and window) are great too. Also make the basement, college child's room, loft area, space under stairwell, or even the attic into a functional office space. With the trend of more people telecommuting and the growth of at-home businesses, this can be a very valuable investment that will improve the appeal of your home.

❑ **AI:** _____

👍 Upgrade the garage only if it will increase productivity or enhance trade work business that will produce income. If you have a three- or more car garage, convert the third or more stalls into an office or additional bedrooms.

Here are energy improvement hints from Pacific Power's "Bright Ideas: A Helpful Guide to **Managing Energy Use in Your Home**:"[3]

❑ Move your equipment to a dedicated circuit. Avoid putting sensitive devices like personal computers, routers, modems, and DVD players on the same circuit as printers, copiers, furnaces, air conditioners, and kitchen appliances.

❑ Install a quality surge protector or uninterruptible power supply (UPS). You may also consider main circuit panel protection. At a minimum, you need a surge protector.

❑ Use timers to turn lights on and off when you're away from the home or on business trips. Plug-in timers cost ten dollars or less. Inexpensive wall-switch timers can be used to control lights and fans in bathrooms.

❑ Replace or repair an appliance if the cord is frayed. Never exceed the cord load rating. If the cord or its plugs become hot, unplug the cord immediately and use a heavier cord.

You might also upgrade to an energy efficient refrigerator, as well as washer and dryer. A front-loading clothes washer uses less water and is easier on clothes than a top loading agitator washer. Put front loaders on a pedestal or blocks if bending over is a health issue for you.

❑ **AI:** _____

👍 Add an attic fan to lower the whole house temperature by turning it on at night to draw in the cooler air. Also consider purchasing a few portable rotary fans, which can be useful in the warmest areas where you spend the most time. To keep the cold breeze out and warm air in, consider buying a floor tube insulator that goes at the bottom of the externally facing doors. These can be purchased at discount stores and come in styles to match a variety of décors.

**Duct tape** is your friend! This is the universal tool of the handy man. Masking tape and plastic ties are also useful repair tools. These can be great for quick fixes to secure items together and long-term maintenance for extending the life of items at relatively no cost.

👍 If you are skilled in a trade, it is best to do the simpler improvements yourself. Working on larger projects for the cost of a case of beer, iced tea, and pizza, you might be able to convince neighbors and friends to help you move, paint, or build a deck . . . and be sure to return the favor someday. Trade services in which you have skills and experience that are of value to others.

For home improvement ideas for investment properties that may also apply to your personal home, go to *Part IV – Your Investing Strategy,*

*Chapter 15: Investing in Real Estate, The Benefits of Real Estate Investing, Techniques to Fix Up Investment Properties.*

## Working with Contractors

Get at least three competitive free bids from contractors. Require referrals and follow up with their clients for feedback on past job performance. It is important to avoid lawsuits and liens against your home. Investigate their history involving workers' compensation claims and pending and prior legal actions. When interviewing contractors, verify that they are licensed, insured, bonded, and certified. *Bonded* coverage is important because it ensures that if you pay your contractor and they do not, in turn, pay their sub-contractors who did the work, you cannot be held legally responsible to pay the sub-contractors.

❑ **AI:** _____

👍 In almost every case, do not pay for labor before the work is complete. Large jobs can be divided into smaller deliverables and payments. It may be necessary to pay for material, but this should not be the norm. Get receipts up front.

👍 Pay for pizza on Friday or buy lunch one day a week for the work crew. This is the right thing to do for people working hard for you, and it will keep them out of the bar during lunchtime.

👍 Be sure the contract mandates that onsite workers will not do anything you find offensive such as obscene language, alcohol consumption on or near the job site, smoking in the home, or working without their shirts.[10]

For more details, go to Contractors State License Board, "What You Should Know Before Hiring a Contractor" at *www.cslb.ca.gov*.

---

[10]   No bare beer bellies or "plumber's crack!"

## Home Maintenance and Upkeep

### A Clean House Is a Happy House

Neat freaks and clean freaks are a great match. Clean and messy people may not be the ideal match. Do not be an enabler of sloppy people. "Less mess means less stress."[4] Guess which one I am: clean, neat, or messy? Not only should you keep your own home environment clean, but also all other places you visit like hotel rooms and a friend's home.

Cleaning up saves you money by prolonging the life of items. Keep a nice absorbent washcloth in the bathroom sink drawer. After you wash your hands or face, clean inside and around the sink. This has two benefits: 1) It helps to dry up water to prevent the build-up of mildew, and 2) The sink will be clean for your guests. The cleaner an item is, the nicer it looks, even if it is inexpensive or old.

❏  AI: _____

👍 Please use nontoxic, biodegradable environmentally safer cleaning products. Many stores carry brands like Clorox Green Works® (*www.GreenWorkscleaners.com*) and Simple Green® (*www.SimpleGreen.com*) all-purpose nontoxic products. Also consider store brand environmentally friendly cleaning products.

👍 Getting 10 percent discounts on dry cleaning[11] for ten items or more is a must. Save up and take in expensive items like comforters, dresses, suits, and items needing sewing repair. This can result in big savings. In many cases, you do not have to wash a clothing item after wearing it once. Set a criteria for when something is dirty, and you can tell how many times you can wear it before it needs to be washed or dry cleaned. Keep a recently worn clothes pile in the bedroom closet, a dirtier pile by the hallway closet for working out, and then finally transition into a laundry pile.

---

[11]    Go to green dry cleaners that use nontoxic chemicals.

Have people remove their shoes or sneakers before walking on your carpet or rug. You can create small signs asking people to "Please Remove Your Shoes" or "No Shoes." Definitely ask ladies to remove their pointy high heels before walking on your hardwood floors. A shoe tree at the front door is a good subtle hint. Have a bunch of furry, comfortable slippers on hand for those who might want to borrow them to protect your floors and their feet warm.

❑ **AI:** _____

👍 You can install plastic walk strips in the front door walkway or foray. For heavy traffic carpets, place a wool blanket or simple rug over it. This will protect the carpet from getting soiled and worn. Wash the blanket/rug every month in the washing machine on delicate or permanent press setting. This is cheaper than shampooing the entire carpet every year or replacing it.

## "You Need to Get Some Smell in Your House"

Modern buildings are constructed so tightly that pollutants are trapped inside. Is your household air full of pollutants from litter box smell, pet odors, pet dandruff, sick family members, smokers, garbage, mold, mildew, etc.? Have you ever noticed how refreshing the air is when you are in the mountains or by a waterfall, or how revitalized you feel after a thunderstorm? Clean air is vital to a healthy body. Many basic illnesses of the body and psyche are the effects of advancements that have led to restriction of the body's biological ability to heal itself.

"There are usually at least 4,000 negative ions per cubic inch (which is optimal) in outside environments. On the other hand, there are only a couple hundred negative ions per cubic inch in the typical indoor household. The reason indoor environments lack the electrical 'nutrients of the air' that we need is that today's 'airtight' homes and buildings prevent them from treating the air inside."[5]

👍 Nature's own cleansing process, which uses activated oxygen, is left outside. Oxygen is a powerful detoxifier, and when it is lacking, toxins begin to devastate body functions. When your body has sufficient oxygen, it thrives. We can look at oxygen deficiency as the single greatest cause of all disease.

I recommend the XygenAir™ Home Purifier, which brings nature's way of rejuvenation inside and can reenergize a household with freshly oxygenized air for greener living. The XygenAir purifier is the size of a smoke detector. For details or to order, go to:

*www.xediadirect.com/dwortham* and click on "Clean Air."

❏ **AI:** _____

## The Home

To focus where to save on your utility bill, here is residential energy use percentages (based on a 1,500-square-foot home with family of four for a six-month period):[6]

| | |
|---|---|
| • Electric heat | 42% |
| • Central air conditioning | 21% |
| • Electric heat pump | 10.5% |
| • Water heater | 10% |
| • Refrigerator | 4% |

## The Kitchen

**"Let's play a game."** Twenty percent of refrigerator energy use is due to opening the doors to load and unload food or browsing the contents. See how fast you can open and close the door without the condenser turning on. Just open the door as little as possible to see what you need to get and make quick choices. Close the door quickly with your other hand or foot and verify that it is tightly sealed. Put a sign on the refrigerator door handle saying "CLOSE ME" or something funny. If you have kids, let them create the sign, as this will get buy-in from your family.

## Kitchen energy-saving checklist and energy efficiency tips:

❑ "Keep the refrigerator and freezer coils clean (on the back or bottom of the appliance). Check and vacuum them at least twice a year. Carefully read the owner's manual instruction first."[7]

❑ "Don't install your refrigerator next to the dishwasher or oven. The heat produced by the dishwasher or oven can add heat to the refrigerator if it's placed nearby, causing the fridge to run more frequently to maintain the low temperature. Look for (or rearrange, if possible) a kitchen layout that places the fridge far away from the dishwasher and oven, allowing the fridge to be significantly more energy efficient."[8]

❑ Recycle your used refrigerator or freezer and get a rebate from the energy company which could be about thirty-five dollars. Rebates are also available for washers, dryers, furnaces, air conditioners, water heaters, insulation, and multi-speed pool pumps. If an appliance is in good working condition, sell it.

👍 To air-dry dishes open the door of the dishwasher at the end of the last rinse cycle, and pull out the dish racks to dry naturally rather than using the heated dry cycle. To reduce the dry time down to an hour or two, run a portable fan on the dishes while they sit on the racks. You can also hand dry them with a towel.

👍 Small tabletop toaster ovens are more efficient than the larger conventional ovens.

Here are more kitchen energy tips from Pacific Power's "Bright Ideas: A Helpful Guide to **Managing Energy Use in Your Home**:"[9]

👍 Keep your refrigerator or freezer full, but not overloaded. Place foods slightly apart on shelves, making sure they do not block the unit's interior air vents.

👍 Cover all liquids stored in the refrigerator. Moisture can be drawn into the air, forcing the unit to work harder.

👍 Make sure the freezer door seals properly.

👍 Top-freezer models are typically the most efficient. Features like automatic icemakers and through-the-door water and ice service add 10 to 25 percent to the cost of operation.

👍 Run the dishwasher only when it is full to capacity, but not overloaded. Choose the shortest wash cycle that will clean your dishes, and scrape off food before loading it into the dishwasher. Wait to use your dishwasher until nighttime on hot and cold days. You will avoid or add heat in the house during the hottest or coldest time of the day.

👍 Consider using a microwave oven, small portable electric frying pan, grill, or broiler instead of the oven.

In most cases, gas appliances are more energy efficient than electrical. This is true for ranges, ovens, water heaters, and clothes dryers. Depending on the price of energy in your state, natural gas can be three to six times less expensive than electricity. Gas is also typically much cheaper than oil and coal heating.

👍 Wash off soap suds with cold water, which will save money versus rinsing with warm or hot water. This is what dishwasher and washing machines do.

👍 Make only enough ice to fill the tray halfway, and then turn it off until more ice is needed. Clean the tray with mild soap and dry it with a towel. This way the ice will not taste funny toward the end, forcing you to throw it out.

Here is a way to extend the life of used ice cubes. If you have a beverage and have some ice left, put the glass in the freezer. Cover the glass so food does not fall in it. Then when you want a drink, the glass will be frosty with the partially used ice, and since the glass is cold as well, less ice will be needed.

👍 Experiment with making a solar oven. They can reach temperatures of 275 degrees. This is free energy, but it can take twice as long to cook food. For building instructions, go to *www.solar-cooking-oven.com* or *www.SolarCooking.org/plans*. Also consider buying a glass solar tea pot with a clear lid to brew loads of inexpensive iced tea.

👍 When drinking tea at a restaurant or café, wrap the teabag in a paper napkin and take home to be used again for hot or iced tea. When there is no more potency left in the tealeaves use them as compost in your garden.

**Take Two**: Never again buy paper napkins! Instead, mooch a bunch of them when you get take-out. Always ask for extra or grab them yourself. When dining at restaurants and fast-food places, get a few extra paper napkins too. Just use what you need and take home the rest. If a napkin is only slightly used, take that home as well. You can save money and trees at the same time.

❑  **AI**: _____

Just for fun, make a game out of matching certain napkins when eating a specific group for food cooked at home. For example: for a hamburger, use McDonald's or Wendy's napkins; for a burrito, use Chipotle Mexico Grill or Taco Bell napkins; and for lasagna, use Pizza Hut or Round Table napkins.

👍 If you have a big paper towel and don't need the whole thing, tear it in half to double its use. Heck, use these free napkins in the place of paper towels. For one person, these napkin and towel ideas will save at least three dollars a month. For a family of four, this can represent annual savings of about $150 per year.

## The Bathroom

"Verify or install energy-efficient shower heads and faucet aerators. They reduce the amount of water released from a tap by up to 50 percent, with almost no noticeable difference in pressure. Turn off faucets immediately after use."[10] A low-flow showerhead's pressure offers the same great shower using less water.

❑  **AI**: _____

👍 Showers are great for getting clean (Duh!), relaxing, and relieving stress or pain, but they should be limited between five to ten minutes. A quick two minute shower can be refreshing too. "For each minute you shorten a shower, you save 2.5 gallons. Fixing running toilets or dipping faucets can save thousands of gallons per month."[11]

**"Don't drop the soap."** Get a hanging soap rack for the shower. Also, get soap dishes with water drains for the bathroom and kitchen sinks. These will allow the soap to last longer because it will not be exposed to water from the shower or sitting in water on the countertop. An additional benefit is to stop mildew buildup in the corners of the shower and countertops. Of course, use the soapy water in the soap dish before it gets stagnate.

👍 If you spread out and hang bathroom towels, they will dry quicker and avoid getting smelly or mildewing. Hang them over the shower rails or add more towel racks if you have a large family. This will keep them fresh longer and reduce the need to wash them as often.

👍 Do not totally dry yourself off before putting lotion on your body. If you remain slightly damp, the lotion will spread more uniformly, soak into your skin better, and seal in the moisture that is on the surface of your skin, saving you lotion and ultimately money.

We all know to squeeze as much toothpaste out of the tube as possible by curling up the end of the tube. A binder clip can be used to keep the tightly wound end of the tube from unrolling. Here are some really cheap ways to get the most out of items:

- 👍 Unscrew and remove the top or cut open the end of the tube to squeeze out all of the toothpaste.
- 👍 To get all of the lotion out of the bottle, unscrew the lid and hit the bottom like a ketchup bottle.
- 👍 For lipstick, remove the pump and use your finger to get at all of it.
- 👍 For makeup, use a brush to scoop out the remaining product.

## The Bedroom

👍 "Install a ceiling fan to circulate air above the area you spend most of your time in like living room and bedroom(s)."[12] "In the winter, set the fan to run in a clockwise direction, which will pull the warm air from the ceiling and push it down toward the floor, subtly raising the temperature in the room and causing the heating system to work less. In the summer, have the fan run in the opposite direction, which will maximize the circulation benefits of the fan."[13]

**Waterbeds are Retro!** Prevent heat loss and reduce your waterbed electric use by up to 20 percent by covering it with a bedspread or comforter when you get out of bed. Adding an extra blanket or quilt will act as a thick layer of insulation to save more energy. Cleaning the waterbed lining and putting treatment solution in the water every six months or as directed will extend the life of the mattress and prevent bacteria growth. Before leaving the house, verify that any electric blankets[12] and heaters are turned off.

Want to take an active part in recycling? Bring existing bedroom sets, furniture, fixtures, and clothes back in style. Disco is back! If you don't believe me, you should check out the disco ball above my black lacquer waterbed!

## The Outside

👍 "Pool and spa covers save energy and money. Seventy percent of pool heat loss is by evaporation. Using covers can keep the water ten degrees warmer, which reduces pool heating costs up to 90 percent."[14]

Don't waste water by overwatering your lawn. Zero landscaping is great for the environment and saves on lawn maintenance. Up to half of the water is lost to evaporation, wind, or overwatering. Another contributing factor is water loss on sidewalks, driveways, and buildings. Only an inch of water a week is necessary in many regions. Keep a five-ounce cat food or tuna can outside, and if rain or watering fills it to the brim each week, you don't need to water anymore or not at all.

❑ **AI:** _____

👍 Buy or borrow a manual push-blade mower that is nice and quiet to operate. Push mowers with no engine are easier because there is little maintenance, no preparation, and no gas necessary. As an added

---

[12]   Do <u>not</u> put electric blanks on a waterbed!

benefit, they are cleaner for your lungs, and you get a total body workout to boot. I borrowed one of these from my friend Charlie when I lived in Denver. My grandmom had one of the first electric mowers with an extension cord, which I ran over. Nowadays, there are cordless electric mowers, but I prefer the push-blade mower because it gives you a workout and is quiet.

👍 "If you want lighting on at night for safety reasons, consider photocells (daylight sensors), which automatically turn lights on at dusk and off at dawn. For ten dollars or less, you can buy a screw-in adapter for either inside or outside lights. Also consider timers if lights only have to be on part of the night."[15] Any light toward the sky only contributes to light pollution and wastes money on energy.

## Lights

Replace all incandescent bulbs with compact fluorescent light (CFLs) bulbs. CFL bulbs use 75 percent less energy and last ten times longer. Replacing incandescent bulbs with compact fluorescent lamps provides the same amount and quality of light. By just replacing a 100-watt incandescent bulb with a 25-watt CFL can save at least ninety dollars over the life of the bulb. They work in most standard light fixtures.

❏  **AI:** _____

"Operating up to 1,000 degrees, halogen torchiere lamps burn a lot of electricity and can pose a serious safety threat. ENERGY STAR® torchieres run cooler at around 100 degrees and reduce energy by over 80 percent."[16] I've burnt my arms way too many times on a halogen lamp. Replace the lamp with a CFL bulb!

Get free energy-efficient light bulbs or discount coupons from your local power company. Instant rebates are available at participating retailers. A negative byproduct of CFLs is that they contain a small amount of mercury, so proper disposal is a concern. Many home improvement stores will accept them to recycle at no charge.

👍 "The cost effectiveness of when to turn off lights depends on the type of lights and the price of electricity. Incandescent lights (or bulbs) should be turned off whenever they are not needed. Nearly all types of incandescent light bulbs are fairly inexpensive to produce and are relatively inefficient. Turning the light(s) off will keep a room cooler, an extra benefit in the summer. Therefore, the value of the energy saved by not having the lights on will be far greater than the cost of having to replace the bulb."[17]

👍 "The cost effectiveness of turning fluorescent lights off to conserve energy is a bit more complicated. For most areas of the United States, a general rule-of-thumb is that if you leave a room for more than fifteen minutes, it is probably more cost effective to turn the light off. In other words, if you leave the room for only up to fifteen minutes, it will generally be more cost effective to leave the light(s) on. In areas where electric rates are high and/or during peak demand periods, this period may be as low as five minutes."[18]

"Use energy-saving holiday light strands. They reduce energy consumption by as much as 90 percent compared to the traditional lights and can last up to 50,000 hours."[19] That is a lot of blinking! Buy solar power lights or decorations that consume no electricity.

❏ **AI:** _____

👍 Go out of your way to read with natural light and turn off the interior lights. Pull the blinds up or shades back and read by the window. Also read outside on the porch, in the back yard, or at the park. If your electrical lighting bill is high, you can read at a friend's home, at the library, in the car, or even at work during off hours.

**Heating and Cooling**

Fireplace and wall heater unit pilot lights use energy and will heat the room during the summer. This little amount of heat can warm up your place and cost more money than you think. A 400-BTU-per-hour unit costs over five dollars per month. Turn off the fireplace pilot light during the summer and other warm days. Furthermore, turn off all pilot lights when on extended trips.

❏ **AI:** _____

Here are even more **energy-saving tips**:

❑ Keep furnace and air conditioner <u>clean</u>, <u>lubricated</u>, and <u>properly adjusted</u>. Clean and replace the filter regularly, as instructed by the owner's manual. A clean and well-maintained unit runs much more safely, efficiently, and inexpensively. Dirty filters reduce air flow and make your furnace work harder. This could save you up to 5 percent.

❑ <u>Install a programmable thermostat</u>: You can set it to turn the temperature way down or up at pre-programmed intervals when you're at work or sleeping. It'll cost you only $75, and it could save you over $150 a year.

❑ Use <u>insulating</u> shutters, blinds, or drapes and keep them closed during winter nights to help keep the heat in. They provide an extra layer of insulation. Close them in the summer or on overcast days to help keep the room cool during the day, saving 8 to 15 percent.[13]

☝ <u>Free heat</u>: Use passive solar heating on sunny days to help warm up rooms. Open the shutter, blinds, or drapes on windows facing the sun to let the sunlight in the room. Then at night, close them to retain indoor heat. Up to 15 percent of your heat can escape through unprotected windows.

## Appliances

Buy energy-efficient appliances! More efficient appliances cost more, but you make up the extra cost and then some over the life of the product. This can save tons of cash on your power bill. **Home energy-saving checklist and appliance energy efficiency tips**:

❑ Remember to select an <u>energy-efficient model</u> ENERGY STAR labeled refrigerator, washer, dryer, and other appliances

---

[13] The extra benefit from closing blinds and drapes is to protect items inside the home from strong ultraviolet rays. Sunshine fades the color from couches, furniture, clothes, carpet, rugs, linoleum, artwork, and paint.

incorporating advanced technologies. Save 10 to 50 percent of the operating costs. "A refrigerator manufactured before 1993 uses twice as much energy as a new ENERGY STAR-qualified model," said Richard Karney, ENERGY STAR Program Manager at the U.S. Department of Energy. ENERGY STAR products are manufactured by most major manufactures and are widely available. For more information, go to *www.EnergyStar.gov*. Rebates are also available for multi-family dwellings (MFD).

❑ "Installing a water heater blanket and insulating the five feet of both the hot and cold pipes can reduce operating costs by up to 15 percent. Before installing the blanket, read the water heat manufacturer's manual and blanket installation instructions. For gas water heaters, leave three-inch clearance around both the access door at the bottom and the gas flue (the metal exhaust pipe at the top)."[20]

❑ "When shopping for a washer, look for the following efficiency features: water level controls, 'sub-saver' features, spin cycle adjustment, and large capacity. For double the efficiency, buy an ENERGY STAR qualified unit. These models use 60 percent less energy, 40 percent less water, and less detergent."[21]

❑ **"What's your astrological sign?"** Aquarium pumps, heater, and lighting consume as much as 150 kWh and cost two to fifteen dollars per month. Consider phasing out this hobby of collecting exotic fish, birds, and reptiles as pets.

Here are more tips from Pacific Power's "Bright Ideas: A Helpful Guide to **Managing Energy Use in Your Home**:"[22]

❑ When purchasing a new dryer, look for humidity or moisture drying control, which can reduce costs by 10 to 15 percent. "Tumble action" reverses the spin direction during the cycle and dries clothes 10 percent faster.

❑ Chances are that standby power is costing you money. Estimates show that 5 percent of electricity used in the U.S. goes to "standby" power. You can make a big step toward energy and money savings by plugging electronics like computers, printers, faxes, televisions, and cell phone chargers into a power strip that can be turned off when your electronics are not in use or when they are fully charged.

New "smart" power strips make saving money and energy easier by sensing when your electronics are idle and cutting off the power flow to them. Devices like the WattStopper and the smart Strip Power Strip can be ordered online.

☞ Turn off and unplug appliances when you are away on business trips. These include faxes, microwaves, air filter, and fans. You will also want to turn down the air conditioner, heater, and dimmer switch on any clocks.

**Reducing Power Factor Cost** by Motor Challenge[23]

**What is Power Factor?** "The power factor of an AC electric power system is defined as the ratio of the [reactive] power (watts) flowing to the load to the apparent power (volts) in the circuit."[24] Low Power Factor is expensive and inefficient, that reduces your electrical system distribution capacity by increasing current flow and causing voltage drops.

**Cause of Low Power Factor:** Low Power Factor is caused by inductive loads (such as transformers, electric motors, and high-intensity discharge lighting), which comprise a major portion of the power consumed in homes, offices, and large industrial complexes. The increase in reactive and apparent power causes the Power Factor to decrease.

Some of the **benefits of improving your Power Factor** include:

•   Your utility bill will be smaller. Utilities usually charge a penalty fee to customers with Power Factors less than 0.95 that can be avoided by increasing your Power Factor.
•   You may experience voltage drops as power losses increase. Excessive voltage drops can cause overheating and premature failure of motors and other inductive equipment.

Techniques for **correcting your Power Factor** include:

☞ Minimize operation of idling or lightly loaded motors.
☞ Avoid operation of equipment above its rated voltage.

👍 Replace standard motors as they burn out with energy-efficient motors.

👍 Install capacitors in your AC circuit to decrease the magnitude of reactive power.

 Capacitor suppliers and engineering firms can provide the assistance you may need to determine the optimum power correction factor and to correctly locate and install capacitors in your electrical distribution system.

## Xedia's Electricity Management System

👍 I recommend investigating Xedia's Power Factor corrective solutions. "Xedia's XPS Electricity Management System improves the Power Factor by reducing the amount of reactive power that the load draws from the utility company. This is accomplished by supplying the reactive power locally at the load by the use of specially designed capacitors. These capacitors store the reactive power needed for stabilizing electric current within an inductive load. Therefore, the amount of electricity purchased from the power company results in lower utility costs if the Power Factor clause is enforced or the utility charges for the apparent demand."[25]

"A poor factor can result in wires and motors overheating, shorting the life of appliances and equipment. When Power Factor is improved, motors will be more efficient due to them starting with less stress and running cooler, thus prolonging their life expectancy."[26] If you experience any "static noise" on your phone or TV, the XPS system may reduce or eliminate the static by reducing noise on the power line. Power line noise and voltage spikes can damage sensitive electronics equipment like computers and mobile devices. It can even cause data loss on cable or DSL Internet connections and can even cause light bulbs to burn out. XPS reduces electromagnetic fields (EMF), as well as electromagnetic radiation (EMR). EMF and EMR have been shown in clinical studies to have potentially negative effects on people's health.

The XPS Systems improve the Power Factor for commercial and residential accounts, thus reducing the amount of power required which reduces the utility bills. For details or to order, go to *www.xediadirect.com/dwortham* (click "Energy Conservation").

❏ **AI:** _____

## Office

Do you notice how so many of these saving items fall into "office" and not general "household?" There is a good reason for this. You are moving through the process from leisure to business, from consumer to producer. This will be the home office for running your business and managing your investments, not just your household.

### Get Organized by Going Paperless

**Avoid Missed Payments and Late Fees:** Use online e-bill services to reduce stress. This service should be user-friendly, fast, convenient, secure, and <u>free</u> through your checking account as a centralized service. This will assist you in staying organized, saving on stamps, and avoiding late charges.

You can automatically have a payment made for the same amount every month on the same day. This is great for bills that do not change frequently, like cable or HOA dues. More importantly, this saves you time and worry so you can focus on productive money-making activities. No more walks to the mailbox by a certain time! This will also save you money on envelopes, paper, and printer ink. Set up the automatic notification option that will e-mail you when a payment is due, delivered, and paid.

❏ **AI:** _____

👍 If you do miss a payment, call your creditor or service provider and ask to have the penalty charge and interest removed. They will usually accommodate the request, at least the first time or two.

Have you ever missed a payment because the bill got buried beneath a stack of papers? Go **paperless** as there are many statements and bills that are best to be electronic. I still prefer paper statements for my retirement plan, bank, mortgages, and other financial investments because it forces me to read them before filing them away. For records and taxes, you probably need a paper copy anyway, so let them print it for you. Beware that many companies are charging twenty dollars or more per year for paper statements to be delivered. In these cases, elect statements delivered via e-mail and print them yourself.

❑ **AI:** _____

**Print Less:** To save paper, use double-sided printouts option (Finishing: "Print on both sides"). Also save scrap paper on which only one side was used and feed into printer to use the other side. Buy paper and envelopes made from 100 percent recycled paper. 100 percent post-composite is best with soy-based ink and chlorine free but comes at a cost. Any percentage (even 50 or 20 percent) of recycled paper is a good start.

Cut back on pop culture, Hollywood, gossip, glamour, and news **magazines**. Transition to investment, financial, wealth, health, fitness, marketing, and self-development magazines. Guys, totally let go of nudie mags! If you have not met the right person yet, how about investing in your retirement and health, which will make you more attractive? Or, give that $9.99 plus tax[14] to a tax-deductible charity each month.

❑ **AI:** _____

☝ Cancel (or at least greatly reduce) your magazine subscriptions. An alternative is to read magazines online if it limits your number of overall subscriptions and the price is greatly reduced directly from the publishers or service like eMagazine at *www.eMagazines.com*. Do the same for newspapers or reduce to the weekend or Sunday edition only. I love *The New York Times* Sunday paper, but it is so big it can take me ten days to read . . . and I hate getting the ink on my fingers. So, I reduced the frequency of subscriptions, subscribed online, or canceled my subscriptions altogether.

---

[14]   This was field trip research for the book.

☝ Try buying magazines as a group and sending them around with a distribution check-off list the way offices do. Share the cost and good conversations about articles among neighbors.

**Electronic Mail:** Sending e-mails versus using postal mail and sending text messages versus leaving voicemails are great timesavers. These are growing trends. Be well informed of any texting, e-mail, and Internet access fees on your mobile device.

☝ At least once a week verify that your spam e-mail folder does not have e-mail senders that do not belong there before deleting these messages. Yes, you probably get dozens of spam e-mails a day like I do, but if you catch one important message, it is worth the time. I sometimes find my own e-mails in the spam folder! You can use speed keys functions like "shift" to delete multiple selected messages at one time.

Create folders to save important e-mails. Flag (⚐) or star ( ✵ ) e-mails that require follow up. Also, create an e-mail signature line with your contact information and website.

❏ **AI:** _____

Put a weekly calendar event in your e-mail account calendar (Outlook, Yahoo!Mail, Gmail, Hotmail, etc.) for managing your business activities. Add a meeting, event, or task to your calendar reminders that might include "Pay Bills," "Call Clients," "Organize Office," or "Workout." Block off two hours for these, and make them recurring/repeating meetings. Also categorize and color code these placeholders. It is best to mark it as "Private." Finally, set a reminder ten minutes prior to the event.

❏ **AI:** _____

☝ **Beware of E-mails or Phone Calls from the IRS:** "The number of e-mails and phone calls from people claiming to be from the IRS has greatly increased. The IRS will never use an e-mail to contact you for the initial contact. They will never ask you to verify your Social Security number. Never give your Social Security via e-mail! Make sure you know who you are talking to on the phone before giving your Social Security number."[27] Also beware of scam e-mails from Federal Bureau of Investigation (FBI), banks, and Princes from Africa, as well as e-mails regarding: account alerts, confirmations of your account, notifications, priority messages, CAPITALIZED messages, foreign-language messages, blank subject title, and announcements that you've won a lottery, contest, or drawing that you didn't even enter!

## Productivity Tools

Invest in tools that will increase income. These tools can be carpenter tools, computers, and computer software and peripherals, a sewing machine, business clothes, desk, promotional material, etc. Evaluate that these tools will provide a good return on investment (ROI) in the desired timeframe. Efficiency and effectiveness are key elements to utilizing your progressive cheapness into real savings that you will immediately turn into profit.

### Internet Service

Call to update your current plans with your Internet, phone, cable/satellite, and energy providers. Always ask for introductory rates for new service members, even as an existing customer. Beware that special rate may run out after six or twelve months, and you will need to call them back once the offer expires to get the rate again. This may take several attempts before you reach the correct customer service agent that can help you, so be patient and nice. If you call twice and do not receive good results, ask for the cancellation or disconnection department. Use competing providers and technologies to plead your case as to why you deserve this special offer. Because they know you are investigating switching to a competitor, they will typically have access and authority to provide deeper discounts and promotional rates.

❑ AI: _____

**It's a Triple!** Consider combining your cable/satellite, telephone, and Internet service through a single physical media access like phone line, coax cable, or satellite signal. This is called "*Triple Play*" or a bundled service. The quality of this service has improved dramatically over the years and is offered by local telephone, long-distance, cable, and satellite providers. It is less expensive than getting all of these services separately through different providers.

❏ **AI:** _____

## Phone Service

**Ring Ring!** Call people long distance during off peak hours (normally nine p.m. to seven a.m.) and weekends for better rates or free calls. Stop buying ringtones! They require a fee and sometimes a membership that can cost twenty dollars per month, but even spending one dollar or a quarter is silly. Many times, in order to play a ringtone, you have to connect to the Internet there may be a charge or pay a licensing fee. Just use the standard rings already on the phone or create your own.

"If you go over your cell phone minutes, upgrade your plan. If you're ever over on your cell phone minutes or getting 'out of calling area' during a 'normal' month, call your cell phone provider and upgrade your plan to include more minutes to cover those other calling areas. Don't get eaten alive by overage fees. Get a plan that covers your actual cell phone usage."[28]

There are specialized Voice over IP[15] (VoIP) services offered via a broadband service with a special modem that your home phone is connected to like Vonage (*www.Vonage.com*). There are also Internet phone services on your computer that are even cheaper with great international rates like from Skype (*www.Skype.com*), but the voice quality may not be quite as superior as having a dedicated modem-based service. Skype also has a really good chat service.

❏ **AI:** _____

👍 Beware that 411, 511, and operator-assisted phone services may charge heavy fees. Go online or dust off the phone book to get this information.

---

[15]    *IP*: Internet Protocol. VoIP is the voice component of the bundled service mentioned in the previous section.

The National Do-Not-Call Registry gives you a choice about whether to receive telemarketing calls. You can register your home or mobile phone at *www.donotcall.gov* for free. Your registration will be effective for five years, and telemarketers should not call your number once it has been on the registry for thirty-one days. If they do, you can file a complaint at *http://complaints.donotcall.gov/complaint/complaintcheck. aspx?panel=2*.

❑ **AI:** _____

## Home Office

Make every room a growth room, especially if you spend a majority of your time in it. The room layout should be about growing your business, managing your money, expanding your skill set, speaking with clients, responding to e-mails, and blogging. This can be achieved by having the following tools: wireless high-speed Internet access, laptop/tablet, mobile phone with e-mail, text, and web capabilities, and a comfortable chair.

❑ **AI:** _____

## Telecommuting

If possible, telecommute (work remotely from home or local satellite office) at least one day a week. Fridays are becoming popular for telecommuting. This may work best because other peers may also be working remotely that day. On the flipside, be flexible, because this may also be a reason to select a different day so there is enough coverage at work. Telecommuting will take the appropriate technology, work ethics, and trust. Being able to VPN (Virtual Private Network) from home via broadband high-speed Internet to access your work Intranet[16] may be critical. Enhance working at home by getting a video camera for web collaboration and videoconferencing. This is great technology to stay connected at work and with family. Cameras are now being built

---

[16]    *Intranet* is a company's private IP network. There are security measures in place like firewalls and private IP address schemas to block the public from accessing their network.

into laptops and mobile devices to make communicating via video even easier.

❑  **AI:** _____

☝ As a mobile worker, having the ability to forward your work phone to your home line or cell may also be a requirement when you are not in the office. Telecommuting is not just saving money in coffee, lunch, <u>gas</u>, tolls, parking fees, parking tickets, and time driving to work, but also in the preparation time getting ready for work. Most insurance companies provide auto insurance discounts for telecommuters, and this is a NICE cost-saving benefit! I have had online access to work for twenty years, and I have been a telecommuter for over ten years.

If you are not yet a telecommuter, prepare your case for telecommuting. For suggestions on how to present your proposal to your employer, read QuintCareers.com, "Making Your Case for Telecommuting: How to Convince the Boss" at <u>*www.quintcareers.com/telecommuting_options.*</u> <u>*html*</u>. For additional input, go to The Telework Coalition at <u>*www.telcoa.*</u> <u>*org*</u>.

Another option is working a compressed week, perhaps four ten-hour days. This will reduce the time and money spent traveling to the jobsite too. When I did this, I chose Wednesdays; first, because others had not requested that day, but also because I did not want to appear I just wanted a three-day weekend by taking off Fridays. I spent my Wednesdays volunteering at Habitat for Humanity (<u>*www.habitat.org*</u>), and there were no complaints from coworkers!

❑  **AI:** _____

**Protecting Your Computer While Saving Energy**

Effectively manage your computer with the features and tools built in to the operating system. "According to the EPA, only 5 percent of laptop and desktop computers used in the U.S. have their energy efficiency settings enabled. This may be unnecessarily costing you money, since it is easy to change. An article on Greener Computing at <u>*www.greenbiz.*</u> <u>*com/computing*</u> reported that General Electric saved $6.5 million in electricity costs a year simply by changing its computer setting."[29]

Set your computer screensaver to blank to save energy. Verify that login password protection is enabled upon startup or resume. Add the computer lock icon on to the toolbar.

❑ **AI:** _____

👍 Before leaving the job or going to bed, put the computer on "Standby" or "Sleep" mode. Note that if file backup is set up at night, it may not work if the computer is in these modes. Another alternative is to turn off the monitor or at least reduce the screen brightness.

Become familiar with keyboard shortcuts for common actions, especially those for copy (Crtl c), cut (Crtl x), paste (Crtl v), save (Crtl s), undo (Crtl z), browser refresh (F5), and spell check (F7). They are faster than using the mouse. Download and use free productivity-enhancing utilities. For example, use the mouse wheel to scroll a window in background without having to change the window focus. For details how to enable the mouse wheel, go to WizMouse at *www.antibody-software.com*. There is also free screensaver and photo gallery management software available on the web.

**Protecting Your Assets**

Take some "**Tips to Prevent Identity Theft**" by Charles Schwab: *Charles Schwab On Investing*, stated "It's important to safeguard your personal information. Data breaches increased 47 percent [in 2008] and affected 35.7 million American. Forty-three percent of identity theft results from lost or stolen wallets, checkbooks, and credit cards, and 11 percent were committed online. Here are some things you can do to protect your information from criminals:"[30]

❑ Shred account statements and any financial documents before you throw them away.
❑ Maintain up-to-date anti-virus, anti-spam, and personal firewall software. For a review of the latest security software, go to *www.cnet.com*.
❑ Don't carry sensitive personal information such as your Social Security card with you unless you are going somewhere where you absolutely need it. Identity theft

commonly results from information found in lost or stolen wallets, purses, mail, or paper records.

 ☝Provide financial information only when you are on a secure website. A secure web address will begin with the letters "https" (instead of the usual "http") and will often display the small padlock icon.

Add identity theft coverage to your home owner's or renter's insurance policy for a cost of about twenty-five dollars a year.

❑ **AI:** _____

## Office Supplies

☝ Try buying store-brand ink cartridges and then refilling them two to three times. The key advantage is if the cartridge does not hold the ink, the store will find that out first and not charge you. I had limited success with the refill used cartridge kits. Note that the cartridge ink level messages may not be communicated on your printer display using non-manufacturer products.

☝ Beware that most ATMs and local shipping stores charge a surcharge for stamps. Supermarkets and office stores do not charge extra. Some membership wholesale stores even provide a discount on a roll of stamps like Costco which cost twenty-five cents less per roll. Of course, the U.S. Post Office vending machines only charge the cost of the stamp. However, online and mail-in orders from the Postal Service may start to charge for shipping, how ironic!

Giving postcards in person or putting on them on the door will save on postage, especially from overseas. Don't put any items in anyone's mailbox without postage, as that is illegal.

# Food

## Buying Meals

### Ordering Tips

👆 Order take-out meals with less fillers such as rice, noodles, and salads in order to get more of the main meal with protein. This is perfect for Chinese, Vietnamese, Mexican, Greek, and vegetarian meals. Get food to go instead of wasting time sitting in a restaurant, and you will often get bigger portions. Call ahead so the food will be waiting for you when you arrive. Besides saving time, you save money because the tip will be less because you are not dining in (though you should still leave a little tip for the cook).

**It's a Double!** Double up on meats when ordering "healthy" take-out to get more bang for your buck. This can make a really full meal or even be split into two meals for a small price increase. This is great for sandwiches, burritos, burgers, and gyros. Normally, the extra meat is a standard order item for only one to two dollars. Places that do not have this standard option will typically charge less. Just say, "Please charge me whatever you think is fair. I just love your food and am hungry as heck. Thanks!" Double cheese is not worth the additional charge of usually more than a dollar. Add extra low-fat cheese, bacon, or guacamole when you get home.

In 2011, the leading sandwich restaurants are competing with subs for only five bucks, so ordering with double meats make this a really good deal. Pizzerias are also offering rival specials of ten dollars per pizza pie with multiple toppings. What super deals if you eat them healthily and do not order the extra sides and a beverage!

👍 If you must eat fast food, watch for deals. Order off of the dollar menu at restaurants like McDonald's and Burger King. Also, don't buy a soda and French fries. Many fast-food restaurants make up to 50 percent of their food profits from soda and fries. Make your own fries at home and grab a healthy beverage from your fridge. Don't be fooled by "value meal" prices. Only get value meals if you can get free substitution of juice, low-fat milk, or bottled water instead. Play the "health guilt game" with the cashier if you have to.


## Saving on Meals

Go online for coupons you can use at your local favorite "healthy" supermarkets, restaurants, take-out, and fast-food spots. This can save money unexpectedly, and it becomes free money. For example, Popeyes Chicken at _www.popeyes.com/locator.php_ and Safeway have online coupons at _www.safeway.com/ifl/grocery/coupons_. Do not use coupons to buy junk food or get a free soda.

❏ **AI:** _____

👍 At most, only eat out one meal during the five-day workweek and only once on the weekend. Eat out during off hours to avoid the lines and possibly get discounts or extra portions. Take extra food from work events or leftovers from the break room home for dinner or leave it in the fridge for lunch the next day. If you leave it at work, be sure to put your name on the container to claim ownership.


## Eating Healthy Meals

👍 "Junk food is a common expense for children and even adults. Resist that urge to take the easy route. Instead, buy inexpensive and healthy snacks to keep on hand. Buy a yogurt or an apple instead of candy. Buy rice cakes or bananas instead of potato chips. Not only are healthier options often cheaper, they are also better for you, reducing health care costs over one's lifetime."[31]

👍 Typically, most of the fat in fried and baked chicken is in the skin. I recommend removing much of the skin before eating. Do this right away so you are not tempted to eat it. First start with a goal to remove 35 to 50 percent of the skin. Also, with extra napkins firmly pat down both sides of the fried food to remove more of the oil. Use more napkins than less. This is a great trick for removing grease from pizzas and breakfast meats as well. If you are at home, work, or in a restaurant, this is a necessary technique that you must do. Your health is not negotiable. Most people will comment, "What a great idea!"

Years ago, I was at a Country Western bar with my good friend Howard, having dinner and waiting for more people to arrive. He ordered a T-bone steak, and I ordered a rib-eye steak. Ten minutes after the food arrived, I looked at his plate, and it was totally clean. He ate the steak quickly, including the gristle and fat. Shocked that he ate the fat and gristle, I explained the dietary and weight issues of eating all of the fat. Avoid eating animal fat to reduce the amount of calories and reduce "bad cholesterol." Also, when preparing a meal, cut off most of the fat, skin, and gristle before cooking.

The good news is that a year later, we barbequed up a few steaks, and he did not eat any of the gristle or fat. I was so proud of him. This proves that we all have the ability to listen, learn, and adapt.

## Buying Food to Cook

### Growing and Gathering Your Own Food

Plant an organic garden to grow your own vegetables, fruits, spices, and herbs to save money and eat healthier. Sell or trade whatever you do not eat. Many herbs and spices will grow year round. Swiss chard is a hearty green that is harvested and will grow back several times well into the fall. As a kid, I grew chard for my guinea pigs rather than buying lettuce at the store. If needed, use chicken wire fence to protect your crops from varmints (a.k.a., vermin). Utilize your outdoor fence to grow vine veggies like sweet peas, string beans, tomatoes, grapes, strawberries, cherries, and cucumbers.

❏ **AI:** _____

If you live in a city or condo, you can still have a garden. If you have a small back porch, balcony, windowsill, or sunny space in your kitchen, you are all set. If your place is dark and does not get a lot of natural sunshine, buy energy efficient lights for hearty, small plants that will assist them in growing faster.

❏ **AI:** _____

👍 If you have roof access or some kind of landscaping around your building, talk to your landlord or Home Owners Association (HOA) about growing on the roof or growing edible landscaping. "'Graze the Roof' is an edible community-produced vegetable garden on the rooftop at Glide Foundation, a progressive (nonprofit) church in San Francisco. The project is an experiment in local urban, sustainable, Do-It-Ourselves food production."[32] Graze the Roof produces hundreds of pounds of fruits and vegetables annually. The project is intended to stimulate healthier dietary choices and strengthen the connection between people and their food source. For more details, go to *www. glide.org/page.aspx?pid=400*.

Go to an orchard to pick vegetables and fruits. This is much cheaper and more natural and healthier than buying produce from a store. Growing up in Jersey, we often picked apples, tomatoes, and strawberries at a local orchard. It was fun, I can admit it now. We picked what we wanted while getting exercise. You can also get great deals at local vegetable, animal, and dairy farms. These are also fun places for kids to play and learn.

❑ **AI:** _____

👍 Pick wild berries, onions, and dandelion greens (excellent for salads) alongside roads, paths, or in fields (just make sure it is not a State-protected area). Fishing and crabbing can provide cheap meals

and entertainment. My college mates and I went clamming in the Long Island Sound and cooked the clams that night at our graduation party. They tasted yummy with butter!

John Hamilton ("no neck") and Darryl ("stud" with $99 Johnny Carson suit) at NYIT 1988 Graduation.

## Buying Organic

**Cheesy Poofs** : Organic food has more nutrients with fewer chemical additives, making it safer to eat than non-organic food. Look for the USDA[17] Organic Seal or the words "Made With Organic Ingredients." Buy store-band snacks like pretzels and cheese puffs from health food stores like Whole Foods 365, Safeway O Organics, Trader Joe's store brand, and locally owned neighborhood markets. Always first look for organic store-brands and buy the items with best price per ounce value.

👍 A good tip is to start cooking brown rice or French fries at home and then buy meat, poultry, and fish from the hot buffet at health food stores, local grocery stores, or New York style delis. Only get the meat and poultry with no bones or pick the meat off the bone if necessary. Do not get any heavy veggies, rice, pasta, or cheese; add these when you get home. Get enough food for at least two meals. And don't forget to get plenty of those store napkins by the buffet table while you're there!

**"Whole Paycheck"** is the common name for Whole Foods because their high-quality, healthy foods can be expensive. You get what you pay for, and you are what you eat. In spite of the accusations that you will spend your whole paycheck on one shopping trip, this is <u>not</u> really true. There are good deals at Whole Foods.

This idea that your "whole paycheck" is going to food means you are not earning enough income or shopping shrewdly. Don't blame the store for providing quality products; blame yourself for not being able to afford it. So what is the solution?

1. Use the cheap tips to saving money while shopping. Shop and cook wisely while eating healthier foods to improve your physical wellbeing.
2. The savings will be invested in growing your net income.
3. Also produce passive income with investment yields, a profitable business, and positive cash-flow rental properties.

---

[17] *USDA*: United States Department of Agriculture.

👍 In many cases, less expensive organically grown wines are really good. One famous bargain wine is called Two Buck Chuck, and yes, it only costs two dollars per bottle. There are a wide variety of white and red wines with a full-body taste from Charles Shaw that can be purchased at Trader Joe's. In 2010, Whole Foods introduced "Chuck to Chuck" a promotion for Three Wishes wine only $1.99 per bottle. My friend Krisjon recommends another good inexpensive wine called Sea Breeze, which sells for $2.50 per bottle at Safeway—that's *only* seventy-five cents per glass! Inexpensive wines can also be found at discount stores like Wal-Mart, Costco, Sam's Club, and Rite Aid.

Less expensive wine is also good for hosting events, picnics, and barbeques, as well as keeping it on hand at home. Since you are hosting friends for free, there should be no complaints. One fall evening, I went to an art gallery, and they were serving Two Buck Chuck. There were cases of it, and since the wine was so cheap, the proprietor was able to pour a full glass and not just a taste.

## Buying Food and Beverages Cheaply

👍 Buying frozen vegetables can be a better value, fresher, and tastier than canned vegetables. Frozen veggies are cheaper per pound and better for the environment because they are not packaged in cans that have to be recycled. Fresh vegetables and fruits are preferred, if "the price is right." Fresh vegetables and fruits with no pesticides are always healthier but will not last as long. Put these vegetables and fruits in GreenBags™ to prolong their freshness.[18]

👍 The price per ounce for eggs of the same size is a good bargain. This may not correlate to eggs of different sizes like small and extra large. Ounce for ounce, jumbo eggs are the best deal. Plus, the largest eggs are sorted as jumbo, so there may be much greater chance of getting a BIG egg at a super price. You may even get two yolks in one jumbo egg. Check this out the next time you are in the grocery store or farmers' market.

---

[18]  Refer to the next section (*Storing Food*) for ideas of how to extend fresh vegetables and fruits shelf life.

👍 Use the deli scale to weigh the same-priced cooked rotisserie chickens, meatloaf, ribs, prepackaged meals, etc. to get the heaviest one. Beware of false high weight readings from excess water, juices, or bones. If the store charges per pound, see if you can drain the water and juices before it is weighted.

Here are some cheap easy meals to prepare: soup, casseroles, pot roast, salads, fruit, grain cereal, spaghetti and meat sauce, homemade pizza, and breakfast for dinner. I've found great deals for huge packages of turkey franks from wholesaler warehouse. Just verify the franks are not full of fat, nitrates, or artificial flavoring.

👍 We do not dilute but intensify things that will provide better performance. Do not buy beverages that brag about having more than 10 percent juice. They are full of water, corn syrup, and sugar. Get pure 100 percent juice that is rich in vitamins, not juice cocktail with only 27 or 20 percent juice because it is on sale. The price will be slightly higher, but the health value and concentration of juice that is not diluted more than makes up for it.

Drink purified or filtered water from home and stop buying bottled water to save money and reduce waste. For more reasons why go to Brita at *www.filterforgood.com*. Many cities and towns have very good quality water right from the faucet. Check with your county or the Environmental Protection Agency (EPA) at *www.EPA.gov*.

❑ **AI:** _____

Make iced tea or lemonade with little or no sweetener and water taken from your home purified/filtered system instead of buying soda, fruit juice, or sparkling water. This is healthier and cheaper, plus it tastes better when it's homemade—especially if you let the sun do the brewing for you.

❑ **AI:** _____

👍 Buying samples will typically save you money, but check the price per ounce.

## Storing Food

Eating green hamburger meat is <u>not</u> recommended or wise. Trust me! Learn from my costly lesson. In this section, you will find tips to prevent meats, vegetables, and fruits from spoiling.

On average, an American family wastes over $500 in food per year because of food going bad before cooking. Move items like cheese, bacon, sausage, extra butter, and hot dogs into the freezer so they do not go bad. Put these items into **freezer bags** to prevent freezer burn and to keep all the food from tasting the same. Of course, I recommend buying generic brand bags. Furthermore, it is a good idea to place baking soda (which removes bad odors) in both the fridge and freezer, and replace it every three to six months.

❏ **AI:** _____

👍 Separate bulk items into small portions (for example; steaks, fish, chicken, bacon, cheese, and butter) in several freezer bags to be easily defrosted for eating later. You can also reuse these bags. Use the same bag for the same food type. Rinse the bags with hot water and let the inside dry out before storing for future use. Cook two to four meals at a time and freeze them for easy reheating.

Definitely put veggies and fruits in Evert-Fresh **GreenBags** (or a similar product), which absorb and remove damaging gases. Most fruits, vegetables, and flowers release ethylene gases during the natural ripening process after harvest. Exposure of the produce to these gases accelerates aging and deterioration. GreenBags are made with natural materials, known to extend the life of the produce by absorbing and removing the ethylene gases that cause normal deterioration. This also works for bananas, mangos, and potatoes. There are special bags that work specifically for cheeses, meats, and cold cuts. Yes, I saw this on a late-night infomercial, but it works (I use them!). They are not expensive. You can buy these bags at *www.EvertFresh.com* or stores that have an "as seen on TV" aisle.

❏ **AI:** _____

This concept was originally for arctic explorers. "Evert-Fresh bags promote healthy eating by minimizing moisture formation, water droplets, and fogging that produce bacteria growth. The green color filters out harmful Ultraviolet light, reduces Vitamin C loss, and maintains temperature control."[33] Get as much air out of the bag as possible, make sure the produce is dry, and then fold the bag closed (do not use ties). These bags are washable and reusable.

The body of the fridge is the coldest area to place perishables. Most of the cold air comes from the back of the fridge and freezer, so items in the door lose their coldness first. Do not put milk, juices, or eggs in the fridge side door. Do not put meat, chicken, or ice cream in the freezer side door. If the door is accidentally left ajar, this will be the first place to get warm, and these costly items spoil quickly.

❑ **AI:** _____

👍 Consolidate when putting items in the fridge to reduce the amount of time the door is open. Stack up items before placing them in the fridge. This will save you money, energy, and time. Also, if the fridge is not full, reorganize the items together. Then turn down the coldness on "crisper" and "bread" compartments that are not being used.

Keep perishable food items like bread, muffins, butter, and spreads in the refrigerator to extend their freshness and shelf life. Also, store opened items like breadcrumbs, grated parmesan cheese, and some spices in the fridge.

❑ **AI:** _____

# Cooking

## The Range: Frying and Boiling

Use lids on your pots and pans to reduce the cooking time. Cooking in a frying pan with a glass lid will keep your food moister and will cook both sides of the food. Plus the glass lid will allow you to view the cooking progress without removing the top and losing heat. If the lid is not a perfect match, that is fine. It can be a larger lid, pan, or even a used piece of aluminum foil.

❑ **AI:** _____

👍 Adding a dash or two of salt will make water and other liquids boil quicker. Watch that the contents do not boil over and mess up the stovetop! Do not turn up the gas flame too high on a stove burner that is beyond the size of the pot or pan, as this will result in wasting heat and gas.

👍 For cooking medium-sized dishes, choose cooking on a stove range over using the oven. Using one burner will save a lot of money versus heating the entire oven.

**Gourmet-Like**: Combine foods while cooking. Add veggies at the end process of boiling pasta or steaming rice. Just lay them on top and put the lid back on. This will be your "steamed veggies." To make "roasted vegetables," you can add veggies in the stove while cooking the main meal. Placing bread or buns on top of the food with a lid or directly on the lid will warm and soften them while saving energy at the same time.

**More Bacon, Less Fat:** When buying breakfast take-out or fast-food burgers, cook your own bacon and sausage at home. Besides saving between one to three dollars per meal, you can follow this healthy cooking technique to reduce the fat and nitrate content of your meal:

1. Cut away much of the fat before cooking.
2. Microwave for sixty seconds before cooking on the stove to reduce the frying time and remove some grease.
3. When the meat is about half-cooked on the stove, rinse it under hot water and drain to remove the grease. Drain the water and grease into a spaghetti strainer to catch any meat that falls out of the pan. Repeat this process again when food is three-quarters done to remove even more grease.
4. Add any seasoning and spices _after_ the last rinse. This way, they are not washed away and wasted.
5. When removing the cooked bacon or sausage from a pan, put it on the napkins and firmly pat down with more napkins to remove the remaining grease.

This also works very well with steaks, SPAM, corned beef hash, and other fried meats with high fat content. Also do this for ground beef that is used for casseroles, sauces, and Sloppy Joes. With meat that is 93 percent lean (or greater), not all of the steps are necessary.

**Get SPAMmed** : SPAM and corned beef hash are not just for breakfast anymore. These are very economic dinner meals that require little preparation. Buy cheaper international and generic brands or similar products that are sometimes called "luncheon meat." They can be just as good or better than the leading brand, though they may have a different texture and taste.

The Great Wall of SPAM

**Get Sauced** : Here is a good technique to get all of your tomato paste, tomato sauce, or other sauces out of a jar or can. Once you empty the sauce in a pot, rinse it out with a little hot water and empty it into the pot. For jars, put the cap back on and shake. The goal is to get all of the sauce out, not to water down the sauce. Most of this water will evaporate anyway. Mom's secret ingredients to enhance general store-brand tomato sauce is to add a little sugar, Tabasco®, crushed red pepper, garlic, oregano, and red wine.

[As with many ideas in this book, you can improvise and use your best efforts. Don't avoid experimenting, and it may take a few tries. You can customize and perfect later what best fits your personality and situation.]

## Baking

**Bag It**: Cook turkeys, chickens, roasts, and ribs in oven bags. This will enable you to cook the food in half the time. They are self-basting, which makes the food more tender and juicy with no effort. For delicious details on cooking with Reynolds® oven bags, go to: *www.reynoldsovenbags.com*.

❑  **AI**: _____

👍 **Preheating** the oven before cooking is way overrated. Why waste all the heat and time waiting for the right cooking temperature? Put your food in first and <u>then</u> turn on the oven. This is proven safe for most foods like meats, poultry, potatoes, and veggies, though it does not work well for baking cakes, pastries, and breads. Turn off the heat just before the food is completely cooked and use the remaining heat to finish it over the next ten or fifteen minutes. Turn down the thermostat in the home when you are cooking so your oven can pull double-duty. In the winter, once you are done cooking leave the door ajar to heat the home.

👍 You can defrost and partially cook food on the stove with no extra fuel by placing it on the hot spots while cooking in the oven. Just find the vents or the hottest spot and place food in metal or microwaveable containers. Near the end of cooking, transfer the food into the oven to completely cook it with the other food. Great candidates for this are potatoes, fries, veggies, and rolls. Even if this saves you half the energy, it is still a bonus with little effort.

👍 "Turn on the oven light when you need to look at food. Whenever you open the door on the oven, as much as 25 percent of the heat inside is lost, and a significant amount of energy is used to build that heat up again, likely extending the cooking time. Instead of losing the heat that way, turn on the oven light when needed and use a meat thermometer. This way, you can look through the glass to visually inspect the food and read the thermometer without opening the door and losing heat."[34]

👍 Bake a frozen or homemade pizza instead of having one delivered. Add your own extra cheese, oregano, red crushed pepper, etc. Furthermore, customize it by adding bacon, spinach, broccoli, and other veggies to spruce up the pizza to make it better and healthier than any leading delivery brand. Remember to put the tip that you would have given to the delivery person toward your emergency fund or into your daily one-dollar kitty jar[19] as savings.

## Nuking

Use the microwave oven for reheating leftovers and cooking small quantities of food rather than using the oven. "Don't use the stove when the microwave will do. For many simple purposes, the microwave oven is much more energy and time efficient than the stove, often using 75 percent less energy for the task and adding less heat to your home."[35]

👍 It is a good idea to "loosely" cover food in the microwave with a paper plate or napkin to heat the food quicker. A splash of hot water will also assist with this as well as keeping the meal moist.

👍 Microwave multiple dishes at the same time. Halfway through cooking, you may need to rotate the dishes, as heat distribution in most microwaves can be uneven, and the middle is usually the coolest spot. If your microwave doesn't have a built-in rotating plate, to save time from having to turn the plate, buy a standalone turntable and place in the microwave. This will assist in evenly cooking the food without your intervention.

👍 The microwave is a great place to keep food warm after cooking or take-out until you are ready to eat. Be careful not to accidentally turn it on with metal objects in it or when it is empty.

## Cooking Family Style

Growing up in a family with two brothers, we cooked a lot of food at once so there were leftovers for the next day or two. Do not cook one turkey burger, hamburger, or potato; cook two or four and wrap the extra for a later day. If you are going to heat the oven, cook two to four

---

[19]  Kitty jar concept is explained in *Chapter 11: Investing in Debt Reduction While Increasing Your Saving, Planning to Save While Changing Habits, Save One Dollar a Day Investment Plan.*

times the quantity of what you will eat for that meal or combine cooking with a whole separate meal. This is perfect for larger families and a very useful time saver for couples and single people. There will also be dollar savings in energy costs.

❑  **AI:** _____

**Get Scrappled**: As mentioned, breakfast meals make great dinners and are easy to cook. Cook enough to have extra for breakfast the next

morning or lunch. Dinners with scrapple and pork roll meats are a simple meal for kids to learn how to prepare. I make killer cinnamon French toast, which is another easy dinner meal.

This looks like meat, right?

Teach your children and partner to cook. This is not an option but a requirement. Have them specialize in at least five dishes each, and rotate the cooking duties.

❑  **AI:** _____

## The Fallout: Maximizing Leftovers

There are <u>no</u> leftovers because you planned to cook extra food. Bring the extra meals into work. Change your attitude for scraps not eaten or fed to the dog to a proactive approach of planning future meals to save money, energy, and time while eating healthier.

✍ "Refrigerate your leftovers in [glass] containers[20] with tight-fitting lids. Avoid storing leftovers in metal or enamel containers and cookware. In time, the salts and acids in the food can damage the container surface.

---

[20]   Rick Bywater says, "There is some concern these days about storing food in plastic containers because of BPA (Bisphenol A). Canada has outlawed BPA in baby products, and there is movement in the [U.S.] along those lines. The best container for leftovers is a glass container."

Worse yet, metal containers can cause food to spoil quickly and possibly lead to health problems for you and your family."[36]

👍 Buy caps for unfinished beverage cans. Get different sizes that fit can, bottles, and jars. To improvise use aluminum foil or saran wrap with a rubber band. Also get the clips for open potato chips and other bagged snacks. You can get these items free by volunteering and also in charity race's or tournaments' gift bags. If you do not have any, use paper clips or clamps. This will keep your food fresh much longer and may reduce the amount you eat at a sitting because you know they will not go stale.

How much money have you wasted eating out for lunch? Let's add up one summer of lunches and a drink at the local restaurant just on Fridays. The food, beverage, and tip is fifteen dollars. There are ten weeks in the summer, so that is $150. In ten years at only a 5 percent return, that would be $244; at 7 percent, it would be $295. In twenty years at 5 percent return, it would have grown to $398; a whopping $580 at 7 percent! Now, if that is two lunches for the summer at 5 percent return in twenty years, it's $796. Saving the investment of $20 lunch every Friday of the year with 7 percent return in twenty years, your retirement plan or business would be worth $4,024!

So think out loud today and ask yourself, "Is that greasy burger and drink worth the ability to fund my early retirement?" I cannot hear you! I still cannot hear you!!! Now, let's also do this today at work for the year by eating at the desk just two days of the week: $20 lunch twice per week equals $2,080 in savings per year. Invested at 10 percent return in twenty years will worth 13,455! Seek support with a coworker to eat bagged lunches from leftovers together.

❑ AI: _____

## Special with Love

Make dishes like your mom and dad made when you were growing up. Many times, these were tasty meals made from scratch to save money. This will reduce the amount of processed food you consume. How about that Shake n' Bake pork chops, lasagna, leg of lamb, grilled trout, pot roast, chicken salad, and birthday cake? I can remember Mom's chicken cutlet, Dad's barbeque ribs, Grandma's Thanksgiving turkey, Auntie's seafood casserole, Uncle's gumbo, and your neighbor's goulash. Are you getting hunger? Try eating baked potatoes versus instant mashed potatoes, homemade mac and cheese versus that from a box, long grain brown rice versus plain white rice, and a bowl of high-fiber cereal versus a donut. You and your budget will be healthier!

I, too, am working to improve my eating habits. I just looked in my cabinets and found some of the products just mentioned. If a "food" item has to be encased in tin foil or plastic that are used in space travel, this may not be the healthiest choice. Check for a two-year or more expiration date; if it's there, that product may contains preservatives. Also check to see if most of the calories come from carbohydrates and sugar versus from fiber and protein.

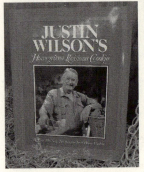

**"Aye! I'm glad for y'all to see me, I garontee."**
Food is one of the largest expenses, especially dining out. If you are not a good cook, take a cooking class, join a frugal cooking group, and/ or buy a cookbook: *America's Home Cooking: Easy Recipes for Thrifty Cooking* by Chris Fennimore or *Homegrown Louisiana Cookin'* by Justin Wilson at *www.justinwilson.com*.

❑  AI: _____

**Spice It Up!** Using spices will add favor and zest to ordinary, bland, and store-brand foods. There are also a multitude of health benefits from spices and herbs by providing nutritional value, supply vital minerals, and have a positive benefit to health. Spices and herbs have more disease-fighting antioxidants than fruits and vegetables.

Learn more about "**Health Benefits of Spices and Herbs**" by permission of InDepthInfo at *www.InDepthInfo.com*. "Spices, especially herbs, have long been used for medicinal purposes throughout the world. Moderate doses of many herbs can positively affect digestion, heart, brain functioning, and more. InDepthInfo has compiled a list of herbs with a brief comment about the health effects of each one:"[37]

- Allspice is thought to be efficacious in the case of stomach ailments and as an aid to digestion.
- Caraway is thought to help with bronchitis and may have properties that help reduce bloating and cramping.
- Cardamom is said to relieve stomach problems and heartburn.
- Cayenne (red) Pepper is sometimes used to stimulate the circulatory as well as digestive systems.
- Chives health benefits include anti-inflammation, anti-carcinogenic, and antibiotic.
- Cinnamon is known to be a strong antiseptic. It also has anti-microbial and anti-clotting properties.
- Cloves are good for digestion and can even be used as a mosquito repellant or to help with toothaches and mouth sores.
- Dill can kill some intestinal bacteria and also helps to calm a nervous stomach.
- Garlic has similar properties to onions in that it can act as an antibiotic and anti-microbial. It is thought to help prevent heart disease and strokes.
- Ginger helps digest high-fat foods and breaks down proteins, making it very good for digestion. It is also thought to combat arthritis.
- Nutmeg helps stimulate the brain and also works as an anti-inflammatory. Use nutmeg in moderation, though, as it is toxic in high doses.
- Parsley may reduce the risk of cancer and be effective against atherosclerosis.
- Peppermint has been used to treat morning sickness and motion sickness, as well as general nausea.
- Saffron may be taken to ease fatigue. Some believe it strengthens the cardiovascular and nervous systems.
- Turmeric (a spice commonly used in curry) is thought to ameliorate the risk of gallstones. It also has anti-inflammatory properties.

"The health benefits of any particular herb or spice may vary from person to person. They also can have short-term or long-term effects. Most spices are not consumed in large amounts, so the average person will not notice their effect. Even so, moderation is a virtue, and large doses of any spice or herb to achieve a desired health benefit should not be embarked upon without consulting a physician."[38] For additional herbs that address anxiety, stress, headaches, and panic attacks, refer to Rosemary Gladstar's *Herbs for Reducing Stress & Anxiety.*

👍 Here is a great way to get the feeling of eating a roast when you are having a hamburger. If you live in an apartment, open the front door into the hallway in the evening to get the smell of other people's gourmet dinners. This is especially good on Sunday when people are home cooking fancy family meals and you are eating a frozen TV dinner. It's even better to put a fan in the front door to draw in the yummy aroma. Now, that's cheap!

## Cooking with Wine

You can store opened wine for weeks in the fridge, even red wine. If you are going to use it for cooking, it will last for months to years without tasting vinegary . . . yes, I said years! Heck, I still have the Tawny Port Wine that was trucked over the Rocky Mountains when I moved from Colorado to California ten years ago! I just used it to marinate short ribs and there is still a little left. Put the cork back in the bottle and stand up the wine in the fridge door.

👍 If you consume a lot of good or expensive wine, get a cork remover and vacuum sealer. The pump creates a vacuum seal by extracting the air that breaks down flavor and locks in the taste to preserve partially consumed wine for another day.

## Shopping Tips

### Spending

👍 Are you a shop-a-holic? Is shopping your rush? Eliminate this temptation. If your kids are bored, don't take them to the mall; instead, go to the library or park. If your friend calls and wants to go shopping say, "No thank you. I am working on my business plan," "No thanks. I am working out," or "No thanks. I am on a budget," and no more explanation is required. People will get the point and normally respond, "Me too. I understand." Spend-a-holics waste money while shop-a-holics waste money, energy, and time. If this is you or somebody close to you, let's start to turn this around now.

Stop being "ghetto fabulous" or "yuppie fabulous." No more wasting your life savings on tire rims, flashy jewelry, expensive watches, huge designer purses, pocketbook-sized dogs, and newest luxurious cars while renting a home. Guys, opening the car door for women will get you much further in receiving respect from your date than showy items you bought on credit.

**Clearance / On Sale!** Always start at the clearance rack. As you enter department stores, first look for Clearance and On Sale signs. These signs should draw you like "a moth to a flame." Shop at wholesale, outlet, liquidation sales, and temporary warehouse stores. Also, check out discount spin-off stores like Burlington Coat Factory, Loehmann's, Nordstrom Rack, and Ross. You should use similar money-saving tactics when buying food and clothes. Buy generic and avoid overpriced big brand names when you can.

👍 If your tastes are high-end designer clothes, shoes, and accessories, join online membership wholesalers that sell them at a deep discount. Try JackThreads at *www.jackthreads.com*, Reverse at *www.reverse-reverse.com*, and Gilt Groupe at *www.gilt.com*. These memberships are free, but some websites charge for special memberships to get early access like Ideeli™ at *www.ideeli.com*. If you have expensive tastes, these websites will save you a lot of money and the trouble of window shopping. There are many other specialized websites to investigate as well.

Do not be enticed by offers that provide a discount after you buy a certain number of items. For example, "Take off 20 percent on any four items or more." Stay away from incentives of a discount over a specified dollar amount like "10 dollars off any purchase of $100 or more." Finally, beware of offers of a free gift if you spend over an advertised dollar amount. Just spend what you originally planned.

## At the Store

### Shopping with a Purpose

"**What is your purpose?**" When shopping, put together a list before leaving home. Bring a pen to check off the items. This is really useful when cooking for the holidays, special dinners, and if you have a large family. Here is something different: Investigate "Smart Shopper" at *www.SmartShopperUSA.com* to create a list that you print and take with you to the store to assist you in staying on task and budget. There are also smartphone shopping list applications (apps or aps).

❏ **AI:** _____

Window shopping is <u>not</u> a money-making activity but frivolous entertainment. Your purpose in life will intertwine into everyday actions and behaviors, not just pinching pennies. Cheapness will become an integral part of your life and second nature behavior. Go to specific stores to buy certain items for the best value. Always shop with a purpose and not out of habit, boredom, or desire.

### Store Discounts and Savings

I prefer to use store flier promotions to review what I need that week over clipping individual coupons. Circle the items of great value. Write in any other items you need on the front page. This will keep your eyes focused on buying only what you planned to buy. Again, when shopping, bring a pen with you and check off each item. Take notice of the active start and end dates of the promotion. In your head, keep your eyes focused on the BIG picture needs, not your daily wants.

**Use Coupons Beyond Their Expiration Dates:** Sometimes, five-dollar, ten-dollar, or 20-percent-off store coupons may not have a real expiration date. The printed date may be extended a few weeks to indefinitely. Many companies have a policy that allows these extensions for products and services. Use your charm while asking the cashier or customer service person if you can still use expired coupons. Coupons can save you significant money.

Make sure you are pleasant and can still pay if they do not accept multiple coupons for the same purchase. You may need to have separate purchases to use them. Bring cash to speed up the checkout process. Do not call for a supervisor right away, if at all. Being cheap does not have to be embarrassing, uncomfortable, or confrontational; it is just practical. Please bring extra coupons to give to a nice person in the parking lot or behind you in line.

👍 Many local department stores, restaurants, and fast-food joints give **military personnel** and **first responder discounts**. You may need to ask for this discount and wear your uniform to impress the point that you deserve a discount because you protect this country and our neighborhoods. This is the least we can do for you.

Buy **store-brand products** like garbage bags, mouthwash, detergent, shaving cream, juice, soup, veggies, etc. Just compare the containers and ingredients to your favorite leading brand. Also buy store-brand napkins, paper towels, breads, frozen food, canned food, beauty care products, nontoxic cleaning products, etc.

❏ **AI:** _____

## Buying in Bulk

**The Incredible Bulk**: Buying in bulk is a great cost savings, but make sure it is actually cheaper and the quality of food is still good. These should be cheaper per unit. If not, don't buy them. Being on sale is another great bonus! As mentioned previously in this chapter, have a plan to put perishable foods in freezer bags—especially meats, poultry, and fish. Use GreenBags for fruits and vegetables. Do not buy junk food or food with little nutritional value, including candy, pop, and chips because they are cheaper. If you do buy snacks, get the light items with no preservatives, 0 grams of trans fat, high protein, and high fiber.

👍 Double up on discounted items like steak (good quality and low in fat), poultry, fish, soap, green products, etc. Buy four or more pounds of lean ground beef to get the bulk price, and freeze it in meal-sized portions. Make pre-made hamburger patties to keep in the freezer to fry or grill when the mood strikes for a take-out cheeseburger. You can buy pre-made patties of hamburger, turkey, and salmon from the store that only costs a little more. This can be less mess and more efficient for small families, couples, or singles.

👍 Buying and cooking in bulk is a great way to manage your time and energy. Buying in bulk will also save you trips to the store, which reduces the chance of a car accident as well as the temptation of buying unnecessary items. You can get bulk items at wholesale stores with no membership fee, warehouse clubs, depots, co-op, and super department stores. I bought a ten-pound bag of potatoes for only ninety-nine cents and a five-pound tube of lean Angus ground beef for only eight dollars at a wholesale warehouse. What deals have you found lately?

**Frugal Shopping**

**"Shopping Tips"** by Trent Hamm:[39]

- 👍 Set a time goal when you walk in the store door. If you're entering a store when you're likely to be distracted (like a clothing store, an electronics store, super department store, or bookstore), set a time goal when you need to check out and leave the store. This will reduce the opportunities you have to be distracted by impulse buys and keep you focused on the items you're intending to purchase. One effective way to do this is to set the alarm clock on your watch or on your phone so that it beeps loudly, reminding you that it's time to get out of the store and making sure you're not dawdling.
- 👍 Master the other "ten-second rule." Whenever you're in a store and you pick up an item, hold it for ten seconds. During those ten seconds, ask yourself if you really need it and also if that money wouldn't be better used in some other way. You'll almost always find yourself putting that unnecessary item back on the shelf and walking away, quite proud that you didn't waste your money on something so unnecessary.
- 👍 Don't buy any items in the checkout aisle. Stores love to load their checkout aisles with impulse buys: candy that's

attractive to both children and adults, magazines aimed at tickling your fancy by shocking and surprising you enough to pick them up and add them to your cart, and small, overpriced versions of very common purchases such as batteries [and gum]. The easiest rule-of-thumb for protecting your wallet or purse is to not buy anything at all in the checkout line. Once you head for the checkout, nothing else goes in your cart unless it's on your list.

👆 Fill in your <u>rebate and registration forms</u> immediately online or with the card. Keep the warranty and receipts where you can logically find them.

👆 Always ask for a rain check when you go to a store for their advertised deal and the shelf is bare. While you're at it, ask for two rain checks. They are usually valid for thirty days.

## Buying Online

Always start <u>and</u> end online shopping at the "Clearance" or "On Sale" page. Shopping online will assist you to remain focused on that one item you need. This will save time and definitely energy in comparing pricing and driving around town. There are smartphone apps to assist you! Online outlet stores have great deals if you look hard enough like The Sportsman's Guide at *www.SportsmansGuide.com*. They are especially good for out-of-season or off-season items. Online discount stores have also everyday common items like jackets, kitchenware, watches, chairs, computer equipment, and furniture. In addition, there are specialty items like air filters, security systems, exercise equipment, and car accessories.

Verify if your company has an employee discount program for its or its' affiliates' products and services. If you work in a store, this is great for in-store items or to reduce the price of tickets and services. Many people take jobs for these benefits. Check to see if your member clubs like airline premier mileage or AAA have free online discount programs. For these programs, sign up to receive e-mail notifications of special promotions.

❑ **AI:** _____

Use comparison websites like *www.PriceGrabber.com* and *www. Amazon.com* to shop for the lowest frugal price. This will calculate the bottom-line price to include sales tax and shipping. Sites like eBay and Yahoo are also great websites to compare prices. Never pay retail prices again!

❏ **AI:** _____

To get collective buying power, join local discount alerts like *www. Groupon.com*. You will usually get prepaid discounts of at least 50 percent, and are good for six to twelve months. There are daily alerts. Each offer will expire by midnight (11:59 p.m. local time), so act quickly. Not to worry, because there is a countdown ticker on the website. There may be a limit to the number of tickets or items one can purchase. Groupon is in over 170 cities worldwide. They will provide a refund of an unused advanced purchase if a restaurant or store goes out of business.

❏ **AI:** _____

👍 Use your credit cards or airline miles for business trips. You can use points accumulated from hotel and rental car preferred member programs as well. Go online to search and print out the equivalent rate for your records. Don't forget to verify with your Certified Public Accountant (CPA) that you can write off the value of the airline ticket, hotel room, and ground transportation expenses.

## Shopping for Food

👍 Compare price per ounce on food, soft drinks, and alcohol. This is standard practice in most large supermarkets, but not at mom-and-pop local convenience and some warehouse stores. Also compare the calories per unit and the amount from fat. In general, try to get the highest amount of calories with more protein, and less sodium and fat (not necessarily zero). Items that are dense in volume with lower cost per ounce are winners, and taste the same!

**Pavlov's Dog :** If you have some treats that you like, rather than go to the local convenience store to buy them, go to larger grocery store to buy them in bulk or at least "semi-bulk." This is better than paying too much on a whim or in answer to a craving, and it saves you money for real needs. For example, buy your favorite ice cream, beer, coffee, soda, hot dogs, cookies, snacks, etc. at the discount store. This should drastically reduce your impulse buying.

❏ **AI:** _____

Bring your own grocery bags to get a few pennies back when checking out. You can earn a bag credit for two to five cents in many grocery stores. Do not totally fill the bags; if you use more of your own bags, that will increase the bag credits. Also double up the bags and let the checker know. If you forget to bring bags, most stores have bins in the front where people return used plastic bags to be recycled. Grab a few of those bags and use them. Reusing is always better than recycling. This is fantastic for the environment and will add a little change in your pocket that will be invested later. Furthermore, buy reusable canvas or nylon bags for only a few dollars (compare prices because these bags do go on sale). Beware, some stores have been charging two to five cents for their plastic or paper bags! This is a growing trend, so be informed.

❏ **AI:** _____

Don't stand still and be lazy when the cashier is scanning your items. Stop acting like you are verifying that the prices are correct. You are not fooling anybody except yourself. Bag your own groceries and items! The checkers are not there to service you but to provide a service to you. This is respectful and will also speed up the checkout process—and you will not feel badly about getting a few extra cents per your own bags.

👍 Check your receipt to verify that you are not being billed for any hidden charges and that club membership discounts were applied. One time I failed to ask the cashier before cashing out if she had deducted my bag credits. She forgot, so I said, "No worries. Just get me next time. Or better yet, please give it to the person next in line." The cashier and the next person in line will never forget me.

## Shopping for Small Items

👍 There is great value in older, discontinued, refurbished, and floor-model equipment. However, you need to do your research. For refurbished units, see if they have a warranty or ask the salesperson to include it for free. For floor models get them to extend the return policy from thirty to ninety days. The nice part of refurbished and floor models there is no assembly, but you need to have a large enough vehicle to remove it the day of purchase. I still have a floor-model Precor® 855e recumbent exercise bike that has been burning calories for fifteen years and saved me $250!

Here is another way to save money by going retro. Keep your old sports equipment. There is no need to upgrade it. If required, take the equipment to a shop for maintenance. I still have my Heart skis from high school. I am taller now than they are. This is good news because they are ideal for skiing around moguls and between trees. Since I rarely play golf, I still have my MacGregor clubs from 1990 that only cost eighty dollars, and I keep them in a red bag my friend Mike gave me. Keep quirky old items rather than acquiring new stuff that may have less character. You can win at the game of life when you spend less on toys by not buying new items that you infrequently utilize.

**Smelling Good!** : Really, does perfume and cologne go bad? I think not! Even if there is a slight change in scent over the years, are you and others going to notice it? No way! Would somebody else have the nerve to tell you? Definitely not, especially if that person is close to you. Perfume and cologne will last for over a decade with minor changes in scent, so never throw them out.[21] Storing them in a cool area away from direct sunlight will increase their lifespan. However, oil-based scents and massage oils may go rancid over time.

Two for the price of one (twofers) are remarkable!

---

[21]  I have had Issey Miyake L'Eau d'Issey Pour Homme eau de toilette for fifteen years and Caesar Man Palace Reserve cologne for twenty years, and they still smell sweet!

## Shopping for Large Items

**SLAM!** You need to put down a large down payment for a personal vehicle, especially for a want or luxury car, massive SUV, boat, etc. For many people in the U.S., a car is a necessity. I like to drive too. Pay more than creditable down payment like 20 to 50 percent. This will lower the loan interest rate and increase the leverage to negotiate a lower price with the salesperson. Pay extra principle per month to pay off the loan before it is due. Slam the door on long-term and huge car loans! Note that you must still continue contributing to your 401(k) while taking advantage of any investment deals. You really need to pay cash for vehicles that cost $10,000 or less and for toys like yachts, weekend road bike, RVs, ATVs, pools, jet skis, and entertainment centers.

**Bed Bugs:** Do not lease or get store financing for beds and furniture because you will be tempted to buy more than you need. Always pay cash for these "wants" and "needs" without touching your emergency fund. Do not use department store credit cards. Don't get lured or suckered into buying with interest-only or gift coupons for a future purchase. These incentives may tempt you into getting more stuff, a bigger model, the complete set, or more expensive type than you originally planned or need.

☞ When furniture gets worn or torn, get it reupholstered instead of buying a new couch or chair. Reupholstering can also be useful to repair car seats.

I heard about IKEA home furnishing store years ago. Feedback from a few people was that their furniture was a lot of work to put it together and the quality was poor. My experience is that this is not the case at all; it is just the opposite! I have been very pleased with the price, quality, choice, assembly instructions, and customer service. Go to their website at _www.IKEA-USA.com_ to view their simpler furniture, office, and household items, not just the pricey perfect model kitchen. At their store, look for red ticket items on sale.

👍 There are very good bargains at government, police, and estate auctions, as well as street fairs and flea markets. Look in the estate section of newspapers, as well as, searching online.

Top piece bought at Indonesia cultural auction and bottom piece at the Black Arts Festival. Really, I don't have nightmares!

## Shopping for Medicine

Buy generic and store-brand medicines and vitamins instead of name brands. Check the shape of the container and ingredients to see if they match the leading brand. Typically generic and name brands are produced by the same manufacturer.

❑ **AI:** _____

👍 "Ask your doctor about generic drugs. Now that many pharmacies are offering four-dollar generic prescriptions, you can save quite a bit of money merely by asking your doctor whether or not there is a generic version of your prescription available that will work for your condition. In many cases, the generic is a perfect equivalent of the name brand prescription, thus substituting the generic for the name-brand prescription can save you a great deal of money at the pharmacy."[40] Many healthcare providers' default prescriptions are generic drugs, and they charge extra for name-brand medicine.

**"Oh Canada, Eh."** Order discounted medicine online from drug and department stores, as well as online only companies like DrugStore.com. Also consider buying medicine from Canada. These prescription drugs are much cheaper than filling a prescription at a pharmacy. Even the U.S. federal and state governments are investigating this option to reduce medical costs, especially for programs like Medicaid and Medicare.

Wikimedia Commons, Ian Muttoo

*www.richmondzoo.blogspot.com/2008_12_01_archive.html*, December 2008

👍 For very reasonably priced eyewear, go online to investigate Zenni® Optical. They have a very wide selection of eyeglasses. Once you have your prescription, lens type, and frame width, go check them out at *www.ZenniOptical.com*.

## Shopping for Music

Keeping it real by going back to original, older items can be fun and save you from buying more stuff. This may be like listening to records or tapes, getting books from the library, and wearing an old dress from high school. You can also check out movie DVDs from libraries. All of this at no cost to you.

👍 Whenever you can, buy used CDs and DVDs, but look for scratches first. Also verify that there is a money-back guarantee and easy return policy. They should be in "like new" or better condition.

👍 Go **old-school** by keeping older media technologies and getting music or games cheaply. Keep your old CD player, cassette player, turntable, Xbox, PlayStation, and VCR, because you can buy used and discounted media at a huge discount. When other people upgrade, they do not need the old items, so they will give or sell them to you cheap. Also think of the distributors and stores that need to get rid of old stock. To save money, don't trade in your DVD player for new a Blu-ray™ player yet. Wait until the last minute to replace it so you can extend its life and the life of your DVDs. Have fun utilizing your old music. Listen to commercial-free radio on Thursdays, CDs on Fridays, records on Saturdays, and tapes on Sundays.

This is the Walkman I wore in my NYIT graduation photo. Yes, I still use it occasionally, mainly for shock value and also to regress back to my college punk rock, heavy metal, new wave days.

Another alternative is to utilize effective **modern music devices** which hold more music, and saves you energy and space. Determine if you can combine systems. Try not to buy new music yet. The common practice is to convert records and CDs to MP3 files, and save them on an MP3 player like a laptop, or more commonly an iPod.

☝ Using services like satellite, high-definition radio, or downloading music to your iPod or another MP3 player are great, but this will cost you. Sirius/XM Satellite Radio is an excellent system to listen to music without having to buy music but there is a yearly subscription. These radios offer over two hours of storage capability to replay past songs. This playback feature enables you to skip the music you do not like and replay your favorite songs. Along with the radio, there is also the same access to channels online at _www.SiriusXM. com_. This is really cool when commuting to work, traveling, dance, events, or business parties. Pandora® is an Internet radio provider with a free basic service where you can create a playlist at _www. Pandora.com_.

☝ How about **FREE college radio stations**? They have live streaming and archived podcasts. Here is the trick: Whenever you go to another state, start at 88 FM and use the manual dial to slowly work your way up to 92. It is refreshing to turn on the radio and realize that 95 percent of the music is something you've never heard of before. There are so many new things to explore, and the world is continuing to grow. Call small local and college radio stations to win free tickets and entry to concerts, bands, and events.

National Public Radio (NPR) at _www.NPR.org_ and Minnesota Public Radio (MPR) at _www.MPR.org_ have good news broadcasts and talk shows. YouTube is an excellent way to watch all genres of music videos for free at _www.YouTube.com_.

# Shopping for Stuff for Other People

## Saving on Birthday Gifts

Gifts are not about the amount of money but are about the value of love that went into them. You cannot put a price tag on love. A special gift like a body massage, neck rub, foot rub, listening more, cooking dinner, and snuggling costs you nothing more than time, but it is often more appreciated than any material gift.

👍 Giving flowers to your loved ones is a special gift. Pick out the freshest, cheapest flowers and plants at a wholesale flower market. Farmers' and flea markets are good places too. However, they typically get their items from the flower market. To get the best price, it is more economical to go directly to the source. Pay cash to negotiate the best deal. Plants, orchids, sunflowers, and exotic flowers last longer and are cheaper than roses.

Say "Heck no!" to Birthweek! *Birthweek* is when a person receives a gift every day during the week of their birthday. Just celebrate for one day and reduce the amount of consumer presents. Women, rather than having a birthday dinner party for yourselves, do something that has more meaning, something you made happen like getting a promotion, starting a business, expanding your business, buying a property, publishing an article, or graduating.

**Happy Birthd:** I found a "Happy Birthday" sign hanging from a tree in a city park. The family did a poor job of cleaning up after themselves. I was so excited that when I pulled it down from the branch the "ay" was torn off. Nevertheless, the idea is to reuse decorations year after year for the same or different family members. A new party theme is not needed each time; it will only cause you to spend money on items that will be discarded.

At an early age with children and at the beginning of a relationship, play down birthdays. Bake a cake and have a small party at the house or park. Do not cater parties at an all-the-rage pizza parlor or hire a creepy clown. I still have the burns on my forearm from baking cakes very early in the morning for my parents—but those were memories in the making!

❑ **AI:** _____

👍 Do not celebrate pet birthdays. No matter how little the cost, it does add up. Give the time and money to a needy child instead. View pets as a want or luxury, not as a need.

## Saving During the Holidays

Not every holiday has to be celebrated. Focus on the original reason for the holiday. Exchanging a few presents is fine, but why spend more time and money on Santa Clause, Rudolph, and Easter bunnies? You may be thinking, "Bah, humbug," but the truth is, this will leave your family more money to invest.

👍 During your lifetime, how much money has been spent on Christmas (or other holiday) clothes, gifts, cookies, decorations, cards, etc.? Just decorate one or two rooms. There is no need to decorate the kitchen, hallway, bathroom, bedroom, or laundry room. Also limit the amount of outside decorations and lights. There will be no more block competition as to who can draw the most electricity. Remember to use energy-saving LED (light emitting diode) light strands and solar powered decorations. How about organizing a block clothing or food drive with your neighbors instead? Helping people in need is more important than helping the electricity company, right? Use the decorations your kids make at school or buy used ornaments from garage sales or thrift stores. Do not blow your monthly expense budget on holiday decorations and events.

Do not go overboard when it comes to birthday and holiday gift giving. Agree in advance to limit the number and dollar amount of gifts. Parents, just get one large present per child. For large families, do one gift per person with a price limit, like thirty dollars. For extended family members, do a present draw for one person.

❏ **AI:** _____

👍 Put your skills like carpentry, craftwork, sewing, and culinary to work by making gifts for people. If you are a musician or DJ, create a mix CD. Everybody loves music!

Ask people what they <u>need in order to be happy</u>, not what they want. This will simplify the holidays. During the winter holiday season, spend more time volunteering at your place of worship and favorite charities. Be merry but money wise.

Do not buy wrapping paper or holiday cards ever again! Use free wrapping paper and cards sent in the mail from charities soliciting donations. Use the cards for holidays, birthdays, congratulations, and get-well-soon occasions. Reuse boxes, wrapping paper, ribbons, bows, gift bags, wine bags, and decorative tissue paper. Heck, grab these items from your apartment recycle bins. Don't ask . . . you know I did. Newspaper makes great wrapping paper (especially the comics). Have all family members adapt this by making a game of who has the most interesting article.

❏ **AI:** _____

👍 Do pets celebrate the holidays? I think not. So why spend money on presents for them? The dog be fine with its current chew toy. Try a tree branch for the dog and old shoelace for the cat. If you simply must give a present to your furry friend, limit it to a discounted food treat or one cheap toy from the entire family.

## Combining Celebrations and Cheap Gifts

**Combine anniversaries and holidays** into one celebration. If it's within two weeks, just do it, even sibling birthday parties.[22] This will save on dinners, presents, and decorations. Start combining birthdays with anniversaries, religious, national, and cultural events:

- Dad's birthday with Independence Day or Thanksgiving
- Son's birthday with Cinco de Mayo or Chinese New Year
- Her birthday with girls' night out or Valentine's Day
- His birthday with the Super Bowl or World Series
- Do not combine bachelor and bachelorette parties, or there might not be a wedding!

☝ Send multiple birthday and anniversary cards in one envelope. This will save a little on postage and stationery.

**Cheap Gifts:** An easy cookbook that s/he can use to feed themselves might be appreciated. Many single parents are on tight budgets, so a cookbook would be a thoughtful gift. Put it in a basket with some spices, oven mitts, and maybe a few cooking utensils, including a meat tenderizer. I also suggest a book on saving money and investing . . . like their own copy of this one!

Gifts Under Twenty Bucks:

- For a beach lover: a nice beach towel and a suntan lotion
- For a book lover: a book and a coffee mug
- For a child: an educational money game
- For a teenager: a budget application for their smartphone
- For a couple: a bottle of wine and a candle

☝ Get a cheap bottle of wine or champagne at a local grocery or liquor store, and at the checkout stand, ask the clerk or cashier to put a higher price sticker on it. For a $6.99 bottle, have them make up a price of $16.99. They will get a kick out of it. Don't forget to leave the price tag on the bottle. When you give the present, make sure the beneficiary

---

[22]   Not favoring one child over another.

sees the price tag, and act surprised and embarrassed that you left it on the bottle.

**The Lamp Gift**: Transference can occur via spreading the love. If you receive a present or gift that you will not use or have too many of them, then re-gift (yes, this is a word) it to somebody else. Reuse the same wrapping paper! Re-gift Christmas, holiday, birthday, work anniversary, and work promotion presents. Wine, books, pen sets, cologne, and unworn clothes are good candidates for re-gifting.

But do not go too far with re-gifting. One Christmas, I took an old lamp from my bedroom, wrapped it up, and gave it to my brother. The lampshade even had a bulb burn in it, and the bulb was not included. We opened our presents in the morning, and by dinner, there was a stack of lousy previously used presents by my bedroom door, including the lamp. Still, I have not given up on re-gifting because it is a smart, economical way to reuse items. Just be sure you aren't giving gifts that someone might find insulting or have given to you (Oops!). Don't forget to take off the original name gift tag!

## Giving Producer-Type Gifts

All of this money saved for everybody will be directed into growing savings, generating income, expanding the business, funding college, and/or building wealth. During the holidays, extra funds need to go to reducing expenses, lowering debt, investing in the future, and/or giving back to the community. This is a family discussion you need to have at the kitchen or dining room table.

❑ **AI:** _____

**Stocking Stuffers**: There are <u>no longer</u> Christmas Savings Plans; that is in the past. There are *only* retirement plans, business plans, and college funds! Are we there? Panama's economy is driven by consumer goods primarily because of the Panama Canal ship traffic. Their government takes 10 percent from everybody's salary and puts it directly into a mandatory Christmas Savings Plan. Then, they release the accounts in November for people to buy presents to fuel their consumer-based economy. Talk about a few controlling the many! If you have Christmas Savings Plans, cancel them and put those monies into a recurring investment for each family member.

❑ **AI:** _____

Buy your spouse and kids shares of a stock or mutual fund for the holidays, birthdays, and special celebrations. How about giving children and young adults a savings bond, a CD, a contribution to their college fund, or setting up a custodial IRA? Put the purchase transaction statement in their stocking or in a "free" greeting card.

❑ **AI:** _____

👍 Also give government savings bonds for baby showers. This will send the parents and guests a strong message about where your mind is. When the baby grows up, s/he will be reminded of you, far beyond when that toy gets broken or they grow bored of it. My parents gave us United States savings bonds as children. On my last visit home, my dad gave me a twenty-five-dollar savings bond that he found in my mom's safety deposit box.

👍 Even better than a CD or savings bond would be to start a Roth 401(k) if they earn an income or family members and friends can contribute to their 529 college savings plan. To make this process easy, invite people to contribute to an online 529 gift registry.

👍 Grandparents, aunts, and uncles should also give investment gifts, not toys or cash. For small graduation, housewarming, and special occasion gifts, give a book that promote money management, wealth-building, fitness, or green living with a used ribbon or wrapped in newspaper. Financial planning software systems or other educational products are also great choices.

👍 Many colleges provide computers to students. If they do not, a Mac or PC would be a great graduation present. The cost can be split between several people. This again sends the message of the importance of investing versus spending.

For your spouse or partner, give gifts that s/he can use to grow his/her business: a computer, printer/copier/fax machine, business suit, tools, software, save, advertising materials, or a business trip. You can also provide services in kind, like creating a website, editing their book, painting the office, updating their filing system, handing out flyers, and record keeping. Buy productive gifts that will be used as business tools and can be used as a legal tax write-off.

❑ **AI:** _____

👍 Furthermore, focus on growing yourself and your business over the holidays and at big media events like the Super Bowl, World Cup, NBA and MLB playoffs, NASCAR races, parades, graduations, derbies, concerts, and weddings. Use these events as income-producing activities, not downtime—the bars and promoters sure do. Instead of buying stuff for the holidays, take the family on a business trip. Bring work with you, and you will continue to be a producer. Holidays are the time to update your business plan and execute the marketing plan to build the business.

## Beauty Care

Everyone, men and women alike, should get haircuts less often. This will save on time, effort, and money that you would waste in the salon or barber shop. You can trim your hair at home.

👍 **Ladies**, silver hair is sexy! Natural, strong, and smart is a beautiful combination. Refrain from going to hairstylists to dye, frost, or highlight your hair often. Go to beauty schools for a cheap haircut and styling. The cheap haircut shops like Supercuts or Great Clips offer low prices and provide good service, and you will often find coupons for these places in your newspapers or mail. Ladies, also try cosmetology schools for a free makeover, including pedicures and waxing (Ouch!).

Women, cut back on your spa days. If you are going once a week, change to every other week. If you are going every other week, move to once a month. If you are going once a month, go to every other month. You get the picture. Schedule these appointments well in advance to refrain from the impulse to just go because you have had a bad day[23]

---

[23]   Jeffrey Combs, "I never have a 'bad' day. Just a few challenging moments."

or an "I deserve it" moment. Do more self-maintenance and treatments. Take turns with a girlfriend, and treat each other at your homes.

❏  **AI:** _____

👍 **Men**, if you're spending more than twenty-five dollars for a haircut, you're paying too much. Don't splurge on a shave. CeCe, who is my barber, charges only fifteen dollars, and I give a five-dollar tip. He invites me to BBQs and city music events, which I attend. Go to barber schools or training barber shops for free haircuts or under ten dollars. Don't forget to tip for a job well done.

Gentlemen, shave your face less frequently. If you shave every day and the growth is not too bad, try shaving every other day. If possible, avoid shaving on the weekends. Try the Save A Blade® razorblade sharpener that sharpens dull blades. Disposable razors can be very economical if bought in bulk and are really cheap when combined with the blade-saver tool, which also makes them a little greener. My preference is to use shaving gel over shaving cream because gel spreads easier and requires a lot less product for a closer shave, making the can last longer.

❏  **AI:** _____

## Clothing

### Shopping for Clothes

Always, always, always buy clothes on sale at the store and online. How many times have you bought something at retail price just to see that a month later, it's on the discount rack for half or less of what you paid for it?

Ordering through a catalog is a good way to narrow the selection and keep you from browsing too much. Only look at the discount e-mail and catalogs promotions that advertise worthwhile sales and sales sections or inserts. Guys, several times a year, Victoria's Secret and Frederick's of Hollywood will send out special discount catalogs. This is a great time to stock up on gifts for her (of course, it is really for us guys) because these discount catalogs are not sent out before winter holidays and Valentine's Day.

👍 You can buy slightly oversized footwear on sale and then just wear a pair of thick socks or two pairs if necessary. This technique is best for hard-soled and stiff shoes. In stores, buy shoes, boots, and sneakers off the racks of open boxes. Footwear on these racks is greatly discounted as compared to a style organized section.

## Saving with Style

Buy clothes at the end of the season or in the off seasons because stores have bigger promotional incentives to deplete their inventory. Break out of the trap of thinking you need to have different outfits for every season of the year. It is not necessary to wear distinct clothes for a certain season of the year. Most people don't care.

You do not grow out of clothing fashions; you grow into a new style. If you grow out of pants or long-sleeved shirts, just cuff them to make cutoff shorts or short-sleeved shirts. If your pants are too short, try wearing matching socks or high-top shoes to hide your high-waters.

👍 If you are missing buttons, no problem! Just alternate which buttons you use like in this illustration. This works better for casual, fun, and stylish shirts and does not work as well for dresses or dress shirts. Still, it's a style choice!

👍 Group items together when one part of a set is missing. This is great for men's socks and women's bras and panties. If the match is not that close, do it anyway and make a fashion statement out of it. This also works well for suits, jackets, paints, gloves, and belts. Try earrings and other jewelry too. Come on! Who will notice?

👍 Get cheap jewelry and spice it up to look more expensive than it really is. Customize by adding your own flair with beads and glitter. I am not really good at this, but once I bought a cheap Native American necklace with plastic imitation bones. The technique was to soak the necklace in a cup of tea for an hour to get the plastic bones to look like real bones.

✎ Wrinkled clothes are in style now. Really, they are! I started this trend, in my mind, twenty-five years ago, and it is finally back. You will look cool while saving time and energy by not ironing as much.

This is not just for men. Ladies, it is stylish to be cheap. If you can look good in an old sweater and jeans, then work it, sister! This is a state of mind with purpose. If you feel hot on the inside, others will sense it too. It will translate to the outside beauty while saving money on clothes and energy on not shopping.

**You Heel:** Women, please do not wear super-high heels shoes or uncomfortable boots when walking around town. Yes, they may look sexy, but you should not be in pain. It will slow you down or cost cab fare to go even a few blocks. High heels are nice, but I prefer a lady who still looks "hot," even when she's going somewhere in a hurry. Wear practical shoes or boots that enable you to still walk fast and sexy. Remember, time is money.

## Saving by Extending the Life

**Hand-Me-Downs:** Secondhand clothes are a super savings for families, and you need to encourage your kids to accept this. Growing up, my brothers, cousins, and neighbors all exchanged hand-me-downs that was coordinated by our parents. You need to foster this sharing. It is important that brothers and sisters get along and like each other. If this is the case, they will support one another because the younger kids will look up to the older ones, and they will want their brothers' and sisters' old clothes. This is the pull technique. I am assuming boys want their brother's clothes and girls their sisters', but you never know.

Notice the high-top sneakers to hide the high-water pants. Also, the shirt is not buttoned at the top and bottom because the buttons are missing. The disco shirt is my older brother's from the 1970s, and the chef pants are from when I cooked in a college cafeteria to work off my student loan.

Wear clothes to the last threads. When clothes, shoes, sneakers, and purses become old or out-of-style, convert them to a different use. If you think an item is getting worn out, redirect its role to when and where you wear it. Wear them at different places or activities than you did before. Demoting your clothes like this will make them last another year or more. Re-categorize clothes, shoes, and accessories to another role so they live on. Convert work clothes to after-work clothes, from dinner clothes to lunch clothes, and from fitness center outfits to home workout ensembles. Make specialized roles like sleepwear, housecleaning, playing sports, and working out. Of course, you can wear beat-up clothes for lying around the home, painting, fixing the car, gardening, and yard work.

❏ **AI:** _____

When clothes start getting torn up, use them as underclothes around the home, as well as for sleeping, working out, or rags for cleaning. These items will eventually go to charities like Goodwill, The Salvation Army, churches/temples, homeless shelters, or to needy families you know. Note that Goodwill is open seven days a week, and The Salvation Army will do pickups at your home. I suggest you give them a little tip . . . and always get a receipt!

❏ **AI:** _____

👍 When your underwear gets too worn out to wear anymore, wash them one last time and store them away. When you go on a vacation, pack the old underwear. As you wear them on your trip, throw them away after they have been worn. This frees up valuable room in your suitcase for souvenirs, gifts, etc. on your return trip.

**Fixing Holes:** If you have a hole in the bottom of a sock, turn the holey part inward 90 degrees so it is less likely people will see it. Once there is no more hope to hide it because it is too big, retire the sock to be a duster.

**Staples :** Check this out . . . many people in the Northeast and Southern California love sweat pants and sweat suits. Of course, I have a few pairs. They are still in good shape and have another good ten years left in them. However, the pockets have holes in them from carrying keys. This also happens with jeans and shorts. This is a problem because important things like keys or a cell phone may fall out. A simple solution is to staple the pockets closed. Problem easily solved! If you are good

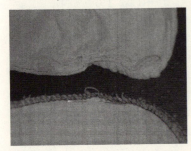

at sewing and can do it quickly, great, but if not, just get out the office stapler. It will take four to six staples to repair the hole, depending on its size. When you wear and wash them, just do a quick maintenance check.

You can barely see the staples.

👍 Other cool ideas to extend the life of clothes are as follows: use safety pins to hold up pants or skirts, Band-aids on glasses, and masking tape on sandals if the soles become unglued.

👍 Resole good quality shoes and boots. This is a savings for both men and women. I have several pairs that I've had resoled at least twice. Use a shoehorn while putting on shoes, boots, <u>and</u> sneakers so you do not stretch out and damage the back part with your fingers while forcing your heel into the shoe or sneaker. This will extend their lives.

Buying high-quality items at a discount can be of great value, especially if they have a very long life expectancy. Italian shoes and belts might last for ten years, a couch for fifteen, a car for twenty, and a spouse forever. Certain countries specialize in quality items at a good price that you can buy locally or on the web.

# Save by Dressing Cheaply

### Free Clothes

Have a clothing- (not wife-) swapping party. Check to see if your friends have been to or know of any parties close by. These can be fab-u-lous!!! Do a TS (Tie or Tool Swap) for men, or SS (Shoe Swap) and PS (Purse Swap) for women. You should do all types of swapping like videogames and movies. Also work with neighbors or go online to swap. There are Meetup groups at *www.Meetup.com* that coordinate these swap and networking events.

❑ **AI:** _____

Meetup is the world's largest network of local groups and makes it easy for anyone to organize a local group or find one of the thousands already meeting face to face. More than 2,000 groups get together in local communities each day, each one with the goal of improving themselves or their communities. Meetup's mission is to revitalize local communities and help people around the world self-organize. You can join various groups or create your own.

☝ Now this is a real stretch, but how about getting clothes that are cleared from school lockers? At the end of the month or school year, all

items are discarded. Gyms and clubs do this too. Why let these forgotten clothes go to waste?

Darryl the night before a big hike. The t-shirt is from the end of the high school year locker cleanout. I still have this t-shirt and the pants. My first sports car that drove me to financial hardship is in the background. Now I drive a much more fuel-efficient car, which I have had for over twelve years and the car has less than 50,000 miles on it.

**Cheap Wardrobe Management**

If you own a lot of clothes, shoes, sneakers, belts, purses, and jewelry, first have an immediate moratorium on buying anymore. Be happy with what you have. Can you do this? Then decide if you really need them. If you do not, sell them, trade them, and then as a last resort, donate them. Even just four or five items is a good start and will bring in a little income or reduce your tax base. If you decide you truly need them, that is fine. Just maintain that collection and do not add to it. Enough is enough! Create different combinations to give you the feeling of a fresh wardrobe.

❑   **AI:** _____

How many shoes do you really need? Do with fewer pairs and free up that space, both physically and mentally. For now, stop adding to the number. Ask yourself, "Do I really *need* that pair, or is it really about my girlfriends, insecurities, or that 'high' I get while shopping?" Find something else to talk to them about that is focused on wealth creation. On the high side, ladies, let's agree that twenty-five pairs is a good number of shoes <u>and</u> boots. Men, let's agree on fifteen pairs, including sneakers. If you only wear a pair once or twice a year let it go. Ask yourself, "Is it going to make me more money or improve my health?" If not, the answer is easy: It's a want, not a need. Start reducing the inventory now!

❑   **AI:** _____

❑   *Which comes first?* **WANTS** _____ or **NEEDS** _____

There has been much discussion on reducing your wardrobe expenses. Quality is important and has its role in life. Extremely expensive clothes and designer-label dresses and suits are basically a no-no. Under $250 dollars for an outfit (not just a jacket or a dress) your profession requires (not desires) is fine, but more for clothes worn a few times a year is not a good investment unless it brings in more business or closes deals.

☝ Re-wearing clothes a few times without washing them is fine, just like you do with a jacket, sweater, and sneakers, as long as you do not sweat in them. If you do, it is wise to lay the clothes inside out to air out overnight. Also check for ring around the collar and foul odor. If you find these, it's time to toss it into the hamper or use it in a workout.

👍 "Many detergents now on the market come from ultra concentrations. This means you don't need to use as much for a standard-sized load. You may have a tendency to add a little more simply because the recommended amount seems too small to do the job. You're throwing away your money when you do this."[41] Use a little liquid fabric softer purchased at the dollar store and also fill the cup up with two-thirds of what the instructions suggest.

👍 When putting clothes in the washer, make sure they are untangled by putting them in one piece at a time to get them clean. It is a best practice to first fill the washer with water; then add detergent, softener, and bleach; cycle to mix for a few seconds; and finally add the clothes. "When you remove items from your washing machine, shake them out before you put them in the dryer. Shaking untangles clothing and decreases drying time and also protects clothing."[42] This will also reduce the clothes from being wrinkled.

👍 Use permanent press drying cycle and set the dampness setting near less dry. Usually the setting just under normal will dry the clothes fine except for denim jeans or towels, which you should hang to dry once pulled from the dryer. Stop the dryer on the air fluff tumble cycle. There is not much value from these twenty minutes. Untangle clothes when removing them from the dryer and hang them immediately so they do not wrinkle. Also consider drying clothes outside on a clothesline or indoors on a drying rack.

👍 Reuse a fabric softener sheet two to three times. On the fourth load, use two older sheets together. On the fifth load, use those again and then discard them. You can also start by tearing a sheet in half and use one for each load.[24] On the third load, use the first half and the second half on the fourth load. At your apartment complex, reuse discarded fabric sheets from other tenants as long as you live in a sanitary environment with clean neighbors.

---

[24]   Verify that the lint filter is securely in place so the torn fabric softer sheet does not caught in the filter.

Clean your dryer lint filter after every load. "A clean filter helps air circulate more efficiently, so clothes require less time to dry. A clean filter also puts less stress on the dryer, which may help it last longer."[43]

## NO FUR

Does wearing a fur coat make you classy? Depending on the size and type of coat, it requires from a dozen to over a hundred creatures to make one coat! Buying an expensive fur coat is crazy and cruel. Do you have an old fur coat in your closet? Is your mother's rabbit coat or mink stole stored in the basement or attic? If you do, give it to charity to benefit other people in need or animals in distress as a donation that you can write-off on your income tax return. This is a powerful transition from consumer to producer that affects others positively. Do not continue the old-fashioned trend of passing the coat down to the next generation as a family heirloom.

❏ **AI:** _____

**WARNING!** These websites may exhibit unpleasant photographs and videos, but I encourage you to check them out if you would like to donate, volunteer, or learn more about their programs.

👍 Give the fur back to the animals. If you would like to see that old fur put to a good use, donate it to The Humane Society of the United States' Coats for Cubs program. The fur will aid and comfort wildlife. All of the furs received by The Humane Society of the United States are sent to

wildlife rehabilitators. They use the furs to warm and comfort orphaned and injured wildlife. Fur is a unique item that I recommend donating over selling. To donate a fur, go to: *www.humanesociety.org/ coatsforcubs.*

Alpine Meadows Wildlife Rehab

👍 Many of the coats retrieved by People for the Ethical Treatment of Animals (PETA) go to homeless people who can't afford to buy their own coats. Every year, PETA holds a few "fur kitchens" at homeless shelters around the country. They have even shipped hundreds of furs to help warm the women and children freezing in Afghanistan and Iraq. The coats are marked so they are not easily resold and charitable fur donations are not exploited for profit. To donate a fur, go to: *www. furisdead.com/donate.asp*.

It is unfortunate to show this photo, but this is the cruel truth behind the fur industry. It's important to shine light on these cruel and unnecessary practices. Lynx in leg-hold trap, FurBearerDefenders. com

☞ Check your favorite clothing store to see if they have a coat donation program that provides discounts on your purchase. In 2010, ABC *Good Morning America* and Burlington Coat Factory had a program called "Warm Coat & Warm Heart Drive." For a donated coat, you received 10 percent discount on your entire purchase. Their focus is everyday jackets. It ran from November through mid-January. For details, go to *www. OneWarmCoat.org* or *www.burlingtoncoatfactory.com/content/coat-drive*.

❑ **AI:** _____

# Entertainment

## Cheap Dining

Know all of the local joints in your neighborhood with discounted menus. Go on a walkabout to discover new cheap eateries and places to market your business. This is an excellent networking opportunity while getting some exercise! Stop in and speak to the small business owners and make a connection.

## Twenty-Dollar Date Night

A date for only twenty bucks? This is very doable. Find a few places to take your significant other or a date out for dinner for twenty dollars that are special. Once you have found several spots that you both enjoy, become regulars and get to know the owner and manager to get discounts or extra food. A happy hour (HH) bar menu is another cheap option during a specific time. If you cannot find a place for dinner, switch to lunch, which will have a cheaper menu. If it is not HH, do not buy any alcoholic beverages. Just drink tap water or hot tea, which is usually free. Have a drink at home or at a nearby happy hour bar before or after the dinner date.

❑ **AI:** _____

Vietnamese, Thai, Greek, Mexican, and Chinese (with no MSG) food can be inexpensive and healthy. Japanese, Cuban, Indian buffets, and hamburger joints (flame broiled) can be really cheap too. Different geographical regions will have their specialties at competitive prices, like seafood in Boston and Seattle, Chinese food in Manhattan and San Francisco, Mexican food in southern California and Arizona, BBQ in St. Louis and Texas, Italian in New York and New Jersey, and Southern food in Alabama and Louisiana.

You might wonder, "What if my date thinks I am cheap?" What does it even matter? What is important is what you are doing with the savings. Explain your investment strategy. Let him/her be a part of it to realize the long-term benefits.

✍ We all have heard of Seniors' Early Bird Specials that start by 4:00 p.m. Many restaurants also offer special family days, allowing kids to eat for free on specific days or hours to bring in extra traffic.

**No Tax**: Ask your local eating establishment if they have a neighborhood discounts for regulars. This is typically on the entire meal including drinks. The discount is normally 10 percent, which will cover the tax and a little more. The Chieftain Irish Pub in San Francisco is one of my favorite spots, and it offers terrific food, along with the added benefit of this discount and HH. Don't forget to tip on the original selling price and not the discounted check.

**Go Fish**: Put your cards in restaurant fish bowls to win free lunches. You just never know if you'll win. The prize is usually a lunch or two. This year, I won at a Mexican grill, and it was for six lunches! Recently,

I was at the same grill and ordered my famous BIG A*S BURRITO with double meat, and the manager comped it. I was way happy this was free, and I left a two-dollar bill tip in their tip jar. Yes, you need to tip at anyplace that has a tip jar, even if all you can give is loose change.

## Tipping

**"I don't believe in tipping. I believe in over-tipping."** Always tip and tip well! Hand people the bill(s), especially if you are tipping a bartender. Look that person in the eye as a sign of respect and thank them again. Tips are a significant source of income for bartenders, waitresses/ waiters, maids, and cooks.

👍 Only tip 15 to 20 percent for the food and beverage bill, <u>not</u> the total bill. You do not tip for the tax portion. I tip at 20 percent for decent and great service. For people I know that give me special treatment or excellent service, the tip is 25 percent. So, on a total check of fifty dollars with 8 percent sales tax of four dollars, the tipable bill is forty-six dollars. Rather than giving a ten-dollar tip for 20 percent tip, give nine dollars. That dollar saved goes in your kitty.

For room service, tip as usual for good personal service. If the service charge is already included, this entire amount is typically not toward the tip for the server and chef. If the service charge is 20 percent, sometimes they are only getting between 10 to 15 percent with the rest going to the hotel, so you will need to include an extra tip to make up for this. Verify this with the person that brought the food to your room. This will enable you to make another connection and a chance to pass out another business card.

Don't forget to leave a tip on the table at a paid or free buffet like the ones in casinos or hotels. Also tip the meat carver and omelet cook a buck or two (per serving).

If you are only drinking free water at a bar, be sure to tip twenty-five or fifty cents for the server.

If you have a drink at a bar or club, walk your empty glass back to the bar. Also push the glass as close to the inside of the bar as possible so the bartender does not have to reach too far to get it. This is just being polite and shows that you respect their service. Also this gives you one last opportunity to thank the bartender and make a connection.

Recently, I brought my glass back to the bartender and pushed it to him just before leaving. I did not want another drink and was just returning the glass. The bartender was nice and just poured me another drink, even though I did not ask. It was a freebie, which was not my intention. Of course he got a two-dollar tip. Good favors happen to good people, and good people in return deserve tips!

For special service from people like bartenders, bellhops, and maids offer a two-dollar bill. Eventually, you will give them a business card within the two-dollar bill. You can get two-dollar bills at your local bank. If they are out, just ask the teller to order a stack of ten for you. There should be no charge.

❏   **AI:** _____

👍 Tip airline flight attendants a dollar for a drink that you purchase and give them a two-dollar bill for free alcoholic beverages. Two-dollar bills are good luck in many cultures, and if you mention that, they will typically accept it.

👍 Tip performers on the street. This has an emotional impact on other people walking by too. You can also distribute your flyers while you're there. Also tip musicians and bands at local performances, especially those who perform at free events.

**Real Tip:** If you get a lot of packages delivered to your home office, show your appreciation to the delivery person. Give your FedEx or UPS drivers a ten-dollar gift certificate for a local health food store that serves hot meals as a winter holiday present. This is an East Coast tradition with a West Coast twist! Of course, I do this as a gesture of friendship and admiration. Last year, a driver gave me a bottle of wine . . . and I'm sure it did not come off his truck!

Get the most out of over-tipping. Strategically use tips to get more products or better quality of services that outweighs the amount of the tip. For example, tip well for the first beverage so the next round will be even "stiffer" or to get the HH extended for you. Another example is heavily tipping waitresses to allow substitutes or extra side dishes. Also target tips to market your business and self.

Once you become wealthy, double your tips for everybody!

## Cheap Drinks

### Drinking Cheap at Home

Alcohol is a big part of the expense of dining and entertainment. Beware of buying a lot of beverages when eating out. The price will quickly add up, and you can get it cheaper elsewhere. If you want really good alcoholic beverages, buy a bottle on sale at your favorite discount store. Then save money by drinking it at home with friends instead of spending money on drinks at a high-end bar or elegant restaurant. Having pre-drinks before going out is much cheaper, and you can make the cocktails exactly how you like them. This has the added benefit of spending more time at home working on money-making activities while saving energy. Invest in or build up your own little mini-bar at home with both discounted decent and high quality alcohol.

❑ **AI:** _____

👍 Always buy cheap beer, well drinks, and house wine. Buying a "top-shelf" cocktail once in a while is fine if the price is greatly discounted. There may be health benefits of liquor that has been filtered multiple times, making it easier for the liver to process and reducing a hangover the next morning. I am haunted by every nine-dollar cocktail I have ever bought. They fly around me with white wings in my nightmares, heckling me that I should have gotten the four-dollar well drink, which is just out of reach.

### Drinking Cheap on the Town

**OTD**: Buy cheap beer and put it in a small brown bag ("street bag") to drink on the street and in parks. This is a great savings of buying one or two drinks in a bar or club. Just have them on the street while walking,

<u>not</u> driving, over to your favorite hang-out. It is best for these to be cans over bottles because of the danger and mess of broken glass. Some cities allow or tolerate this, but don't flaunt this. Check with your city or county first. At the liquor or grocery store, a great price on beer will include the tax or can/bottle deposit. This is called *OTD*, which stands for "Out the Door." This is the final price and a great deal!

👍 Drinking on the train, subway, bus, and cab are other great pre-date or pre-event savings. This is a cool way to get a jump start on the night. Again, check that it is legal or tolerated and try to stay with cans that are concealed. You'd be surprised at all the places where it is allowed. In a

taxi, ask the driver if s/he is fine with this. Pass part of the savings along and give him/her a little extra tip for being accommodating. Remember to dispose of your trash.

Darryl brown-bagging it in London.

👍 Make your own double when you're out on the town. Buy a couple of small bottles (50 ml) of alcohol and leave them in the freezer. Get the plastic bottles, which can cost as little as one dollar (OTD) for decent, two dollars for good, and four dollars for premium liquor. Buy a drink at the bar, not just a soda or juice. The bar, club, or restaurant needs to make money too. Drink a little of it and then go to the bathroom or a secluded corner and pour a bottle into your drink. **Double your pleasure**, but be careful not to get caught and that nobody sees you throwing out the bottle.

👍 It is always good to keep a flask handy to bring to bars and events. They make flasks in all different shapes, so you might get one in the shape of a cell phone in a leather case with belt clip. Deceptive flasks do not work everywhere, trust me. Do a web browser search[25] for them. Sometimes it is easier going with two small bottles in your pockets,

---

[25]    Examples of web browser search engines are Google, Yahoo, and Bing.

briefcase, purse, or bra. Don't do this if it is strictly prohibited in the establishment.

In family restaurants that don't serve alcohol, ask if you can bring in your own wine and if they will waive the corking fee. Also local restaurants, cafés, and pizza parlors may allow you to bring in your own alcohol. This is best for people you know or regularly visit. Don't expect it, but you never know until you ask.

Join wine-tasting social clubs. For twenty bucks per event, you can taste varieties of wine for a few hours. It is much cheaper than spending the day in Napa Valley, California (wine country) and it is an excellent opportunity to network.

❑ **AI:** _____

👆 If you are not drinking alcohol, get a soft drink and mention that you are the designated driver. You may get a free soft drink, or at least free refills.

### *"Do NOT Drink and Drive! Drink Responsibility."*[26]

**Happy Hours**

**"The early bird catches the worm."** Only indulge in happy hours with discounted drinks for a specified time. Seriously, do not negotiate about this with people. Always ask if there is a drink special or happy hour, even if there is not a sign posted. Ask this no matter where you are—at pubs, lounges, hotel bars, night clubs, boat parties, street

---

[26] "In 2007 the number of alcoholic liver disease deaths was 14,406 and alcohol-induced deaths, excluding accidents and homicides was 23,199," according to the CDC at _www.cdc.gov/nchs/fastats/alcohol.htm_ (April 27, 2011). "In 2008, there were 13,846 alcohol-related deaths," according to the National Highway Traffic Safety Administration at _www.alcoholalert. com/drunk-driving-statistics.html_ (April 27, 2011). According to MADD at _www.cheshireherald.com/node/331_ (April 27, 2011), "Also in 2008, there were over 500,000 people were injured from drunk drivers."

festivals, neighborhood block parties, restaurants, symphonies, and even weddings. You just never know. Especially look for happy hour specials on a first date (in case there is not a second), business trips, and even if you are not paying. Set the tone that you value money and are bold enough to ask for what you want. It shows you respect yours and other people's money.

Specials are not just for drinks. They may also have free food or a short discounted bar menu.

Typical HHs occur Mondays to Fridays from 5:00 to 7:00 p.m. Don't assume seven o'clock is the standard end time. There are many so-called "happy hours" that start at 4:00 and end at 6:00, so verify the end time. Find extended happy hours that last to 8:00 or even 9:00 p.m. Also, identify places that have happy hour on the weekend which is great for a dinner date and watching sporting events.

❑  **AI:** _____

👍 There are also reverse or late-night happy hours that start at 9:00 and go to 11:00 p.m., or start at 10:00 p.m. and go to 1:00 a.m. To find happy hours in your area, use City Search at _www.CitySearch.com_ or Google it. There are Meetup groups that specialize in hosting happy hours.

Not all happy hours are equal. There are many variations:

- An extra beer with bucket of beers during a sporting game
- Bottomless Bloody Mary or Mimosa Sunday brunches
- Discount on draft beer, well drinks, and house wines

- Half off everything behind the bar (yeah!)
- Special only on item(s) on the board or menu

Five-dollar Cosmo at Orson in San Francisco which is a hidden jewel in SOMA. The vibe is cool with music you haven't heard before, at least not in a restaurant.

👍 If you are out with friends or on a date, do not make a big deal about happy hour prices until the hour is almost up or you are paying. Set your cell phone alarm fifteen minutes before HH is over to remind you to get the last discounted prices. Beware of the premature end time, and remember to watch the bar clock. Understand your environment, as many neighborhood bars run on bar time with clocks running ten to fifteen minutes fast. While other establishments' time is directly linked to the cash register clock with no ability to extend the happy hour.

This just happened to me in Tulsa. I arrived with plenty of time to get the last HH call, but the bartender said I was too late. The bar clock was eighteen minutes fast. I pleaded with the bartender and showed her my cell phone time of 6:52 (yes, p.m.). I mentioned that I had just called an hour ago and was told happy hour went to seven o'clock. She pointed to the bar clock, which showed 7:10. I turned up the charm, and in the end, I got two light beers for only three dollars. I gave her a two-dollar tip for extending the HH and stacking[27] the second beer. To make the experience even better, she mentioned that there is free pizza by the window (yum!).

👍 When staying at a hotel, check at the front desk to see if there is a manager-hosted happy hour. There will probably be free food and many times free drinks. These happy hours are typically from 5:00 to 7:00 p.m., Monday through Friday. Some are just one day of the week while others are seven days a week. Upscale and chain hotels often have happy hours at the lobby bar.

👍 Remember to tip the bartender as if you were buying at the regular price. Fold the bill twice to be a quarter of the size before handing it to the bartender. Do not leave it on the dirty sticky bar countertop. Watch for them to come back around. They will remember you the next time you return and maybe give a discount, free drink, or extend the HH. Heck, just ask if they will extend the happy hour for you for an hour or even all night. This really works. I know because countless bars have extended this courtesy to me. Make the connection! If they like you,

---

[27] *Stacking* is when you buy an extra drink for yourself before the discount special ends—stacking a new beverage behind your current beverage.

there is a good chance this will happen to you. It's about friendship and trust. Everybody wants to be liked and appreciated.

## Cheap Entertainment

### Cheap Movies

Only go to **matinees** with discounted tickets to watch movies, especially new, 3D, or IMAX® features. Using regional coupon books for discounted movies is a great thrill. College and independent film festivals will have lower ticket prices. Never pay full price for a movie ever again! If you're feeling festive, order an ice slushee-type and have them add ice to the bottom. Once you're seated, pour in a little booze from your flask. This makes the fifteen minutes of previews bearable! Remain low-key so you don't get caught. Do not abuse the situation by getting drunk in the theater and disturbing other people.[28]

BYOPC : If you get hungry during the movies, bring your own snacks like trail mix, a bag of chips, a box of candy, a chocolate bar, fruit, or home-popped popcorn with butter (of course). This will save you from the temptation of buying the expensive food at the theater concession stand. However, bringing a cooler of soda pop or a bucket of fried chicken may be a stretch. Again, watch out for the ushers and clean up the evidence when you leave the theater.

Have a movie night at home. Break out the old DVD or even VCR tapes. It has probably been a long time since you have watched those movies. To get to the twenty-first century, use a Digital Video Recorder (DVR) or TiVo® to store movies to be viewed later. This will allow you to fast forward through the introduction, commercials, and boring parts. There are also free movies on cable and satellite on-demand services. Check it out to save money and energy.

❑  **AI:** _____

👆 Don't forget to multitask while watching movies at home. Sit there with your laptop working on your business. At least open mail, organize

---

[28]   Of course, talking softly during a movie is totally acceptable.

records, file office papers, pay bills, and create marketing material while enjoying movies and television programs. Your family or date will probably help if you ask and explain your motives. How can they say "No"? They are lucky to have your company. Teach kids to master this skill at a young age with grace.

👍 Check for free outdoor movies hosted by the city or indoor movies hosted by local bars.

## Cheap Clubbing

Join mailing lists to get on the guest lists of bars and clubs to pay no or a reduced cover charge. Get to know the cashier, manager, or owner so you do not have to pay. You will need to tip them or at least offer to buy them a beverage. As previously mentioned, tip two-dollar bills to local bouncers in the establishments you frequent. They may give you preferred door treatment and not make you wait in line, and they may even waive the admission fee.

❑ **AI:** _____

👍 Get to the club early to get in for free or get a discounted entry fee. For example, get in free before ten o'clock or ten dollars before eleven o'clock. If you're on a date or with a friend when the cover is ten dollars, ask for fifteen dollars for two people. Mention that you will tip the bartenders well or give them a two-dollar bill.

👍 Have your own DJ music and dance party. Pick out some music and dance around your home with a beverage. Have fun parties by yourself, with a date, or together with other couples on the weekend versus going out and spending money at a club. You can also plan small dance parties around satellite or online radio weekly shows. Some of the specialized DJ music parties are disco, house, punk, club, hip-hop, new wave, 80s big hair, and Top 40 hits.

**BADA BING!** Say NO to nudie bars, guys![29] Go out on a date instead of going to a strip club, even if the date is with your wife. Buy a few

---

[29]   This also applies to ladies.

scented candles and light them around your home. Women will think
you are romantic, even if you tend not to be. Get candles that are

encased in glass to reduce the chance
of fire. Incense is another great way to
set the mood and will diminish any foul
smells in your place. The combination
of candles, incense, a clean place,
flowers, and a kiss at the front door will
increase your odds dramatically. You
know what I'm getting at (wink-wink!).

**Cheap Events**

👍 Listen to free jazz, reggae, blues, world beat, country, rock bands,
symphonies, DJs, and watch plays in the park. There are many of these
free outdoor events during the warmer seasons to hand out flyers for
your business; have your partner and kids help. College performances
charge much less than mainstream shows.

There are many cheap and fun public places to explore:

- 👍 <u>Events</u>: parades, marches, rallies, carnivals, dances,
  independence celebrations, county fairs, church choirs, New
  Year's celebrations, and book readings
- 👍 <u>Museums</u>: modern art, Southwestern art, heritage, design,
  natural history, academy of science, children, aviation, military
  base tours, factory tours, and the Capitol
- 👍 <u>Parks and Reserves</u>: hiking, swimming, rock climbing, biking,
  rollerblading, military memorials, concerts, symphony, Japanese
  gardens, botanical gardens, feeding the ducks, bird watching,
  and sun bathing

👍 Check your community or recreational center bulletin board for
inexpensive activities. After-school activities and neighborhood
programs are offered at great price value. Take a date or the kids to a
free cultural event, national landmark, or government buildings. Here
are a few examples of events with free admission (subject to change):

- First Wednesday of the month at San Francisco Zoo
- First Friday of the month from 4:00 to 7:00 p.m. in New York at The Museum of Modern Art
- First Saturday of the month at Denver Art Museum
- First Sunday of the month at San Francisco Asian Art Museum

Other cities have similar promotions. There will be a donation box when you walk in, and I suggest you give a buck or two per person. It is a charitable gift, so ask for a receipt or make a note of it.

State parks, state fairs, natural preserves, beaches, rivers, and lakes are also cheap sources of entertainment. Get on the weekly e-mail calendar of events for *www.CitySearch.com*. Websites like *www. sf.funcheap.com* and *www.sfgate.com* offer endless great ideas and free or low cost events in the San Francisco Bay Area. Similar online event calendars exist for most cities and towns.

❏  **AI:** _____

👍 If you want to enjoy expensive outdoor concerts, listen from just outside the open stadium or arena. Bring a chair to sit and relax on the street, in an adjacent park, across in an open space, or nearby on a friend's patio. If needed, pay to get into the parking lot to get really close to listen to the music outside. You can also enjoy tailgate festivities and watch the game on portable TV without a ticket.

👍 Get a journalist's pass for free entry and special privileges into conventions and other paid marketing events. Bloggers with active websites classify as journalists. There may be free samples and extra benefits. You can also get access to special parties with free food, drinks, and excellent networking opportunities.

👍 To save on concerts, sporting events, and amusement parks, go directly to the ticket promoter or sponsor for discounted tickets or coupons. This may be online, at the store, or on the back of the product box/can.

**Live Vicariously through Others:** Watching others enjoy themselves will save you money. Enjoy local sporting events like marathons, rugby, soccer, and tennis. You can even seek some thrills from heated competitions like kickball, Big Wheel® racing, and surfing. Improvisation, poetry reading, amateur standup comedian, and open mic nights are cheap forms of entertainment that will have you laughing. Once again, just make sure you are multitasking with a money-making activity.

👍 I encourage happy, simple things like music and exercise as a cheap thrill. Find small things that bring you much joy. They do not have to cost anything. Take a date walking around a lake, jogging on the beach, or hiking in the mountains. Bring a picnic basket or backpack with lunch and wine as an extra bonus. That is romantic!

**"On belay. Belay on. Ready to climb. Climb on. Climbing!"**   Going

to free events is not a free pass to spend a lot of money on food. Make time to cook and take food with you to city events, concerts, parks, hiking, and climbing. Eat cheaply and healthy whenever possible.

Darryl climbing the Longs Peak Mountain east face ascent in Colorado at 14,259 feet.

👍 Look for discount signs for food, clothes, art, jewelry, and crafts at events. "After a street fair or festival ends, go up to some of the food booths and find out what they're doing with all the food they didn't sell. Sometimes you can score some free food, or they might sell it to you cheap."[44] You can get plates of food for just a few dollars, a deal on handmade soap, and twofers on beers. Eat similar food that you will get at a street fair before you go there. This will remove the temptation to buy expensive food at public events. You can buy chicken skewers at a local grocery store for under three dollars versus eight you will pay at a fair or carnival. Even bringing your own water, beer, iced tea, or ice cream to a festival will save many dollars. Teach your children this habit and ask for their support. Tailor this for different types of fairs and ethnic events.

**Cheap Sports**

**Saving at the Game**

If you love sports, enjoy games that are cheaper. Rather than going to expensive Major League games, go to high school, college, minor league, amateur, and preseason games. These tickets are cheaper with better seats than at Major League sporting events. For more ideas, check out "10 Affordable Ways to Get Your Sports Fix" by Bob Cook at *www.nbcsports.msnbc.com/id/27209782*.

❑ **AI:** _____

👍 Try buying tickets below face value from scalpers <u>after</u> the game has started. Go late to sporting events to buy cheaper scalped tickets, because the price drops dramatically once the game has begun. Bring a map of the stadium or arena so you do not get ripped off. This shows that you know what you are doing and are exercising "street smarts." Pay less by talking to a few scalpers before settling on a price. Verify the ticket date is correct. In many cases, scalping tickets is legal as long as it does not involve selling the tickets for much more than the face value and certain distance from the box office. Sometimes the local bars will have people trying to get rid of tickets too. Check the message board behind the bar or with the bartender.

👍 Go to games with seat price discount promotions. There are also free tickets if you donate a gift of non-perishable food or an unwrapped toy. Avoid the free stuff promotions that are meant to sucker consumers in with bobble-heads, bats, or fan towels for the first 2,000 attendees. Having to wait in line for hours to collect "free" junk and then wait again until the game starts is a waste of time.

Do you really need the expensive box seats, all that junk food, and three large beers? That is money lost that you can never get back. If you are in good spirits with good company, you can easily spend half that money and still have a great time. Cancel, sell, or partner on season tickets, but if you must buy them yourself, only purchase discounted ones that are cheaper than individual tickets.

Play sports on organized leagues instead of just watching them. It will be a lot cheaper on your wallet and healthier for your body. For pickup games and matches go to your local and community parks that have basketball, tennis, and volleyball courts. Many city parks offer community swimming pools at little or no cost.

❑ **AI:** _____

**Splinters:** Buy or make cheap food to bring to sporting events. When you are skiing bring a sandwich in your pocket to be eaten at lunchtime at the lodge. When I lived in Denver, my friend Ed and I went to Colorado Rockies baseball games together. When walking from the parking lot, we would look for the "burrito lady." She was set up with a cooler on the sidewalk across from the stadium in downtown Denver. We would only pay a buck twenty-five for a hot breakfast burrito. We loaded up so we did not buy the expensive ballpark food. You can also go to the local grocery store to buy cooked meals to put in your backpack to carry into the game.

☝ Before you go to a game, look for bars near the stadium or arena that offer drink specials. Save money by consuming less at the inflated prices during the game. Cattycorner from Coors Field stadium, we visited a bar called Splinters from the Pine and drank one-dollar Coors Lights before baseball games. Yes, I said a dollar! Just across the street in the stadium, the same beer was six fifty, and that was back in 2000. You would think since Coors Brewery had the stadium naming rights, they could sell their beer to fans at a discount, but fat chance!

### Saving at the Races

☝ Many horseracing tracks have one-dollar promotional days. The domestic beer, hot dogs (not made from the horses), parking, and programs are only one buck each. These days can be on Fridays for date night or Sundays with the family. This is a fun outing at little cost. You will meet a diverse group of people, which provides extra entertainment. Just bring some work during the lows between the races. Don't bet on every race or eat too many dogs.

**Life after Racing:** Greyhound dog racing is another alternative with promotional days, but it has a bad history due to the killings of so many dogs. Many states in the U.S. have banned greyhound racing, and others have passed legislation to improve the treatment of racing dogs. "After the dogs are no longer able to race or as soon as they no longer consistently place in the top four, the dog's race career ends. The best dogs are kept for breeding purposes [lucky them]. According to the industry numbers, upwards of 2,000 dogs are still killed annually in the

U.S. while anti-racing groups estimate the figure at closer to 12,000. Other greyhounds are either sold to research labs or sent to foreign racetracks, sometimes in developing countries."[45]

"Organizations such as Greyhound Pets of America (*www. GreyhoundPets.org*) and Adopt-a-Greyhound (*www. Adopt-A-Greyhound.org*) try to ensure that as many of the dogs as possible are adopted. In addition to actively cooperating with private adoption groups throughout the country, many race tracks have established their own adoption programs at various tracks."[46] These are the thoughtful race tracks you should consider attending.

👍 For car races, go to the event sponsors' stores, sponsors' website, or local supermarket to save on tickets. Seats can be discounted 50 percent or greater.

## Transportation

### Saving Money on Your Vehicle

### Do You NEED a New Car?

Do you really <u>need</u> that expensive $40,000, $55,000, or $75,000 vehicle, or do you just <u>desire</u> it? The more expensive a car is, the higher the maintenance, insurance, and license plate fee. Children want things they do not need. Is a fast red convertible, fully loaded black slick sedan, massive SUV, or minivan with all of the extras more important than your family's future? Is it worth having to work into your sixties and seventies before being able to retire?

Drive your vehicle several years or 25 percent longer than you initially planned. Drive it as long as it is safe and reliable. A safe car does not have to be expensive or the latest model. What were you planning to do with the old car anyway? Send it to the junkyard, sell it, or trade it in? Just keep it longer! Do this for your current car and your family members' cars too. This will be a substantial savings for you and your family over a lifetime.

❑ **AI:** _____

"Staying away from car payments by driving reliable used cars is what the average millionaire does. That's how s/he became a millionaire."[47] In 2010, Warren Buffet drove a 2006 Cadillac DTS, and Bill Gates had driven his Porsche for ten-years.[30] Before you buy a new car, ask yourself the following:

- "Am I fully funding my 401(k)?"
- "Am I fully funding my children's college funds?"
- "Do I have full medical, dental, and life insurance coverage?"
- "Can I buy a home or an investment property?"
- "Can I invest in a business to exponentially increase my income?"

Depending on your answers to these questions, you may want to reconsider taking out a loan for a new car or truck. Save at least $10,000 before spending any money on a new vehicle, and invest these interest payment savings in one of the above opportunities.

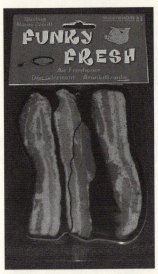

**Smells Like Bacon:** Buy air fresheners to make your old car smell new. These fresheners come in fun shapes and interesting aromas.

👍 "A new car typically loses 20 to 40 percent of its value as soon as you drive it off the lot."[48] "The average vehicle loses 60 percent of its value during its first four years."[49] Buy a new vehicle with the intention of keeping it for at least fifteen years. If you buy a used vehicle, buy it with the intention of keeping it for at least ten years. If you use mass transit a lot or telecommute add five years to keeping your vehicle. If you take the time to think about it, you'll realize that many people are still driving the exact car model you got rid of so many years ago, so you probably could have driven that vehicle a little longer. How much money would it have saved to still be driving that green Gremlin or purple Pinto, not

---

[30]    This information may be out of date but you get the concept.

to mention how cool you looked in it with fuzzy dice hanging from the rearview mirror?

With a new car, it is worth to investigate getting a five-year service/repair extended warranty and at least a two-year warranty for a used car. Check with a competent accountant to see if it can be used as a write off, since warranties for business assets may be tax deductible.

"Consumer advocates, noted experts, and a good calculator will confirm that the car lease is the most expensive way to operate a vehicle."[50] Ask yourself, "Why do I need to have something new every four years?" This is related to people, cars, and other material items in life. What is all of the passion, obsession, and pride over a car? It's not like you made it. You probably bought it off a lot or on the web like everybody else. That does not make you unique. It is YOU and the close people surrounding you that make you special.

"Upgrades should have mass appeal, but personalizing adds little to the resale value of a vehicle. In other words, go for the premium wheels and rims, but don't opt for souped-up mega wheels that will only appeal to a small audience. Just because you spend $4,000 on extras doesn't mean your vehicle will be worth $4,000 more. Many add-ons make driving more pleasant, but they don't necessarily add value."[51]

👍 "Install your own car extras. If you're mechanically inclined or a good friend or relative is, pass on options such as air conditioning and CD players. You can probably install them yourself for much less than the dealer will charge."[52] Remember, even if you're trying to save by not having that CD player installed, do not drive with ear plugs to listen to music. It is dangerous because you cannot hear the outside surroundings, and it is illegal in most states.

## Vehicle Maintenance

Keep your current car running efficiently, cleanly, and safely. This will increase the life of the car and your enjoyment of it. Follow the manufacturer's recommended maintenance and oil changes schedule (every 3,000 to 7,000 miles for most cars) to ensure the vehicle will last longer. A local mechanic may have less expensive maintenance suggestions.

Use dealer coupons on scheduled maintenance and routine oil changes. Always work with the service manager and ask for a discount or promotions if no coupons are available. Bring the manager a Danish pastry to show your appreciation. Try to use expired coupons, but it is best to mention this when scheduling the appointment to see if they will honor it or have a better deal.

❏  **AI:** _____

Shop around for the best gas prices online, use phone apps, and walk around your neighborhood. Drive to the next town if necessary. In general, I would <u>not</u> suggest putting regular unleaded gas in your car. I alternate between premium and super premium to save money. This is a good balance of putting quality fuel with high octane in your car so it lasts longer while cleaning the engine, which hopefully leads to less maintenance and repair costs. This also allows you to put the lowest-priced gas you can find in the tank and not necessarily the more expensive gas from the major brand suppliers. Most of the gasoline in the U.S. is refined by three major oil companies anyway. Check with your mechanic and owner's manual for their recommendations.

👍 In modern vehicle models, gas caps can still be continuously turned once they are on. When you think it is on, give an extra twist. This will make sure it is 100 percent on, and no more air will get in the gas tank. I had a situation in which I did not fully put the gas cap on, and the maintenance light came on. The mechanic had to reset the computer system to turn off the light, which cost me $250.

**"My mama didn't raise no dummy!!!"** Look for creative methods to increase the life and usage of your vehicles. Think outside the box by watching a car repair show, asking a friend for ideas, or going to local non-dealer privately owned mechanic shop. A man found a very creative solution when his car air conditioner broken down, and he took it to the auto repair shop. The mechanic told him it would cost $1,400 to fix the A/C. He just laughed at him and said, "I can fix it myself for a whole lot less than that!"

**Land Shark:** Name your car and talk to her/him. This will make you more loyal to keeping the car in good condition and holding onto it longer. It has been said that people who name their cars are less likely to be in an accident. Of course, all of these ideas also apply to trucks, SUVs, RVs, bikes, boats, motor homes, etc.

❑ **Vehicle's name(s):** _____ _____

If your kid needs a car to get to/from college or work, get them an auto that is simple, cheap, reliable, and safe. A brand new car is not necessary. During my last year in college, the school dramatically raised the price of room and board,[31] so many of us decided to move off campus. I needed a car to get to campus, and I bought an orange Toyota Corona for $200 from my neighbor. Thanks, Mr. R! I painted large white fins on the side doors, "LAND" on the hood, and "SHARK" on the trunk. So she was christened *Land Shark*.

My second car was a black Datsun five-speed stick shift, and the metal undercarriage of the body was getting a little rusty. This car cost a whopping $500 and ran well. At a car wash, I spray painted the rust with black Rust-Oleum® so it did not show. Protecting the steel from rust increased the lifespan of the car another year.

👍 Car-share members[32] can save more than $500 versus car owners because they don't pay for gas, maintenance, or insurance. What would you do with an extra $500 a month? In *Part IV – Your Investing Strategy,* I give you plenty ideas of where to invest it.

---

[31] *Board* is the food service cost at college that is billed by semester.

[32] For car-share details, go to the *Getting Around Smartly, Driving Green* section a few pages later in this chapter.

## Vehicle Insurance

If you work remotely part- or full-time, call your insurance company to recalculate your vehicle's annual driven mileage down to reduce the premium cost. Use mass transit to get to work, or drive very little you should qualify for low-mileage discount. Even just telecommuting once or twice per week, you may still qualify for this discount. Some other great discounts include having a superior driving record, renewal history, parking your car in a garage, having a car alarm or anti-theft system, and also military discounts for people who are serving in the Armed Forces.

❑ **AI:** _____

👌 If you do not drive much see if your insurance company has a "pay-as-you-drive" option. They verify the mileage driven, just like rental car companies, and adjust the premium rate accordingly.

Combine your personal insurance, car, and home policies. Many people still maintain insurance with separate companies for their automobile and home. Negotiating each of them separately may seem like a good deal, but the insurance companies offer significant discounts when policyholders have more than one policy with them. There is typically a discount for having multiple policies with the same insurance agent, though not necessarily the same company. An agent can only sell a policy in the state in which they are licensed. For example, this means they typically cannot provide a multiple-policy discount if the property is in another state.

❑ **AI:** _____

There are also discounts for having multiple cars on the same policy. A 10 percent discount is fairly common. As an added bonus, your billing will get simplified. The insurance company can usually align the policy expiration dates as well. However, if the other person has a poor driving record and is frequently late on payments, let them correct their issues before combining policies and taking on any extra liabilities.

❑ **AI:** _____

Pay auto insurance by electronic automatic withdraw payments. Insurance companies may charge you more if you pay monthly, quarterly, or semi-annually over annually. While there may be a small one- or two-dollar monthly fee involved, it is worth the convenience, but ask to get the fee waived. The local agent may not have the control, but corporate will have that authority.

❑ **AI:** _____

Compare prices and coverage every year. Also do this analysis if your living situation changes like getting married or moved. If you change insurance companies before the first policy is over, that company is required to refund the remaining prorated balance.

❑ **AI:** _____

## Getting Around Smartly

### Driving Safely

✋ Drive in control and not with anger. Using the "just missed traffic accident scenario" helps to cope with traffic and slow drivers. When you are stuck in traffic because of an accident, just be grateful you were not hurt in it. *Visualize* being in the traffic in your car and not being involved in the accident, and go back to a safe place. That person on the side of the road getting towed could have been you. Also think of that slower driver that abruptly pulled in front of you as slowing you down so you do not get a ticket. Try this to calm your road rage and driving anxiety. Be happy you are not that driver in a fender-bender or getting a ticket for speeding.

Don't forget the "courtesy wave" to a fellow driver that lets you pull in from of them. Do a pre-wave followed by another wave once you are let in. Smile and make eye contact, even if you have to use the rearview mirror, so that they know you are being sincere. Never flip anybody off while driving, no matter how bad the situation may be. Just relax and breathe—if you do, you will win.

**"I'm an excellent driver."** Pledge, "I will never be at fault in a car accident."

❑ _____     _____
   **Signature**                                  **Date**

If you do happen to cause an accident after making this promise to yourself, just start over with a new date and pledge it again.

My mom and dad were never in a car accident. This is a combination of offensive and defensive driving skills coupled with patience. We can do the same, right? Safety is not an accident.

👍 To alert people, beep your horn twice before backing out of any parking space and when driving out of a garage or a hidden driveway. For safety reasons, turn on your headlights when driving in tunnels or in the mountains.

Bikers, bicyclists, skateboarders, and rollerbladers always wear your helmets, no matter how short the trip or how long you have been riding! For bicyclists, there is a clever device that locks your helmet to your bicycle so you don't have to carry your helmet with you while shopping, eating, or are just out and about. Check out this innovative product at *www.theHelmetLock.com*.

❑ **AI:** _____

## Save While Driving

**Turn off** the radio and lights <u>before</u> starting your vehicle. Also verify that the DVD monitor, navigation system, and other electronic devices are <u>off</u> before starting the engine. If they are on when starting the car, they will drain the battery, which will require it to be replaced sooner than necessary.

❑ **AI:** _____

Use car fog lights only when they are needed because they are expensive to replace and are distracting to other drivers. Of course, please use head—and fog lights when driving in the rain, fog (duh!), snow, and other severe weather conditions. Driving with fog lights on for no reason is illegal in most states. The point is not to be wasteful and always be screaming for attention.

👍 Stop the engine while idling for more than ten seconds. It's better to turn off the engine and then restart it. If you are in the parking lot or garage talking on your cell phone, turn off the car as quickly as possible. Do not dilly dally or fuss around while the engine is burning up gas and oil. As soon as the car is in park or neutral and the emergency brake is on, turn off the engine. Then you can turn off the lights, radio, electronic gadgets, and close the windows.

**Mass Transit**

👍 Use mass transit and walk; you will avoid the risk of getting speeding and parking tickets. Ride your bike, take the train, or ride the ferry. Take the bus rather than a cab, unless your group consists of three or more people, in which case a taxi may be cheaper and quicker.

👍 Go online to Craigslist or specialty websites to get discounted commuter checks or tickets. People who are not going to use them will sell them to you at a reduced price.

In 2010, Mayor Michael Bloomberg was the second wealthiest person in New York City.[53] He frequently takes the subway to and from work. If mass transit is good enough for billionaire Mayor Bloomberg, it is good enough for you. The key is not just the money savings compared to taxi fare or parking garage fee; the key is to being productive while saving money. Time on mass transit is time for growing yourself or your business. This is the perfect opportunity to build your mind and business, in addition to saving on transportation costs while connecting with potential clients.

**Driving Green**

**Car-sharing** programs are similar to car rentals, the main difference being that you can use the car-sharing vehicle for as little as half an hour. The cars are located in your community rather than at a central car rental location. In short, car-sharing services are a unique cross between a rental car, car ownership, and cab service. They have options for personal, business, and college use. There are a wide range of vehicles, including two-door, mini-van, electric, hybrid, sport, luxury, SUV, and truck.

👍 "The **benefits of car-sharing**" by Zipcar:[54]

- Carefree – No maintenance, no servicing, no parking hassles, and no cleaning.
- Convenient – A car when you need one, and some programs have various models to suit your changing needs. Some motorists use car-share as a "second car."
- Environmental – Improves air quality. Each car-share vehicle replaces four to eight privately held cars.
- Low Cost – Pay only for the hours you drive, a fraction of the cost of owning a car, and cheaper than owning a car if you need a car for fewer than 7,500 miles per year.
- Practical – Reduces the number of cars in the city and car usage of individuals by as much as 50 percent.

**Zipcar** (*www.Zipcar.com*) is the world's largest car-sharing and car club service. This can be a cost savings for business trips, holidays, or extended stays as compared to renting a car. How does car-sharing compare to car rental? Average car rentals cost between forty to sixty dollars a day, plus more charges for mileage, insurance, oil, and gas. Car-sharing is less expensive because you can rent by the hour, you have reserved parking locations, there are no line-ups or papers to fill out, and there are no pick-up or drop-off constraints. This is definitely reducing $CO_2$ omissions!

"According to research conducted by GreenZebra among the 200,000 North American members of Zipcar:"[55]

- Paying by the hour means car-sharers plan their trips efficiently with 90 percent of members driving less than 5,000 miles per year.
- Over 40 percent of members decided against purchasing a car or ended up selling theirs.

**Buy Fuel Efficient Vehicles:** Cars with standard manual transmission (a.k.a., stick shift or five-speed) tend to be more fuel efficient than cars with an automatic transmission. The long-term maintenance of replacing the clutch of manual transmission is usually lower than servicing the automatic transmission. There are federal and sometimes state tax write-offs or tax credits for electric, hybrid, and other fuel efficient vehicles.

❏ **AI:** _____

Another idea is to buy a car or convert an existing car to run on vegetable oil. You can get this used oil from restaurants, kitchens, park events, amusement parks, and street fairs. There are groups that coordinate these exchanges. If you are handy, build your own electric car. They can drive up to 500 miles per charge.

## Travel

### Saving While Planning a Trip

Check websites like Lonely Planet™ at *www.lonelyplanet.com* or buy a travel book to plan a trip. I also recommend getting a travel book for where you live to find free, fun events. Two informative and fun book collections are *Broke-Ass Stuart's* guides at *www.BrokeAssStuart. com*[33] and *The Cheap Bastard's* guides at *www.TheCheapBastard. com*. These types of books and websites provide local free or low-cost activities, sights to visit, and out and about places, eateries, and entertainment. You will be surprised at what exists right in your very own back yard!

❏ **AI:** _____

👍 Travel off season to get the best airfare and accommodations rates. You may need to travel during the winter or rainy season, so bring the appropriate clothes.[34] In addition, try not to travel over school and holiday breaks. Yes, you may have to take off time from work or take the kids out of school, but there are technological solutions to these hurdles. For example, bring a laptop to remain productive and

---

[33] Check out Broke-Ass Stuart's new show on IFC, "Young, Broke, and Beautiful."

[34] When people visit San Francisco during the summer, they are surprised that it is the foggy and chilly season, and the unprepared tourists end up buying high-priced fleece sweatshirts. The fall is the nicest weather in San Francisco. During your trip, schedule a coaching appointment with me!

join conference calls via Internet phone or cell phone with unlimited minutes and free roaming. To have the ready access to connect to the Internet, get a wireless data card for your laptop or a data plan for your smartphone. Treat these as flexible workdays. Off travel days like Wednesdays, Saturdays, and Mondays will have great savings with more flights, hotel, and rental car availability at lower rates. For example, travel to Maui on Sunday and return on the following Monday or to Vegas on Wednesday and return on Saturday morning (just stay up all night).

👍 Travel with a date to save money on hotel, transportation, and entertainment (if you know what I mean, wink-wink!). Do not go into debt for a trip. Pay cash for business and family trips. Use a debit card for required charges like booking travel arrangements and use cash for food and entertainment expenses. If a credit card is necessary, make sure the trip is paid off at the next billing cycle. If there is still a previous balance on the card because you're adding the travel expenses, then you also need to pay the interest and finance charges.

**Saving on Airfare**

Fly the "**red-eye**" flights overnight to save a night on having to get a room. *Red-eye flights* depart late at night and arrive early the next morning. If these flights are under-booked by the airlines (there are a lot of available seats) or if you buy them at least fourteen days in advance, the tickets are cheaper than flying during peak business travel times. Tickets are discounted because airlines need to get their planes and crews to other airports for the next day of flights.

❑ **AI:** _____

👍 This may require freshening up in the morning when you land or sleeping overnight at the airport. Just be prepared so you can be comfortable. Bringing food from home or the local deli on the plane is a must for these long trips because meals are either pricey or are not served at all. Doesn't it get to you when somebody walks on the plane with freshly purchased French fries? That smell always gets my attention, and if you are lucky enough to sit next to that person, they may eventually offer you a salty fry or two.

I am writing this at 5:00 a.m. in Dallas Fort Worth airport (DFW). This is my first sleepover at an airport, and it was by choice to save money by not getting a hotel room. When I landed at 12:30 a.m., I got settled in a quiet space behind the gate check-in podium. I rolled out the yoga mat I had packed in my carry-on bag and loaded the yoga DVD in my laptop. You should have seen the looks from people unloading from my flight watching me do downward dog and triangle poses. It was a great workout! Then until 2:30 a.m., I wrote my book and developed a marketing strategy for my energy conservation business. Finally, I was ready to get some shut-eye.

My sleep was short lived. TSA[35] personnel were starting work at gate security and woke me up at 4:30 a.m. I went to brush my teeth and pick out the afro. When looking in the mirror, I was reminded why these flights are called red eyes. My eyes were bloodshot, but it was still well worth the savings.

**Ask, and You Shall Receive:** You need to feel you deserve good things to happen to you, and they will eventually, but a lot sooner if you ask. On a business trip, I was upgraded to First Class on the flight out. The Westin hotel allowed me to work out as a non-guest for free prior to my business meeting. On the return, United Airlines changed my ticket from a connecting to direct flight at no charge. All of these positive experiences enabled me to be more productive, travel more cheaply, and remain happy. This was the same successful trip as the red-eye flight to DFW that I just mentioned.

Go online to the airline website that you travel frequently and set up e-mail notification for flight status and early check-in. Have these messages sent to your e-mail address <u>and</u> mobile phone. These alerts are a noteworthy energy and stress saver during that day of travel; tracking the status of your flight departure times.

❑ **AI:** _____

---

[35]   *TSA*: U.S. Transportation Security Administration.

## CHAPTER 7: $AVING YOUR MONEY
### (STRETCHING THE DOLLAR)

## Saving on Lodging

Get competitive hotel rates from online travel agencies like Hotels.com, Travelocity.com, and HotWire.com. These sites are really good to find affordable rates for business trips on short notice. Their rates are very similar with the same availability, so decide which online agency you prefer by their user interface and how accommodations information is displayed. Occasionally, verify that they still have comparable rates. Your credit or debit card will be charged when booking the reservation, so educate yourself on their cancellation and refund policies.

❏ **AI:** _____

When shopping for hotels online, change the search sort by price "lowest to highest." I like to remove the one-star ( ⭐ ) and five-star ( ⭐ ⭐ ⭐ ⭐ ⭐ ) hotel ratings and search again. All of the other expenses at five-star hotels will be higher too. Just say "No" to FIVE-STAR hotels!

👍 Once you decide on a hotel, go directly to the website of the hotel for special promotions. This is especially valuable for the major hotel chains, smaller hotels, motels, and casinos. Booking directly with them will typically have a twenty-four or forty-eight-hours before arrival cancellation policy. This flexibility may be best for certain situations, even if the rate is slightly higher. After you have stayed at a privately owned hotel or motel, call them directly for cheaper rates because the hotel and you both will save on booking fees. Ask for special loyalty rates, best available price, AAA, AARP, or AMEX discounts, and a complimentary room upgrade. Paying cash will also allow you to negotiate a lower rate.

**BnB:** Staying at bed-and-breakfasts (B&B) in big metropolitan areas and beach towns is typically less expensive than staying at hotels. In addition to a lower room rate, you will also save on restaurants, parking, and movies. This can be a quaint romantic getaway. Like privately owned motels, get B&B owners' numbers via the web to call them directly to save money on the room and get special accommodations. For international online B&B reservation services, check out *www. airbnb.com*.

👍 Camping is also a frugal alternative. For really long road trips and outdoor weekend events, renting or borrowing an RV can be an economical option.

### Saving on Rental Car

An economy model vehicle has the lowest rental costs and will save on gas. For long road trips, get a rental car contract with unlimited mileage. Even if an upgrade is complementary, stay with the small fuel efficient model to save on gas. When renting a vehicle, put the absolute cheapest regular gas in the tank. Never return a rental car without a full tank of gas, as rental car companies will charge the highest price for gas and may charge for a full tank to fill a gas tank, even if you returned it only half-empty.

❑ **AI:** _____

👍 As alternatives to renting a car, utilize mass transit. This is especially beneficial for getting to and from the airport. Carpool whenever possible. For a quick day trip, explore using car-share. Walking is great exercise for short excursions of a mile or two.

### Save While on the Trip

What are your favorite vacation memories? They are typically the less adventurous, less expensive things, like snorkeling in a lagoon with barracudas, jogging on the beach with your loved ones, or walking through a new city, neighborhood by neighborhood.

👍 "When traveling, use the **'peak-end' rule**. One particular trait of the human psychology is known as the 'peak-end' rule. Our memories of something are defined by the peak of that experience and also the end of that experience. In other words, when you think back to your vacation in a year or two, you'll likely just remember the best thing you did and the very last thing you did, along with a few other scattered nits. So, when you plan your vacation, instead of jamming each day with amazing things, just plan one peak experience, the real centerpiece of your trip, and one great experience near the end of the trip. Fill the rest of this trip with experience options and also relaxation, and you will create an incredibly memorable vacation without shelling out the cash for nonstop and exhausting activities."[56]

👍 "Use a digital camera with a large memory card instead of film. Travel with a digital camera or mobile phone that can take pictures. Invest in a huge memory card and feel free to snap plenty of pictures."[57] This will save money and time compared to traditional cameras with film. Plus you can upload photos to your website or Facebook while on the trip.

👍 Double-bag your toiletries (lotions, perfume, hair products, etc.) while traveling to prevent them from leaking on your clothes. You can get plastic zipper bags at any airport in the gate security line. Always get a few extra. They make good sandwich bags!

👍 Do not forget to eat a big meal before leaving to the airport. Get a hotel room with a refrigerator and microwave. Bring food with you or shop at a grocery store in town. Commit to eating cheaper on trips than at home. This is not the time to fatten up.

👍 In Singapore, Tokyo, and London, I went to convenience stores to get cheap prepackaged meals. You can use their microwave to warm them up and eat right at their tables. Most large cities throughout the world have convenience stores and gas stations that sell cheap precooked meals. In Taipei, Taiwan there were 7-Elevens everywhere, even three of them on my hotel block. The prices for a hot dog and generic beer were only fifty cents each!

## Working Out on the Trip

Bring workout clothes, equipment, and DVDs on all trips. It will save you the time of driving to a local gym and save money on a day pass. More importantly, it will help you maintain your fitness routine. For workout aids, pack shortened yoga mat, straps, bands, wrist weights, your 35-pound dumbbells (just kidding), etc. Take an older mat that is thin and cut it down to size to fit in your carry-on luggage so you can do Tae Bo™, cardio, Pilates, abs, and advanced yoga poses. Of course bring those workout DVDs. You can watch them on your laptop while watching a television show or on the hotel's DVD player. Don't forget your sneakers and athletic socks.

❑  **AI:** _____

Also travel with AB Force® (*www.ab-force.com*) or other small abdomen rolling device like the GoFit Abdomen Dual Exercise Wheel® to get a quick upper and core body workout. Find an open space by the bed, living area, or kitchenette. Place a towel under your knees, and go to work! Rolling back and forward will tone the lower abs, upper abs, and back muscles. Go to the left at the ten-o'clock position and right side at the two-o'clock position to work the obliques and arms. Alternate going

AB Force

straight forward, back, left forward, back, straight forward, back, right forward, back, straight forward, back, and then repeat. Do this for three sets of ten repetitions or continuous duration of two to five minutes. Do more if you can to get an even better burn or less if your time is limited.

❑  **AI:** _____

When going through airport security with the AB Force and wrist weights, remove them from your carry-on luggage and put them in a separate bin.

👍 If there is no gym in the hotel and you have enough room in your luggage, pack Bodyrev® Perfect Pushup™ tool for a tough workout. There are a variety of exercises you can do to work different muscles. If the room is small, do pushups in the hallway.

👍 With your laptop, logon to your cable or satellite provider's online on-demand service to watch exercise videos. Some hotels even have fitness channels like Discovery Fit & Health (FitTV) and AcaciaFitness with workouts you can perform in your room for free, or they may at least have a channel with twenty-minute infomercials advertising exercises.

👍 A fantastic free exercise is to walk the stairs in the hotel several times. You can get a quick leg, butt, and cardio workout with little preparation. To get a better burn, take two steps at time. When I was in Vegas, I did this workout at the Pink Flamingo. I also did the stairs workout on a trip to Tokyo of 110 stairs—twice!

When traveling, don't get pressured into long dinners or just vegging out in front of the TV. Do not use working on the computer as another excuse to not honor your commitments to a regular workout schedule. Put the computer in sleep mode or turn off the television: then go for a run, work out in the hotel gym, work out in your room before going to dinner, or walk after dinner.

After the tragedy of 9/11, I needed a different environment to reboot my system, so I took a trip to Taipei. The airfare and hotel were cheap. For exercise I ran around a spectacular park and jogged over to a larger park with over five temples built in the 1980s. The Chiang Kai-shek Memorial Hall opens at 10:00 a.m., and I had thirty minutes to kill, so I did tai chi in a beautiful garden with a class full of elderly women. It was fun, and they were much better than me. How often do you see a 200-pound Black man doing tai chi in downtown Taipei? They probably see this all the time, I'm sure.

Precisely at ten o'clock, two impressive guards marched out and opened two huge doors. As we walked into the hall, there was only a striking three-story impressive bronze statue of Chiang Kai-shek, the

 former president of the Republic of China.[36] It was an unforgettable experience. This is a perfect example of free exercise and experience at the end of the trip.

Wikimedia Commons, Denglong

## Saving in the Room

Bring movies to watch on your laptop or portable DVD player in the rooms. This will save you from being tempted to order expensive

---

[36] This was built five years after the leader's death. There are no political or social views associated with me visiting Chiang Kai-shek Memorial Hall.

on-demand movies. Always keep a few movies, television series, and exercise DVDs in your luggage or briefcase just in case you take an unplanned trip.

❏ **AI:** _____

Secure your valuables at all times. Use the security steel cable to lock your laptop and briefcase. Use the hotel safe if it is available. Many hotels do not charge to use them. Lock your computer login, too, whenever you are away from it. Set up a screensaver timer so the computer will log out when it is inactive for a certain period of time. Many Personal Digital Assistants (PDAs)[37] also have this option, which should also be enabled.

❏ **AI:** _____

**"Housekeeping!"** When staying at a hotel or motel, do not have the housekeeper clean your room every day. This will save on tips, the time for you to get ready for her/him to clean, and will be better for Mother Earth. Put up the "Do Not Disturb" sign so they do not come in to clean.[38] This should also increase the security because thieves will think someone is in the room. If staying by yourself in a room with double beds, just use one bed for the trip. Don't dirty up both beds.

🖐 Get soap, shampoo, and conditioner every day from the maid's cart. Do not get fresh towels every day and only take them when you really need them, just like at home. Only open one bar of soap and use it for both the shower and sink. Like a carnival game, have fun throwing the bar from the shower and trying to land it the sink without popping out. Choose the deodorant or fancy bath soap, which is usually the large bar. It should last the whole trip. If the soap is in good shape on checkout day, dry it and pack it with you. Also bag used shampoo, conditioner, and lotion bottles. This habit saves the hotel money and

---

[37] *Personal digital assistants* are handheld wireless appliances that combine computing, cell phone capabilities, and Internet access. There are personal organizer applications on these devices. BlackBerry®, iPhone®, Android™ ("Droid"), and Google Phone (Nexus One®) are examples of PDAs, also known as *smartphones*. Tablets are also considered PDAs.

[38] Marriott Hotels have clever "Do not disturb" door handles that read: "Brain Storm: It's really coming down in here. Better wait 'til it clears up."

resources because people use less soap and have fewer bars and bottles to throw out, which is good for the environment.

👍 You can use the cheap hotel soaps for your bathroom hand soap at home. Also use cheap soap when you first rinse off in the shower and then finish the shower with your good soap. This technique can be applied to hotel shampoo, conditioner, and lotion as well.

Please tip well <u>when</u> you have maid service! At the hotel or motel, leave the tip on the pillow so the maid can see it. Do this each time the room is cleaned and not just on the last day so you get good vibes and service throughout the trip. Do not tip for the days there is no service. Be generous—it feels good! For normal rooms, leave three to four dollars per cleaning. For condos, suites, upscale hotels, and large rooms, leave at least five dollars per cleaning.

❑ AI: _____

👍 If you stay in a small bed-and-breakfast, leave a five dollar tip at the end of your weekend stay, because there is no daily maid service. An alternative to tipping is to give a gift or bottle of wine that you can drink with them. In foreign countries, if tipping is not their custom (like in Europe, Asia, and Central America), still tip a little but at a much lower rate (one or two dollars) than in the U.S.

## Make Trips Productive

Growing your mind, knowledge, and business while traveling to create a productive trip. Always be prepared to grow your business and knowledge when traveling. Start packing two days in advance so you do not forget anything. Bring work and business reading materials with you, especially for long trips on airplanes, trains, buses, and cruises. This will be uptime, <u>not</u> downtime. Time parked on the airport tarmac or sitting in the boarding area will be productively utilized. Once, on a flight, I was so committed I requested the flight attendant to ask the pilot to slow the approach to the airport so I could get more work finished.

❑ AI: _____

One winter I was on a Greyhound bus for twenty-five hours from Houston to Denver. It was a very long but productive trip. I got a lot of reading completed for work and my personal development. However, there was a group of passengers smoking cigarettes in the back of the bus. They did not listen to my complaints or heed the warnings by the bus driver, and then started smoking marijuana in the bathroom. To overcome this issue, I bought their compliance with a few Tanqueray gin and tonics drinks that I packed in my bag. Then we all got along like family, and I was a hero.

👍 No more pure leisure vacations, trips, or honeymoons! Seriously research and buy investment property and land on these trips. Take short trips so you can stay connected with your career or job. Combining business and personal trips is strongly encouraged, but keep these expenses separate. Pleasure activities, visiting family, and taking in a show with friends are NOT business expenses. Only deduct business-related expenses like attending a trade show, marketing your business, or meeting with clients.

Remember to pack your power cord for the computer, the phone or PDA charger, and the laptop security cable with the lock and key.

❑   **AI:** _____

Keep a one-to-three outlet plug converter with third grounding prong in your briefcase. When all of the outlets are taken in the airport, conference room, older hotel room, or coffee shop, you will be able to use the outlet prong to plug into. People will always let you plug in to convert from one to three outlets. Just use one (the second outlet) and let somebody else use the third . . . and you just made two connections (the original outlet person and the third one). You will never have to suffer from a lack of available electrical outlets again.

❑   **AI:** _____

# Going Really Cheap

## Buying Cheaply

Learn to love **dollar** and **ninety-nine-cent stores**. Be sure the item is really worth a dollar because the price is set to benefit the store more than you. At a dollar store in Arkansas, I bought a string of orange Halloween lights for only twenty-five cents and used them at Christmas. Now that's a great deal! Some Goodwill stores have half-off and/or dollar days plus twenty-nine-cent racks. To save more money, make your own costumes and decorations for parties.

Buy used household items and office supplies at **yard sales**, curbside sales, fire sales, thrift stores, secondhand stores, and discount stores in foreigners, immigrants, and homeless neighborhoods. Yard and garage sales are typically held on Saturdays and sometimes on Sundays. Find garage sales and discounted items in your neighborhood, go to *www. CraigsList.com*.

**Fleas**: Great deals can be found at swap meets and flea markets. You can find almost anything there, both new and used, including produce. I still have my Frank Zappa, Meat Puppets, and Cramps t-shirts that I bought at the Englishtown Flea Market when I was in college. They were three for ten dollars. Of course, they're a little snugger these days, but they're perfect for forward and back bend yoga poses.[39] Women think it's HOT . . . or maybe not! My family also sold items at that flea market. We cleared out a bunch of stuff from the basement and made a few bucks.

**Pawn Shops** have many super deals and are fun to visit if you have an item you need. There is a lot of fascinating history there. I got a grocery walker cart from a pawn shop to complete my homeless person Halloween costume, and it was a hit. People thought I was a real homeless guy off the street and even gave me change in my cup. The irony is, somebody broke into my apartment garage and stole a few

---

[39]   Check out my photo in *Chapter 16: Invest in Yourself and Family, Your Mind*.

items from some of the units' storage closets. My closet was untouched, but they took back the grocery cart!

You don't have to buy everything. **Trade** things you do not need anymore for items you need. You can also trade for services you need, offering your valuable skills in return. These services might include tutoring, baby/kid/pet-sitting, auto repair, computer repair, and lawn care. Use your time efficiently when you are the caretaker.

**Borrow** expensive items like vacuum cleaners, snow blowers, heavy gardening tools, and power tools from your neighbors. Also borrow items you do not use often like wax paper, spices, a wok, a fondue set, and a tux.

Also consider **sharing in a purchase** of large items with a close friend. This is a huge savings! But first create a simple written binding contract that is to be signed and dated by all purchasing parties, and a copy of the contract should be given to each person.

## Cheap Support Groups

Join the local **Freecycle**™ group, an e-mail group where people give away things they don't want or receive things that others are getting rid of. You can find everything from kids' clothes, to toys, furniture, tools, and more. You can OFFER things to others who need it and request things you WANT. There are currently 4,937 groups and 8,404,766 Freecycle Network across the globe. It is a grassroots and entirely nonprofit movement of people who are giving (and getting) stuff for free in your community. It's all about reuse and keeping good stuff out of landfills. Membership is free! Go to *www.Freecycle.org* and find a community near you.

❑ **AI:** _____

Be daring and start **bartering** in your community. For example, you have a child that needs tutoring in math and you cannot afford it, but you are bold enough to approach a person that you know is a tutor. Ask if s/he is willing to tutor your child in exchange for the child doing a thorough housecleaning or cutting their lawn once a week. It works, and you should customize it to fit your situation and skill set. This is similar to trading but in a more organized manner. Join local exchange, swapping, and bartering networks like Googlegroup and Yahoogroup where many people post their items for sales and services they can provide.

❑ **AI:** _____

## Just Plain Cheap

**Keep It Clean**: There is no sense throwing out bars of soap when they get really small. To get the full life out of soap, wrap up several used baby bars to make a larger one. Combine facial, bath, and hand soap bars. Merge them with the new large bar or rubber band all of the small

ones together using a band or two. Once used, let the soaps dry together; they will merge together as one bar, and eventually you can remove the rubber band. Give it a chance. If it does not work the first time, try it again.

☞ Reuse dental floss if it is in good condition.[40] Just rinse it and allow it to dry. Beware not to overuse it, or it can get stuck between your teeth. Learn from my past experience.

**Pocket It**: Rather than buying a fancy earpiece for your cell phone, try this low-tech solution. Place the call and select speakerphone. Then put the phone top down in your top front shirt pocket so the speaker and microphone is facing up toward your mouth.

Sometimes you just have to walk away. Do you really need it? What helps is knowing what you should be doing with that extra money. Then the buying decision is easy because you have long-term goals that require funding.

*"If you can believe it, the mind can achieve it" ~ Ronnie Lott*

---

[40] Check with your dentist first. This could be a good way to get more floss when visiting his/her office.

# CHAPTER 8: SAVING YOUR ENERGY (INCREASE PRODUCTIVITY)

*"Success is almost totally dependent upon drive and persistence. The extra energy required to make another effort or try another approach is the secret of winning." ~ Denis Waitley*

## Eliminating Things

**"One Less Thing."** Less stuff equals fewer things to clean, maintain, and worry about. There needs to be a reward that affects at least one of your goals in life. You may have to say "<u>No</u>!" to campaigns, other people's get-rich-quick network marketing scheme, or the latest millionaire infomercial program.

People who have daily drama are needy, and unwilling to change, are on their own. You cannot save every person or animal. There is NOT enough time or money to do so. However sad it may be, in some cases, nature will take its course. Without hesitation, save and rescue people in unsafe or dangerous situations.

Once troubled people have taken action and sought professional help, then you can provide advice and support. This is a little harsh, but you cannot help others until they help themselves. Stop being seduced into others' unhealthy relationships. Don't enable this bad behavior or allow yourself to be sucked into their mayhem. You may need to put yourself first and walk away. This will enable you to focus on your areas of improvement and goals.

## Focusing

👍 My goal is to replace women's cigarette holders with PDAs like a Blackberry, iPhone, Droid, or another smartphone. Rather than burning time smoking, you'll be spending time being productive. Use a jog or a brisk walk as a great physical excuse to help you quit smoking or reduce the amount consumed per day.

Also use exercise to reduce the amount of alcohol you drink at night, especially on vacation. Morning workouts can help you put a time limit on partying the night before and be back to the hotel room, say by midnight. At home, sign up for regularly scheduled fitness classes on Saturday or Sunday mornings that will keep you from staying out too late. Attending an early-morning religious service or volunteering will also help set a curfew the night before.

❏  **AI:** _____

## Less on the Wedding

### Planning the Wedding

**Bridezilla!** Go with less and smaller on a wedding, please. Think of the future and not just the wedding day. It's about people having fun, not just you being the center of attention. Friends and family will be happy if you are happy. They are not expecting a grand ballroom gala or seven-course meal. At the end of the day, the only thing that counts is the deeper commitment to your partner.

**Pay cash** for the wedding, especially for the rings and the honeymoon because these are truly wants! Have the cash allocated upfront without diving deep into your savings. You will get a better discount with NO interest and finance charges. Any chump with decent credit can charge a big diamond ring and a wedding hall; even my rabbit received credit cards in the mail with "Mudbone Wortham" imprinted on them. Using credit is not a showing of love nor does it prove he can provide for his bride or their future family.

✍ No bridal registry at expensive niche or department doodad stores is necessary. Instead, tell your guests to get your gifts at business-oriented or home improvement stores. Set up a wish list account at an office or bookstore where people can pitch in online, but not at stores where you can buy doodads or specialty expensive home décor. You don't need to be tempted to buy a widescreen TV, fancy dining room set, or something else you don't need.

👍 If you prefer cash because you are building for your future, just ask for it. Be specific about what the money will be used for, and even add a picture of the house, college, or business where the money will be spent.

👍 For invitations, use the online Evite system at _www.Evite.com_ or postcards. It will save **energy** and be easy to update. In the invite, give an indication of what the cash or business gift will be used for.

Buy a new or <u>used</u> modest wedding dress with no complicated head veil or train. Of course, if your mother's or sister's dress fits or can be altered to fit, wear it. You can also rent or buy a prom dress. You can even look on eBay, Craigslist, and Yardsellr or go to yard sales! The week after the wedding, sell the dress to pay for the honeymoon. Do not plan to save it for your oldest daughter. What if you have all boys or no kids at all? If you still have your dress, sell it today.

❏   **AI:** _____

👍 Have the best man and groomsmen wear black suits with inexpensive matching ties and not rent tuxedos. The bridesmaids can wear black dresses and matching shoes. This way, they do not have to rent or buy clothes, as most of them probably already own a black suit or dress that fits them well. Even if they do have to buy it, it will be something they can wear again and again—not the case if you force them to buy an expensive lime green taffeta nightmare!

👍 Keep it simple and just have a best man and one bridesmaid. There is no need for a "cast of thousands." If your choice is going to cause a problem between jealous siblings or friends, choose a grandparent, but don't expect a wild bachelor or bachelorette party!

👍 Do not waste time and energy on an engagement party or a wedding shower! Combine it with the bachelorette party.

👍 Have your wedding at a park, college, workplace or conference room, barn, hall, or parents' home. Also, you can make the flower arrangements and bridal bouquets yourself by buying the flowers and supplies at a flower market or growing them yourself. There is nothing wrong with a keg of cold beer and boxes of decent wine.

☝ You can cook the food for the wedding. The guests would love a home-cooked meal. What are your best dishes? Few people can cook baked ziti with hot/sweet sausage and chicken parmesan like I can. Can you barbecue ribs and chicken or cook your own cultural/ethnic dishes? Make it a theme wedding using these dishes. My friend's mother cooked a delicious Hungarian spread for her daughter's wedding, and it was delicious!

☝ Catered buffet or family-style meals are cheaper than individual plates with servers. Consider a few healthy choices plus options for vegetarians and vegans that are less expensive than meat dishes. Make or buy several sheet cakes or dozen of cupcakes, as these will be much cheaper and feed more people than the fancy tower wedding cakes. It is all about the roses and icing anyway.

Decide up front to have a collaborative wedding, including support from your guests. Guests will be more than happy to help with making flower bouquets, table arrangements and favors, baking cakes, bringing food, seating guests, and decorating. You need to ask your guests in an organized manner and well in advance. Inform them this will be an elegant but modest wedding and that you will be paying cash to save money for the future. Be respectful with your requests and do not blow your money on silly expenses like a stretch limo and an elaborate hall. People may be offended and not willing to help out if they feel you are spending money unwisely.

❑ **AI:** _____

☝ Don't hire a DJ. Instead, create a playlist, load the music to your iPod, and connect to a good quality portable sound system. Ask a friend to DJ for you. Have a well-organized playlist or be online to honor guests' music requests. Also have friends rotate as bartenders. Offer them a gift card for your appreciation, though they probably will not accept it.

☝ Have friends bring their camcorders to film the wedding in order to save the money you would have spent on a professional film crew. For the wedding ceremony, it is fine to have a professional still photographer, but not necessary for the reception. There is no need for pre- and post-wedding pictures at places where the actual wedding ceremony was not held. Putting inexpensive disposal cameras on each table. Only print out the pictures you want.

**BYOSS**: Nowadays, it is better to throw sunflower seeds at weddings than rice because it has been discovered that rice can kill wild birds if they eat it. Sunflower seeds can feed the hungry uncle during the ceremony and feed birds afterwards! Eco-friendly nontoxic bubbles are also becoming a new trend.

👍 Going with a green wedding will reduce many of the traditional rituals

and associated items that will be thrown out the next day. Using reusable plastic ware, cups, and containers will save money. Have the ceremony and reception at the same location. Encourage people to carpool, and do not get a limousine.

Siberian Wedding, Wikimedia Commons, Cyrille (Suleiman) Romier, Flickr, Jacopo Werther

Here are more great ideas to save money on a wedding:

- Gloria Dawson "7 Tips for Planning Your Green Wedding," at *www.thedailygreen.com/green-homes/latest/tips-plan-green-wedding-50051408*
- Jeremy Vohwinkle, "How to have an Affordable Wedding," at *www.financialplan.about.com/od/planningforlifestages/a/saveonwedding.htm*
- Sami Grover, "How to Go Green: Weddings," at www.treehugger. com/files/2007/04/how-to-go-green-weddings.php

**After the Wedding**

👍 You can make thank-you gifts for people, but many people do not expect a gift; your invitation to participate in the wedding is a gift in itself. I suggest encouraging people to choose from several charities (provide a short list to choose from) and making a matching donation. This is much better than giving them a gift for giving you a gift. If you have fifty people at your wedding and everyone pitches in twenty-five bucks and you match, that's $2,500 to your favorite charity! Both you and the other parties can take a tax write-off.

Make sure you are both investing in your retirement plans and eliminating debt, plus have separate Wills. If you are already married, verify this is happing and if not do it now.

❑ **AI:** _____

## Less TV

News is in the past, and you need to focus on the future. This includes watching less media events, entertainment news, and both local and national broadcast news. Much of it is usually negative and is not that enlightening, educational, or informative. Focus on being a part of the solution with an answer. It is important to stay current on events, but there are free online media resources to get the information quickly. The Internet is a faster method to gather more information that is tailored to your goals and a great way to filter out of the doom-and-gloom reports. However, if watching the news, sports, or entertainment is necessary for your job, career, or business, that is excellent, but not for just hobbies or recreation.

❑ **AI:** _____

☝ You need to get away from the noise of life at regularly scheduled intervals. This time is to be spent on income and wealth-creating activities. Get your weather forecast from the Internet rather than waiting for it on your local news. Just do a web search for your city or zip code: good sites are *www.wunderground.com*, *www.weather.com*, and *radar.weather.gov*. This is more productive than waiting for the local news weather forecast which waste your time by teasing you with introduction forecasts and then going to commercials. Instead, watch positive self-help and business development programming.

Watch less or no sportscasts. Stop watching college draft announcements. Do not watch preseason games, countdowns, or pre- or post-game interviews and shows. Do not get tricked into watching all of the network coverage when the game starts much later—verify the actual start time. Stop playing fantasy sport leagues! Turn off qualifying rounds broadcasts for racing and golf. Just watch the race or tournament. If there are two games on a day or weekend, just choose to watch one. You do not have to spend all Saturday or Sunday watching sports. Also, refrain from watching poker tournaments until you are independently wealthy and volunteering a whole heck of a lot. Over a year, this will equal out to a huge energy and time savings. Use this newfound free time for income-producing activities.

❑ **AI:** _____

**"I can't hear who?"** Watch all sports with the sound <u>muted</u> at home. This quiet space will allow you to focus on more important things such as reading a book, listening to self-help CDs/MP3s, listening to educational material, or speaking with your children. You will build your business while still enjoying sports with the sound off. While watching regular programming, mute show introductions, commercials, and credits. This saves energy by not pumping watts to the television speakers or your surround sound system. Plus this will provide you with silent time to concentrate. To remove the temptation, turn off the surround sound system.

❑ **AI:** _____

👍 Utilize DVR or TiVo technologies to record programs and play them back later, skipping the boring or irrelevant parts. For newscasts, fast forward through all the trivial stories, weather, and commercials. These technologies are perfect to speed through games to get to the last quarter and races to get to the most exciting final laps, especially the crashes. Fast forward, keeping an eye on the scoreboard. When it changes, stop, go back, and see what happened. Also skip over huddles, halftime, timeouts, penalties, cautions, etc.

Block out the hours you are going to watch programs so the TV is not always on. Remember to combine marketing your business online, opening mail, paying bills, and working out. It is fine to talk on the speakerphone while working out, unless you are swimming.

❑ **AI:** _____

## Less on Pets

If you have more than two pets reduce your livestock size. To contain future growth, spay or neuter existing pets and donate found animals to shelters. Have your children work at a rescue organization that places animals in other homes rather than bringing them into yours. If you have a large, difficult, or high-maintenance animal, consider donating it to a better-suited home for the animal's sake, as well as your own. It will save you money, energy, and time.

❑ AI: _____

👍 Reduce the over-busy household and ark of various pets. Use this strategy to create focus and reduce the chaos. Rather than getting another pet, why not have your kids create outdoor habitats in your yard for wildlife like birds, butterflies, bunnies, snakes, toads, squirrels, fish, or whatever lives in your neighborhood? And don't just try to attract these critters, but document them for a school, Scouts, or 4-H science project. Volunteering at a zoo or animal shelter will enable you to make a positive contribution to animals.

Pets can be energy guzzlers, especially exotic animals. These creatures are best left in their natural environments rather than you trying to re-creating their environment in your home. Pets can provide much comfort and joy, but you may have to make a hard choice. This is directed toward your current furry situation, especially if you have more than you can handle or the cost is more than thirty-five dollars a month. Strongly consider selling or giving away all of your exotic pets.

❑ AI: _____

Fish are best suited to be swimming free in the oceans, lakes, and streams . . . or served on a dinner plate. Birds' wings should not be clipped so they cannot fly. Please do not cruelly dispose of fish or any animal. This includes letting domesticated pets "free" in a pond or the woods when they have not learned to live in the wild (do not do this). Give pets to a friend, shelter, or government agency where they can be cared for.

👍 If you already have pets, another suggestion is that when you have a baby, give away one pet so you can focus on the children by reducing the distractions and expenses. Do this for each addition to the family.

Energy can be better spent on a host of other things. For example, working out, calling relatives to check in, improving job skills, learning another language, listening vs. talking communication skills, writing a blog, bonding with your boss, doing homework with your children, making whoopee with your partner, and organizing your files. These are good energy investments. How about all of the money saved? What is the point of getting very large or exotic animals? Can you be happy with just one dog, a cat, or a <u>rabbit</u>?

👍 Adding large and many small pets can complicate the order in the home. Having two dogs can sometimes more than double the complexity.

Do you always have to have two or more cats? How many cats can you pet at one time? How about just the one cat? They rarely get along anyway. Also say "NO!" to high-maintenance, fancy purebred cats like the hairless Sphynx that looks like an oversized bald rat; these can cost from $800 to over $3,000!

Get a dog that has long legs so you can walk with them at a fast human pace. They can be a great jogging partners. Beware of tiny, cute, high-maintenance "pocketbook" or "drop kick" dogs that walk slow because of their tiny legs and have to be taken for a walk four times a day because their bladders are so small. You pay the bills, so if you must have a pet, get one that can keep up with you. Of course, say "NO" to vicious dogs that have a history of attacking people, killing babies, and are aggressive toward other dogs.[41]

Please rescue average-sized pets (not the size of a pony) that have a long life expectancy and are low maintenance. Adopt a well-trained free or very inexpensive animal from a kill shelter and not a "puppy mill" store. Focus on simple animals that may be a mixed breed. Greyhounds

---

[41]   Do NOT support dog fighting, cock fighting, or bull fights!

are good pets if you have a large back yard or a lot of time to walk them every day. A temporary pet may be more fulfilling to some people, such as training a guide dog (a.k.a., seeing eye dog). Are you as willing to reach out to help others as you are to take care of an animal? Walk a little old lady across the street. Volunteer at a nursing home or deliver meals to people that are unable to leave their homes.

❑ **AI:** _____

When I was I kid, my brothers and I found a stray German Shepherd. It was a playful dog, but it had ticks and probably fleas. Dad came home from work and said, "We are not keeping the dog." There was little debate. The next day, the bitch[42] was delivered to the shelter where they found her a good home. Did I mention that my brothers and I are allergic to dogs? Sometimes you have to make the courageous decision and say "No." Think with your heart and mind for long-term happiness and needs (yours and the animal's), not just for short-term gratification and wants.

**Put Pets in Their Places:** "Dogs and cats take their toll on a bed. Just because your 80-pound German Shepherd believes your bed belongs to him doesn't mean that you should allow him to lie down on it every day. Likewise, your cat may love to use your mattress ticking or, better yet, the box spring, as a scratching post. Placing a mattress cover or fitting sheet over the box spring discourages scratching—but keeping kitties and dogs out of the bedroom will solve these issues altogether."[58] Dogs and cats can be hard on carpets and rugs. Dog claws can also destroy hardwood and vinyl floors. Cat claws can maim bed posts and couches. "Your pet can wake you and prevent you from getting back to sleep."[59] They don't have to get up for work the next morning. Don't let your pet train you and sleep in your bedroom, in the kids' bedroom, or on the couch.

❑ **AI:** _____

👍 You should have no large pets or exotic pets in extremely small living spaces. This includes urban cities, apartments, and condos. Be respectful to your neighbors and verify that your dog is not barking, yipping, or howling when you are not home because it is lonely or

---

42    Relax! This is the name for a female dog.

another dog walked by the window. This is not fair to the dog or your neighbors. Do not leave the television on for the dog or cat when leaving the house. If they must have a human voice in order to keep them calm and quiet, turn on the radio. It will use a lot less energy.

Dogs can also be rough on car seats. Do not let your dog be a human and sit wherever it wants. Their claws scratch the leather, they slobber on the windows, and their fur gets everywhere. Do these activities add to the resell value of the vehicle? Get a pet barrier to keep the dog in the cargo bay or back seat so it won't disturb you while driving and dirty up the vehicle. Have them sit on an old blanket. For animals in the back seat, you can also get a special dog seat belt to keep them from jumping around.

❑ **AI:** _____

**No to Pet Cemetery:** When a pet dies, don't have a formal ceremony or pay for a funeral or cremation. Find a cheap method of disposing of their body.

Feed pets natural food with no artificial additives and preservatives.

❑ **AI:** _____

## Being Faster

**"Move it or lose it, sister!"** Walk and move faster while burning more calories. Test walking 5 percent faster. Then the following week, increase the pace by another 5 percent. Continue increasing at this rate for the next two weeks. By the end of the month, get the total increase to 20 percent. This includes all your body movements and not just walking. Do it in the street, at the store, at work, and at home. You will be surprised how easy it is, and you will work up a sweat. More importantly, you will get more accomplished. This is a critical factor to being more productive.

❑ **AI:** _____

👍 Time is constant, and it is the one thing we cannot produce or change. Walking really fast will give you one to two times of your time back. Jogging will save you five to ten times as much. Why walk when you can run? I just did it, and it felt great! Rather than walking the four blocks to my place, I ran wearing dress shoes, and now I am writing my book gaining ten minutes back to my life.

✋ Think of places where you can cut corners like parking lots, department stores, lawns, in your home, hiking, and walking across town. Do this every time you can, even with a date or business partner. Stop following the sidewalk or pathway. Why is grass there in the first place if not to be walked on? Walk on the grass and save a bunch of steps. We are individuals, so let's make our own paths. Save the energy to be used in a more effective manner.

👍 The fastest way to get from one point to another is a straight line. After I finished a 5K race, a fellow runner shared that thought with me. You are looking way ahead to plan your course. When you are walking, use the straight-line method to get somewhere quicker and use the saved time wisely. This also applies while driving or riding to save gas

 and time. Think as if you are racing at a NASCAR oval track, IndyCar road race, or NHRA funny car drag strip.[43]

Courtesy of Englishtown Raceway Park

**Jaywalking** saves a lot of time and energy. Do this in the most efficient linear path possible. In many cities and towns this it is common practice and legal, or at least flexible and tolerated. Educate yourself on the local jaywalking laws. Be safe and look both ways several times.

❏ **AI:** _____

Look ahead to see when the light is going to change. Time your speed to cross the street. Just picking up the pace by walking faster will save you from waiting for the light to change. If you don't think you can make the light walking or it is starting to change, do a slight jog to beat it. Be

---

[43]  As a teenager, I cooked food, sold soft drinks in the grandstands, and even pulled a double-shift on a garbage truck one night at Englishtown Raceway Park.

careful! Even if it is not necessary, do a light jog when jaywalking. You should always be looking for ways to convert energy saved to income producing activities.

Men, please lead your lady while crossing the street. Be mindful of the direction of traffic. Remember to put yourself between her and the traffic, especially crossing one-way traffic (men toward traffic) and walking on the sidewalk (men toward the street). Lead her, this will save time when crossing diagonally to walk a straightest path to the next spot. If walking by yourself, watch for other people crossing the street to see if they need assistance. Also watch their back to protect them so they are not hit by a vehicle.

❏ **AI:** _____

**"I talk fast, I think fast, and I act fast."** If you want something completed quickly, give it to a productive and busy person. You want to be the go-to person that people can trust and expect to get the job done, so move it! This will raise your importance to others and economic value to your employer.

## Being Quicker

**Double Down**: Use both hands at the same time more often. You may have to make this a conscious decision before you get really good at it and it becomes natural. No doubt, this will speed up a simple task that you take for granted. This is good when washing dishes, packing, gardening, typing, etc. As a lefty, I tend to use the dominant hand more than just using the right hand when an object is closer or when using both hands together is more efficient. This is a great time saver. Plus, when your hands are full, use your foot to push something or close the door. Start mastering this skill today.

❏ **AI:** _____

👍 I prefer to take my car to a quick automatic carwash that takes less than five minutes and costs under ten dollars rather than washing it myself. Washing your car at home saves money but not necessarily time, unless you have kids that you can put to work.

As soon as you enter an elevator, push the "close door" button and then select the floor. These seconds saved will add up to minutes over time. Be polite and don't close the door on other people or just after a person leaves the elevator.

## Doing More

Keep focusing energy on a money-making activities to educate yourself or grow your business. Bring self-development, business, or educational books to read during the slow period and intermissions at sporting events. There is a lot of down time during football, soccer, hockey, lacrosse, and baseball games. This includes professional leagues and your kids' games. Your loved ones will have to accept this productive behavior of successful people like us. Matches, races, tournaments, concerts, and plays are also great candidates for this strategy. Please do not fill in programs or scorecards during a game.

❑ **AI:** _____

**Read fifteen minutes** every morning and evening versus making coffee, watching news, or a late-night show. Reading before going to bed can help settle the mind to prepare for a nice night of sleep. Stop reading lengthy biographies, celebrity news, gossip rags, political hacks, and sports magazines. Refrain from only reading long novels, fiction, fantasy, and mystery books. First, read books that millionaires read on career development, business management, financial planning, personal growth, health, fitness, marketing, and sales to increase your financial literacy, profitability, spirituality, and motivation. You will be famous, at least in your own and your family's eyes, if you choose to be. Doing it yourself is better than reading about somebody else doing it.

❑ **AI:** _____

👍 Open up your junk mail to look for gifts, mailing labels, coins, unused postage stamps, sticky notes, wrapping paper, greeting cards, etc. Do this while watching TV, speaking on the phone, or on the toilet. If you are really busy, delegate this task to somebody else, but it needs to be completed regularly.

Please be productive at cafés and coffee shops, and don't just read the paper or surf the net. Stop waiting in long lines to buy an expensive gourmet latte. Can't you drink juice or home-brewed organic coffee at your home, enjoy a homemade breakfast, and pay a neighbor to use their wireless network? Many cities offer free wireless in public buildings like libraries, community centers, recreation centers, downtown, in parks, in open spaces, and into your home. Also check government buildings, though many times they will charge a daily fee. For a list of free Wi-Fi spots in California, go to *www.wififreespot.com/ca.html*. Many other cities and states have similar free access programs.

❑ **AI:** _____

**ABC (Always Be Connected):** A good time-management methodology is needed to stay productive, and it is important to be connected to your resources. Life can be less complex by using advanced technologies like the Internet, cell phone, PDA, PC, MAC, tablet, and cable or satellite TV. Utilize them to your advantage by remaining connected and engaged in your investments. All parents would benefit from having a PDA to keep track of children's events, performances, practices, games, and assignments. Use this for your notes of ideas and tracking action items to remain productive.

❑ **AI:** _____

iPhone, iPad, Android, Blackberry, Google Phone, or other **smartphone applications** can be very effective tools in saving you energy. Here are just some of the apps that increase productivity (all may not apply to you):

❑ Comparing prices and creating a shopping list      __/__/__
❑ Creating and managing a budget      __/__/__
❑ Finding real estate deals, analyzing, and
  funding them      __/__/__
❑ Managing real estate investment properties      __/__/__
❑ Organizing contacts and databases      __/__/__
❑ Quick access to banking and brokerage accounts      __/__/__
❑ Taking notes and voice recording ideas      __/__/__
❑ Tracking business and travel expenses      __/__/__
❑ Tracking fitness training and dieting progress      __/__/__
❑ Tracking goals and objectives      __/__/__

# CHAPTER 8: SAVING YOUR ENERGY
## (INCREASE PRODUCTIVITY)

❑ _____   __/__/__
❑ _____   __/__/__

*"Begin each day as if it were on purpose." ~ Will Smith*

# CHAPTER 9: SAVING YOUR TIME (INCREASE EFFICIENCY)

*"When nothing is sure, everything is possible."* ~ Margaret Drabble

## The Importance of Time Management

**Less Is More!** Time is constant, but money is exponential in both the upward and downward directions. Spending less **time** on your favorite consumer activities will open up more time for revenue-generating activities. You need to do <u>less</u> eating, drinking, smoking, golfing, shopping, watching television, talking, planning, coffee breaks, etc. That time recovered will be spent doing <u>more</u> reading, praying, meditating, exercising, growing, working smarter, networking, giving, listening, spreading compassion, doing for results, and reaching your goals.

**Time Is Money!** Your time will be invested, not wasted. Once time is spent, it is gone forever, but investing time will have long-term enduring implications. This is a critical trait of business owners and investors to achieve compounding growth and passive income.

**Networking** will enable you to have more time by leveraging other people's time. You never know who you will meet or what new information you will learn and what an instrumental impact this could have on your life. Take the time to make a direct and meaningful connection with someone today. It can be in person, on the phone, or via the Internet. Such networking can convert an opportunity into a revenue-producing event.

❏  **AI:** _____

While we can do many things ourselves, it is sometimes wise to transfer responsibility to someone else to save time and money. The cost might be low with superabundant rewards where your time will be well spent on other tasks with more meaningful results. Delegating responsibility while getting more accomplished is the key to success. Provide them with support and advice. You need to analyze your trade-off criteria to make a fast decision yourself or wait for your delegate to respond.

What <u>activities and chores</u> can you **delegate**, and to <u>whom</u>?

| | |
|---|---|
| _____ | to _____ |
| _____ | to _____ |
| _____ | to _____ |
| | ❑ **AI:** _____ |

## Getting Time Back

**Let me show you how to make time.** Do things <u>once and only once</u>. Touch a piece of paper or item only one time. Think ahead and combine activities to improve your efficiency. Avoid making multiple trips when only one is necessary. This includes walking up the stairs, crossing the room, making a trip to the printer, and journeying to the store. It can be as simple as throwing something in the trash, opening the fridge, folding clothes, picking out clothes, writing on an envelope, watching a movie, or asking a question again. Work harder to increase effectiveness. Do more at one time like packing more densely, intensifying your workouts, gathering information more quickly, and making more decisions at once.

👍 Work hard to save time. Again, a lot of time is wasted eating, drinking, and smoking. While you are reducing these consumptions, also reduce the time spent on them. In other words, waste less time by eating, drinking, and smoking <u>faster</u> but responsibly.[44] Put an ice cube in hot coffee, tea, or soup to reduce the temperature so you can drink it faster. This will be a behavior change, and you can invest the saved time in yourself, your family, and your business.

**Cook Faster and Eat Quicker:** Use technology and tricks to speed up the cooking process. Break spaghetti in half before boiling it. This will save time because you'll be able to boil and eat the spaghetti quicker. Adding a dash of salt will make the water boil more quickly. Remember to boil water and liquids with the lid on to bring to a boil quicker and keep the heat in. Once the pasta is done, rinse it with cold water to remove the starches so the pasta does not stick together. Putting a

---

[44]   This is <u>not</u> gorging, binge drinking, or chain smoking—just responsibly spending less time consuming the same amount.

little oil or butter in the water will also help prevent pasta from sticking together.

👍 To save energy and time, crush your cornflakes with your hand in a bowl before eating them to minimize the chewing action before swallowing. The best way is to open the box, remove the bag, open it slightly, and crush the whole bag. Then wrap the bag with rubber bands. Experiment with other foods like cutting up spaghetti and lettuce before chewing.

Eating a meal should be enjoyable, not a project. Serve all of the food courses at once. Don't wait for that late person before you to start eating. Go to short dinner parties. Arrive late and leave early. This does not need to be an all night affair when there is money to be made.

Ice Cube: Use thawing trays to defrost frozen food. These absolutely work "as seen on TV." An ice cube will start visibly melting in seconds, right before your eyes. This will reduce thawing time to at least half. To reduce the time even more, place another tray on top of the food item for faster temperature transference.

❏ **AI:** _____

Have you ever taken a roast, hamburger meat, or something else from the freezer that morning with the good intention of cooking it but then you have to work late, a coworker wants to meet for dinner after work, or you are just too tired to cook? So you put the thawed food in the fridge and get busy or forget about it, and the food goes bad. How many times has this happened to you? Thawing trays will prevent this kind of waste because you will be able to defrost a nice, healthy meal in an hour or two just before you are ready to cook it.

👍 How many times have you cooked a nice hot meal and needed to wait for the pot or pan to cool before eating or storing in the fridge? Maybe it got late or you had somewhere to go and just put it in a little warm. Instead put the pot or pan on the defrosting plate/tray so it will defuse the heat. Within several minutes, the temperature drops, and the food is ready to eat. In a few more minutes, the food is ready to go in the fridge without wasting energy and negatively affecting the other surrounding food. The quicker the food is cooled, the longer it will last.

This little efficiency improvement and cost savings will enable you to run your household more effectively, which is a key trait to managing your investments and businesses.

**Mall Rat:** Again, stop window shopping as a regularly scheduled recreational event. Shop when you *need* to, not because you *want* to. If this is a family, friends, or dating event, try to focus on a more natural setting. How much stuff do you really need to be happy, abundant, and productive in life?

👍 Avoid mega malls that are so large they have their own zip codes or it takes half a day to shop at a few stores. It is not necessarily that the stores are expensive or inherently "bad," but the newest vogue items are seductive and soon-to-be not hip. You can get good deals at small malls with discount department stores in them. Be a more targeted shopper, and do not wander around looking to spend your cash, but save money. When shopping, walk faster than normal. This will burn more calories while reducing the chance of you browsing for items you do not need.

**Watch less** TV and movies, and play fewer videogames. Reduce the amount of time watching (or just stop watching altogether) the following types of programs: dancing and singing competitions, paid programming, celebrity, vanity house, pimped-up car, game, reality, judge, and late-night shows. These shows are addictive and have a "cliffhanger" and teaser effect that will make you fall into a cycle of watching too much TV just to see who gets voted off next week. Also, avoid enticing movie previews by going to the movie theater fifteen minutes later than the listed start time.

❑ **AI:** _____

Stop watching soap operas, trivia, model, bachelor, or housewives shows. This will free up large amounts of time. Do not watch repeat shows and movies you have seen many times over. Avoid placing a TV in the bedroom, office, or kitchen.

❑ **AI:** _____

**"Kill two birds with one stone."** Don't get guilted into long phone calls by friends and family. Keep phone calls short, precise, and focused with a predetermined time to end the conversation. Always be prepared to multitask while on rambling calls. This is a good time to check e-mails, pay bills, and do household chores. Set a time limit on how long you can talk. Get an egg timer or set a timer on your cell phone or wrist watch. If it ends sooner, even better, and when you need to go, you need to go. Just say, "I need to finish some work," "I want to help my kids with their homework," or "I'm running over on my minutes" to end the call.

Remember to multitask when you are driving the kids to school, on vacation, working out, jogging on the treadmill, walking in the park, painting, mowing the yard, raking the lawn (don't use a leaf blower!), doing housework, washing the dishes, ironing, etc.

❏ **AI:** _____

## Using Time More Effectively

**"Stairway to Heaven."** Take the stairs whenever you can. Don't be that person who is always waiting for the elevator and complaining about it being slow. Practice this in the office, on vacation, and on business trips. This is great because you get an unplanned workout and get there faster. Just be safe if you are alone and take extra precautions at night.

👍 Also walk up and down escalators, especially moving walkways, even if you are walking with somebody else. Pass people on the left, even if there is no room, assume you have the right and ask them to move. Just say, "Pardon me" enough in advance so that you do not have to stop and can pass in stride. Then say, "Thank you." They do not control your time. Busy people like you and I are on the move.

**Two Places at the Same Time**: Get duplicates of items you use often so they are close when you need them. Have two or more of important items that you use all of the time in separate places that you frequently visit. This will reduce the time spent to get the item and make it more likely that you will use the item when needed. One example is having a toothbrush and toothpaste in all of your bathrooms as well as in your travel kit. Other great examples are dental floss, mouthwash, lip balm, makeup, vitamins, facial creams, eyeglasses, and keys.

❏ **AI:** _____

Get two remote controllers so you can change the channel and volume from the other room. This is great when you misplace a controller for your cable/satellite box, TV, stereo, radio, and iPod docking station. It prevents wasting time running back and forward between rooms or up and down the stairs to change the station. Don't forget to buy an extra power cord for your laptop and charger for cell phone. Get two of each: one set for use in your home office, and another that you keep packed away in your briefcase for trips.

❑ **AI:** _____

👍 This strategy is also useful for getting two or more of your favorite items that you use a lot. For example, get two pairs of the style of shoes or jeans you wear all the time. Also get multiple pricy beauty care and common household items. Get them only when they are on sale. You benefit by buying now because with inflation, these items may cost more later. Just buy the items you prefer and not other items that you will rarely use.

👍 When eating at home or dining out, use two napkins to eat more efficiently. Put one napkin on your lap to catch the food and another on the table to be readily available to wipe your mouth. Just ask the server for an extra napkin or grab one yourself.

**Five Bucks on Black**: You should be planning for your future, not gambling it away. Greatly reduce the amount of time, money, and energy that you spend betting on games and races or buying lottery tickets. It can be fun and a stress relief, but start the reduction process now. Gambling less gives you more time to be productive. This is more about time and energy versus money, so if you make money and grow your business while enjoying fun entertainment, that is perfect! Keep shifting the energy and time saved to investing in yourself, your family, and your community.

Wikimedia Commons, Logan Ingalls, FlickreviewR

Switch your poker night and girls' night out to business development nights. If you need to get new friends, do so. You would be surprised by how many of your current friends will jump at the opportunity to change and do more producer activities. If not, go to forums on Craigslist, Facebook, or other online bulletin boards to meet like-minded individuals. Join frugal, wealth-building, and real estate message boards and groups.

❑ **AI:** _____

Change your perspectives to developing yourself and growing a business. Think of these things as fun. This is not work but a necessity. Convert coffee or tea breaks into *reading breaks*. Turn smoke breaks into *walking breaks*. Finally, turn lunch hours into *learning hours*. Many companies have break rooms with ping pong, fuzz ball, darts, and cable newscast to relieve stress and encourage teamwork. Utilize the time as a wealth-building mini-workshop. How about financial literacy activities over playing games? Increase your understanding of personal finances, business structure, banking institutions, real estate acquisitions, and government regulations.

❑ **AI:** _____

Check to see if your company has brown-bag lunch financial planning or real estate educational workshops. If not, start a club. Ask local banks, brokerage firms, mortgage lenders, and realtors to give workshops onsite at no cost to you. They can also conduct webinars or teleconferences to reach more people with less overhead. Inquire if they have existing programs online or Internet podcasts that you can access to accomplish the same goal.

❑ **AI:** _____

Be humble and ask for other people's support. Keep your break-time activity partners. When I worked at AT&T, my great friend Mike was my mentor. We would go for walks during lunch or in the mid-afternoon break, and on those walks we networked and discussed philosophy. He invited me to be the vice president of a groundbreaking nonprofit organization (Colorado Environmental Action Exchange) that connected companies and governments to partner with schools to create environmental programs. An activity partner has the potential to turn into a business partner.

# CHAPTER 9: SAVING YOUR TIME
## (INCREASE EFFICIENCY)

👍 "As you get older, you recognize what is valuable, and time is at the top of the list. Time is more important than gold or big houses or fast cars. It's the most valuable resource we have. Unfortunately, we are taught at a young age to trade time for money. That's the message our public education system teaches our kids. [John Dessauer] proposes we change that mindset. Instead of teaching kids the linear way of earning income—the 'time-for-money' exchange—we should teach our kids the miracle of passive income, of doing something once and getting paid for it time and time again. Passive investments do the work for you by freeing up time to do more investments."[60] To learn the benefits of passive income, go to *Chapter 15: Investing in Real Estate, The Benefits of Real Estate Investing*.

*"The ability to concentrate and to use time well is everything."*
*~ Lee Iacocca*

# Part III: Generating Savings ($ET) Endnotes

[1]   MicroGiving at *www.microgiving.com/blog/2009/02/5-tips-to-change-your-bad-spending-habits-and-have-more-for-charity* (May 1, 2011).

[2]   Wikipedia at *www.en.wikipedia.org/wiki/World_energy_resources_and_consumption* (May 1, 2011).

[3]   Pacific Power, "Bright Ideas: A Helpful Guide to Managing Energy Use in Your Home", July 2008, pp. 26, 11, 27.

[4]   Jeff Davidson, *The Joy of Simple Living: Over 1,500 Simple Ways to Make Your Life Easy and Content*, Rodale Press, 1999, p. 82.

[5]   Xedia Technologies, Inc.

[6]   Pacific Power, p. 2.

[7]   California PUC and PG&E, "A Step-by-Step California Guide to Smarter Energy Use", 2008, p. 5.

[8]   Trent Hamm, *365 Ways to Live Cheap: Your Everyday Guide to Saving Money*, Adams Media, 2009, p. 15.

[9]   Pacific Power, pp. 5, 12, 13, 14.

[10]   Ibid, p. 9.

[11]   San Francisco Public Utility Commission (PUC) at *sfwater.org/mto_main.cfm/MC_ID/16/MSC_ID/382/MTO_ID/597* (May 1, 2011).

[12]   Pacific Power, p. 7.

[13]   Hamm, p. 101.

[14]   California PUC and PG&E, "Save Energy in Your Home as Easy as 1, 2, 3", October 2008.

[15]   Pacific Power, p. 11.

[16]   California PUC and PG&E, "A Step-by-Step California Guide to Smarter Energy Use", 2008, p. 6.

[17]   U.S. Department of Energy, Energy Efficiency and Renewable Energy, "When to Turn Off Your Lights", at *www.energysavers.gov/your_home/lighting_daylighting/index.cfm/mytopic=12280* (May 1, 2011).

[18]   Ibid.

[19]   California PUC and PG&E, "Save Energy in Your Home as Easy as 1, 2, 3", October 2008.

[20]   Ibid, p. 5.

[21]   Pacific Power, p. 14.

[22]   Ibid, pp. 6, 15, 14.

[23]   U.S. Department of Energy, Motor Challenge, "Reducing Power Factor Cost Fact Sheet", 1996.

24  Wikipedia at *www.en.wikipedia.org/wiki/Power_factor#cite_note-0*

25  Xedia Technology at *www.xediadirect.com*.

26  Ibid.

27  Timothy J. Mayclin, CPA, *Tax and Business Services Newsletter*, November 2009.

28  Hamm, p. 202.

29  Matthew Wheeland, "Green Computing at Google", GreenBiz.com, May 2, 2007, at *www.greenbiz.com/news/2007/05/02/green-computing-google* (May 1, 2011).

30  Charles Schwab, "5 Tips for Prevent Identity Theft", *Charles Schwab On Investing*, Summer 2009.

31  Trent Hamm, *365 Ways to Live Cheap: Your Everyday Guide to Saving Money*, Adams Media, 2009, p. 50.

32  GreenZebra at *www.theGreenZebra.org*.

33  Evert-Fresh Green Bags.

34  Hamm, p. 13.

35  Ibid.

36  Davidson, p. 71.

37  Will J. Rayment, "Health Benefits of Spices and Herbs", permission of In-Depth Info.com, at *www.indepthinfo.com/spices/medicinaluses.shtml* (May 1, 2011).

38  Ibid.

39  Hamm, pp. 194, 5, 195, 87.

40  Ibid, pp. 136-137.

41  Davidson, p. 180.

42  Ibid, p. 185.

43  Ibid, p. 186.

44  Stuart Schuffman, *Broke-Ass Stuart's Guide to Living Cheaply in New York*, Falls Media, 2008, p. 142.

45  Wikipedia at *www.en.wikipedia.org/wiki/Greyhound_racing* (May 1, 2011).

46  Ibid.

47  Ibid.

48  Dr. Phil, "An Action Plan for Eliminating Debt", at *www.drphil.com/articles/print/?ArticleID=233* (May 1, 2011).

49  Michelle Warren, "Add-ons that Don't Add Value to Your New Car," Bankrate, at *www.bankrate.com/finance/auto/add-ons-that-don-t-add-value-to-your-new-car.aspx* (May 1, 2011).

[50]  Dave Ramsey, *The Total Money Makeover: A Proven Plan for Financial Fitness*, Thomas Nelson Publishing, 2003, pp. 87, 34.

[51]  Warren.

[52]  Davidson, p. 232.

[53]  Jennifer Glickel, "David Koch Replaces Mayor Michael Bloomberg as Manhattan's Wealthiest Man," DNAinfo.com, at *www.dnainfo. com/20100922/manhattan/david-koch-replaces-mayor-michael-bloomberg-as-manhattans-wealthiest-billionaire* (May 1, 2011).

[54]  Zipcar at *www.Zipcar.com*.

[55]  GreenZebra at *www.theGreenZebra.org*.

[56]  Hamm, p. 218.

[57]  Ibid, p. 217.

[58]  Davidson, p. 144.

[59]  Ibid, p. 148.

[60]  John Dessauer, *Real Estate H²O: Quenching Your Financial Thirst in a Parched Economy*, Dessauer Publishing, 2008, pp. 40, 41.

# PART IV – YOUR INVESTING STRATEGY

*"To have an abundance of wellbeing in the **Five Pillars of Wealth**:
<u>Financial</u>, <u>Relational</u>, <u>Mental</u>, <u>Physical</u>, and <u>Spiritual</u>. Without these
five pillars, you might be rich, but you'll never be wealthy. Growth
brings wealth." ~ James Arthur Ray*

## CHAPTER 10: THE IMPORTANCE AND POWER OF MONEY

### Creating Wealth

Wealth is not just about accumulating money and big toys. It includes
the ability to **INVEST** in yourself and others. The key is to generate your
own active and/or passive income. Generate enough reserve funds or
residual income to sustain yourself to retire years earlier than planned!

There are many examples of <u>wealth</u>:

- Being 100 percent debt-free
- Being able to care for parents, foster children or adopt
- Being able to donate a portion of your fortune to charity
- Fully funded family's retirement plans and college funds
- One month building villages or teaching as a missionary
- Owning stocks and mutual funds
- Passive income exceeds expenses
- Retire by the date you set
- Your money accumulates compounding interest

Generate income and create wealth by <u>investing</u> in these areas:

- Career or job skill set
- Increasing savings and debt reduction
- Income-generating investments and businesses
- Retirement plan and real estate
- Education, fitness, wellness, relationships, and community

You have to judge which of these wealth-building investments should be funded and their target dates. The motivational questions, behavioral changes, debt reduction, trading-down wants list, vices, passions, goals, and transformation plans will be personalized. A savings of ten to twenty dollars per week put into a growing asset is a big step. Increasingly multiply these savings over the coming months and years to **generate more money to invest**.

You need to create a balanced investment portfolio. In volatile markets manage your risk with a portfolio comprised of different equities. It will be up to you to determine the mix and percentages, but a sample might look something like this:

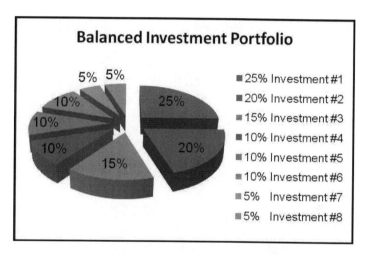

This is an example of eight investment components:

1. Pre-Tax IRA, SEP IRA, 401(k), or 403(b) Retirement Plan
2. Home-Based Business
3. Real Estate
4. After-Tax Non-Retirement Plan Account
5. Emergency and Savings Accounts
6. 529 College Savings Plan
7. Donating and Volunteering
8. Health and Wellness

Your portfolio may be comprised of fewer or more investments. You may start with two investment components and end with five or start with five and end with over ten directed investments, many of which are mentioned above. What your balanced portfolio looks like will be determined by your individual circumstances. Your situation will change, and so will the investment mix over the years.

**You don't have to be a millionaire to be wealthy!** It is what you can do to support your community and assist others. Wealth, for me, would mean being able to leave work to help in Haiti after the 2010 magnitude 7.0 earthquake, Indonesia after the 2004 Christmas Indian Ocean tsunami, and New Orleans (locals pronounce "Nawlins") after 2005 Hurricane Katrina. My company did not stop me; I did. Also having the resources to fly supplies in to these disaster areas would be real wealth that saves lives.[45] What does being wealthy mean to you?

New Orleans Saints Superdome—September 2, 2005, FEMA, Jocelyn Augustino

## The Family and Money

Marriage is the greatest of partnerships, and it requires deep commitment. Of course you must take this love seriously and cherish your mate. There also needs to be a commitment to achieving BIG dreams together and growing your collective Inner Economy. Have a candid discussion on spending versus investing. Don't play the tit-for-tat game of spending that has you saying, "You golf with the boys, and I will go shopping with the girls . . . I get a new truck, and you get a new fully loaded sedan . . . I will remodel the kitchen, and you get new expensive lawnmower." In most cases, these are

---

[45]   After Hurricane Katrina, former Vice President Al Gore chartered 2 planes to evacuate 270 people from New Orleans Charity Hospital.

expenses not investments. Remember that non-investment items need to be purchased with cash and not credit cards or a loan.

👍 The U.S. divorce rate is over 50 percent and growing. Most of those marriages fail due to financial reasons. My goal is to reverse this trend and keep more couples together to raise their children and retire early together. No matter what stage of marriage or a relationship you are in, this is an opportune time to have this discussion. Let's change it from a money discussion to happiness, dreams, life goals, and investments discussion. Express your deep desires and what the family is willing to trade to get there together. There was a reason why you're together in the first place. Redirect spending from consumer habits to producer habits. The passion will now be invested in eliminating debt, increasing your retirement plan, growing the business, and paying for school.

Honest, frank, and open communications should enhance your relationship while you pave a smooth path forward together. This is not about control, but influence. You are not competing against each other but working together to meet your common goals. Be nurturing and compassionate without lecturing. Also, do not be self-absorbed or have self-hatred. This is not about power, but about owning up to your financial commitments and personal responsibilities to yourself, to each other, to your children, and to the life you have built or are building.

❏ **AI:** _____

Parents are responsible to help their children go to college, vocational and trade schools, etc. This includes the moral support, motivation, homework assignment, and financial assistance they will need to gain a skill set and education while getting good grades in the process. Every time you have a baby, this must be taken into account. Make or reaffirm this commitment today.

❏ **AI:** _____

👍 Parents, please do not pierce your baby's ears until you add at least $5,000 to their college fund and start a savings account for them. Your children looking adorable is not as important as their future. It is about the kids and not you, so stop buying cute baby clothes and start investing in their future even before they are born. It is never too late or too early to start. Even five bucks a week or fifty a month will add up and slow the temptation of buying stuff they don't need and are really only <u>your</u> wants.

## Spending Money Wisely by Investing It

You are transforming from spending and wasting money to investing and growing money. Investing wisely is the key to success. Profitable companies do not squander money, so why should you consume their products for quick satisfaction with no long-term benefits? This money management wisdom will be balanced by your principles, giving you flexibility to become financially free and retire early.

The vast majority of wealthy people are debt-free, especially from bad debt, while the strongest global companies have an excess of cash reserves. The key is **spending less than you earn**. Break this down per month. "Winning at money is 80 percent behavior and 20 percent head knowledge. If you're not paying cash, you're paying too much."[1]

👍 In the Cashflow 101 board game, there is an opportunity card for your brother-in-law to borrow money with no collateral or time commitment to repay the loan. I have never seen a player take this deal, but we always talk about. It usually brings up bad memories of past experiences. There is a similar deal with your sister-in-law; I removed that card from the deck because it was repetitive. The players got the message with an unknown return-on-investment because there were no terms to pay off the debt. The point is, beware of loaning money to family members and friends. My dad said, "Only loan money if you do not need it or expect it back." I also removed the $4,000 widescreen TV and $17,000 boat doodads cards from the game. We have a choice in life not to buy luxury items and instead focus on acquiring assets.

I host a Cashflow game once a month. It reminds me of property management tasks I need to do, as well as reconfirms my diverse investment strategy. In addition, my focus is having a deeper impact on committed individuals while playing the game. We have fun and grow our investment portfolios together. I recommend that you host a game playing with like-minded entrepreneurs.

❏  **AI:** _____

*"Play now and pay later, or pay now and play later."* ~ Chad Wade

# CHAPTER 11: INVESTING IN DEBT REDUCTION WHILE INCREASING YOUR SAVINGS

*"The person who says it cannot be done should not interrupt the person doing it." ~ Chinese proverb*

## Planning to Save While Changing Habits

### Transforming Behavior

"Looking good is when your broke friends are impressed by what you drive, and being good is having more money than they have. You have to reach the point that what people think is not your primary motivator. Reaching this goal is the motivator."[2]

Is it important to:

- Buy a new sports or luxury car that depreciates 20 to 40 percent as soon as you drive it off the lot?
- Buy jewelry so extravagant that you only wear it once a year, to be accompanied by an armed guard?[46]
- Have a store deliver and install your new modern kitchen?
- Have furniture so fancy you cannot enjoy sitting on it?
- Have season tickets or fifty plus pairs of shoes?

Or is it important to:

- Be 100 percent debt-free and pay cash for a used car?
- Buy a home where you can write off the county taxes, mortgage interest, insurance, and even depreciation?
- Donate at least 100 dollars per month to charities?
- Have one million dollars of assets in your retirement plans?
- Send children to college without sacrificing your future?

---

[46]   Maybe I'm exaggerating about the guard, but you get the point.

Which list is smart investing and the preferred behavior of a producer? It is more pleasurable to check your portfolio performance online than looking at a shiny car in the garage.

## First Steps in Addressing Debt

"First step, you will have to be current with all your creditors. If you are behind on payments, the first goal will be to become current. If you are far behind, do necessities first, which are food, shelter, utilities, clothing, and transportation. Only when you're current with the necessities can you catch up on credit cards, car loans, and student loans."[3]

❑  AI: _____

To pay bills and loans, choose automatic withdraw payout options that have no fee. Select to pay bills five days before the due date. It feels good and takes a proactive approach to happily managing money. If, for some reason, the payment does not draft, you have a few days to correct the problem before you are hit with late fees and penalties.

❑  AI: _____

**Five-Dollar TIP**: For each credit card that you pay off in full every month, pay an extra five dollars. If $100 is total amount due (not the minimum required payment), pay $105. This will illustrate that you are overpaying and may help your credit score. In the next payment cycle, it will be a credit. Keep adding back in the same five dollars. Now you are lending to the lenders, and it feels good.

❑  AI: _____

Always—yes, ALWAYS—pay more than your minimal payments on all debts, both good and bad. Even if this debt is to your father-in-law, best friend, or neighbor, pay them extra per installment too.

❑  AI: _____

✋ You should not loan money to a person you are dating. If you do, against my advice, make sure there is a binding promissory note with repayment terms, the note is signed and dated by both parties and a witness, and both parties have an original copy. When it comes to financial dealings, whether you are on the borrowing or lending end, always capture the details in writing. If this is a really large amount, get something of the same or greater value for collateral. If you don't want to take my word for it, watch a few episodes of *Judge Judy* or *Judge Greg Mathis*[47] to see why.

## Creating a Budget

Create and maintain a budget to track your expenses and investments. This will also help you stay on track building savings and paying off debt. It takes a lot of willpower to stick to a strict budget. Could you do it for a week? If you track your expenses for just one week, you will have a good idea where all that money is going. Tracking for a month, you might find quick areas to save money. Many people are surprised when they discover how much they spend on small things like that coffee, going out to lunch, cocktails, shoes, or premium movie channels. "John Maxwell said, 'A budget is people telling their money where to go instead of wondering where it went.' You have to make your money behave, and a written plan is the whip and chair for the money tamer."[4]

Create a budget spreadsheet in Microsoft Excel, use Intuit Quicken personal finance program, or on smartphone application. Make this a project for your kid, a friend, or neighborhood college student. Wasteful consumption patterns, hoarding, and collecting can be controlled through successful budgeting. There are many different types of budget templates that you can download for free, including weekly, monthly, and yearly formats. Specific budget templates like household, personal, business trip, retirement, and college are also available. It is important to know where and how you are spending your money. A visual diagram that can be easily updated will help you quickly realize the benefits by cutting expenses.

❑ **AI:** _____

---

[47] I previously mentioned that you should reduce time spent watching judge and reality shows, but there is valuable content in some of them.

Here are resources that can assist you in creating a budget:

- CNET's monthly expense calculator 1.1 (Windows) at <u>download.cnet.com/Monthly-Expense-Calculator/3000-2064_4-10896867.html</u>
- Frugal Village's online monthly budget table at <u>www.frugalvillage.com/budget.shtml</u>
- Suze Orman's monthly expense budget calculator at <u>www.oprah.com/article/money/personalfinance/pkgyourmoney/20081119_expert_suzeexpense</u>

## Cash Is King

Let's discuss the advantages of using cash versus credit cards. "When you pay cash, you can 'feel' the money leaving you. This is not true with credit cards. Flipping a credit card up on a counter registers nothing emotionally."[5] Using cash instead of plastic has a more immediate effect of loss. This is money lost that cannot be recovered. It is hard to value something you cannot see.

It is important to carry some cash with you. You never know when you will need it. In general, cash speeds up the checkout process. It drives me crazy when I am in line at a grocery store and the person in front of me uses a debit card for a banana and pack of gum. Using a debit card may be easier to track and categorize items online, so this is fine. Always keep a few twenties on you for small purchases like dining out, clothes, sodas, coffee, and emergencies.

❏ **AI:** _____

Cash will provide opportunities to negotiate. American Express (AMEX) charges the merchants 4 percent fee of the purchase price. The other major credit card companies like VISA and Master Card charge the merchants between 2.5 to 3 percent. Banks also charge merchants for each debit transaction. You can negotiate at least with this and ask them to pay the sales tax as well. Just ask, "Can you please be flexible with that price since I can pay in cash?" This works for both products and services for smaller stores and privately owned businesses. Cash is warm, and debit and credit cards are cold. Carry all denominations (ones, fives, tens, and twenties), but be careful not to show people how much you have. Protect your "hand" just like you do in a poker game. I just did this buying a bed mattress and saved $80 off a $300 purchase!

❏ **AI:** _____

👍 Think of the connection that you've made by placing cash tips in somebody's hands versus on a plastic credit card. This also gives you the opportunity to look in the person's eyes to make a connection and a friend while they say, "Thank you." Wealthy people carry cash with them, and so should you.

**Nuts** : Stash money around your house and car in case of an emergency or if something unexpected comes up, just like a squirrel stores nuts in the fall to prepare for a harsh winter. Put bills in the dresser drawer, car glove compartment, safe, briefcase, back of the wallet, hidden section in

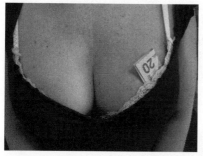

purse, luggage, and bra (just joking a little about the bra, but my mom did this when I was growing up!). Saving cash should be a part of your investment portfolio.

❏ **AI:** _____

This is not my Mom but a willing participant.

👍 When you are jogging, put a twenty and a few business cards in your pocket. If you get hurt or lose your keys, you will have money for a cab ride and to make a call. If you need to buy water, you can, and the cards are good for networking and identification purposes.

In 2008, I was in Tokyo, where they only have access to ATMs in post offices during business hours—surprising for a country known for global financial institutions. I was running low on cash, and the post office was open on a Saturday. Good news, right? The problem was that their ATMs have different keypads than I am accustomed to here in the States. The bottom line is, I could not get any of my money. Fortunately, I had stored eighty bucks in my luggage, so I was able to eat and go clubbing that weekend.

👍 Note that when traveling out of the U.S., ATMs usually provide the best exchange rates as compared to hotels and exchange booths. This is what I witnessed while traveling aboard.

## Save One Dollar a Day Investment Plan

**"Here, kitty, kitty."** Save one dollar a day to invest in <u>addition</u> to your existing automatic deposit allocations. It was Oscar Levant who said, "A dollar saved is a dollar earned." Dave and Tom Gardner, stated "The value of a dollar is huge when it's invested and compounding, and that's exactly where your dollar should be and what it should be doing."[6] Every day, put one dollar in a jar with lid, small container, or better yet, a safe. It's just a buck. Call this your "*kitty*." Invest that dollar soon, and it is not just to be a one-to-one gain. There is a factor of profits to every dollar saved. This also has a huge mental impact when you are deciding to buy a diet soda or coffee. This will represent two or four days of savings in a single decision. Passing on a shirt or eating dinner out will be one month of savings. This is not hard. After a year, this will amount to $365 that will be wisely invested. To stay on track, get a one-page yearly calendar. Mark off with a highlighter the days when you put money in.

❏ **AI:** _____

The best strategy is to put a few dollars in several times a week to stay connected with the need to save consistently. Don't be frustrated if you get behind, just kick in a ten or a twenty at once, or over the next week to get caught up.

Saving a daily dollar in the kitty is a given. Agreed? Let's go further with this idea. Multiply this by all family members. Yes, this is for EVERY member of your family. Agreed? Roll this plan out to them. A family of four will be able to reinvest $1,460 annually which is an example of a grand slam. Furthermore, there is the added benefit in the gain of compounding interest or growth year over year. Be each other's accountability partners, this is not a competition. Remember, <u>each</u> person decides where to <u>invest</u> their savings. As long as you describe what investing is and provide examples, they will choose wisely. That is transforming to producers as a team! If you are not married encourage your partner or the person you are dating to join you in this daily saving ritual.

❑ **AI:** _____

**"I'm going to have a treasure bath!"** After you have collected a good amount of money in your kitty, you should treat yourself to a money bath, your own version of Demi Moore and Woody Harrelson in *Indecent Proposal* or Mel Brook's *History of the World Part I*. Then, invest this money when you get $25, $100, or $200 saved. This money is not to be spent on wants and needs, just investments like mutual funds, real estate, and your businesses that work for you while you are sleeping.

 But it can also go into any investments like an emergency fund, reducing debt, office supplies, wellness, and education. Track the investments from these funds by keeping all of the receipts, transactions, statements, or by making a note of what you invested in from the kitty. Just leave them in the kitty along with the current and past calendars. I suggest that you wash your hands with antibacterial soap after the treasure bath though, because money goes through a lot of hands!

❑ **AI:** _____

Now you will reward yourself by watching your investments grow every month . . . and get the popcorn on sale. If you are not able to start saving a dollar a day now in the kitty, start with fifty or twenty-five cents. Just have a plan and write down when you will get to a dollar. Remember, investments are compounding from what you contributed and the earnings! They are increasing with no or little effort from you. Pick a targeted annual increase of 5 to 15 percent.

## Debt Reduction

### Attacking Bad Debt

**"Don't write a check that you're a*s can't cash."** Sacrifice to pay off debt. Do not avoid your debts and responsibilities. Deal with them today, honestly and head-on. Live within your means, and do not over extend yourself, financially.

***Pro Rata* Debt:** "If you cannot pay creditors what they request, you should treat them all fairly and the same. You should pay even those that are not jerks, and pay everyone as much as you can. Many creditors will accept a written plan and cut special deals with you as long as you are communicating (maybe even over-communicating) and sending them something. *Pro rata* means 'their share', the percent of total debt each creditor represents. That will determine how much you send them. Then, send the check with a budget and Dave Ramsey's The Total Money Makeover *Pro Rata* Debt sheet [see back of Dave's book] attached each month, even if the creditor says they will not accept it."[7]

👍 Save yourself hundreds of dollars in interest payments on credit cards by directing extra savings appropriately to pay off the cards quickly. The largest interest rate debts are your main priority, as they are costing money and not saving. Also work on an emergency fund at the same time. Until all of your credit cards are 100 percent paid off and you have an emergency fund, you need to use a debit card and pull funds from your checking account. The use of a debit card will discourage your bad spending habits with credit cards and prevent you from dipping into your savings account.

By reducing your credit card debt, you can save over $700 if you transfer your card with a $2,000 balance and an 18 percent interest rate to a different card with an 8.25 percent rate. Or take advantage of one of those 0 percent transfers with a new card and save even more. But make sure you pay them down before the term period ends and the interest rate goes dramatically up.

❏ **AI:** _____

👍 Remember, once you pay off the credit, department, and gas cards with crazy high rates, DESTROY them. Don't settle for just cutting them up. Have a card-melting party each time. Put it on a stick and toast it over an open fire like a marshmallow.

## Systematically Paying Off Debt

Choosing to pay even a little extra on the required loan amount can save you thousands of dollars. This strategy works the same for mortgages, student loans, auto loans, or really any loan that allows you to prepay the principal. For example, suppose you have a $10,000 student loan at an interest rate of 7 percent and a repayment period of ten years. If your first payment on that loan is due January 1, 2011, you would continue paying through December of 2020. Your monthly payment would be around $116, and at the end, you would have paid $3,933 in interest charges.

If you paid just $30 extra a month, making the payment $146, you would pay the loan off in May of 2018, two and a half years early, and, your total interest paid would be $2,800, saving you $1,133 in interest charges. If you paid an extra $60 each month, with a payment of $176, the loan pays off in just under six years in November of 2016. The total interest paid would be $2,180, saving you $1,753. Clearly, making the additional interest payment can save hundreds to thousands of dollars, even on a small loan.

❏ **AI:** _____

Pay a little extra principal on your mortgage. You'll save thousands on interest paid per year. Did you know that paying just $100 extra a month on a conventional thirty-year at 6.5 percent fixed interest rate $200,000 mortgage will save you over $55,000 over the life of the loan? It will also pay off the loan five years early. That's worth looking into, right? Just have this extra amount added to the total payment withdrawn by the lender or directly from your bank.

❏ **AI:** _____

When you get a bonus or tax refund, you can even send in a check toward paying off extra principal. This is a good idea, but you must also have it automatically deducted every month. Do not solely rely on writing a big check to pay down the principal once a year with your income tax return or bonus. If you have extra money, that's great, but what if you owe money to the government or do not get a bonus from your employer? Paying down the principal earlier in the year will save on accumulating interest in the long-term. Add annual and semi-annual contributions to accelerate this systematic method.

❏ **AI:** _____

## Automating Paying Off Debt

Set up monthly automatic withdrawal for mortgages and loans. The lender will give you the option when you want the "draw," but you need to ask them for the last draw date without a penalty. It will be on the tenth or the fifteenth of the month. Some lenders charge a fee for setting a draw after the fifth or tenth. For my personal home, it does not matter because there are always enough funds in my checking account, so they pull it on the fifth (earliest option). For rental investment properties, have them draw later in the month on the tenth or fifteenth (latest option), depending on the mortgage company policy. The later date on the investment property is because the tenants' rent checks can come in by the fifth of the month, and then it takes several days for their checks to clear.

❑ **AI:** _____

👍 Apply additional principal each month to every property. The largest amount goes to your home because no matter what happens, you have a place to live. The rest of the extra savings are invested across the investment property mortgages with the most going to the highest interest rates and the least going to the lowest interest rates. The type of loan and terms are also factors when distributing the extra principal payment amount across multiple properties which is discussed in *Planning for the Future Now, Debt-Reducing Scenarios* section with instructions.

It is easy to move your additional principal payment UP and down. Lenders usually require a minimum of fifteen days for the changes to take effect. There is NO tax advantage to paying the principal of a loan. On your taxes (Schedule E), you are able to deduct the interest paid, but not the principal. You need to take this into account when considering this method. For many real estate investors, this is a long-term buy-and-hold strategy to own a property outright by paying off the mortgage early and then living off the rental income.

👍 If you have an interest-only loan and are paying extra principal, the total loan principal amount will decrease. This means you may be paying just a little less interest each month. It may only be a few cents to a dollar, depending on the loan amount and interest rate. If you are paying extra principal, then you are serious about paying down the loan faster, so the lender will not be able to apply all of the amount you requested toward paying down the principal balance.

Here is a solution: Have the mortgage consultant lock in a fixed total amount. Here is an example with interest $500, escrow $200, principal $100. Change the principal of $100 to total payment of $800 per month. You need to monitor this because if the escrow goes up, less money may be going toward the principal. This is not a huge issue because escrow accounts are analyzed annually, and the lender will provide thirty to sixty days notice. To create a list of your loans and how to balance the extra funds toward principal, go to *Planning for the Future Now, Debt-Reducing Scenarios and Documenting Your Debts* section.

❏  **AI:** _____

## Recovering from Too Much Bad Debt

I was fresh out of college and working for a great company with good salary, but my expenses were too high. I overextended myself by buying a new Mazda RX7 sports car and upgrading to a big loft. I was quickly in over my head, drowning in more expenses than I expected. Inevitably, several months later, I ran out of money and only had seven dollars left in my checking account to last the week . . . and it was only Monday. What a sick feeling it is to be so broke! Have you been there? Maybe you're there now!

I was sitting on my floor with my pet rabbit eating rice with a little butter and pepper. Yes, Mudbone and I were both eating out of the same bowl—it

was pitiful. My neighbor Amy caught us in the compromising position and took us both out to dinner. I ate lasagna and Mudbone enjoyed a calzone (he loves cheese).

Mudbone Wortham

That was a wake-up call. I quickly moved to a cheaper house and got a roommate to split the rent, utilities, and household expenses. In addition, I temporarily reduced my percentage allocation to my 401(k).

This is an example of how upgrading to a larger home or getting a new car can put a person in a financial hole. This hardship and embarrassing situation could have been prevented. I learned from this mistake and grew from this lesson.

## Debt-Reducing Scenarios

The philosophy of savings in this book is targeted on the future of investing in your Inner Economy. A part of this investment is paying down your bad and good debt, but this is not the only component. You also need to increase your income with your newfound time. Finally, you need to create wealth through businesses and investments with your newfound energy.

☝ As discussed, multiple strategies should be implemented at once. Of course, the primary savings will go toward paying off and eventually eliminating bad debt. Put most of the money toward the card(s) and loan(s) with the higher interest rates, but also put a little on the other card(s) and loan(s) proportionally from highest to lowest rates. Group debt by credit cards, department stores, loans, home mortgage, and investment property mortgages.[48]

Example of $1,000 per month to pay off bad debts with the same balance:[49]

- $700    Credit Card A at <u>25 percent interest rate</u> with $5,000 balance ($100 minimal payment required)
- $200    Credit Card B at <u>20 percent interest rate</u> with $5,000 balance ($100 minimal payment required)
- $100    <u>Department store card</u> at <u>15 percent interest rate</u> with $5,000 balance ($100 minimal payment required)

---

[48]    For an alternate solution by Dave Ramsey, check out "Chapter 7: Baby Step Two: Start the Debt Snowball" in *The Total Money Makeover: A Proven Plan for Financial Fitness*.

[49]    Numbers are for illustration purposes only.

✍ If the terms and conditions of credit and department store cards are similar, treat them the same when paying them off. The difference is the interest rate, so $600 more money is applied to Credit Card A—compared to $100 on Credit Card B and a minimal payment on the department store card.

Credit cards have a little higher priority because that frees up available credit and the ability to charge again in case of an emergency:

1. Once Credit Card A is paid off, increase extra principal on Credit Card B to $600 and $100 extra toward department store card.
2. Once Credit Card B is paid off, divert the entire $1,000 toward the department store card.
3. Once you pay off the department store card, destroy it. You probably only got it because the first time it was used, you received a 10 percent discount for that purchase or rebate on the next purchase.

Example of $1,000 per month to pay off bad debts with different balances:[50]

- $800 Credit Card A at <u>25 percent interest rate</u> with <u>$5,000 balance</u> ($100 minimal payment required)
- $150 Credit Card B at <u>20 percent interest rate</u> with <u>$2,000 balance</u> ($50 minimal payment required)
- $50 Department store card at <u>15 percent interest rate</u> with <u>$1,000 balance</u> ($50 minimal payment required)

✍ The balance comes into play in three scenarios that may change the allocation of funds:

1. The term (due) interest rate is going to rise, so Credit Card A receives the bulk of the extra principal amount ($700).
2. You have a lot of loans and recurring credit, some of which you want to close (though not all) to improve your credit score. For instance, close Credit Card B but not A.

---

[50] Numbers are for illustration purposes only.

3.  Balance is really low (department store card), then pay it off first and have one less account to worry about.

Example of $4,000 per month to pay off property mortgages:[51]

- $950    Thirty-year home mortgage loan at <u>5 percent fixed interest rate</u> with $100,000 balance ($800 minimal payment required)
- $950    Thirty-year investment Property A mortgage loan at <u>7 percent fixed interest rate</u> with $100,000 balance ($800 minimal payment required)
- $1,000  Thirty-year investment Property B mortgage loan (first) at <u>7 percent variable interest rate</u> with $80,000 balance ($800 minimal payment required)
- $1,100  <u>Fifteen-year</u> investment Property B home equity line of credit (HELOC) loan (second) at <u>10 percent variable interest rate</u> with $20,000 balance ($400 minimal payment required)

👍 Because each housing market is different, it may not be clear when a home will be sold, so extra principal is spread across all of the mortgages but not evenly. Home mortgage and investment Property A have addition principal paid on both the same ($150) personal home is priority but since investment Property A interest rate is higher than the home mortgage they cancel out. More extra principal is put on the investment mortgage for Property B ($300) and not Property A because B is a variable interest rate loan. This carries some uncertainty and risk because the rate can go up in the future. The largest proportion of extra funds is applied to the investment Property B HELOC loan ($700) because it has the highest interest rate at 10 percent, the rate is variable, and loan balance is the lowest.

Example of $2,000 per month to pay off good and bad debts with difference balances and terms:[52]

---

[51]   Numbers are for illustration purposes only.

[52]   Numbers are for illustration purposes only.

- $900   <u>Thirty-year home mortgage loan</u> at <u>7 percent interest rate</u> with $100,000 balance ($800 minimal payment required)
- $400   <u>Five-year car loan at 10 percent interest rate</u> with $20,000 balance ($250 minimal payment required)
- $700   <u>Credit card at 20 percent interest rate</u> with $5,000 balance ($100 minimal payment required)

👍 The goal is to pay off the credit cards first and then the car loan. Set a goal to pay off credit cards within six to eight months, five-year car loans in three years, and thirty-year mortgages in twenty years. If maxing out your credit cards is a recurring problem for you, nip it in the bud by destroying the cards once the debt is paid off. As illustrated, it is wise to also pay off good debt like a mortgage because these are for long-term assets that should appreciate in time, providing security for you and your family, but getting rid of bad debt with very high interest rate is the top priority.

Once the credit card is paid off, continue the example of $2,000 per month to pay off good and bad debts with difference balances and terms:[53]

- $1,000   Thirty-year home mortgage loan at 7 percent interest rate with <u>$92,000 balance</u> ($800 minimal payment required)
- $1,000   <u>Five-year car loan</u> at 10 percent interest rate with <u>$16,000 balance</u> ($250 minimal payment required)

👍 This scenario will pay off the car loan next at an accelerated pace. Then, increase the amount extra from $100 to $200 toward the principal of the home mortgage while dramatically increasing the car loan from $150 to $750. At the same time, increase your retirement and personal investment funds from other money saving activities. Finally, once the bad debt is also paid off, plan to put those funds toward building a business and buying real estate.

---

[53]   Numbers are for illustration purposes only.

## Documenting Your Debts

Pull together all of your accounts that have unpaid balances. Create a list of these accounts. Decide on the savings per month that you will invest to pay off the debt <u>principal</u> (not the interest or minimal balance, because you are already doing this). For example, if you save $400, you will spend it across all of the debt with the highest interest rate getting the largest portion. Time is of the essence! Spread the money proportionally according to the interest rate and other factors illustrated in a previous section, *Debt-Reducing Scenarios*.

_____'s Debts List ___/___/___

(from highest to lowest interest rates)

| Debt Owned To | Amount | Interest Rate/Type | Terms | Extra Principal | Date to Payoff |
|---|---|---|---|---|---|
| _____ | _____ | _____ | _____ | _____ | _/_/_ |
| _____ | _____ | _____ | _____ | _____ | _/_/_ |
| _____ | _____ | _____ | _____ | _____ | _/_/_ |
| _____ | _____ | _____ | _____ | _____ | _/_/_ |
| _____ | _____ | _____ | _____ | _____ | _/_/_ |
| _____ | _____ | _____ | _____ | _____ | _/_/_ |
| _____ | _____ | _____ | _____ | ❑ AI: _____ | |

## Building Up Your Savings

### Funding the Emergency Fund

Everybody needs to have an emergency fund or reserves! Don't let emergencies derail your ability to fund investments. "Important **emergency fund strategies**" by Dave Ramsey:[8]

- Most of America uses credit cards to catch all of life's emergencies. Some of these so-called emergencies are events like Christmas, [birthdays, and vacations]. An emergency fund can turn crises that used to be huge, life-altering events into mere inconveniences.

- An emergency is something you had no way of knowing was coming, something that has a major impact on you and your family if you don't cover it. Emergencies include paying the deductible on medical, homeowner's, or car insurance after an accident, a job loss or cutback, medical bills resulting from an accident or unforeseen medical problem, or a blown transmission or engine that you need to repair in order to function.

👍 Whether the emergency is real or just the result of poor planning, the cycle of dependence on credit cards has to be broken. The first "Baby Step" to your "Total Money Makeover" is to begin the emergency fund. A small start is to save $1,000 in cash fast! If you have a household income under $20,000 per year, use $500 for your beginner fund. Fully funded emergency funds cover three to six months of <u>expenses</u>, not your income. This will typically range from $5,000 to $25,000.

👍 If you have a "steady, secure" job where you have been with that company or government agency for fifteen years and everybody is healthy, you could lean toward the three-month rule. A real estate agent should have a six-month fund, and a healthy postal worker who has been in her job for years and plans to stay might keep a three-month fund. Customize your emergency fund to your situation and to how your spouse deals with the feeling of risk.

There are financial institutions that allow you to get a high-yield interest and still able to access the funds when necessary with minimal or no penalties. Use a money market or interest-bearing savings account[54] as

---

[54] Verify that all of your banking, brokerage, and retirement accounts are Federal Deposit Insurance Corporation (FDIC) insured. *FDIC* is an independent agency of the United States government that protects you against the loss of your deposits if an FDIC-insured bank or savings association fails. Basic coverage limit for single, IRAs, and other certain retirement accounts (owned by one person) is $250,000 per owner. For more details, go to *www.FDIC.gov*.

your emergency account. Leading banks and stock trading companies will store account funds in a money market for you that earn higher interest rates. Credit unions usually offer higher interest rates, lower service charges and lower rates on loans as compared to traditional banks, and they may even waive maintenance fees. Investigate moving your checking and savings accounts where you—not the bank—earn interest on <u>your</u> money.

❏ **AI:** _____

Get a free savings account that incurs interest to store your emergency fund. Transfer "extra money" from a checking account where there is no or low interest occurring to the savings account with a higher interest rate. I have implemented this for my business and personal accounts. For most free checking accounts, there is no interest paid unless a significant minimal balance is maintained. Open a free savings account that earns interest. Go online to move money from savings to checking when needed.

❏ **AI:** _____

During the process of writing this book, I came to realize that cash in my brokerage account was not earning any interest and the free checking account was in a money market earning very little interest. So, I bought several stocks and opened a savings account with interest. Extra funds sitting in the checking account were transferred to the savings account. As a producer, you will become the bank and investor that earn interest from others.

"Automatically build an emergency fund. Simply instruct your bank to automatically take a tiny amount out from your checking account each week ($10 or $25 dollars, for example) or monthly (perhaps $50 or $100) and put it into a savings account."[9]

❏ **AI:** _____

"The Roth IRA is unique. It's almost the perfect margin-of-safety product. The reason is, it's both a long-term retirement savings plan and a parking place for emergency money."[10] There may be a penalty for early withdrawal of the earning, but not for the contributions.

❏ **AI:** _____

## Managing Bank Accounts

Set up separate savings and retirement accounts for different goals and businesses. Name these accounts appropriately to quickly identify them. Give them fun and interesting names so that when you access the account online or review the statement, it makes you smile and challenge yourself to grow the account balance size.

❏ **AI:** _____

I recommend using duplicate style (carbon copy) checkbooks instead of single-part wallet style checkbooks. They only cost about an extra five dollars per box, and it is worth it. My bank does not charge for checks for preferred customers with a certain balance. Duplicate checks make an imprint of the check on a carbon copy so you can check it off when it clears. There is also a small check box for donations, which will simplify recording your taxable contributions during tax session.

❏ **AI:** _____

"Don't tolerate bank fees. Check your [three] most recent bank statements. Do you see things like maintenance fees, mysterious monthly fees, check-cashing fees, minimal balance fees, debit card minimal activity fee, and other fees that seem inexplicable to you? These fees are unnecessary and cost you money. Call your bank and ask to have them waived and removed going forward. If you don't get a clear answer as to why it can't be waived, politely ask to speak to a supervisor."[11]

❏ **AI:** _____

There is a fee for insufficient funds <u>per</u> check. This adds up quickly if precautions are not taken. Investigate getting overdraft protection on your checking account(s). There should be no charge to activate this service. Also, call back periodically to increase the overdraft limit if there are a lot of monthly withdraws like a mortgage and car loan. However, this overdraft fee can be very high, sometimes thirty or forty dollars. You will be charged for insufficient funds and another fee for overdraft per check! The charge may not be deducted the day it occurs, but on the next day. At least the check did not bounce. If you catch it and put funds in to cover the negative balance, you may still be charged the next day. At first, it is a little confusing viewing the account balance and fees online.

❏ **AI:** _____

👍 Don't attach the emergency fund or brokerage trading account to your checking account to protect you from overdrafts, because then your emergency fund will get spent on impulse purchases. It is fine to have overdraft protection from an interest-bearing savings account that is not intended for emergency events.

**Deposit This**: The choice is yours between the extra charges or the backlash of your credit score being affected by bounced checks. Furthermore, Chase and other banks have e-mail alert services that notify you when an overdraft happens. They will send an alert when your account is below a certain predetermined amount like $1,000. You can select alert options for outgoing wire transfers and when ATM withdrawal amount is exceeded. This is an extremely proactive way to manage your resources by notifying you when to deposit more funds in an account, which is better than borrowing money for overdraft funds. Alerts can also be sent to your mobile device.

❑ **AI:** _____

## Improving FICO Credit Score

"Know your credit report and what it means. Countless businesses utilize your credit report to assess how trustworthy you are. From the obvious (car loans, home mortgages, credit card rates) to the surprising (insurance rates), your credit report (and scores calculated bases on the content of your report) has a great deal of influence on the amount you have to pay. Even worse, errors on your credit report can cause all of your rates to go up, costing you a lot of money. Fortunately, it's easy to access your credit report for free, check for and correct errors on it, and ensure that it remains strong in the future by following these tips:"[12]

❑ You can get your credit report for free, no strings attached, from the federal government once a year at: *www. AnnualCreditReport.com*.

❑ Correct any errors on your credit report, debts you paid off that aren't reported, and stuff that you have never seen before.

"FICO scores are usually intended to show the likelihood that a borrower will default on a loan; a separate score, the Bankruptcy Navigator Index (BNI), is used to determine the likelihood of a borrower declaring bankruptcy."[13] Find ways to increase your Fair Isaac Corporation (FICO) credit score. This will increase your ability to borrow money with better terms and lower interest rates.

"**Boost Your Credit Score: Five Ways to Improve Your Credit**" by *Charles Schwab On Investing*:[14]

1. Pay your bills on time                      [35% of score]
2. Keep credit card balances low               [30% of score]
3. Increase the length of your credit history  [15% of score]
4. Minimize new credit requests                [10% of score]
5. Maintain different types of installment     [10% of score]
   and revolving debt

❑ **AI:** _____

# Planning to Invest Your Savings

The key to investing is savings. An effective savings strategy, coupled with a smart investing strategy, will help you to meet your financial goals. Every dollar saved now helps you to be in command of your current consumption, by which the size of the income that you think will be required for retirement is lowered—not by the government or your employer, but by you.

If you are new to investing, start with conservative equity mutual funds in which professionals manage the selection of an assortment of investments. Mutual funds tend to be at lower risk for sharp swings over time than stocks and real estate, because mutual funds are many blends of stocks, bonds, and cash. These funds can also target your retirement date, called "*Target Funds*" or "*Lifecycle Funds*." They start off aggressively, are heavier in stocks, and become more conservative and heavier in bonds and cash toward the year you anticipate to retire like 2020, 2030, or 2040. Target funds typically have low management fees, around 0.5 percent.

❑ **AI:** _____

👍 It is critical to have a diversified portfolio and a mixed asset allocation among different investments based on your situation and goals. Don't put all your eggs in one basket! This appears to be sound judgment, but you may need to step out of your comfort zone. If A and B are good now, why would you also spend resources on C and D? You may investigate and eventually invest in them all. Once you are comfortable, add growth and value funds from different categories. Hear me . . . this is EXACTLY why this book is focused heavily on the hardworking cheap perspective as well as money-wise principles. This mind shift does not have to be all touchy feely. We are short on time and long on dreams. This works, so direct the increased savings accumulated through implementing cheap strategies across multiple investments!

Do not let life get in the way of contributing to your earlier retirement and happiness. It is interesting that some people want us to live by *their* terms and conditions. This may not be your strategy or the best course of action. You will make your own investment plans without interference. At the end of the day, if you can love yourself and give back, you are winning! Do not worry about all of the daily noise trying to grab your attention and slow you down.

To become wealthy, you need to assertively invest in your business and education. It has been stated that out of the top 1 percent of income earners in the United States, 75 percent of them became rich with business ownership or real estate (excluding inheritance).[15] It truly does take money to make money. This is exactly why I emphasize being progressively cheap to reduce your expenses. In parallel, reducing wasted time and energy will allow you to focus on growing your Inner Economy to reach your life and financial goals. There is nobody else to blame. If there were, they are not listening or don't care. You can make money or excuses, but not both!

❑   **Which do you choose? MONEY ___ or EXCUSES ___**

*"Failure is the opportunity to begin again more intelligently."*
*~ Henry Ford*

# CHAPTER 12: INVESTING IN YOUR CAREER, JOB, AND GENERATING INCOME

*"Don't wish it were easier, wish you were better. Don't wish for less problems, wish for more skills. Don't wish for less challenges, wish for more wisdom." ~ Anonymous*

## Work Smarter to Increase Your Earning Potential

### Enhance Core Competence

Enhance your skills, competence, and performance at your present career or job to get an excellent rating. This should increase your salary and earn you a promotion. Managerial or supervisory positions have more responsibility and accompanied with higher pay. Their bonuses and stock options are higher too. Likewise, sales jobs can pay well, especially if based on commissions.

❑ **AI:** _____

Don't assume a raise at your job will out-pace inflation or your cost of living. The government and corporations give us the lowest increase they can to maximize profits while controlling our temperament, which typically does not include fuel cost increases. Work to be more valuable to get higher raises from your employer. As a business owner, give yourself a raise by operating a profitable company. Get a car allowance for your job or write-off mileage for your business. Making more money or being in a high income bracket does not eliminate the necessity <u>to save even more money to invest</u>.

👍 Please seek pleasure and some satisfaction in your present career or job to outperform your peers. Income is important, and you must work hard to increase your compensation (income, incentives, and benefits). Do not let others—including yourself—belittle your contributions to society. I am <u>not</u> encouraging you to quit your day job; in fact, quite the opposite. My aim is that you are fulfilled in your profession while generating extra income to eliminate debt and invest in steady growth opportunities, all while building wealth.

Increase your income in your career or job by getting better at it. Forget about being on par with your peers. Go out and get MORE than your fair share! Maybe you need to invest in improving your current skill set or acquiring new skills. Build on what you enjoy and things which you are already good at. Ask yourself, "What makes me special? What are my strengths and weaknesses?" List them here so you can analyze them and never forget them:

| **Specialties** | **Strengths** | **Weaknesses** |
|---|---|---|
| _____ | _____ | _____ |
| _____ | _____ | _____ |
| _____ | _____ | ❑  **AI:** _____ |

## Build Your Skill Set

"It is tough getting a job out there these days. And that is why what most people that are unemployed should be doing now is building their skills so that when the economy does recover, they'll be ready and they'll have a heads-up on the competition. This is a good time to beef up your training so that when the jobs become available, you will be in the head of the line."[16]

Judge Greg Mathis

*Judge Mathis*, Warner Brothers, 1999

It may be a huge advantage to learn one or more additional languages. You can take a foreign language class at a community college, community center, or online. The United States Hispanic/Latino population is growing. Plus, the world now operates on a global economy, and countries like Brazil, China, Germany, India, Japan, Russia, and United Arab Emirates are leading the way. Special focus on Arabic, Spanish, Hindi, and Mandarin Chinese languages and their associated cultures may increase your marketability, but this means other languages may be in unique demand because there is less competition. Learning Sign Language will expand the number of people with whom you can communicate. My goal is to be fluent in

Spanish and Rasta M'n. Are there any **languages** you could learn that will benefit you?

_____   _____   _____

                                             ❑  **AI:** _____

To save money and time, take online self-study courses, smartphone apps, or buy a home-study program like Rosetta Stone® at _www. RosettaStone.com_. It worked for Olympian Michael Phelps! Your company may pay for it, or it may be a tax write-off for you. You also may be able to get this software online from your local library. Definitely get a library card to get access to online services like downloading books, music, and software programs.

                                             ❑  **AI:** _____

👍 For free lessons, take weekend workshops. It will be cheaper and more efficient than getting a trainer or consultant. Learn a craft, skill, or how to cook. Also take writing, sewing, yoga, or sports workshops from community clinics. In addition to the skills you will obtain, you will also meet other people in your neighborhood with similar interests, and this can be another networking opportunity.

👍 It is best to create a list of all of the education and skills you will need to meet your goals. You can find an action item tasks of education and knowledge requirements list in *Chapter 16: Invest In Yourself and Family, Your Education.*

If you are unemployed, you need to "stay the course" but make slight adjustments for your situation. **Unemployed person's course correction task list:**

- ❑  Collect all of the funds and benefits from the last job.
- ❑  Apply for unemployment and other benefits you are entitled.
- ❑  Follow my most aggressive CHEAP strategies and push it.
- ❑  Pay your bills on time to not get any late or finance charges.
- ❑  Increase your emergency fund.
- ❑  Continue to pay off your debt balance. If this needs to be decreased, doing it proportionally favors the debts with the highest interest rates but try to pay in full. Also consider reducing or temporarily stopping the payment of extra principal.

❑ Downsize your home to reduce the mortgage or rent. Consider getting a roommate.
❑ Get a deferment for student loans.
❑ Continue to fund your investments at a lower rate.
❑ Look for new work, including a new career path and business opportunities.
❑ Increase your desirability by acquiring new skills.
❑ Exercise more. It's not like you have anywhere to go, and don't play the depression card. Still enjoy your life and smile.

"If you hate your career path, change it. You should do something in your life that lights your fire and lets you use your gifts."[17]

## Work Harder to Make More Money

### Get a Second or Part-Time Job

Get a second and third job, if necessary. **Military** and **civil servant** jobs offer great career paths. The Reserves or National Guard are great opportunities to make extra cash. Activated Reservists and Guards qualify for many of the same benefits as full-time enlisted troops.

❑ **AI:** _____

**Pursue getting a part-time or seasonal job.** This doesn't have to be a painful process. Check out *www.CraigsList.com* or your local newspaper listings (in print and online). Look for something stress-free that feels less job-like. Perhaps there is something you have always wanted to try: barista, baker, babysitter, bartender, beekeeper, bookkeeper, bouncer, boxer, broker, or butcher?

❑ **AI:** _____

Do whatever it takes: dig ditches, shovel snow, clean houses, paint houses, wash cars, walk dogs, house sit, deliver newspapers, serve food, bus tables, wash dishes, work night shift, promoter, sanitation worker, fast-food cook, teller, clerk, temp worker, day laborer, etc. These are all respectable jobs and provide a valuable service.

👍 If you like sewing, repair clothes or sell sweaters. Hem pants or alter wedding and bridesmaid dresses. Many people do not know how to do simple sewing tasks like replacing buttons and fixing tears or ripped hems, and they will pay you for this service in order to salvage their pricey clothes. Start off small with reattaching buttons, repairing tears, and hemming. Make toddler outfits for the special occasions. Become a local repair wo/man that neighbors come to when things need to be fixed. Teach piano, guitar, or some other instrument lessons. Tutor students. Be a superintendent in your complex for free rent while keeping your other job.

**Add hours** to your current job(s) and work paid **overtime**.

❏ **AI:** _____

**Sorry, Dad**: Work at any job, and get a second job plus overtime to generate income so you are not a burden on other people. What was I thinking working half-a*s in the lumberyard the summer before going to my first year of college? I was a lightweight, only worked a few extra overtime hours on Saturdays. I spent twelve bucks on lunch and beverages at the local drive bar on Fridays. My first semester in college, I had to call Dad to ask for more money for tuition. Years later, Mom mentioned that he sold his stocks at IBM to put his boys through college. In case I have not said this recently, "Thanks, Dad . . . and Mom too!!! Sorry for being a mooch that year."

The next summer, I followed my brother Kendall's lead and worked every extra possible minute and brought my lunch to the lumberyard.[55]

This was more money for college tuition and less that I needed from my parents and student loans. My parents never said anything and let me learn to take the right path when I saw it. They set proper guidelines and morals, which enabled me to make great decisions.

---

[55] 👍 BEWARE of the hazardous and toxic chemicals in "treated" lumber that is water resistant or fire retardant. While working in the lumber yard, we handled these woods and were advised to wear a mask and gloves. You should take the same precautions.

This forklift caught on fire when I was driving it, working through the break to earn a few more dollars for my college expenses. I was not hurt, and only several skids of lumber were burned, but the forklift was totaled.

## Make Money from Hobbies

☝ Are you a crafty person? Are you good with your hands and making things? Can you build or repair furniture, cabinets, toys, etc.? Make money from activities that you already do. If you enjoy scrapbooking, sell your service to friends who have plenty of photographs but lack the time and skill. Make jewelry or be a street performer. Sell the items you made or repaired from yard sales, markets, *www.Yardsellr.com*, *www.Etsy.com*, and *www.eBay.com*.

Convert current hobbies into income-producing activities. If you are a hunter, sell the meat that you do not eat. If you are a fisherman or angler, sell the fish. Buy what your buddies have killed or caught and resell it for a profit. Hunt and fish legally, humanely, and fairly <u>without</u> traps, snares, or dynamite. People will pay more for fresh organic meat and seafood with no steroids or hormones. Spend less time on sports and more time creating income from these activities. Become a paid coach, referee, umpire, or judge. If you like model rail cars, buy old trains that do not work and fix them up to sell. Now you are having fun and getting paid!

❑ **AI:** _____

☝ "Hobbies that require a constant influx of money like golfing, skiing, snowboarding, wine tasting, expert art collecting, and sport sea fishing are a dangerous drain on funds."[18] Go to free workshops at Home Depot and Lowes to learn a trade or home improvement skill to earn income from a hobby. You can also take classes at a college or community center, plus watch YouTube instructional videos.

☝ If you play an instrument or sing, join an orchestra or band to make money. Jobs like stage hands, disc jockeys, and sound board workers will also produce income. Dance in performances or shows!

Note that you may need to acquire a business license, set up a business entity, and get the appropriate insurance to undertake any of these endeavors.

❏ **AI:** _____

## Make Money Any Which Way (Legally)

### Reducing Items

**Reduce the clutter** and things collecting dust while getting paid or tax credit for them. When you get close to the recycle phase, first identify if you can sell it online or through traditional methods like yard or sidewalk sales. If you cannot get much value from selling items, donate them. Public libraries love free records, magazines, books, and collectibles; if they cannot add them to their collections for whatever reason, they will sell them on their discards shelf to make money for the library. Also stop adding to wine, art, and other collections. Use up these supplies or donate them to nonprofit 501(c)(3) (a.k.a., 503c) charitable organizations.

❏ **AI:** _____

**RRR to RRRDR**: I am expanding the traditional Reduce, Reuse, and Recycle model to support our needs to succeed to Reduce, Reuse, Resell, Donate, and Recycle. **Resell** and **Donate** have been added prior to the final recycle phase. This has a greater benefit to the environment and increases the life of items while increasing your Inner Economy by generating cash or tax write-offs.

Stay with me . . . these are the principles of this book's teachings:

1. Reduce what you consume.
2. Reuse yours and other people's items.
3. **Resell** items you do not need or want anymore. This includes buying used items to sell at a profit.
4. **Donate** to nonprofit charities for the tax benefits.
5. As a last resort, recycle the item.

✑ Do not throw out packaging for consumed products. Use them to place a food item that will smell bad in a day or two. Reuse bags from frozen fries, bread, produce, and grocery. Also reuse bags and boxes that are shipped or mailed to you to ship other items in. When you recycle, put other material that is going to be recycled into it. For example, you can put cans into a container, plastics into bread or shopping bags, and paper into pizza or shipping boxes. Recycling like this will save on buying trash bags.

✑ Reuse aluminum foil from home use and take-out orders which can be reused many times.

## Selling Items

Have annual **yard**, **garage**, and **sidewalk sales**. Advertise everywhere around your neighborhood, including on billboards at grocery store, school, and community centers, plus Craigslist and online posting groups. Coordinate with neighbors to have a block sale to increase the amount of potential buyers. If you cannot attend, you can still participate. Make an agreement with a neighbor to sell your items so you collect most of their proceeds. Give them 10 to 20 percent of the money collected for items they sell for you. Sell everything you do not use or need. Remember to let your kids keep their earnings from sales of their own items; this will teach them the deprecation value of their possessions as well as hard work. Beforehand, create a plan where to invest their earnings. Use this as the motivation why they need to let go of items.

❏ AI: _____

👍 Also be a bargain hunter at **swap-n-shop**, **pawn shops**, and

**junkyards**. Buy used items really cheap with the intent to resell them for a profit. You may need to fix them up to increase the resell value. Do not hoard junk that can be repaired and sold within six months. I remember getting a car taillight at a junkyard for one-third the retail price. It was fun going to the yard.

Wikimedia Commons, de.wikipedia.org, Stefan Kühn

**Sell collectibles** like dolls, coins, cars, china, baseball cards, stamps, bottles, records, DVDs, comic books, magazines (especially "girly" mags), rarely read books, anything vintage, and war and sports memorabilia collections. There is BIG money to be made if you buy artwork, wines, and antiques at a large discount and have a retail market with buyers established. All collections and hobbies are for sale!

❏ **AI:** _____

**eBay** is a great opportunity to buy and sell products online to earn income. There are many books out there on this topic to teach you how to make a business out of it. This model is distributing business opportunities to individuals from major retailers. I buy a lot of things from eBay and Amazon for my businesses and home. Many times I use the "buy it now" option without bidding if the price is right. This saves energy from placing and monitoring bids. Yardsellr.com is a new local alternative to sell items in your neighborhood.

❏ **AI:** _____

**Get cash for gold and silver.** We all see these commercials regarding generating income from selling used jewelry and silverware. I have not tried it, but transforming stuff to income makes immense sense! Give these entrepreneurs credit for promoting people to generate revenue from used items. It may be a good place to start. There are also local auctions, conventions, and pawnshops who will buy your gold and silver. Shop around to get the highest price.

❏ **AI:** _____

👍 If you are not using the piano weekly or generating income with it, sell it. If it is not in the best condition, consider **donating it as a collectible** to a not-for-profit charity. What other instruments and tools do you have that you are not using? Are there hand-me-downs and family heirlooms that you can sell? It is better that those items are being used rather than taking up valuable space.

👍 Lastly, if you not fully utilizing your **time share** unit, sell it.

## Collect All Coins

**Finders Keepers**: Look for change and dollars on the floors at bars, night clubs, and stores. Create excuses to look for and pick up change and bills. I have found five-, ten-, and twenty-dollar bills before. My friend Clarence found $100! Never walk over change, no matter who you are with. Of course, always pick up any coins in the street, including tails facing up and pennies (even Canadian ones). This is FREE money to be placed in your kitty or immediately invested. While going through airport gate security X-ray machine conveyers, check for change on the floor before and after the X-ray.

Of course, use the change from the penny tray in the convenience store first. Take up to, and over if you dare, ten cents. Even make change from the tray, to your advantage. Go for it and see the look on the cashier's face. So what? It's not stealing. You are going to invest those coins in producing jobs and giving to charity.

👍 Keep change in three places: 1) In your wallet or purse, 2) Right where you leave your wallet or purse at home, and 3) In coin jar, mug, or piggy bank for overflow. I recommend that men get wallets that have change holders and women also do the same for their purses. I buy wallets that have a plastic ID flip pocket or zipper compartment to store loose change.

❑ **AI:** _____

Periodically empty the home change jar and put the coins into emergency, savings, or retirement account, not the kitty. Have a contest with your kids to see who can collect the most change. Do not use the coin exchange machines in grocery stores to sort change because there is a surcharge (in some cases up to ten cents on the dollar!). Instead, put your coins in a roll wrapper and deposit them at your emergency fund. It may take a few months or years to fill a roll. Remember that most banks offer free coin wrappers.

❑ **AI:** _____

If you collect a lot of change, buy your own coin sorter that automatically wraps the change. For the kids, get a fun change sorter machine to encourage them to collect change and then easily deposit into their savings account or college fund. This will be a perfect gift, which is also an investment.

❑  **AI:** _____

*"Don't stay in bed unless you can make money in bed."*
*~ George Burns*

# CHAPTER 13: INVESTING IN YOUR RETIREMENT PLAN

*"It is never too late to be what you might have been." ~ George Eliot*

## Planning for the Future Now

Say and write down when you are <u>going</u> to retire. Pick a specific year or age. Say, "I will retire by 2020" or "I will retire by forty-five." Say it aloud now and write it down, even if your target retirement date is thirty or more years away.

***"I will retire by:"***

❑   _____    _____    _____
    **Target Date/Age**    **Signature**    **Current Date**

Remember that a part of your retirement plan can include Social Security, employer-funded pension, medical coverage, and health savings account. Some people still have pension plans, which is terrific, but with more companies and municipalities outsourcing, cutting costs, and filing bankruptcy, there are no guarantees. The inevitable required changes in Social Security and Medicare age and income qualifications are a whole another issue. These sources of income in our "golden years" are becoming less secure. We need to create our own plans and grow our own economy.

☝ Let's agree that there is no such thing as disposable or discretionary income. To dispose means to get rid of or transfer control of something that is not needed or wanted. This is not the case, correct? Let's call it something else. This money left over after paying monthly expenses is your "**investment fund**." This is more proactive and positive, and it demands respect. You will be less likely to waste it on consumable products and more likely to invest the money in wealth-producing goods and services.

Heavily investing in retirement doesn't mean quitting your job. Feel proud and not guilty about planning to retire early from your employer.

# Types of Major U.S. Retirement Plans

I started my **pre-tax retirement plan** at 2 percent and over the years have been able to maximize my contribution to the extent that extra money is funding after-tax[56] investments. Would you really miss 1 or 2 percent of your income? Put the extra 1 percent into your 401(k), 403(b), Thrift Savings Plan (TSP), pre-tax and after-tax traditional Individual Retirement Plan (IRA), rollover IRA, Simplified Employee Pension plans IRA (SEP IRA), Roth IRA, Roth 401(k), Solo 401(k), 457 savings plan, and/or Employee Stock Purchase Plan (ESPP).[57] Individual states in the U.S. manage state pension and retirement plans for their employees like California (CalPERS) and Texas (ERS). In many states, teachers manage separate plans like California (CalSTRS).

❑ **AI:** _____

401(k), 403(b), and 457 are employer-sponsored retirement savings plans. You need to decide if you want to add both pre-tax and after-tax contributions. Pre-tax will reduce your taxable income, but the taxes are only deferred to a later date set by the IRS. You may also want to fund a **after-tax traditional IRA**, a **401(k)**, or other **employer-sponsored retirement savings plans**, before and/or after you've maxed out the pre-tax contribution. The nice part of funding more than your pre-tax

---

[56]   After-tax and post-tax investing mean the same thing and are used interchangeably.

[57]   *403(b)* is employer-sponsored, tax-sheltered annuity plan. 403(b) and is also known as TIAA-CREF (Teachers Insurance and Annuity Association – College Retirement Equities Fund) for teachers, administrators, and nonprofit employees. *The Thrift Savings Plan (TSP) is* a defined contribution retirement savings and investment plan for Federal employees or members of the uniformed services. The TSP offers participation in the same type of savings and tax benefits that many private corporations offer their employees under 401(k) plans. TSPs have similar contribution and withdrawal rules as 401(k) plans. *Rollover IRA* is a individual IRA account set up with funds roll over from your former employer's retirement plan without any tax implementations is done within sixty days designated by the IRS. *457 Plan* is a non-qualified, tax-advantaged deferred-compensation retirement plan that is available for governmental and certain non-governmental employers.

contribution is that the set-up and administration fees are being paid by the employer's administered plan. Say it: "Nice!" Now this is investing! Use this same model for your spouse's retirement plan. There are multiple action items here.

❏  **AI:** _____

If you are a small business owner without an employer-sponsored retirement plan, how do you plan for retirement? One option is to start a **Solo 401(k)** which is available to self-employed people operating a business. There are two parts: salary deferred and profit-sharing. This plan is perfect for any sole proprietor, consultant, or independent contractor and has the same abilities as a Self-Directed IRA, discussed below. Since you are both employer and employee, the contributions limits are doubled, up to $49,000 in 2011. This option is best for a business that employs your and possibly your spouse, but not if you are planning to hire other employees in the future.

❏  **AI:** _____

👍 **Simplified Employee Pension plans** are great for part- or full-time self-employed people that generate a profit. There are fantastic business tax advantages with this plan.[58] "Establish a pension plan for your small business. You may qualify for a tax credit of up to $500 in each of the plan's first three years."[19]

👍 **Self-Direct IRA** (SD-IRA) accounts are more flexible and have more options than traditional IRA. Self-Direct IRAs allow you to invest in real estate, land, and other business opportunities. Yes, you can still purchase stocks, bonds, and mutual funds. Most traditional brokerage firms do not handle SD-IRA and you need to go to specialize firm to open an account. It is not that difficult to set up, but you need to be educated first. These accounts have high set-up and annual maintenance fees. Self-Direct IRA may also have a fee per transaction and a substantial fee to close the account.

Typically, **ESPP** purchase employees' stock at 85 percent of the value. Employee Stock Purchase Plans can give you an immediate discount

---

[58]  Self-employed people should investigate setting up a Health Savings Account (HSA) that has tax-deductible advantages.

of 15 percent from your employer's stocks. You own these shares and since they were purchased with after-tax dollars you can sell any time, even after you leave the company. Your employer usually pays the expense of managing the plan and your account. In 2011, there is a $25,000 annual limitation for shares purchased in each calendar year. Companies may have a lower limit in the dollar amount or percentage of your income. If your contributions have stopped, it is likely because you have reached the IRS $25,000 limit based on the purchase value of the stock on the first day (offering date) of the plan period or it is your company's policy limit.

❑  **AI:** _____

We are <u>not</u> able to **write-off losses** in retirement plan accounts. However, losses in after-tax personal trading accounts can be written off. "Chris Farrell recommends buying individual stocks in a taxable account. Uncle Sam will share your pain by allowing you the tax write-off if you're wrong."[20] In 2011, the amount of these types of capital loss was $3,000 per year, and the remaining balance could be indefinitely carried forward (carry over) as a tax deduction against ordinary income to the next tax year. Keep good records! I have experienced losses in my 401(k) retirement plan with mutual funds and Roth SD-IRA with real estate investing. Over the years, the funds have been built back up, but we still see dramatic dips in the market. Real estate is at historical lows and in a slow recovery.

❑  **AI:** _____

## Seek Financial Advice

You may need to seek advice from an investment advisor, financial advisor, or Certified Financial Planner (CFP) to amass a diverse portfolio. "An investment advisor can help with the best mix of growth and value stocks and funds."[21] Typically, you can get free access to these advisors or planners through your retirement plan provider, stock/ mutual fund trader brokerage firm, insurance company, and bank.

❑  **AI:** _____

**"A Big Booyah!"** Get access to online investing research and training through these type of companies just mentioned. Also watch the financial programs on the following television stations: CNBC, Bloomberg Television, and FOX Business Network. I also recommend you watch the following shows: *Clack Howard* (CNN), *Dave Ramsey* (FOX Business Network), *Jim Cramer's Mad Money* (CNBC), and *Suze Orman* (CNBC).

❏ **AI:** _____

✍ Even having these programs and shows on as background noise will help train your mind to tune into business-related dialogue. You can also get their archived programs, videos, and podcasts on their respective websites, which are easy to find on Google and iTunes. Be sure to join Dave Ramsey's Yahoo Group at: *Dave_Ramsey_Debt_Beaters@yahoogroups.com*.

Most investments will have some level of risk. Few are 100 percent safe. Government and municipality bonds or money markets are less risky than individual stocks but with lower returns. The more risky a long-term, multi-year capital investment is, the less access you may have to cash out without penalties, if at all. Some of these are notes for oil rigs, skyscrapers, office complex, and other capital intensive projects with a long planning phase. This is input into the creation or evaluation of your portfolio, which needs to have diversity depending on your financial situation, age, etc.

I am assuming you are reading this book because you need to make major changes to create a different life for yourself and your loved ones. This means you are not going to play it conservatively or safely all of the time. You will work hard to take calculated course corrections and dynamic risks with dynamic rewards. This is about your investing knowledge and personal risk assessment. Reach out to a professional advisor to support your goals.

## Understanding Investment Options

✍ "Before you invest, you must ensure that you have realistically assessed your probability of being right *and* how you will respond to the consequences of being wrong. Successful investing is about managing risk, not avoiding it."[22] Cross-investigate stock and mutual fund ratings at *www.MorningStar.com* (one- to five-star rating system). Get insights on past performance from *finance.yahoo.com*, *www.Reuters.com*, or another online independent source.

**Wide-Load to No-Load**: Invest in *no-load mutual funds*—that is, no-load fees on the front and back end. That is get mutual funds that have no sales charges when shares are bought (front-end loaded) or sold (back-end loaded). It is also great not to pay transaction fees for the initial purchase and, of course, never for recurring investments.

However, a transaction fee or short-term redemption fee may apply to no-load mutual fund transactions. Moreover, no-load funds may still incur management fees and 12b-1 fees.[59] Investigate if the fund warrants these charges.

❏ **AI:** _____

Now this is a wide load to avoid! Wikimedia Commons, Versageek, Flickr, mrmonochrome

Example of prospectus summary:

| | |
|---|---|
| Minimum Initial Investment: | $1,000 |
| Minimum Additional Investment: | $100 |
| **Sales Charge:** | **None**, **100% No Load**, and **No Transaction Fees** |
| **12b-1 Fee:** | **None** |

Buy **low-cost** and **low-maintenance mutual funds**. This is easy to miss because the money doesn't come out of your pocket each month,

---

[59] "An extra fee charged by some mutual funds to cover promotion, distributions, marketing expenses, and sometimes commissions to brokers. A genuine no-load fund does not have 12b-1 fees, although some funds calling themselves 'no-load' do have 12b-1 fees (as do some load funds). 12b-1 fee information is disclosed in a fund's prospectus, is included in the stated expense ratio, and is usually less than 1 percent." (InvestorWords. com, *www.investorwords.com/4/12b_1_fee.html*, April 28, 2011)

but keep an eye on the operating expenses of the mutual funds in your 401(k) and other investment vehicles. My rule of thumb is that no fund should cost more than 1 percent, and the combined cost for all your funds should be 0.5 percent or less. For example, if a mutual fund costs you $100, fifty cents immediately goes to the fund manager and you get no growth from that half a dollar. Balanced funds fees may be over 1 percent because they combine many other funds and have to pay their fees too. If you don't believe that even 0.5 percent can make a big difference, you will be pleasantly surprised once you witness the returns.

Note the *redemption fee* for mutual fund shares held for ninety days or less. You will be charged a flat rate or percentage of the amount redeemed (about 2 percent). The duration restriction and percentage may vary. Some mutual funds charge redemption fees to discourage new investors from withdrawing the mutual fund if the fund's net asset value drops unexpectedly.

**Check It—Reinvest It**: To continually passively grow trading accounts when you are buying stocks or mutual funds, check "Reinvest Dividends and Capital Gains." This is an option while purchasing or during the set-up process to reinvest any payout back into purchasing more shares. It is "Reinvest Dividends?" for stocks and "Reinvest Dividends/Capital Gains?" for mutual funds (even if they are made up of stocks and bonds). For stocks, capital gains occur when you sell a stock. Do this for all retirement and personal brokerage trading accounts. There are typically tax implications in non-retirement plans because this first appears as a distribution and then is reinvested. *Note:* If you are retired, you may <u>not</u> want this option because these will be included as actual income.

## Reinvest Dividends? <u>Yes</u> Reinvest Capital Gains? <u>Yes</u>
Now this is POWER!

❏  AI: _____

| Symbol | Name | Reinvest Dividends / Capital Gain? |
|--------|------|-----------------------------------|
| JMCVX | PERKINS MID CAP VALUE FUND INV CL | Yes / Yes |

Dividend Reinvestment and Capital Gains Reinvestment status.

60

---

👆 Note that if the stock or fund is outside of the United States, typically you <u>cannot</u> reinvest dividends and capital gains, so distributions will be made which is a taxable event. This depends on each country's foreign investment laws. Below is an overseas mutual fund that provides the option to reinvest dividends. However, even if "Yes" is selected and submitted, the online brokerage system will not be able to reinvested the dividends.

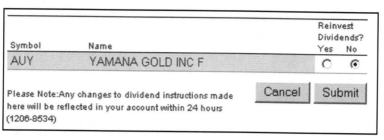

| Symbol | Name | Reinvest Dividends? | |
| --- | --- | --- | --- |
| | | Yes | No |
| AUY | YAMANA GOLD INC F | ○ | ◉ |

Please Note:Any changes to dividend instructions made here will be reflected in your account within 24 hours (1206-8534)

Cancel   Submit

61

"Get your investment records in order so you can make wise year-end sell decisions, either to rebalance your portfolio at the lowest tax cost or to offset gains and losses. Track down reinvested dividends for any stock sold. They'll add to your cost basis and reduce taxable gain or increase deductible loss on the sale."[23]

❑ AI: _____

Verify that your bonuses, rewards, and commission contributions to your retirement and employee stock purchase plans are also enabled. Many companies will have the election option to opt out, but I choose not to. Keep having the company take out the contributions to aggressively grow your retirement plan. Check to see what the default is for your company which also applies to after-tax contributions:

| | |
| --- | --- |
| Pre-tax Bi-Weekly Pay Election | 12% |
| Pre-tax **Bonus / Commission Election** | 12% |
| Roth Bi-Weekly Pay Election | 1% |
| After-tax Bi-Weekly Pay Election | 2% |
| After-tax Bonus / Commission Election | 2% |

❑ AI: _____

---

[61] This is not stock or mutual fund advice.

## Choosing the Right Investment Vehicle

👍 It is essential to reinforce automatically increasing investment contributions. Contributing 6 percent of your salary to your pre-tax retirement plan does not reduce your take-home pay by as much. The contribution is not taxed now, and taxes on the growth are deferred. In other words, taxes are not paid until you withdraw the money. You will have **more money (M²) to INVEST** now because of the tax deductible contribution. This has huge compounding growth benefits over the years. When you retire, it is expected that your income will be less because you are not working. That means your tax bracket rate should be significantly lower than your current tax rate working full-time. For example, you will get taxed at 25 percent versus 33 percent. Your income will be from cashing out your investment like taking distribution from IRA or 401(k) and from recurring passive investment like real estate rent checks. Your expenses should be less since your kids are out of the house and your home is paid off, or almost.

**Autopilot**: For your company- or government-defined pension plan, the fund you contribute will be automatically withdrawn from your paycheck. For other plans likes Roth or SEP IRA, you can set up monthly automatic withdrawals from your checking account.[62] This will keep you on track of reaching your financial goals. There is no charge for this service. There is usually a minimum amount to set this account to take monthly contribution. These contributions are typically $100 to as low as $25 or a percentage of your paycheck. There is a minimum dollar amount to open the account or invest in a mutual fund, but it varies with your brokerage relationship and type of funds. Normal funds vary from $1,000 to $2,500. In special cases, it can be from less than $100 to a lot more like $10,000.

❏ **AI:** _____

Please take advantage of **employer 401(k) matches**. It is common for plans to have a one-to-one match up to 6 percent. If your employer matches retirement plan contributions, do everything you can to take full advantage of that match. It is FREE money that will grow exponentially

---

[62]   Automatic contribution do not assure and do not protect against loss in declining markets.

over the years! Wouldn't you say "Yes" to free money? If you don't want it, give it to me.

❑ **AI:** _____

👍 If your investment strategy is after-tax contribution to your 401(k), check if your employer still matches funds. They probably will not, but you can try it for a pay period or two to see if they match. You will be taxed on their contribution since it is after-tax. Once your pre-tax contribution limit is reached, the after-tax election will continue to be deducted if you plan allows it, which it probably will. Power is being inquisitive and applying lessons learned!

Did you know you can **automatically increase** your retirement and children's 529 college savings plan's contribution percentage rate each year? Your increase will be processed each year in the month you or your plan specifies, unless it would exceed your plan's maximum contribution percentage or you choose to stop the increase. This proactive initiative will make you reach your annual investment goals and keep pace with inflation without any effort.

Set up annual or quarterly increases in saving measures to reduce your bad debt to zero and also reduce good debt. These regular increases will also be applied to your retirement plan and capital business investments. For the sake of illustration, let's use a retirement plan. In 2011, the maximum pre-tax personal annual contribution was $16,500 ($22,000 if you are over age fifty) and will likely continue to increase. If you are not contributing now, start at 2 percent of your paycheck. If you are annually contributing under $10,000 do a yearly increase of 2 percent of your paycheck and contributing $10,000 or more do an increase of 1 percent. As just stated, this election can be automatically set up in your retirement <u>and</u> brokerage accounts. Also manually increase the contribution when you get a raise. Before you know it, you will be fully funding to the maximum contribution of that plan and may need to start another retirement plan (like SEP IRA) for your business!

❑ **AI:** _____

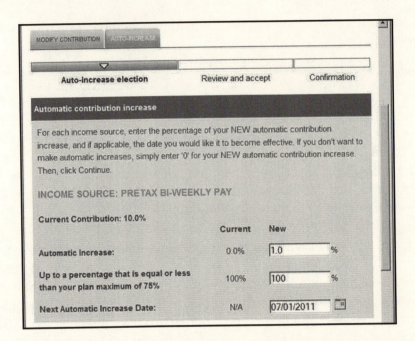

👍 Get funds to start businesses and buy real estate from your after-tax stocks, mutual funds, stock options, Employment Stock Ownership Plan, or Employment Stock Purchase Plan. *Charles Schwab On Investing* stated, "Don't be tempted to borrow against your 401(k) to pay off those credit card debts. If you lose your job, you'll probably have to pay the loan back within ninety days, or it will be considered a distribution. And remember, while you hope that it will never come to this, if you go through bankruptcy, creditors can't touch the money in your retirement accounts."[24]

**"Don't Believe the Hype."** "An investment operation is one which, upon thorough analysis, promises safety of principal and an adequate return. Operations not meeting these requirements are speculative. If you overestimate how well you really understand an investment or overstate your ability to ride out a temporary plunge in prices, it doesn't matter what you own or how the market does. Two factors in good decision making are well-calibrated confidence and correctly-anticipated regret."[25] For higher advertised ROI, the higher the risk may be so conduct extra research and due diligence. For great investing conversations join Benjamin Franklin's Yahoo Group forum at *The_Intelligent_Investor@yahoogroups.com*.

## Monitoring Your Retirement Plan

**Buy low, sell high.** The stock market in 2008 provided perhaps the biggest gut-check for investors in a generation. Furthermore, the S&P 500, NYSE, and NASDAQ averages were flat for the first half of 2010, up modestly toward to end of the year, a big 6 percent gain the first quarter of 2011,[63] and 7 straight weeks of loses in the third quarter. With the huge fluctuation in the markets you need to regularly monitor and modernize your portfolio. Follow these suggestions from *Janus Report* **"Keeping Your Eyes On the Horizon**:"[26]

1. Keep your emotions in check
2. Continue to invest
3. Stay diversified
4. Avoid trying to time the market
5. Review your long-term investment strategy

At a minimum, perform a monthly review and quarterly rebalance of your target allocations and current distributions. To make this easier, sign up for weekly and monthly e-mail subscriptions of your stocks and mutual funds percentage updates. This will keep you regularly informed of your account performances and balances. After the markets closes on Friday, you will receive an e-mail that shows your account performance for that week. It is wise for you to review this report before the weekend begins. There may also be monthly mutual fund performance summary. To a snapshot of all of your stocks and mutual funds performance for a day use a tool like My Yahoo! or iGoogle Stock Portfolios.

❑ **AI:** _____

When reviewing your account, it will indicate if dividends are reinvested or not. Two points to bear in mind:

👍 If there was a merger and you have a new symbol, your previous decision to reinvest may not be carried forward, so you will need to make the change again.

---

[63] "This is the biggest first quarter market gain in thirteen years," Fox News, March 31, 2011.

☞   Remember, for multinational mergers you will probably not be able to reinvest dividend for stock and funds outside the U.S. but might be able to do so with capital gains.

**Just a Pinch More Can Make a Difference:** If you increase your regular monthly IRA contributions by $100 over thirty years with 6 percent annualized growth and interests compounding monthly, it will add $100,000 to your retirement plan.[64]

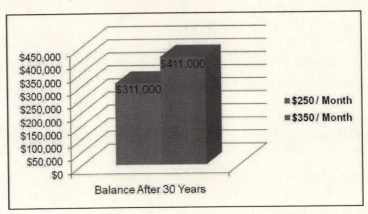

For tracking your progress and make any necessary modifications document your retirement plans.

_____'s Retirement Plans List ___/___/___

| Plan Provider | Plan Type | Expected Returns | Current Total | Amount Per Month | Fully Funded (Y/N) |
|---|---|---|---|---|---|
| _____ | _____ | _____ | _____ | _____ | __/__/__ |
| _____ | _____ | _____ | _____ | _____ | __/__/__ |
| _____ | _____ | _____ | _____ | _____ | __/__/__ |
| _____ | _____ | _____ | _____ | _____ | __/__/__ |
| _____ | _____ | _____ | _____ | _____ | __/__/__ |
| _____ | _____ | _____ | _____ | _____ | __/__/__ |

❑  AI: _____

_____

[64]   This is a hypothetical example and does not represent any particular investment. Example does not account for taxes and inflation.

Utilize a retirement plan calculator to estimate how much money you will need to retire and by what year. Forecasting with your current investment balance and contribution amount may predict the year you can retire at the lifestyle (withdrawn per month) you choose. For example, CNN's retirement planner calculator helps you estimate how well your savings program is preparing you for retirement. First, they help you figure out how much you'll need. Then, CNN provides your chances of getting there. If it looks like you are falling short, they offers some suggestions for improving your plan. For details, go to CNN's retirement planning tool at: c*gi.money.cnn.com/tools/retirementplanner/retirementplanner.jsp*.

❑ **AI:** _____

*"It is never too late to start, but it is always too late to wait."*
~ *Jeff Olsen*

# CHAPTER 14: INVESTING IN YOUR BUSINESS

*"Never tell people how to do things. Tell them what to do, and they will surprise you with their ingenuity." ~ General George S. Patton*

## The Dream and Advantages of Business Ownership

**Create a Business!** Do you want the "American Dream," to be a business owner and work for yourself? This is hard work and a lot of responsibility. You deserve the opportunity to be an entrepreneur and control your destiny as a business owner in free enterprise.

It is not your responsibility to improve and feed this consumer-driven economy.[65] Yes, we all need the essentials and a few joys of life. Your responsibility is to gradually grow your Inner Economy by being a business owner, property owner, and assisting others in need. You recognize this economic model and don't blame others for your current financial situation. You are accountable for your actions and your family's success. People should be consuming your goods and services, and not the other way around! Be a business leader in your profession and community.

There are HUGE **tax benefits when it comes to owning a business**. Your business will reap the rewards of economic stimulus, tax credits, and tax write-offs from government. These funds will increase your profitability or be reinvested into to building your business. In general, paying taxes is a good thing because it means you are making money. You can feel good about it, especially if the government is spending our money wisely, though this is not always the case. We, as voters, need to monitor politicians and get involved in politics to advance our interests.

---

[65]   It has been stated that consumer spending accounts for 70 percent of U.S. economic activity.

# Starting a Business

Sarah Caron said, "It might seem counterintuitive to start a new business when the economy is in the dumps, but a recession can actually be the ideal time for launching a company. In fact, many well-known and successful organizations were born during an economic slump. Why do these companies succeed? Usually it's because the founders recognized a market need and filled it. Identifying that need—whether it's related to entertainment, travel, or even streamlining how businesses operate—is the key to any thriving enterprise, regardless of the economic climate in which it begins."[27]

**What business(es) do you want to start?**

❑ _____  __/__/__

❑ _____  __/__/__

❑ _____  __/__/__

Dave Ramsey's "**Three Rules for Starting a Business**:"[28]

1. Start part-time and don't quit your day job.
2. Don't go into debt to start a business, start with cash.
3. The more information to make the decision whether to go forward or not, the better.

Starting a new business venture is a risky proposition, especially during these turbulent times. "Tim Mayclin's *Tips for Starting a New Business*, practical suggestions to help you succeed:"[29]

👍 Be realistic: Don't expect your business to be immediately successful. In fact, you should be prepared, both mentally and financially, for the worst-case scenario. Recent statistics from the Small Business Administration (SBA) show that about one-third of new business startups fail to make it through two years, and over one-half fold after four years. Give your business time to grow and prosper.

👍 Minimize the risks: Even if you're encouraged by the initial results, don't tie your fortunes completely to this undertaking.

If you're still gainfully employed somewhere else, keep your job and operate the new venture as a sideline business.

👍 <u>Carve out a niche</u>: Your business should fulfill a specific need that is difficult for chain stores or other broad-based businesses to meet. If you try to compete directly with the corporate giants, you're likely to lose.

👍 <u>Choose the proper form of ownership</u>: Depending on your circumstances, it may be best to operate the business as a C corporation, a partnership, an S corporation, a limited liability company (LLC), or a sole proprietorship.[66]

Startup Nation's "**Ten Steps to Start a Business**:"[30]

| | |
|---|---|
| ❑  Create a life plan | __/__/__ |
| ❑  Choose a business model | __/__/__ |
| ❑  Create a business plan | __/__/__ |
| ❑  Select a business structure | __/__/__ |
| ❑  Create key business assets | __/__/__ |
| ❑  Find the funding | __/__/__ |
| ❑  Organize logistics | __/__/__ |
| ❑  Find great people | __/__/__ |
| ❑  Establish a brand | __/__/__ |
| ❑  Market and sell | __/__/__ |

**Create a Business Case:** "A **business plan** precisely defines your business, identifies your goals, and serves as your firm's resume. [For medium and large companies] the basic components include a current and *pro forma* balance sheet, an income statement, and a cash flow analysis. It helps you allocate resources properly, handle unforeseen complications, and make good business decisions. It provides specific and organized information about your company and how you will repay borrowed money. A good business plan is a crucial part of any loan application. Additionally, it informs sales personnel, suppliers, and others about your operations and goals. Elements of a business plan: 1) Description of the business, 2) Marketing, 3) Finances, and 4) Management."[31]

---

[66]  For more details, go to *Operating Your Business, Selecting the Correct Entity* section later in this chapter.

"Marketing takes time, money, and lots of preparation. One of the best ways to prepare yourself is to develop a solid **marketing plan**. A strong marketing plan will ensure you're not only sticking to your schedule, but that you're spending your marketing funds wisely and appropriately. A marketing plan includes everything from understanding your target market and your competitive position in that market, to how you intend to reach that market (your tactics) and differentiate yourself from your competition in order to make a sale."[32]

Even small business owners need to create business and marketing plans. These can be simple plans at first. Business owners need to build a feasible economic model and design accurate profitability projections. Furthermore, you need to find funding for your new business or to expand your existing business. Finally, do all of this while building long-lasting relationships to leverage win/win partnerships to generate business.

❏   **AI:** _____

Use federal, state, county, and city/town government resources to create your plan. For starting a small business, go to the U.S. Small Business Administration at *www.SBA.gov*.

## Business Ideas

It is vital to have several sources of income, called Multiple Streams of Income (MSI). This can be in many combinations:

1. Full-time and part-time job(s)
2. Full-time job and home-/Internet-based business(es)
3. Traditional business and part-time job(s)
4. Traditional business and home-/Internet-based business(es)
5. Several part-time jobs
6. Part-time job and home-/Internet-based business(es)
7. Monthly withdrawals from retirement plan and rental income

❏   **AI:** _____

✍ For a 2011 hot list of businesses, go to StartupNation at: *www.startupnation.com/hot-business*.

## Provide a Needed Service

**Offer Services to Your Neighbors:** Does it look like your neighbors need help? If their grass is always too high or garden full of weeds, offer to take the burden from them for a fee. Walk from block to block to see who house needs painting. How about being a pool cleaner or a traveling beauty solon? How many of us cut lawns, shoveled snow, babysat, and waited tables for money while we were growing up? I worked at a Christmas tree nursery pruning trees in the hot summer and cutting them down in the chill of winter. These jobs are still an opportunity to make money.

❏ **AI:** _____

👍 Another creative idea is to set up a water filtration system in your home. Many companies are installing these systems versus buying bottled water or five-gallon water tank stands. If you have a five-gallon tank, you can go to discount grocery stores to refill the bottle. Besides saving money on buying bottle water, you can also sell purified water to neighbors in small towns, rural, or reservation communities. This idea can be applied to other homemade beverages, dishes, and deserts. Remember to get a business license and work with a professionally certified company.

## Direct-Sales Opportunities

Big business opportunities include direct network marketing and distribution. There are over sixteen million Americans involved in direct selling opportunities. Most of these businesses have a Multi-Level Marketing (MLM) aspect of recruiting new members to make money. This is an exponential growth trend because of the accessibility of Internet and the explosion of mobile devices apps. Buying a franchise is another opportunity available to the masses.

I am a proponent of direct marketing <u>without</u> the primary focus of building a team or the "pyramid" tier structure. Focus on products and services that solve a person's issue or business problem, not just on getting more people to join your downline without justification from your past sales performance. If operated properly, this business can generate income to build emergency fund and retirement plans.

**"If it doesn't make sense, it probably isn't true."**   Basic integrity asks, "Does it pass the smell test?" Don't get bamboozled or hoodwinked by promises, scrutinize the data and facts. Beware of get-rich-quick-schemes and gurus that promise getting rich is easy. It takes little to no money and effort, but they pressure you into buying something first if you are serious about their opportunity. These might be acquaintances selling you on a dream by you just sharing the market opportunity idea with other people, sending a video link to watch, or bringing potential clients to a briefing. You see these infomercials late at night. They also have wealth-building seminars every month near you.

What **products**, **services**, and **markets interests** do you have that are franchise, home business, or network marketing opportunities?

☐ _____    __/__/__
☐ _____    __/__/__
☐ _____    __/__/__

## Patent Pending

**"That's Mine!"** We have all had some innovative ideas in our heads for years. What magnificent ideas do you have? "It's not easy to think about ideas as property, but for some businesses, it's vital. Most of us have had an idea for a new product or service only to dismiss, postpone, or neglect it. Sometimes we later find that others had the same idea but took it to market before we did. By that time, it is too late for us to take advantage of the idea. Ideas are relatively easy to come by, but inventions are more difficult. It takes knowledge, time, money, and effort to refine an idea into a workable invention, even on paper. Turning an invention into an innovation—a new product accepted by the marketplace—takes a lot of effort and a little luck. There are substantial barriers in the path of those who pursue innovation. Overcoming them requires careful planning and plenty of input from others."[33] Write your ideas down and patent them. Then sell or development them for BIG profit.

"Hundreds of thousands of inventors and innovators file each year for protection under U.S. patent, trademark, and copyright laws. However, it can be hard to decide which of the three vehicles is most appropriate for the protection of a particular invention. Although a single product or service may require a patent, a trademark, and a copyright, each category protects a distinct aspect of a creative work or expression. People who may not be interested in protecting their own rights must still take precautions to avoid infringing on the rights of others."[34] First determine what type of intellectual property protection you need: 1) patents, 2) trademarks, or 3) copyrights.

Generically, "a **patent** is a set of exclusive rights granted by a state (national government) to an inventor or their assignee for a limited period of time in exchange for a public disclosure of an invention."[35] A patent is an intellectual property right granted by the Government of the United States of America to an inventor "to exclude others from making, using, offering for sale, or selling the invention throughout the United States or importing the invention into the United States"[36] for a limited time in exchange for public disclosure of the invention when the patent is granted.

There are three type of patents:[37]

1. Utility patents may be granted to anyone who invents or discovers any new and useful process, machine, article of manufacture, or composition of matter, or any new and useful improvement thereof.
2. Design patents may be granted to anyone who invents a new, original, and ornamental design for an article of manufacture.
3. Plant patents may be granted to anyone who invents or discovers and asexually reproduces any distinct and new variety of plant.

In the United States, patents are filed with and granted by the U.S. Patent and Trademark Office (USPTO). Check to see if your ideas have been patented in USPTO databases at *www.uspto.gov* or use Google Patent Search at *www.google.com/patents*. If your idea is not there, go for it! Filing online for patents at *www.uspto.gov* is cheaper and faster than mailing in applications.

❏ **AI:** _____

👍 You will probably need a patent attorney at some point in this process. Transition your savings into funding the development of a patent. If you are requesting additional moneys from investors to build your  invention, a business case may need to be created. Income from successful patents can fund real estate purchases, your children's college fund, and charities.

Darryl at San Francisco Decompression 2009 funky street party. Notice my Nolo's *Patent, Copyright, and Trademark* book that I read on a light rail. I made a great connection with a patent attorney on the train over to the music festival. In my left shirt pocket are bookmarks that I handed out to folks . . . and yes, that is a McDonald's fanny back. Pretty cool, huh?

"A **trademark** includes any word, name, symbol, device, or any combination, used, or intended to be used, in commerce to identify and distinguish the goods of one manufacturer or seller from goods manufactured or sold by others, and to indicate the source of the goods. In short, a trademark is a brand name."[38] You need to identify the goods and/or services with which the mark is used or will be used.

In the United States, trademarks are filed with and granted by the U.S. Patent and Trademark Office. Check to see if your ideas have been trademarked in USPTO databases at *www.uspto.gov*. If your idea is not there, go for it. Filing online for trademarks at *www.uspto.gov* is cheaper and faster than mailing in applications.

❏ **AI:** _____

"**Copyrights** protect works of authorship, such as writings, music, and works of art that have been tangibly expressed. In more details, a copyright is a form of protection provided to the authors of 'original works of authorship' including literary, dramatic, musical, artistic, and certain other intellectual works, both published and unpublished. The 1976 Copyright Act generally gives the owner of copyright the exclusive right to reproduce the copyrighted work, to prepare derivative works, to distribute copies or phonorecords of the copyrighted work, to perform the copyrighted work publicly, or to display the copyrighted work publicly."[39]

In the United States, the Copyright Office (a division of the Library of Congress) registers copyrights at *www.copyright.gov* which last for the life of the author plus seventy years. Again, filing online for copyrights is cheaper and faster than mailing in applications.

❑  **AI:** _____

List your **patent**, **trademark**, and/or **copyright ideas**:

❑ _____  __/__/__

❑ _____  __/__/__

❑ _____  __/__/__

For more details, refer to Nolo's *Patent, Copyright and Trademark* and Nolo's *Patent It Yourself*. Nolo explains the processes better than the government. Here are additional resources:

- For more details on patenting your ideas, go to: *www.uspto.gov/patents/resources/types/index.jsp*
- For more details on trademarking your goods and/or services, go to: *www.uspto.gov/trademarks/index.jsp*
- For more details on copyrighting your work, go to: *www.sba.gov/smallbusinessplanner/start/protectyourideas/serv_copyrtfaq.html* or *www.copyright.gov/circs/circ1.pdf*

## Operating Your Business

**Document Partnerships:** Because memories fade and people have different interests in mind, create contracts between you and your business partner, clients, suppliers, and employees. Depending on the nature of your business, this may be a simple one-page agreement. Make sure there are lines to print and sign the names of all parties, including lines for a witness. Search for free contract forms and samples from the web, ask your CPA, or buy a book at an office store. For customized contracts, go to a paralegal, who will be less expensive than an attorney.

❏ **AI:** _____

## Setting Up Your Business

"Mark J. Kohler's **basic goals for legal planning** are to: 1) Protect our assets, 2) Save taxes, 3) Build wealth, and 4) Keep the process as simple as possible. The following steps can be implemented on a day-by-day basis to protect the all too valuable corporate veil in an affordable, easy, and simple manner:"[40]

- ❏ Set up your company properly and maintain its records: Filing the Articles of Incorporation with the appropriate state agency is important. It is also vital to have corporate books, bylaws, stock certificates, initial minutes, and regular director and shareholder meetings with minutes.
- ❏ Document your business transitions: Use the company name on all of your transactions rather than your individual name.
- ❏ Use the company name in all advertising and correspondence: If you set up a company, you need to let the public know about it in your transactions, or they will assume it is you they are doing business with and not your company.
- ❏ Separate checking: Set up a separate checkbook for each company you form and do not co-mingle your personal and business transactions.
- ❏ Ownership of company property: Please do not own your business property personally or have your business own your personal property.

## Selecting the Correct Entity

"Let's reduce the chance of a lawsuit and, if a claim arises, minimize the damage. Asset protection is not just to simply protect you from a lawsuit, a claim originating from a car accident, or having someone hurt on your property. The liability could arise from a partnership gone bad, a disgruntled employee, divorce, or even one of your family members in a car accident."[41]

☝ "Please don't try to select the entity you need on your own. You have (or should have) advisors to help you make this decision. This process also doesn't have to be an all-or-nothing, expensive, and time-consuming project in which you are held captive by your legal advisor. There are five primary considerations to address when determining which entity best fits your individual needs:"[42]

- Asset protection exposure
- Tax-planning opportunities
- Flexibility and partnership goals
- Raising capital
- Administrative issues

Which entity works best for you will depend on your situation and business goals. More than one entity may be necessary. For details about business entities, refer to Mark J. Kohler's *Lawyers Are Liars: The Truth About Protecting Our Assets!*, "Appendix A—Business Entity Descriptions and Matrix."

❏ **AI:** _____

## Paying Taxes

Pay your dang taxes! Have integrity and do not lie or cheat. Be 100 percent accurate and honest on your taxes. Do not "fudge" the numbers or just make things up. Filing clean income tax returns will let you sleep at night. The biggest tax write-offs are owning real estate and being a business owner, but we want these transactions to make money and the businesses to be profitable. Always seek accurate, competent advice from a licensed professional.

Focus on long-term capital gains investment. In 2011, this tax rate is 15 percent. Short-term capital gains are taxed at your current tax rate, which is much higher than 15 percent for most Americans. Create a plan for handling short-term and long-term capital gains and possible losses.

❏ **AI:** _____

**2011 Federal Tax Brackets:** Your tax bracket is the rate you pay on the "last dollar" you earn as a percentage of your income. Here are singe status tax rates and the income ranges where they apply:

| Tax Year: | 2011 ▼ | | |
|---|---|---|---|
| Filing Status: | Single ▼ | | |
| **If your taxable income is between...** | | **your tax bracket is:** | |
| 0 | and 8,500 | 10 | % |
| 8,500 | and 34,500 | 15 | % |
| 34,500 | and 83,600 | 25 | % |
| 83,600 | and 174,400 | 28 | % |
| 174,400 | and 379,150 | 33 | % |
| 379,150 | and above | 35 | % |

Courtesy of *www.MoneyChimp.com*

Future tax rates will inevitably change. "As of [the end of 2010], the plan for the future was to leave the lower tax brackets alone and raise the top two brackets to where they were during the 1990s. The cutoffs for the top brackets are to be raised so that singles making above $200,000 annually or families making above $250,000 will be the ones affected by the higher rates."[43] For your tax bracket, go to: *www.moneychimp.com/features/tax_brackets.htm*.

"Identify actions to take before year-end to minimize your income tax bill. Accelerating deductions, delaying income, contributing to retirement plans, and taking investment losses are just a few of the strategies you might want to consider. There are also tax credits that require careful planning or they may be lost. Plan year-end purchases of new or used business equipment to take full advantage of the higher expensing limit of $250,000 for [2010]. Purchases of new equipment (not used) can qualify for first-year 50 percent bonus depreciation."[44]

❑ **AI:** _____

## Insurance Policy Coverage

"Most of us already recognize the powerful benefits of insurance and maintain a variety of insurance policies. Please make sure you have proper auto, home, health, and long-term care insurance; and not only having the right type of policies, but coordinate your insurance to save money and obtain better coverage."[45]

❑ **AI:** _____

"The cost of multiple policies can appear to be significant as you add up the premiums on a month-to-month basis. Mark Kohler encourages that you do not get frustrated and combine all of your insurance into one big mess in your mind. Realize each insurance policy has an independent and separate purpose. Don't throw the baby out with the bath water just because one type of insurance may seem exorbitant or unnecessary. Please analyze each one of your policies independently of the other."[46]

"Consider Mark Kohler's **six types of insurance**, which are not exhaustive of all the potential types of insurance a business owner may need:"[47]

- ❑ General liability insurance: This is a policy to cover the general "slip and fall" that could take place in a business, the general unforeseen liability that could happen to anybody.
- ❑ Malpractice or errors and omissions: Typically, this is a policy for the professional practitioner to cover accidents or losses incurred from their advice or services they provide.
- ❑ Director and officer insurance: If you have a nonprofit or a large company that employs or solicits the assistance of individuals on a board of directors, it is very common to maintain a policy to protect your board members should something go wrong in the business.
- ❑ Workers' Compensation: This is must for the small business owner. In fact, it's illegal in most states for an employer to have employees and not carry Workers' Comp. This insurance protects the owner from a claim due to an employee accident.

❑ Property insurance: This could be personal property insurance for the computers in the building, the equipment on the manufacturing floor or out on the job site, or it could be real property insurance for the building you use for your business or investment property you.

❑ Umbrella insurance is an additional policy providing an "umbrella" of coverage over all of your activities that create liability. It provides a second layer of protection in case of an insurance claim or potential lawsuit.[67]

## Safeguarding the Office

**Get Back Up**: Protect your computer from debilitating crashes by backing up file content and programs. This should be at least three times a week. If you are doing a lot of work or are mobile often, back your PC, MAC, or PDA up every night. Also back up the contacts and pictures you keep on your cell phone just in case you lose it or it gets broken. Frequent backups should not damage your computer's hard drive. Buy a separate hard disk drive to back up the files. Less trouble may be an online backup service. Verify that the service also encrypts your data. These providers are great if you travel a lot. For example, check out *www.Carbonite.com*.

❑ AI: _____

At least once a month, perform **disk defragmentation** and **disk cleanup** on your computer to increase the system performance and delete unused files to free up disk space. Apple stated, "The file system used on Macintosh computers is designed to work with a certain degree of fragmentation. This is normal and does not significantly affect performance for the majority of users. You should not need to frequently defragment the computer hard disk."[48]

❑ AI: _____

Verify that a **virus scan** is enabled on your Mac or PC.

❑ AI: _____

---

[67] More details on umbrella insurance are in *Chapter 15: Investing in Real Estate, Real Estate Investing Tips, Insurance Policy Tips.*

Consider getting a **safe** that is fire resistant for at least thirty to sixty minutes of temperatures at 1200-1400°F. It also need to be water proof in case of flooding. Get a model that can be bolted to the floor. Be discreet when moving it into your home as this will help deter a home invasion and place the safe where it cannot be seen, perhaps in a closet. This can be a tax deduction for your home-based business and reduce your insurance policy premium.

❑ **AI:** _____

For more resources, go to "Operating a Business" from the IRS at: *www.irs.gov/businesses/small/article/0,,id=99930,00.html*.

## Marketing Your Business

**ABC (Always Be Connecting):** Use every situation and event as a potential opportunity to connect with other people. Look at bad situations like waiting in a long line, middle seat on a long airplane flight, or working the nightshift as a chance to meet new friends and expand your business. Always look for the possibility to connect by listening, speaking, and collaborating—not just talking to people.

To grow your income and business, you need to increase the opportunities that are presented to you. You will need to grow your network, interactions, relationships, plus social, team-building and teamwork skills, all while increasing face time with people. Like President Ronald Reagan you too can be known as a "Great Communicator" by influencing people to buy your products or services. Join social media sites like *www.Facebook.com*, *www.LinkedIn.com*, *www.MySpace. com*, and *www.Twitter.com*, where you can meet potential clients. I had numerous smiles and positive memories within seventy-two hours of joining Facebook. Expand your knowledge base and access to resources. Have a clear mind that is open to change and experiment with new ideas.

❑ **AI:** _____

Carry a voice recorder to record your thoughts, patent ideas, tasks, and new business contacts. Most cell phones and PDAs have a voice-recording feature. It may record just a minute or over an hour, depending on the model. You can also carry a small notepad.

❑  **AI:** _____

**Get Carded** : You need to get a personalized business card to market yourself and your business. Keep it simple at first and carry at least a dozen cards with you at all times. I recommend that you add a broad or generic title:

- Business Owner
- Entrepreneur
- Life Coach
- Innovator
- Soon-to-be Millionaire
- Real Estate Investor

If you are in the process of acquiring new skills, add the title:

- Business Student
- Chef in Training
- College Student
- Commercial Pilot in Training
- Fashion Design Apprentice
- Stylist in Training

Add what you love:

- Love Baking Cakes
- Love Gardening
- Love My Job
- Love Restoring Classic Cars
- Love Volunteering
- Love Riding Horses

Have fun with it! Adding these sayings to your card will allow people to *visualize* who you are and ask you questions. Use your cards for advertising your investments and business goals to your existing network and new markets. To get your cards professionally made, compare prices and services at companies like OvernightPrints.com and VistaPrint.com. Also check out your local office stores for sale specials. You can even buy a business card software program that will enable you to easily print business cards on your own printer. For large quantities, this is not always the most economical solution because high quality ink and cardstock can be pricey.

❑  **AI:** _____

**SPIDER-MAN**™ : Create your own website to promote your business. Post a blog or create a newsletter to drive traffic to your website. Go

Daddy is a notable web services hosting provider that has affordable prices to create a website at *www.GoDaddy.com*. World Press is a well-known provider of blog hosting services that also has affordable prices at *www.WorldPress.org*.

❑  **AI:** _____

👍 Create your own niche market. You may make the best fudge in the world or have a craft that is unique in your local community. Now you need to let people know about your specialty in your neighborhood, school, workplace, fitness club, cyberspace, etc.

**"That's the bonus of getting out and about."** You never know who you will meet on the bus, train, or just walking around the neighborhood. Opt to get out in public to meet people rather than staying at home. Give out your business cards, bookmarks, flyers, and refrigerator magnets EVERYWHERE! Carry them in your wallet, purse, notecase, briefcase, and vehicle.

❑  **AI:** _____

Early one Friday evening, I did a little food shopping and was walking around my neighborhood. On the way home, I was taking pictures of a gang of rats near the highway on-ramp. Nearby I noticed many people walking into an office space between an auto repair shop and homeless shelter. I wondered what it was and crossed the street to take a closer look. The people were sharply dressed, so I followed them up a steep flight of stairs.

As it turned out, it was SOMA Artists Studios, an art gallery open house with over fifty artists. I made many fantastic connections and enjoyed powerful, amazing artwork. One special networking connection I made was with a

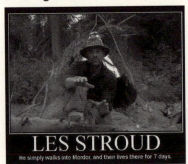

couple and an artist named Brian over a bottle of wine at *www.bgillespie.net* studio. I got corked bottles of wine from under the hallway table and he opened them for us in his studio.

Les Stroud, *Survivorman,* Les Stroud Productions©, 2004

Have an open house to market your business. Model this like the original Tupperware parties that started in 1948 and continue today. Invite your neighbors, friends, acquaintances, and business contacts. This will be a great ice breaker. Make flyers or invitations and hand them out when you see your neighbors. Let them know you are new to the neighborhood and would like to get to know them. If it makes sense, go door to door like an Avon lady. Go for it! Joyfully inform them about your business. Utilize sporting games, holiday parties, and even political events to market your business too. Maximize your effectiveness by inviting people using social media sites and networking groups.

❑ **AI:** _____

## Being Profitable: Going from Red to Black

You need to hustle in this lackluster economy to make your business profitable. Being efficient will merge into your current career or job and into the new business. Shift from spending money on junk to productive objects that create recurring and residual income. Cutting expenses is also an essential tool to utilize.

👍 Networking and exposure to new clients is key to growing your business. Distribute business cards at celebrations including your own and others' weddings. Make the honeymoon a personal and business growth opportunity with your loved one. Combine your anniversary and family vacation with a business trip. Bring self- and business development books to read. If your family cares about you and your goals—which they should—they won't have any issues with you using that time to better yourself.

To increase profitability include your spouse, life partner, boyfriend, or girlfriend as your partner in business. Request that they strongly support your business to succeed, in return they will not be left behind. He or she will need your support to accomplish their goals too. Include other family members and friends, only more guardedly.

❑ **AI:** _____

If you do not have kids, put those savings toward your continuing education to improve your current skill set or to acquire new ones.

Enhance your business development skills to grow your business revenues and profitability. Focus on trade skills and tools that will make you money.

*"Entrepreneurs are simply those who understand that there is little difference between obstacle and opportunity and are able to turn both to their advantage." ~ Niccolo Machiavelli*

# CHAPTER 15: INVESTING IN REAL ESTATE

*"There's no reward in life without risk." ~ Barry J. Farber*

## The Benefits of Real Estate Investing

👍 Owning real estate as an investment automatically makes you a business owner. Treat this as a business, because it is one, by taking the appropriate measures to protect your assets and reduce your liabilities. Real estate is how I and millions of others started our journey creating wealth with other people's money (mainly, the banks'). Be careful not to jump into real estate investing too quickly. Get educated, do your research, and beware of predatory selling and get-rich-quick schemes, particularly online.

High-level benefits of owning real estate investments include: positive passive cash flow, depreciation, appreciation, amortization, tax benefits, and leveraging other people's money and time. Many of these benefits also apply to owning your own home.

**Why Invest in Real Estate?** Real estate is the **I.D.D.E.A.L.** investment vehicle to generate income and create wealth:

1. Income can be generated from rental property. A real estate investment structured with enough of a down payment and rent that exceeds the mortgage plus all other expenses, generates short-term income that is considered positive cash flow. With more properties and higher down payments this income will increase and contribute to lasting residual income. Accelerating paying down the mortgage principal with rental income will decrease the term of the loan and interest paid. Over time, even a highly leveraged, negative cash flow property can turn into a positive cash flow investment. Selling rental properties can generate long-term capital gain profits. Finally, short-term investments like fix-and-flip technique can also generate short-term income which is short-term capital gain.

2. **D** is for deductions, which are claimed on your income tax returns. Since real estate investing is a business, you qualify for a wide

range of tax deductions. These deductions vary depending on the structure of your business entity and investment strategy.

3. **D** means <u>depreciation</u>, which allocates the cost of your property over its estimated useful life determined by the IRS. As soon as you purchase capital investments like a property, office furniture, or computer equipment, it automatically begins to wear out. Its value declines year by year and you get to write-off that loss of the purchase value on your income taxes. Depreciation is the tax deduction to offset the rental income produced by owning real estate.

4. **E** stands for <u>equity</u>, which is the original mortgage amount borrowed less the amount owed on the mortgage to the lender today. If you have a $150,000 mortgage and still owe $100,000 of it, your equity is the difference, $50,000. Equity grows over time if you pay down the principal and not just the interest. This results from the periodic pay down, usually monthly, of the principal amount of an amortized loan. Positive appreciation can add to the equity, while negative appreciation can erode equity, so this needs to be factored into the equation. Aggressively paying down the mortgage principal can more than negate a down housing market that is experiencing negative appreciation over a few years. Over time, your equity can translate into wealth if the property appreciates. Coupling positive cash flow and tax deductions provides the ability to pay down the loan more quickly.

5. **A** is for <u>appreciation</u>, which means the investment grows in value over time. In a solid real estate market, appreciation will happen with little effort from you. Appreciation varies from market to market. Targeted home improvement, can also increase the value. Real estate is a growth asset, and often the largest part of the return is the equity gained through appreciation. Even if there is no appreciation over the life of the loan, the owner would end up with a free and clear property at the end of the loan payment period.

6. **L** means <u>leverage</u>, financing most or all of a real estate deal with someone else's money. A property can be controlled through the use of OPM, other people's money, combined with a small amount of money of your own to obtain 80 percent, 90 percent, or even 100 percent leverage. In the vast majority of deals,

over 100 percent leverage is not recommended.[68] To purchase medium-sized real estate deals and business endeavors, you may have to put down 30 percent and up, reducing the leverage. The key factor is that you profit from the entire deal including the leverage portion that is borrowed money. You can also leverage people's credit, time, and knowledge to benefit your deals.

**Mortgage Principal Reduction:** As the paid equity in the property increases the principal amount of your mortgage amount owed decreases, if the loan is set up to pay monthly principal. For an interest-only loan, you can request the lender to withdraw an extra monthly principal payment like 100 dollars in addition to the predetermined interest payment. If interest is only paid, the principal is never reduced unless you are proactive and do it yourself. Beware that the loan may come due faster than you remember and you will owe the entire balance. I've been there but was able to refinance before the note came due.

Owning real estate is an excellent addition to your income and retirement portfolios that can help reduce your taxable income base. Tax write-offs in rental real estate offset income from your job, business, and in other areas of real estate investing like fix and flip.

Let's expand I.D.D.E.A.L. even further. Here are the **major tax benefits of owning rental real estate**:

1. Appreciation: Real estate is a superb tax shelter because appreciation is not taxable until the property is sold. Consider doing a 1031 Exchange[69] or a Charitable Remainder Trust

---

68    Because loans of 105 percent and higher give borrowers money back at closing you owe more money than the value of the property. This was one of the reasons for the real estate subprime mortgages collapse in 2008-10. These types of loans as well as negative amortization loans were used by speculator buyers and are very rare to get these type of loans now.

69    A *1031 exchange* is a tax deferred exchange of the profits for selling one property and then proceeding with an acquisition of another like-kind property within a specific time frame defined by the IRS.

(CRT)[70] techniques that can defer or never pay tax on that appreciation.

2. <u>Property Tax Deductions</u>: You can write off property taxes. By owning real estate, you create a mechanism to write-off (within income limitations) expenses that are now business related. Property depreciation is a potent tool to reduce income taxes. The IRS allows you to take a write-off for the value of the building, not the land, which is typically over twenty-seven and a half years for residential property. Commercial property depreciation is typically evenly deducted over the length of thirty-nine years. Also write off mortgage interest, closing costs, and refinance charges.

3. <u>Business Tax Deductions</u>: As a business owner, you can deduct business-related operating expenses like office furniture, computer equipment, and machinery. Large capital expenditures can be depreciated over three or seven years. You can also write-off supplies, training HOA dues, utilities not paid by the tenant, home office space, business mileage, business trips, cell phone, and Internet charges. These items can be deducted 100 percent in the first year.

4. <u>Passive Cash Flow</u> is the net return from rental income minus expenses basis each month. Annual and one-time expenses need to be factored in. If the number is positive, this is known as "*positive monthly cash flow*" and if negative, this is known as "*negative monthly cash flow*." The only income you're recognizing on your taxes is the rent collected minus all deductions. Even with positive monthly cash flow, there still may be a loss on your Schedule E tax form because of depreciation and other business deductions.

👍 An *active real estate investor* makes decisions of how to manage or run their real estate investments. This does not have to include daily responsibilities of a property manager, though it can be, but it does

---

[70]  "*Charitable Remainder Trust* is an arrangement in which property or money is donated to a charity, but the donor (called the grantor) continues to use the property and/or receive income from it while living." (InvestorWords. com, *www.investorwords.com/830/charitable_remainder_trust.html*, April 29, 2011)

involve some decision-making. This is different from a *passive real estate investor* who has no involvement in managing the investment. There is a tax advantage of the amount of losses you can write off as an active investor over a passive investor classification. There are even more tax advantages of being a real estate professional like a realtor or full-time investor over an active investor.

You can learn more about real estate tax deductions, go to the IRS:

- "Publication 527 (2009), Residential Rental Property" at *www.irs.gov/publications/p527/index.html*
- "Real Estate (Taxes, Mortgage Interest, Points, Other Property Expenses)" at *www.irs.gov/faqs/content/0,,id=199901,00.html*
- "Rental Income and Expenses - Real Estate Tax Tips" at *www.irs.gov/businesses/small/industries/article/0,,id=98895,00.html*

**Small Deal?** Have a balanced real estate portfolio. For beginners, focus more on cash flow properties than on speculative appreciation. My favorite lesson in playing the Cashflow 101 game is for players to purchase small deals like stocks, mutual funds, and a single-family dwellings until they have enough cash to invest in the big deals. Start with catching small fish with average return on investment, and be patient. These little fish are more plentiful, more obtainable, and easier to manage.

Buy an investment property making positive monthly cash flow where

you can also write off insurance and other tax benefits for an asset that may appreciate in value over time. With investment property, one can also write off expenses like insurance, maintenance, tenant placement fee, and property management fee. Have an investment property become your retirement home when you are ready to retire.

❑ AI: _____

👆 Be aware that investing in land can have high returns but also comes with high risks, so really do your due diligence first and be careful. Despite what real estate brokers and investment clubs tell you, these tend to be long-term investments. Typically, large deals like apartment complexes, storage units, mobile parks, and coin-operated shops require a lot of capital and time. These non-recourse loans typically required 50 percent down. Understand the basics and then graduate to the next level. Start slow with smaller deals. Investigate single-family dwellings (SFD) and duplexes.

Once you are comfortable and have a few successes, then you can move to bigger fish with higher returns like starting a business, owning four-plex townhome, and managing motel. Upgrade your tools to catch bigger fish. Then have enough resources to keep doing big deals so you don't have to go back to small transactions.

❑  **AI:** _____

👆 Real Estate Investment Trust (REIT) is a passive method to investing in properties or mortgages. The investment portfolio can be diverse or specialized. Some REITs provide dividend distributions. This is like a real estate mutual fund and can be purchased on the stock exchange from any brokerage firm.

## Techniques to Fix Up Investment Properties

If your real estate investment strategy is fix-and-flip or buy and hold, improvements may need to be done on the property to increase the value to sell or rent. "Increasing the curb appeal will increase your property value. First impressions are just as important in real estate as everything else. That's because most home buyers will size up a property within a few seconds—before they even go through the front door. For that reason, it's important to spruce up the exterior of your property, it increases 'curb appeal.' Doing so doesn't have to be expensive or a lot of hard work."[49] "The time to repair the roof is when the sun is shining," said John F. Kennedy.

John Dessauer's "**How to Increase Your Curb Appeal**" suggests:[50]

- ❑ Give the property an industrial cleaning by cleaning the sides of the house, windows,[71] porch, garage, roof, walkways, and parking areas. You can use a hose and in many cases a power washer may be necessity. Try to trade from a neighbor for the day.
- ❑ Give the property an external face lift. A good paint job can add thousands to the resale value of the property. It can be the greatest value-producing improvement you can make on a dollar-for-dollar return basis.
- ❑ Pay attention to landscaping. This can be one of the most important aspects of adding curb appeal to your place. If landscaping is done right, it can add up to 30 percent to the value of your home.

Focus on improving the areas of the home that will be most appealing to potential buyers and provide the biggest return on your investment. "According to statistics, women are responsible for 80 percent of the buying decisions when it comes to real estate. And while men (usually deferring to the women) are most interested in whether a house has a garage or secluded office or den, women pay the most attention to the bathroom(s) and the kitchen. For that reason, it is recommended to remodel one of those rooms first—or both if you can afford it with cash."[51]

John Dessauer's "**Investor's Home Improvement Checklist**:"[52]

The Kitchen:
- ❑ Paint or refinish the cabinets and change the knobs and handles.
- ❑ Consider handmade cabinetry, but only if you can afford it. Have them installed by a professional if you cannot do a Grade A job.
- ❑ Open a wall, if possible, to create a pass through or a barstool countertop.

---

[71]  Cleaning both the inside and outside of window, plus removing the screens will increase the natural light into the home by 20 percent to brighten it up giving the illusion of more space.

❑ Update old appliances[72] and window treatments.
❑ Increase storage space if the layout allows.
❑ Change or remodel countertops by adding a Formica laminate.
❑ Install a new sink and faucet.
❑ If the kitchen is antiquated or outdated, consider a bigger overhaul by painting the walls, upgrading the lighting (energy efficient), and installing a tile floor.

The Bathroom(s):
❑ If the bathroom is old and outdated and you can afford it, rip it all out except the tub (unless it's old, an ugly color, or dirty). Leaving the tub makes the job easier, faster, and cheaper.
❑ If you do rip out the tub, consider putting in a soaking or Jacuzzi tub as an upgrade.[73]
❑ Repaint the walls with semi-gloss.
❑ Consider adding tile or half-wall wainscoting to the lower four feet of the wall (or the bottom six to eight inches).
❑ Replace old vinyl with a nice tile floor.
❑ Be sure to caulk where appropriate.
❑ Upgrade lighting (energy efficient), and add mirrored vanity cabinets, wallpaper borders, and nice towel rings as finishing touches.

The Rest of the House:
❑ Paint bedroom closets a bright white, upgrade the lighting, and install a closet organizing systems that includes a shoe rack.
❑ Paint the interior of the house (neutral and earth tones), including the ceiling.[74]
❑ Add ceiling fans with light kits and dimmer switches whenever possible.

---

[72] If you cannot afford to update large appliances, upgrade small appliances like microwave, toaster open, can opener, mixer, and blender.

[73] Make sure this is not too large because it will take a long time to fill it up and take a lot of hot water.

[74] A $15 gallon of paint can be worth $1,500 on the walls.

❑ Follow appraisal rules and install plush carpeting in the bedrooms over a dense quality pad. Choose a color that sets off the walls and baseboard trim.

❑ Install floors throughout the rest of the house with tiles is better than vinyl, but hardwood is the best.

👍 Materials can be bought at large depots like Lowe's, Home Depot, Costco, and Sam's Club or purchased at discount stores like Wal-Mart, Target, Kohl's, and IKEA. Utilize discount days and coupons. Have a phased approach or all-in-one weekend approach. Do not let this effort go on forever. Keep a schedule that continues investments in growing opportunities and paying off debt as well.

For techniques on purchasing multi-family dwellings or rehabbing investment properties, refer to John Dessauer's *Real Estate H²O: Quenching Your Financial Thirst in a Parched Economy*.

For details about building or converting a home to be green, go to *Chapter 17: Investing in Your Community, Go Green to Benefit the Environment and Yourself, Building Green* or U.S. Green Building Council's Green Home Guide at <u>www.greenhomeguide.org</u>.

# Real Estate Investing Tips

### Investing Tips

Real estate investing is risky, but like any other opportunity that requires preparation and precise execution, it can reap rewards with positive results.

### Top Fifteen Real Estate Investing Tips:

1. Create a strategy that enables your short-term income and long-term wealth goals.
2. Take the appropriate and decisive actions that fit your strategy sooner than later.
3. Get educated first and have a mentor (not by trial and error).

4. Get access to an abundance and variety of deals.
5. Find the real motivation why a seller is selling.
6. Verify the numbers yourself by doing thorough due diligence to validate a deal (love the numbers, not the property).
7. Get a home inspection, along with an appraisal, before buying a property.[75]
8. Study the contract, lease, HUD1 statement,[76] and read all the fine print.
9. Be an informed client who drives the deal closing and tenant placement processes.
10. Have the correct amount of insurance and liability coverage.
11. Have an exit strategy prior to entering into a deal, including your primary home.
12. Expect the worst and be prepared for it with cash reserves.
13. Build in a vacancy rate depending on the type of deal and region (at least two months per year for residential property), plus tenant placement and property management fees.
14. Treat investing as a business, not a hobby, by getting a CPA who owns investment properties and a business.
15. Record all expenses on managing your investments.

❑ **AI:** _____

## Common Investing Mistakes

As already stated, real estate can be very risky, and you need to thoroughly conduct your due diligence. All you need to do is watch the news and drive around your neighborhood to see all of the foreclosure signs. There were over 2.8 million foreclosures in 2009 alone;[53] plus over 1 million homes were foreclosed in 2010.[54] How many people do you know that have lost their home? Are you one of those unfortunate people? The number of home foreclosures in 2011 is expected to be higher than in 2010.[55]

---

[75]   A *home inspection* reports the condition and quality of a property. An *appraisal* assesses the value of a property considering any issues (problems) with it.

[76]   *HUD1*: Housing and Urban Development 1 statement documents all closing numbers that are received and paid for both the seller and buyer.

**Top Fifteen Real Estate Investing Mistakes**:

1.  Paying for a business entity before you start investing.
2.  Believing that a Nevada LLC is the solution for every business—set up the appropriate business structure.
3.  Not getting or registering an LLC in the state in which the income property is located.
4.  Believing that you need to be a real estate agent to be an investor (though there are some benefits to that depending on your investing strategy).
5.  That you must buy a property in the state you reside.
6.  Thinking every real estate deal can be closed with no money down. But some loans like FHA and VA[77] can be done with small down payments. Furthermore, deals like "subject to" with potentially no or little down payment.
7.  Forcing a deal to happen because of passion and not logic.
8.  Inflating the numbers or believing the seller's numbers without verifying them.
9.  Fudging your financial numbers to qualify for a loan.
10. Encouraging false appraisal numbers and claims. Instead, give the appraiser your checklist and be present if possible.
11. Not understanding your mortgage terms, knowing when the mortgage payment interest rate will change, and when loan balance is due.
12. Only paying the interest and no principal on a mortgage.
13. Believing that you can accelerate the time it takes to fix and flip a property quicker than the average duration.
14. Treating a vacation property like a vacation home and not as an investment property.
15. Not taking pictures to document the condition of every room before a tenant moves in and when they move out.

❏ **AI**: _____

---

[77]   *FHA*: Federal Housing Administration; *VA*: Veterans Administration.

## Insurance Policy Tips

For owning multiple properties and businesses, an **umbrella policy** is recommended in addition to hazard insurance. Verify that the policy will cover your assets under a different insurer. Also verify that you are not required to switch over car coverage to them (unless it saves you money). A $1 million umbrella policy requires an investment of only about $300 per year and $2 million policy is about $500. If you add in a car, the premium will be much higher. People think umbrella policies only cover liability, but this is not true. The policy mainly covers liability, but it can also cover hazard, which is a smaller percent. This is <u>not</u> in lieu of hazard insurance, which is required by mortgage underwriters and umbrella policy insurers. The umbrella policy company may require a minimum hazard policy coverage like $500,000 on a property.

❏ **AI:** _____


✎ An umbrella policy can include personal property and assets but needs to be accounted for separately via writing from a different bank account. Proportionally pay the amount according to the value of each property. Do NOT co-mingle businesses and personal funds. If you have multiple investment properties that are managed in different entities (for example, LLCs) these also need to be paid from their own bank account too.

For large investments, commercial property such as office buildings and shopping malls, and multiple properties, look into **commercial umbrella policy**. For three or more residential properties, get the commercial type of an umbrella policy, though it may cost $50 to $100 more.

❏ **AI:** _____


Your **landlord policy** should have full replacement cost coverage, including all exterior features like car port, detached garage, shed, fence, porch, deck, etc. This will also cover loss of rental income. Your primary home should have the same replacement coverage option.

❏ **AI:** _____


You should investigate **flood insurance** if you are in a 100-year plain. Depending on where the property is, you may want to look into hurricane insurance and earthquake insurance. If these other policies are required, you should be notified by the realtor, insurance company, and/or loan underwriter. Ultimately, you are responsible and should ask to be sure. The replacement costs value needs to be the same as the hazard policy replacement costs.

❏ **AI:** _____

Add **Ordinance Law Upgrade Coverage** to all of your hazard insurance policies. This is additional insurance coverage in case building ordinance, code, or law changes and repairs are needed to complete a claim to your hazard insurance policy. This option is also referred to as Building Code Upgrade Coverage. Loss payment of rental income will also include the increased costs you incur to repair the damaged structure or to construct a replacement structure to comply with the enforcement of any local, state, or federal law, ordinance, or regulation affecting repair or construction of such structures. This is a small increase in your policy that may cost only fifteen to twenty dollars a year. Get this policy selection for both your investment and personal properties. For older or rundown properties, an insurance company may not allow this policy option.

❏ **AI:** _____

For investment properties, your tenant lease shall require proof of **renter's insurance**. Verify you get a copy of their insurance policy prior to them moving in and if the lease is renewed.

❏ **AI:** _____

## Property Taxes Tips

**Reassess Property Taxes:** "Up to 60 percent of taxable property in the U.S. is assessed at a value that is higher than it should be, according to the National Taxpayer's Union, an advocacy group, with a goal to lower taxes. That means the property is taxed at a higher rate as well. Additionally, the American Homeowner's Association references a *Consumer Reports* article that up to 40 percent of property appraisals have clerical errors in them."[56] In this down housing market, request that your property taxes be reassessed by the county.

❏ **AI:** _____

I obtained a property tax reassessment after the 2001 dot-com bust in Silicon Valley. The value of my condo dropped by $125,000, which was reflected in the equal reduction in the assessment value. I used this extra money to buy more stocks while the prices were low and to supplement my income when companies were suspending bonuses. I recently reassessed my rental properties. One property was reassessed at $14,000 less, which in turn reduced my property taxes.

Check to see if new homestead laws implemented in the tax year provide homeowners an increase in the basic **homestead exemption**. This is available in most states to protect a certain portion of your home value from being vulnerable to taxes, creditors, or bankruptcy. If you are currently receiving an exemption, you may not have to reapply unless there is an ownership change. It is recommended that you check anyway. The new increased amount may be automatically granted to homeowners who are currently receiving this exemption and to first-time applicants who qualify. In many cases, to qualify, you may need to own and occupy the property as your primary residence in that county.

"Some of the exemptions are as follows: people age sixty-two and older, disabled-based income, disabled Veterans, Veterans Surviving Spouse, and un-remarried surviving spouse of a Peace Officer or Firefighter killed in the line of duty. To find out if you qualify for a new county exception, an increased city exemption, or any addition exception based on disability or age, contact your county assessors or homestead exception department. An example from 2009 in Fulton County, Georgia was $10,000 to $40,000."[57] In 2010 basic homestead exemption in City of Atlanta was $30,000 and Georgia statewide school tax exemption is $10,000. There are filing deadlines to be eligible.

❏ **AI:** _____

## Mortgage Tips

Because interest rates are low, this is a great time to investigate **fixed-interest conventional mortgages** for your home and investment properties. If you have not already done so, refinance to principal and interest traditional fifteen- or thirty-year loans. The interest rates are rising, so lock in now while the rates are near an all-time low.

❏ **AI:** _____

Do **NOT** get suckered into signing up for **bi-weekly mortgage payment programs** with an administration processing charge by the lender or an individual selling for another company. There is a set-up charge of several hundred dollars and usually a fixed term to the agreement. You can accomplish the same goal of paying off the loan sooner by setting up an automatic withdraw through the lender and take off an additional $25, $50, or $200 per month without an unnecessary program. Just call the lender to take the extra principal payment each month on top of the normal payment depending on your financial situation and other outstanding loans. You can also set it up yourself from your lender account or draw from your banking account, and the problem is easily solved. This can be set up online, which gives you easier control to move that amount UP and down as your situation changes, all with more flexibility and no startup costs. More details of this technique were covered in *Chapter 11: Investing in Debt Reduction while Increasing Your Savings, Debt Reduction, Automating Paying Off Debt.*

❑  **AI:** _____

Eliminate the need to keep **Property Mortgage Insurance** (PMI) which is about $100 per month for the average size loan. The first step is to call your lender to verify if you have it or not. This may not be noted on the mortgage billing statement. This insurance protects the mortgage company if you default on the loan and the coverage will typically be on the first or primary mortgage. If you put enough money down at closing or have excellent credit, it may not have been required, but the lending market guidelines keep changing.

There are two types of PMI: 1) Paid by the mortgage company and 2) Paid by you, the property owner. If it is the first PMI type, you probably will not even know about it because the mortgage company is paying for PMI coverage. So do not worry about it. For the second PMI situation, call the lender to waive or remove it. It may be that simple. If they will not waive PMI, ask what it will take to get the policy requirement removed. It may require a new credit report and history proving that you are not a risk. If the value of the home has increased or the loan principal balance has decreased, that may be enough to remove PMI payments. In some cases, you may need to pay down the principal to a certain value of the home (for example, 80 percent loan-to-value [LTV]) to get PMI removed.

❑  **AI:** _____

👍 If you are at risk of losing your home or investment property, get Housing and Urban Development's "How to Avoid Foreclosure" material at _www.HUD.gov/foreclosure_.

To gain more knowledge regarding real estate investing education and support systems, go to _www.RetireSoonerThanLater.com/Education_.

❑  **AI:** _____

*"You will miss 100 percent of the shots you don't take."*
*~ Tiger Woods*

# CHAPTER 16: INVEST IN YOURSELF AND FAMILY

*"When one door of happiness closes, another opens; but often we look so long at the closed door that we do not see the one which has been opened for us." ~ Helen Keller*

Wealth is not just about money, but also about mind, body, and energy. When you feel better about your health, looks, weight, and mental wellbeing and have a positive outlook on life, your attitude improves, and you require less stuff. Your positive mind and growing energy will be your new quick pick-me-up with no false highs from supplements. There will be no more need for the coffee ritual every morning to get moving, energy drink in the afternoon after eating a huge lunch, or that extremely expensive pair of shoes when you are feeling blue.

**"The 7 Habits of Highly Effective People"** by Stephen R. Covey:[58]

**Habit 1:** Be Proactive
**Habit 2:** Begin with the End in Mind
**Habit 3:** Put First Thing First
**Habit 4:** Think Win/Win
**Habit 5:** Seek First to Understand, Then to be Understood
**Habit 6:** Synergize
**Habit 7:** Sharpen the Saw

*The 7 Habits of Highly Effective People* starting guidelines:[59]

1. The more proactive you are (Habit 1), the more effectively you can exercise personal leadership (Habit 2) and management (Habit 3) in your life. The more effectively you manage your life (Habit 3), the more renewing activities you can do (Habit 7). The more you seek to understand (Habit 5), the more effectively you can go for synergetic Win/Win solutions (Habits 4 and 6). The more you improve in any habit that leads to independence (Habits 1, 2, and 3), the more effective you will be in interdependent situations (Habits 4, 5, and 6). And renewal (Habit 7) is the process of renewing all the habits.

2.  Personal Ethics: Success became more a function of personality, of public image, of attitudes and behaviors, skills and techniques, that lubricate the process of human interaction.
3.  There is the principle of potential, the idea that we are embryonic and can grow and develop and release more and more potential, develop more and more talents. The principle of growth is the process of releasing potential and developing talents, with the accompanying needs for principles such as patience, nurturance, and encouragement.
4.  *Inside-out* means to start first with self: your paradigms, your character, and your motives. Private victors precede public victories.
5.  As we continue to grow and mature, we become increasingly aware. This is interdependence paradigm of we can do it; we can cooperate; we can combine our talents and abilities and create something greater together. Interdependence is a choice only independent people can make.
6.  Win/Win is a frame of mind and heart that constantly seeks mutual benefits. *Win/Win* means that agreements or solutions are mutually beneficial and satisfying. With a Win/Win solution, all parties feel good about the decision and feel committed to the action plan. Win/Win sees life as a cooperative, not a competitive arena. Win/Win is based on the paradigm that there is plenty for everybody, that one person's success is not achieved at the expense or exclusion of the success of others. Because we think Win/Win, we believe in a synergistic third alternative, a solution that is mutually beneficial and is better than what either of us originally proposed.
7.  Synergy is the essence of principle-centered leadership. It is to value differences, to respect them, to build on the strengths, and to compensate for weaknesses. Simply defined, synergy means that the whole is greater than the sum of the parts.

We will be principle-centered, not self-centered or want-centered. Your desire will be the most critical motivation factor and principles will efficiently drive your decisions, not your lust for more stuff. Have high standards and constantly strive to improve your situation. This transition will take time, but it is necessary to achieve life fulfillment—all while increasing your circle of influence in your personal life, job environment, and business ventures.

## Love Yourself

**"Me, Myself, and I."** You need to love yourself almost unconditionally. There may be things in your past or present that need to be corrected and improved, and that you are not proud of. There are at least four things everybody should love: <u>me, myself, I . . . and money</u>! You really need to love yourself over anything else. This does not have to be 100 percent at first. You need to recognize where you bring value to others and feel good about yourself. "The more respect you have for yourself, the more respect others will have for you."[60] Of course, you can also love your God, savior, prophet, and/or spirit, plus the value money provides.

Impress nobody but yourself. Forget about spending money on expensive clothes, jewelry, watches, purses, shoes, cars, and your spouse just to get a compliment. This is short sighted, and you need to look forward. It is better to be complimented on feeling and looking healthy, giving back to the community, helping others improve their financial situation, and retiring wealthy when you want to. Acknowledge and accept these compliments gracefully. Money and success should not be feared but cherished.

**"Stop calling me 'Jerry'!"** You are going to change direction in life. People will give you a new level of respect and a nickname that you deserve. You are important, and what you do matters. You are of value. Say it! Repeat, "I am valuable" until you start to believe it. Because my last name is Wortham, kids often called me "Worthless" while growing up, so I vowed to make something of myself to prove them wrong—and I did! Recently, a friend from college called me "Worthy." Now that I like! What is your new powerhouse nickname? _____

## Your Soul and Spirit

### Being Fulfilled and Responsible

**Happiness**: Be happy and like it. Do not be a victim that can never be happy. Focus on the little things in life that bring you pleasure. His Holiness, the Dalai Lama said, "I believe that the very purpose of our life is to seek happiness . . . Yes, I believe that happiness can be achieved through training the mind."[61] Being rich and having more possessions is not always better. You need to be fulfilled and happy with less.

"The same reason a person would act badly, is the same reason a person would act good. We, as a society, have to make the choices available, or we will continue to be stuck with the popularity of negative choices. Some of us are not blessed with a supportive home environment. We need to transform defensive behavior related to inferiority, insecurities, and fear"[62] into productive and not destructive energy.

"**Seven Deadly Sins**" by Mahatma Gandhi are guiding principles in life that we should all follow:[63]

| | |
|---|---|
| **Sin 1:** | Wealth without Work |
| **Sin 2:** | Pleasure without Conscience |
| **Sin 3:** | Knowledge without Character |
| **Sin 4:** | Commerce without Morality |
| **Sin 5:** | Science without Humanity |
| **Sin 6:** | Religion without Sacrifice |
| **Sin 7:** | Politics without Principle |

"They cannot take away our self-respect if we do not give it to them," said Mahatma Gandhi.

### Connecting with Others

**Greater Than One**: We are ONE. There is no "us" or "them." Let's remove labels and focus on being human. Include as many people as possible to support your goals, and you, in turn, will support them. The synergy of two people working together is greater than the sum of two people working separately.

We need to be centered, driven by positive life rules. These are "**13 Steps to a Great Dance Team**" by Adrian Flores that can be applied in other life experiences:[64]

1. Do not criticize: No criticizing of yourself or anybody else. Those who criticize stall the success process.
2. Be beautiful: Beauty is an inside job. What people see is enhanced by your attention to them. Make good eye contact, be attentive, and be sensitive to your partners.
3. Acceptance: Accept yourself and others, as well as where you are in the learning curve.
4. Think only of the present moment: Stay conscious of the work you are processing, your partner, and your surroundings. This ability to stay focused on the present moment activity can make the difference in all your personal achievements as well as in **becoming a skilled _____.**
   ❑ **AI:** _____
5. Distinguish yourself: What is your passion? Each of us is a contribution to society, and unless we nurture that special quality in us, we will never be happy . . . .
6. Think hygiene: Personal cleanliness, fitness, and appearance are important.
7. Be of service: Asking for help is just as important as giving help to a team member.
8. Challenge yourself: Push yourself to the next level of accomplishments.
9. Commit to success: Never give up, no matter what.
10. Commit to the group, and the group will commit to you.
11. Only respond to positive behavior: Help yourself by not paying attention to negativity.
12. Perform with the group: Team up with a partner. The benefits include being comfortable in your own skin, confidence, really caring for others, being appreciated, a sense of belonging, being acknowledged, a sense of worth, and a strong connection to society.

13. <u>Be real</u>: Truth and honesty is being real with yourself. A real person can't get into trouble because they are powerful enough to do just what they know is best for them without breaking the laws of the land.

## Smile Now!

**Greeting People:** Walk proudly with your chin up, eyes looking forward (not looking at the ground), chest up and out, and stomach in. Be proactive by always be looking to connect with people. When you shake somebody's hand, extend your hand and arm to them. Be warm and enthusiastic, and move more quickly as you approach them, looking into their eyes. The "bro" shake or fist bump is cool in personal relations, but it is not appropriate for business or people you do not know well. You can use a soft two-hand shake with women. Be prepared for the person that has a firm handshake that usually lasts a second or two longer than most. Start a sentence with the person's name like: "<u>Sue</u>, I will send the proposal tomorrow." I like to repeat their name back twice and associate it with something about that person to help me remember it. To perfect this technique, practice with a friend.

❑   **AI:** _____

Introduce yourself to the person walking onto the airplane and the people who sit next to you. Once they are settled, smile and reach out your hand to shake theirs. Don't wait too long because that wall will start to be built and the cement will dry quickly.

**Smile:** Smiling is free and contagious. Smile at people, make eye contact, remember their names, and get a short life story. For example, if somebody is doing a repair job at your home, get to know all of the contractors and be on a first-name basis with them. Shake their hand, even if it is dirty, or give them a pat on the back. People will show they appreciate the friendly gesture by giving you extra stuff, better or quicker service, and discounts. They will work harder for good people that care about their wellbeing. Try this with your local butcher, customer service person, car repair person, etc.

Two great easy ways to relieve stress and pressure is first simply to SMILE. Relax your jaw and facial muscles. Smile with good posture by standing or sitting tall without slouching. This will reduce stress and give you confidence. Do it now! Another fun way is to skip or dance. Come on . . . skipping was so much fun when we were kids. We should treat ourselves to some cheap fun.

❏ **AI:** _____

A smile always makes you more attractive while releasing tension. At a hotel, I saw the coolest thing. In the bathroom, the soap had "Smile Now" embedded in it. This was really nice soap with rosemary infusion made by Bloom. The box also had the words "Simple Good" and "[Energy]" on it. I give credit to Embassy Suites for having this soap in their wonderful rooms. Their pool, fitness center, and manager's happy hours are also great amenities that made it easier to be productive.

People whose faces show a lot of pain from a hard and stressful life are often the sharpest, nicest, and most caring. They deserve our special attention, even if it is only a smile or a casual, "Hi, how are you doing?" This will challenge you to take a risk on not the most obvious choice. These people are hidden jewels.

**Be Nice:** Go out of your way to open the door for people, including holding elevator doors, even if you are in a rush. This small gesture will allow you to command that space, and people will respect you and see that you are a kind person who is aware of the situation and their needs. This goes for all genders, because contrary to popular opinion, chivalry is alive and works both ways. Guys, I know you are opening car doors for your lady, even if she is driving or leaving in a car. I'm sure you are putting her coat on and pulling out her chair for her, right? If you do not know that person, be polite by saying, "Please allow me" or ask "May I?" Men should be gentlemen at all times! Side note, I love when women hold the door for me.

❏ **AI:** _____

**"Please"** and **"Thank You":** Express your request for service with "Please." Express your gratitude with praise, "Thank you," and the appropriate tip. Do not respond with a belittling or factual response that does not first acknowledge a nice complement. In other words, if someone tells you, "That is a nice shirt," don't answer sarcastically with, "I bought it ten years ago for twenty bucks." Don't answer "Have you being working out?" with, "No, just eating less because I lost my job." Instead, say "Thank you for noticing." Anytime you can honestly respond with a compliment, do it: "What are you doing to stay fit and positive?" Practice saying "Please" and "Thank you" out loud so you feel comfortable making this a natural response.

❑ **AI:** _____

For a blind gesture, say, "Thank you" aloud even if there is nobody there to hear you. It's not silly but thoughtful! Just express your gratitude. It is good practice, and you never know who is listening. If later you know who that person is, you can say, "I said 'Thank you' before, but you were not present, so thanks again." Some examples might be the person that anonymously carried a package from the mailbox and left it at your doorstep, left a discount coupon on your car windshield, or returned your lost wallet. You can also be thankful for services and non-tangible things. Say, "Bless you" when other people sneeze, even if they cannot hear you, because the people around you will.

👍 I like to add "THX" in the beginning of an e-mail, which means "thanks." If replying to an e-mail, replace "Re" with "THX." For example, "THX: Follow-Up Meeting."

**"You're Welcome":** Along with accepting compliments, it is equally as important to be able to accept praise and appreciation. When somebody says, "Thank you," respond with a simple, "You are welcome." If you are providing a service, do not respond, "No problem." Instead, practice saying, "It was my pleasure."

❑ **AI:** _____

**"I Apologize":** Drop the word "sorry" from your vocabulary. Instead, say, "I apologize." As I have learned in my police explorer and business training, there truly is a difference. The only time I use "sorry" is when I must show remorse for an accident I caused, like stepping on somebody's foot, breaking their possession, or in cases of sympathy for someone's loss or death.

❑ **AI:** _____

## Protecting Your Body

**"Danger, Danger, Will Robinson!"** Safety should never be taken for granted. That is not to say you should never take the bus, jog around a lake, shop at flea market, or date online. You need to be "street smart," which will allow you to safely take more calculated risks and be exposed to more opportunities.

👍 Safety comes first. Please stop jogging with earbuds or earplugs! You need to remain alert and listen to your surroundings. I love music, listening to inspirational speakers, and chatting on the phone, but how important is this when your safety is at stake? How about just

using one earplug? Ladies, when jogging, carry a whistle, panic alert, and/or pepper spray (if it is legal to carry in your area) on your keychain or person. If necessary, get trained to use these defensive instruments. Exercise outdoors during the daylight and/or with a partner.

❏ AI: _____

*Lost In Space* 1967, © courtesy of Space Productions and Synthesis Entertainment

👍 Your situation may require you to leave the blinds or drapes closed for privacy concerns. At times, it may also be wise to leave lights on as well. For property protection, get a timer for your internal lights, especially over the holidays and while on vacation. Outside motion-detector lights can also save energy and possibly deter attackers or robbers. These security measures permit you to focus your thoughts on positive money-making activities.

# Your Mind

## Feed the Mind with Yoga

"There is a reciprocal relationship between a supple mind and the ability to shift perspective: A supple, flexible mind helps us address our problems from a variety of perspectives, and, conversely, deliberately trying to objectively examine our problems from a variety of perspectives can be seen as a kind of flexibility training for the mind."[65]

**Namaste:** Yoga has been <u>practiced for more than 5,000 years,</u> and 15 million Americans are enjoying its health benefits. While practicing yoga, you may notice that you sleep better, get fewer colds, or just feel more relaxed. Science is providing evidence of how yoga works to improve one's health, heal aches and pains, reduce the body's recovery time, and keep sickness at bay.

Here are the **wellness benefits of practicing yoga**:

1. <u>Less stress, more calm</u>: You feel less stressed and more relaxed after a workout. Some yoga styles use meditation techniques to quiet the constant "mind chatter" or deep-breathing techniques to focus your mind on the breath.
2. <u>Concentration and mood</u>: The ability to focus are common benefits. After practicing yoga, you may have a positive attitude, be in a better mood, and feel happier.
3. <u>Effects on other medical conditions</u>: Yoga has been used as an adjunct treatment for specific medical conditions, from clinical depression to heart disease. Yoga benefits other chronic medical conditions, relieving symptoms of asthma, back pain, arthritis, and carpal tunnel syndrome.
4. <u>Other benefits of yoga</u>: Studies have suggested that yoga may have a positive effect on learning and memory; slow the aging process; improve energy levels, coordination, and reaction times. The spiritual and emotional dimensions of your practice may encourage you to address any eating and weight problems. Yoga studios are great pick-up spot!

Darryl doing Urdhva Dhanurasana (upward bow pose) in Napa Valley, California in that same t-shirt from a high school locker.

## Addressing Mental Illness

**Seeking Help:** Your mental health is critical to your progress and happiness. Reach deep for the bravery to take the first step and get the appropriate assistance. If you need help be courageous and accept the responsibility of seeking guidance, therapy, medications, and support systems. There are many community services available to you. It troubles and pains me to see people suffer. Everybody deserves a healthy, balanced life.

❑ **AI:** _____

**"What is Mental Illness?"** by National Alliance of Mental Illness:[66]

- Mental illnesses are medical conditions that disrupt a person's thinking, feelings, mood, ability to relate to others, and daily functioning.
- Millions of Americans are affected by mental illness yet remain untreated or under-treated for their conditions. "One in four adults—approximately 57.7 million Americans—experience a mental health disorder in a given year."[67]
- Serious mental illnesses include major depression, schizophrenia, bipolar disorder, obsessive-compulsive disorder (OCD), panic disorder, post-traumatic stress disorder (PTSD), and borderline personality disorder.
- Mental illnesses are not the result of personal weakness, lack of character, or poor upbringing. Mental illnesses are treatable. Most people diagnosed with a serious mental illness can experience relief from their symptoms by actively participating in an individual treatment plan.
- In addition to medication treatment, psychosocial treatment such as cognitive behavioral therapy, interpersonal therapy, peer support groups, and other community services can also be components of a treatment plan and assist with recovery.

**"Getting Through Tough Economic Times"** by U.S. Substance Abuse & Mental Health Services Administration is a useful guide that provides practical advice on how to deal with the effects of financial difficulties on your physical, mental, and emotional health. "It covers: 1) Possible health risks and stress management, 2) Suicide warning signs[78] and getting help, and 3) Other steps you can take."[68]

Be honest with any addictions you have. Seek immediate professional assistance and a support system. Verify that your healthcare provider offers mental health benefits. Call them to validate that treatment for specific disorders are covered under your plan such as substance abuse and eating disorders. If you qualify, federal, state, and local governments plus not-for-profit organizations have resources available. You can get great insight from documentary series like A&E's *Intervention*, *Obsessed*, and *Hoarders*[79] at *www.aetv.com*.

❑ **AI:** _____

For details on OCD, depression, post-traumatic stress disorder, and schizophrenia illnesses refer to *Transforming from Consumer to Producer in 90 Days Tutorial Workbook*.

## Your Education

Education and training are investments in your personal growth. Have a commitment and resolve to learn more. This applies to gaining sophisticated knowledge in a trade, profession, finances, real estate, stock market, mental health, wellness, religion, spirituality, business development, and self-development. Do not classify these as expenses. They are investments in yourself.

---

[78]    Are you feeling desperate, alone, or hopeless? Call the National Suicide Prevention Lifeline at 1-800-273-TALK (8255), a free, 24-hour hotline available to anyone in suicidal crisis or emotional distress. For online resources, go to *www.SuicidePreventionLifeline.org*.

[79]    "If you suspect you are a hoarder, know that you are not alone. It's a condition that can be treated and worked with, like any other flavor of mental challenge. If you are not a hoarder and need to deal with someone who is, please be gentle. Know that they are probably not 'doing it' to spite you or because they are lazy or because they are naturally messy. It will be a healthier process for both of you if you reach for education over judgments or blame." (Beth Crittenden's at *www.OrganizationCoach.net*)

What **educational and knowledge requirements** do you need to meet your financial and personal goals? (all may not apply to you):

- ❏ License      _____    _/_/_
- ❏ Certification    _____    _/_/_
- ❏ Degree      _____    _/_/_
- ❏ Education    _____    _/_/_
- ❏ Knowledge    _____    _/_/_
- ❏ Training      _____    _/_/_
- ❏ Skill Set    _____    _/_/_
- ❏ Tools      _____    _/_/_
- ❏ _____    _____    _/_/_
- ❏ _____    _____    _/_/_

❏ **AI:** _____

Moreover, many educational expenditures can be a tax write-off or credit, especially if you own a business or itemize your tax deductions. "Education does not cost, it pays," said Mauney D. Collins. Every step will reap dividends. The purpose of your business and ventures are to make money! It is not just to have fun and get tax write-offs. "If you think education is expensive, try ignorance," said Derek Bok.

## College Tuition Programs and Scholarships

**Go Buffs!** Look at community, local, state, and online colleges to get the best value for credits. With online courses, you can finish a bachelor's degree in less than four years, not five or more. This allowed me to receive half of my credits from the University of Colorado via one of the first distance-learning systems. Stay focused and on task. During the summer or in the evenings, go to community or online colleges to retake classes you did poorly in. This will help you save on overall tuition costs (but do not do this for curriculum core classes). Furthermore, this strategy gives you the opportunity to take more classes in your discipline and gain more knowledge from the educational institution issuing the degree that will look great on your resume. This will ensure that you graduate on schedule while saving expenses.

❏ **AI:** _____

There are work programs that will pay for all or part of your college. Many companies, government agencies, and military services pay for tuition and other school expenses, including books, registration and other miscellaneous fees. Paid time off to attend classes and for study time may also be available. Ask if the study time can be onsite (library, cafeteria, or conference room) to eliminate the perception that you are at the beach surfing. Make the time and day(s) the same each week and communicate this to coworkers by marking it viewable (not private) on your online work calendar.

❏  AI: _____

After graduating from undergraduate studies, I was offered a job at AT&T Bell Laboratories in Colorado. However, I was required to get my master's degree, or the offer would be withdrawn. At the same time, I received an assistant professor position at Texas A&M University. Work-study program like this pay you a stipend while you receive a free education. My decision was to get into the workforce making real money and accepted the position at AT&T. They had a graduate program

through which selected new hires could work for AT&T during the summer and attend college during the normal school year.

Ralphie V, the CU Buffalo mascot, University of Colorado, Glenn J. Asakawa

These programs are still available in the workforce today. There may be a cap on the amount of total money and/or the amount available to you each year, and you may have to pay first. To get reimbursed for a class, you may need to receive a grade of 3.0 (B) or higher. In addition, there may be a requirement of how long you have to stay with the company after receiving the money. This can be one to two years or more. Any less time with the employer, and the funds need to be returned.

Look aggressively for scholarships and financial aid for college. "Unclaimed scholarships are another great method for funding school. There is more than four billion dollars in unclaimed scholarship money every year. These scholarships are not academic or athletic scholarships either, but are small- to medium-sized dollar amounts from organizations like community clubs."[69] To search for unclaimed scholarships, go to Financial Aid Finder at *www.financialaidfinder.com/scholarships/unclaimed-scholarships-reality*.

❑ **AI:** _____

Along with academic, athletic, and activities scholarships, as well as those for minorities, women, and people with disabilities. There are art, fashion, musician, and acting scholarships too. If there is a profession, vocation, or trade you are interested in, there is probably a grant or low interest loan available. For scholarship lists, services, and software tools, enter this data in your web browser search engine: "lists scholarships online software programs free." Research the results, as well as the "Sponsored Links" or "Ads." Also try Financial Aid Finder's free scholarship search at *www.financialaidfinder.com/scholarships/find-a-scholarship*.

❑ **AI:** _____

There are employers, government agencies, and nonprofit organizations that provide assistance for people to train for and receive their high school General Educational Development (GED).

## GI Bill

**Thanks to the Troops**: We should always salute all the men and women that serve and protect us. Walk up to them, shake their hand, and thank them for their sacrifice wherever they are in uniform like at the airport, grocery store, and sporting events. Offer to buy them lunch or a drink to show them your appreciation for their sacrifice.[80]

The federal government funds education for members of the U.S. Armed Forces. Service members, please get the most out of **"The GI Bill"** by Military.com:[70]

---

[80]  Do not let your political view or position on the wars in the Middle East get in the way of supporting the troops that make sacrifices and take risks to protect us.

- The Montgomery GI Bill is the centerpiece of military education benefits. Active-duty service members and veterans can receive a monthly benefit valued at nearly $40,000. This tax-free benefit can be used for tuition, books, fees, and living expenses while earning a degree or certification (including undergraduate and graduate degrees) or attending trade school.
- It can also be used to pay for independent study programs, required continuing education units, licensing, apprenticeship, and on-the-job training programs.
- Many veterans who served after September 11, 2001, will get full tuition and fees, a new monthly housing stipend, and a $1,000 a year stipend for books and supplies. Also gives Guard and Reserve members who have been activated for more than ninety days since September 11, 2001, access to the same GI Bill benefits.

For more details on the GI Bill and other Veteran benefits, go to *www. gibill.va.gov*. For U.S. Armed Forces news and technology updates, sign up for Military.com newsletter at *www.Military.com*.

❏ **AI:** _____

**Military College Fund:** When signing up for the armed forces, request the college fund incentive. This is targeted for new recruits with Military Occupational Specialties, which are in high demand or unique skills. The college fund is in addition to the GI Bill. I could only verify that the Army and Navy participate in this program.

❏ **AI:** _____

## Your Knowledge and Awareness

**Knowledge Is Power!** We all have different achievements, goals, dreams. You own your definition of wealthy. With the proper knowledge you can realize wealth no matter your income, amount of debt, and educational background.

Now back to Robert Kiyosaki's Cashflow 101 game. In playing you realize it is typically easier to get out of the rat race if your randomly chosen occupation has a lower income with less expenses. For example, a truck driver or teacher has to do fewer deals to accumulate more passive income than expenses as compared to a doctor or lawyer with higher expenses. Since the doctor and lawyer incomes do not support reducing debts, more deals will need to be completed, and it will take a little longer to get out of the rat race. The key strategies in this book illustrate how people with less income need to generate more business revenue and people with higher income need to reduce those expenses.

I encourage you to have your kids play this board game. Anybody ten or older should play it. Even seven- and eight-year-olds will enjoy and comprehend the original 101 version over the Cashflow for Kids. They will learn more if you play the game with them. Have the youngest be the banker . . . and be patient and coach him/her. There is also an e-game software version of Cashflow 101 that is cheaper than the board game. I prefer the board game because of the interaction among the players. Upgrade board and videogames to those that teach financial literacy, business ownership, or acquisition strategy.

❏  AI: _____

**Always Growing:** Multitask with respect and do not apologize for making the most of <u>your</u> time. This is the key to being productive. Multitasking is a trait of millionaires. You need to be in that mindset. Gain knowledge by listening to financial independence, business management, business development, motivational, and other self-help CDs/MP3s while doing other activities.

Transform listening to more self-improvement and business development CDs or MP3 recordings. Listen to less music and talk radio. Your vehicle will be a classroom on wheels, especially for carpooling to work and road trips. As pointed out before, riding public transportation is the perfect opportunity to listen to your electronic developmental material.

❏  AI: _____

**Reduce Your Drama and Anxiety:** As stated before, it is not always about you. Think ahead about how your behavior might have a negative effect on the people that surround you. Also eliminate how other people's drama affects you. It is also not always about them either. A balanced life is imperative to being in harmony. Insulate yourself from their ability to influence your set schedule and goals. If you know people that are causing you grief and aggravation, you may need to release them from your life. Finally, look deep inside yourself to see why you allow them to get any control of your life. Check out the book *The Recovering Drama Queen* by Kathy Shepard.

Reducing drama will also reduce your stress and anxiety levels while increasing your motivation. Less drama will allow your extra found energy and time to be focused on income and wealth-producing activities. Yes, it will take enhancing and strategically using your self-discipline, self-control, self-awareness, self-esteem, and self-confidence. Release your egotistical feelings of greed, selfishness, and anger while maintaining your pride to earn a better life. Receive positive frequencies and opportunities.

Put a positive spin on any situation:

- "I am happy to have twenty-five dollars in my pocket instead of twenty-four."
- "I can do a light fifteen-minute workout, which is better than ten minutes or no workout at all."
- "I lost one pound last week, which is better than none."
- "I am glad to be employed, than collecting unemployment."

Confidence is the key to attracting positive people. It is also important for people to accept who you are and what you believe in. Be passionate and confident in redirecting your limited money, energy, and time to create unlimited potential as an entrepreneur.

## Your Body and Fitness

Exercise is the key to great health. Increased air flow, blood flow, overall circulation, and removes many toxins from your system. "As you increase your body's ability to do more demanding things, you'll find your normal activities much more comfortable and pleasant. You will have more afternoon energy. The fatigue you've felt that's made you 'too tired' to exercise in the past will be replaced by an energy that will invigorate everything you do."[71]

Use your gut, little pouch, love handles, saggy butt, and/or flabby arms to motivate you to workout. Utilize your weight, cardio, and strength goals to remain consistent with your exercise routine. Perform a balanced exercise program with strength and cardiovascular training three to five times a week. Also practice at least one outdoor exercise per week like jogging, walking, biking, hiking, or playing a sport.

❑ **AI:** _____

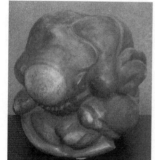

**"Your body is your temple."** Taking care of your physical body and health are very important elements of being a producer. We sometimes seek acceptance from external forces when really all we need to do is look inward to get approval from ourselves. Maintaining a healthy body is a vital trait, which improves your mood.

Inward facing soul meditation pose statue

## Working Out at Home

Working out at home also saves a lot of time and money. Relieve the stress and recoup the energy of having to travel to the gym. Push-ups, sit-ups, and stretching do not require any equipment.

## Simple Exercise Aids

You can enhance your exercise program by adding simple tools mentioned before like the **Bodyrev Perfect Pushup** and **AB Slide**™ roller. Bodyrev Perfect Pushup tool enables full extension and different angle exercises to work multiple muscle groups. Bodyrev also has chin-up and dips bars. I prefer the AB Slide over AB Force for home use because I get a better workout due to its four larger wheels giving more stability that provide active resistance creating a more strenuous workout. The AB Force is less than half the size, weight, and price of the AB Slide and is best for traveling. Like the AB Force, going back and forth works the core stomach muscles, also going side to side tones the left and right obliques. To get a tougher workout, roll the AB Slide twelve inches on the floor before starting the exercise to wind the spring up for extra resistance.

❏ **AI:** _____

**No Pain, No Gain!** Everybody should own a set of **dumbbells**. Even just a few dumbbells will be beneficial. If you have a strong grip, to save money and space, combine smaller dumbbells to make larger weights. My set is from one to seventy-five pounds. You can do so many strength-building exercises with just dumbbells and for an extra bonus get a curl bar with free weights.[81] They are excellent investments that do not cost much and will last decades if properly maintained and kept dry. You can purchase these at any household department stores like Costco, Kmart, Target, and Wal-Mart. For great deals, go to fitness stores that sell gym equipment or garage sales. Fitness centers will also sell their older equipment and weights that are being upgraded at a heavy discount.

❏ **AI:** _____

👍 If you are really busy, focus on toning areas that people see the most like biceps, lats, chest, and forearms for men; and triceps, shoulders, butt, and calves for ladies. Also play to your strengths by targeting muscles that build up easier, such as your shoulders, stomach, and legs. This is because you can spend less time to get great results. My chest and back muscles respond the best, and these are what half of my exercises target.

👍 There is no excuse for not having enough space to work out. Reorganize

Me in my home gym

Photo by Angyl Nihthasu

---

81    For examples of exercises, refer to the *Encyclopedia of Modern Bodybuilding* by Arnold Schwarzenegger with Bill Dobbins.

your home to accommodate your fitness goals. This needs to be a high priority. If a table or couch needs to be moved several times a week, do it. A couple of square feet is enough to work out with dumbbells. You can do most dumbbell exercises sitting in the kitchen chair and can store the weights under the bed. You can jog in place in the living room or stretch on the balcony. You only need a small area to roll out a yoga mat. Another option is to practice some exercises and sit-ups in your bed (and I don't mean the Kama Sutra with your partner, though I'm sure that burns calories too!). Use some of the exercise equipment I suggested to get a great workout using very little space. If a common area in an apartment or condominium is the only space available to you, use it.

## Technology Exercise Aids

✎ Nintendo Wii has an innovative fitness training programs called **Wii *Fit*™** which is an at home trainer that personalizes your exercise routine. This software tracks calories burned and charts your fitness goals progress. There are programs for gaining strength, doing aerobics, and practicing yoga. The Balance Board™ accessory is required because it reads your real-life movements and brings them to life on the television screen. Xbox 360 Kinect and PlayStation 3 also offer similar interactive fitness programs.

Cable and satellite providers will have a **fitness channel** like FitTV that have a wide variety of programming. These providers also provide free **on-demand fitness programs** that cover all major exercise routines. For TV workouts, continue to practice during the commercial and advertisement breaks. For a quick thirty-minute workout, I enjoy FitTV's Namaste Yoga practice.

❏ **AI:** _____

Plan your home workouts around financial newscasts or your favorite programs. Watch these related shows when you are building muscle mass or burning calories. When you are pumping iron, watch a football game, *World's Strongest Man*™, or Mixed Martial Arts (MMA). When riding a stationary bike or jogging on the treadmill, watch a soccer game, tennis match, or bicycle race.

**PIP**: Let's utilize television technology to the MAX. Utilize the picture-in-picture (PIP) feature to watch an on-demand class, DVD, or VCR tape workout exercise while watching a television show simultaneously. This adds a healthy element into your regular TV schedule. Try doing yoga in one window and watch a soothing nature program in the other window. Another bonus is that multiple people can utilize the TV screen at the same time.

❑ **AI:** _____

## Going to the Gym

**The Burn!** Consider canceling your health club membership if you aren't using it. This seems to be a contradiction to being healthy. Utilizing the gym health benefits are cheaper than a major medical bill. First, start going to the fitness center again this week. Don't cancel your gym membership until you evaluate how much you use the health club. Are you getting the most out of it? What was the reason you joined? These should be simple answers that gets you motivated. If not, it is time to consider canceling your membership.

❑ **AI:** _____

👍 Check for membership hidden usage fees. Are you paying for extra benefits at exclusive clubs that you do not use like the pool, basketball courts, and a private locker? Try modifying the contract to exclude these items. Some new offers have a "pay-as-you-go option" rather than monthly fees with multiyear contract terms. This can be great for people that are not as consistent in their routines.

Do not waste money by prolonging the evaluation process. Never say, "It is not real money." Do not let the fitness center or athletic club take the money every month and you end up wasting thousands of dollars before canceling the membership. If you are not going to utilize your membership, cancel it, but first have a replacement plan and investigate less expensive options. Are you going to join a cheaper gym, work out at home, work out at your local recreation center, jog in the park, or row on the river? Have them waive any cancellation fees.

❑ **AI:** _____

👍 If joining a gym for the first time, it may be wise to get a trainer or a really fit friend for the first couple of sessions. Always bring business cards to the gym when working out, to the field when playing a game, and when jogging. Make it a goal to give out at least two cards per workout, game, run, and walk.

Use a hand towel to wipe down machines before and after using them. This will leave them clean for the next person and will extend the equipment's life. Also so you do not train on somebody else's sweat, because that can be downright nasty! Another benefit is that people will respect your thoughtfulness and see you as an authority. This is practice for being a leader. Throw the used towels in the basket and don't leave them on the floor or tossed on the equipment. If a person on the treadmill is running hard and does not have a towel, offer one. Even nicer is to offer a cup of water too.

## Building Your Body with Yoga

**Oma:** United HealthCare® says, "Yoga isn't just about relaxation and meditation. This exercise will not only help you reduce anxiety, it will improve strength and flexibility and increase muscle tone and circulation. If you need some time to relax but don't want to skip a workout, do yoga and get both at the same time."[72] Yoga is a great exercise and as previously mentioned is also a way of life that touches your wellness, mind, and soul.

Here are more **fitness benefits of practicing yoga**:

1. Flexibility: Improved flexibility is one of the first and most obvious benefits of yoga. Asanas yoga poses safely stretch your muscles. Yoga increases the range of motion in joints and increase lubrication in the joints.
2. Strength: Strong muscles protect us from conditions like arthritis and back pain. Yoga improves muscle tone. Weight-bearing exercise strengthens bones and helps ward off osteoporosis and may help keep calcium in the bones.
3. Posture: With increased flexibility and strength comes better posture. Most standing and sitting poses develop core strength. With strong abdominals, you're more likely to sit up straight and stand "tall."

4. Breathing: Deep mindful breathing often improves lung capacity. There are yoga exercises that emphasize deepening and lengthening your breath. This stimulates the relaxation response to help your circulation while improving sports performance, endurance, and aerobic conditioning.

5. Heart: Yoga can lower blood pressure and slow the heart rate. A slower heart rate can benefit people with hypertension, heart disease, and stroke. Yoga exercises that get your heart rate up improve cardiovascular conditioning and can lower your risk of heart attack.

**"Ya' man, relax don't worry."** The only way to be certain that you will benefit from yoga is to try it for yourself. Guys, don't be afraid. Start off at an introductory class or with a beginner DVD with instructions. As a beginner, to understand the history, philosophy, and poses, refer to Mara Carrico's *The Wisdom of the Yoga Journal's Yoga Basics*. At a class, let the yoga instructor (yogi) know you are a beginner and would appreciate any extra instructions and advice as s/he see fit. Use props when necessary.

❏ **AI:** _____

Once you get good at yoga or have gone to a few classes, try practicing at home to save money and time. I have been practicing yoga for over a dozen years and started with a series of seven practice tapes from Yoga Journal. My favorite videos are Living Arts *Yoga for Flexibility, Yoga for Strength, Yoga for Energy*, and *Power Yoga—The Complete Workout*. For more advanced practices, check out Shiva Rea. You can find all of these videos at *www.Gaiam.com*. Yes, I said "tapes" which all

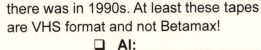

there was in 1990s. At least these tapes are VHS format and not Betamax!

❏ **AI:** _____

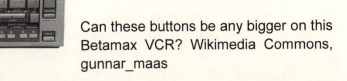

Can these buttons be any bigger on this Betamax VCR? Wikimedia Commons, gunnar_maas

As just mentioned, there are great on-demand practice sessions from the cable and satellite providers, but these exercise classes tend to be more advanced so be prepared. Pilates is also a terrific exercise to do at home or the gym.

❏ **AI:** _____

## Other Forms of Exercise

Go online to find free running clubs. Verify that there is more exercise time than time wasted gathering. Search for free introductory classes for cardio boot camps, strength training, and yoga. Find clubs and classes that are inexpensive or running a promotion. Another option is to trade a service of equal value.

❏ **AI:** _____

Playing recreational sports are excellent and fun form of exercise. Join a league that utilizes public parks or schools so the expense is low. Get a sponsor to subsidize the uniforms and registration fees.

❏ **AI:** _____

**"Dance, Dance, Dance."** Dancing is a fun way to exercise. This can tone certain muscles, burn calories, and raise the heart rate. Great music to dance to includes African, Zumba, capoeira, samba, salsa, tango, house, pole, hip hop, and slam dancing. As beneficial as it is, though, dance should *not* be your *only* source of exercise.

Pull doors open. Do not use automatic sliding doors or door openers designed for people with disabilities. It is not cute or clever, just lazy, and you lose the connection opportunity to hold the door open for somebody else. Also, don't get slowed down being stuck with the slower pace of revolving doors. As previously mentioned, take the stairs and walk faster whenever possible. Train your mind to get the most out of your body for simple everyday activities, and others will notice. Of course, long passionate lovemaking is a pleasurable method of burning calories.

## Sleep, Sleep, Sleep

👍 Make sure you are getting enough rest and sleep, but not too much. This is critical for your mind and body to recover. Exercise can be a simple solution to episodes of insomnia and irregular sleep patterns. Working out regularly improves sleep quality by producing deeper sleep:

- Heightens your brain activity by increasing the amount of oxygen, which reduces stress.
- Eases the buildup of muscular tension and dissipates lactic acid.
- Stimulates your nervous system and release of *epinephrine*, a hormone that creates a sense of happiness and excitement.
- Increases deep sleep pattern as the brain compensates for physical stress.

Twenty to thirty minutes of modest exercise three or five times a week results in better sleep at night and more energy during the day. While more energetic exercise during the day and mild exercise before bedtime will help you fall asleep faster and stay asleep longer.

❑  **AI:** _____

**Like an Elephant**: Power naps are great when you need a natural energy burst. "Sleep researchers say that a nap of twenty minutes or less is ideal because you arise without having engaged in REM (rapid eye movement, a deeper stage of sleep) sleep and you feel refreshed."[73] When you are getting up early and staying up later to increase your income and wealth, naps may be your savior. I like to call these "elephant naps." When was the last time you saw an elephant sleeping? Never?

Exactly! An elephant's power nap lasts about thirty minutes and they sleep no more than four hours a day. That's a lot compared to giraffes that only get five-minute naps and sleep only thirty minutes in a twenty-four-hour period.

ZZZZ!, Wikimedia Commons, Fruggo

## Your Health and Wellness

Health, wealth, and happiness have an integral and synergistic relationship. My message is to be proactive, not reactive, in all aspects of your life. This includes preemptive and preventative care for your health. You are totally responsible for this success or failure. Being healthy will allow you to manage your energy level to match the effort required to meet your goals.

Do not get discouraged if you are not in good shape and have some bad habits. Today is a new day, and the time to change is now, even if you choose to work on only the minimal areas of concern first. Later you will include other areas to be addressed.

## Healthy Habits

Good health is priceless! Living healthy will save you money on medical bills and time wasted lying sick in bed. The key is that you will be able to find new work or work harder to produce extra income and be more productive on your business to create profits. Cut back or stop drinking alcohol, soda, and coffee, eating fast food, and smoking, especially if it is causing health or behavioral problems. Yes, this may be common sense, but we all need reminders. Use working out and spending time with the family as healthy alternatives.

"Exercise boosts detoxification by improving the way tissues use oxygen and dispose of waste products, eliminating waste products in sweat, making weight control easier and combating stress. Yoga is a gentle exercise that can aid the discharge of waste. Relaxation allows you to release both mental and physical tension."[74]

Make sure everybody in your family has medical insurance! Medical bills are the most common reason why people file bankruptcy. Also investigate getting dental and vision care insurance. Always plan in advance to pay cash for doctor, chiropractor, therapist, dentist, optometrist, and specialists. Use the emergency fund for catastrophic medical problems only and not for regular visits or to pay insurance premiums.

❏ **AI:** _____

Investigate long-term disability, dismemberment, and accidental death insurance. Even if your employer provides these types of insurance, you may want to get individual supplement coverage. Depending on your situation, it may be cheaper and a better fit than life insurance. "Think to buy renewable term-life insurance. Do not buy whole-life insurance or any of the 200 other things called universal life, life plus, or so on. With renewable term-life, you pay a small premium each year in exchange for pure insurance coverage. You can cancel the policy at any time. Whole-life, on the other hand, has an insurance component and an investment component. If you want to cancel, you may face a substantial penalty, depending on the terms of your contract."[75] **Warning!**: Whole-life insurance accounts typically are <u>not</u> insured by Federal Deposit Insurance Company (FDIC) or any federal government agency.

❑ **AI**: _____


Parents should speak to their children and teenagers about drugs. For guidance, refer to The Partnership for a Drug-Free America with great information at _www.DrugFree.org_. Stop smoking in the vehicle and at home with your children present or will be, no matter how old they are. Don't ever self-medicate, smoke marijuana, or get drunk around your children.

❑ **AI**: _____


## Healthy Foods

Watch what you eat and drink. I am not saying you have to give everything up. Start with a small reduction or change of 10 to 15 percent. Replace the word "perfect" with "progress."


### Foods to Eat

Buy food with more nutritional value, giving you more energy and fuel for the same price. Buy cereal and snacks high in fiber and protein with less artificial flavoring, sugar, and other empty calories. For example, buy whole-wheat and multi-grain bread versus white bread and donuts. Eat brown rice and beans; these have a lot of vitamins, nutrients, and fiber. Another example is eating an apple or banana versus a Pop Tart or chocolate cake. Read the nutrition facts and ingredients to determine the dietary value.

❑ **AI:** _____

👍 Try frozen yogurt or sherbet instead of ice cream. Convert food items with regular sugar to light items with less or no sugar. It will be just as tasty with less carbohydrates. Replace processed white sugar with pure natural brown sugar which is unprocessed from sugar cane or beets. Do not use artificial sweeteners like saccharin.[82] Substitute instead with honey, maple syrup, or stevia.

**Go Organic:** Eating fresh and raw produce is the best way to obtain daily nutrients. However, the pesticides used on many crops remains a major health concern. By choosing organic foods, you can reap the health benefits of fruits, vegetables, meat, poultry, and fish without exposing yourself to potentially harmful chemicals.

❑ **AI:** _____

Buy store-brand items at major health food stores like Whole Foods or Trader Joe's. These store-brand products at health food stores are organic, packaged recycled material, and cheaper than their large grocery store competitors. Whole Foods has great seafood, vegetables, deli, and sake (rice wine) selections. Trader Joe's offers great frozen food, cereal, and European beer selections, too.

❑ **AI:** _____

👍 Most fast-food restaurants have healthy options like salads, fruit, sandwiches, and vegetarian menu items. It is your responsibility to customize your order to make it healthier by asking for no salt, no MSG,

---

[82] "Many studies have since been performed on saccharin, some showing a correlation between saccharin consumption and increased frequency of cancer in rats (especially bladder cancer) and others finding no such correlation. No study has ever shown a clear causal relationship between saccharin consumption and health risks in humans at normal doses, though some studies have shown a correlation between consumption and cancer incidence." (Wikipedia, *www.en.wikipedia.org/wiki/Saccharin*, April 29, 2011)

to hold the mayo, etc. Order the baked or open flame-grilled options over fried.

United HealthCare states, "Teach your children about good nutrition by playing the MyPyramid Blast Off game at *www.mypyramid.gov/kids/ kids_game.html*. Your youngster can launch his or her own rocket into space by discovering how to eat well and be active. The interactive game is part of a program provided by the U.S. federal government."[76]

❏ **AI:** _____

**Foods to Avoid**

**Running on Empty**: Our reasons why we buy **processed foods** can include habit, taste, and convenience. Avoid consuming empty calories loaded with sugar and sodium. Many processed foods have calories that contain very little protein, minerals, and vitamins for their incredibly high price tag. Resist the temptation. Buy less processed food and more grandmamma-style meals with nutritional value. Save money by buying fresh produce, meats, poultry, and fish to be cooked at home. It is also much healthier for you!

👍 "Eating foods that contain **saturated fats** raises the level of cholesterol in your blood. High levels of blood cholesterol increase your risk of heart disease and stroke. Be aware, too, that many foods high in saturated fats are also high in cholesterol, which raises your blood cholesterol even higher. Saturated fats occur naturally in many foods. The majority come mainly from animal sources, including meat and dairy products. Examples are fatty beef, lamb, pork, poultry with skin, beef fat, lard and cream, butter, cheese and other dairy products made from whole or reduced-fat (2 percent) milk. These foods also contain dietary cholesterol."[77]

"In addition, many baked goods and **fried foods** can contain high levels of saturated fats. Some plant foods, such as palm oil, palm kernel oil and coconut oil, also contain primarily saturated fats, but do not contain cholesterol. The American Heart Association recommends limiting the amount of saturated fats you eat to less than 7 percent of total daily calories. That means, for example, if you need about 2,000 calories a day, no more than 140 of them should come from saturated fats. That's about sixteen grams of saturated fats a day. Find out your personal daily fat limits at *www.myfatstranslator.com*."[78]

❑ **AI:** _____

Do not eat foods that contain **steroids**, **hormones**, **antibiotics**, or **additives**. Instead, eat food derived from animals that are organically fed and humanely raised, handled, and slaughtered. Favor animals that are raised cage free, free range, and in natural environment. Consume foods that are naturally flavored and seasoned, not artificially flavored or colored.

❑ **AI:** _____

To remind you what <u>not</u> to consumer, put a list of calories of your favorite alcohol beverages and unhealthy foods on your fridge.

❑ **AI:** _____

## Healthy Drinks

### Beverages to Drink

**Drink More Water:** "Drink at least six to eight glasses of water each day and more in warm weather or if you are exercising or sweating for any reason. Alcohol and drinks that contain caffeine, such as tea (including green and black green herbal teas), coffee, and cola, do <u>not</u> count as the same volume of water, because they increase the loss of water from the body in urine."[79]

❑ **AI:** _____

The following are "**10 Reasons to Drink More Water**" by Dr. Christina Scott-Moncrieff:[80]

1. Flush out your kidneys and liver, enabling them to remove unwanted waste.
2. Keeps energy levels up: a 2 percent loss of water surrounding the cells of the body can lead to a loss of energy by up to 20 percent.
3. Reduce the risk of developing gallstones and kidney stones.

4.  Relieve constipation.
5.  Reduce the risk of developing a headache.
6.  Make your immune system work effectively.
7.  Keep your brain active: dehydration may contribute to memory loss and senility.
8.  Reduce the feeling of hunger: try water as a snack!
9.  Keep your skin looking good and feeling soft.
10. Control the temperature of the body and eliminate toxins by sweating.

Choose **100 percent natural juices** over soda and **herbal tea** over coffee.

❑ **AI:** _____

## Beverages to Avoid

Drink less and less **coffee**. Brew your own store-brand organic coffee at home and take it to work with you or cut off the daily coffee fix altogether. If you must have coffee, try switching to decaf. "Caffeine increases the production of urine, which may result in the loss of various minerals and vitamins. Symptoms from caffeine include anxiety, panic attacks, insomnia, and in children hyperactivity."[81] Coffee can also darken your teeth and prevent you from getting the required restful sleep.

❑ **AI:** _____

"You may or may not be aware that coffee is one of the leading inhibitors of weight loss. Many studies confirm that your coffee intake may be preventing you from finding weight loss or success due to both psychological and physiological reasons. This is true of both regular and decaffeinated coffee. Perhaps this is why popular weight loss programs, including Jenny Craig™, Physician's Weight Loss™, Weight Watchers™, and The Zone™ all suggest you should limit your coffee intake."[82]

Refrain from buying the **pricy Danish** with your cappuccino. While dining out, pass on the server's coffee and dessert offer. Opt for a salad or fruit instead. Baking your own muffins, cakes, rolls, and pastries from scratch, even cooking from a box (read ingredients for healthy choices), will save money.

❏ **AI:** _____

"Calories from **alcohol** are not entirely 'empty.' Some wines contain Vitamin C, and beer contains B Vitamins. However, the amount of these nutrients is tiny when compared to the number of calories that alcohol provides. Worse still, calories derived from alcohol tend to be transformed into fat that is stored in fatty tissue and in the liver. A nutritionally sound diet contains a good balance of carbohydrates, proteins, and fats, sufficient fiber, and a plentiful supply of minerals and vitamins."[83] If you must drink wine or beer, consume less and try organic bands.

❏ **AI:** _____

**Say "No" to Soda!:** Talk about no nutritional value! Soda has nearly zero. What is the point or excuse? Kids often say, "Well, I am used to it" or "I like the taste," but we are adults and can change. Some of the health risks with soda are obesity, tooth decay, week bones, Osteoporosis, kidney stones, chemicals, and harmful additives. For more details, see an article by Autumn Conley Bittick, "Soda: The Candy We Drink: The Many Risks of Our Dependence on Soft Drinks."

❏ **AI:** _____

Absolutely NO **energy drinks**. It is more important to get a natural energy boost through deep sleep and strenuous exercise than always relying on coffee or an energy drink to keep you alert.

❏ **AI:** _____

☝ If you need assistance in improving your diet, seek consultation from a certified nutritionist.

## Stop Smoking

### Cigarettes

"Most cigarette ingredients can cause long-lasting harm to most of your bodily organs and provide the best reasons to quit smoking. If you take a few moments to read this quit-smoking portal (*www.QuitSmokingSupport.com*), you'll encounter reason after reason to quit

smoking from addiction to odor to long-lasting ill health effects such as cancer, oxygen deprivation, asthma, irritations, infections, and fetus impairment."[84]

Original painting by Montgomery Flagg flickr from Yahoo!, posted by krystalweaver

"Tobacco smoke contains more than [**5,000**] **chemicals**, of which over fifty are known to cause cancer. In addition, smoking is a major cause of heart disease. You may already know this, yet people continue to smoke. This is because smoking is addictive. Like sugar, smoking can enhance the production of the naturally occurring chemicals in the brain that calm mood and decrease sensitivity to pain, both physical and emotional."[85]

"The adverse health effects from cigarette smoking account for an estimated **443,000 deaths**, or nearly one of every five deaths, each year in the United States. More deaths are caused each year by tobacco use than by all deaths from Human Immunodeficiency Virus (HIV), illegal drug use, alcohol use, motor vehicle injuries, suicides, and murders combined."[86] "Cigarettes take another victim every six and a half seconds."[87]

Smoking can age your skin and darken and yellow your teeth. Ladies, isn't that enough reason to stop?!?!? Date and hang out with nonsmokers to help you quit smoking. They will support you while not acting as a bad influence. Jogging, walking, or biking will determine whether or not you have reduced lung capacity from smoking. These are good activities that will assist in the transition.

❑ **AI:** _____

Besides the fact that smoking causes damage to your health, it is a very expensive habit! Cigarettes in New York City have topped more than eleven dollars a pack. In 2010, the average pack of cigarettes cost over five dollars. Smoking a pack of cigarettes at five dollars a day costs $1,825 dollars a year, depending on the brand and taxes. And, that's not counting the resulting increase for life insurance and healthcare costs. If you have no willpower, at least consider switching to a generic brand <u>with</u> filters and save yourself over $365 to $730 a year if smoking one pack a day in the U.S.

❑ **AI:** _____

Cutting back to only half a pack a day for a five-dollar pack of cigarettes will save $912.50 a year. If both you and your partner-in-crime cut back by a whole pack a day, you will save $3,650 annually or two packs a day, the yearly savings are $7,300. This is a lot of money you could use to pay off your bad debt, build up retirement, send children to college, and fund a business or two. Even cutting back by a pack per week will fund your kitty.

I grew up in a smoking family and understand how hard it is to quit. I witnessed firsthand the negative health effects to the smokers and all of us around them. Parents, if you smoke, there is an increased chance that your children will smoke, and there is the health danger of secondhand smoke. "Secondhand smoke causes asthma,[83] which is a disease that cannot be cured."[88] At all times, avoid secondhand smoke. "Even if you don't smoke, your health can be damaged by the passive inhalation of tobacco smoke. Nonsmokers are more sensitive to smoke than regular smokers, and environmental smoke has been shown to have a higher concentration of some toxic chemicals. Smokers can also be motivated to give it up to prevent a child or loved one from suffering the ill effects of passive smoking."[89] To repeat the message, don't smoke in the house or car if children are present or will be later.

❑ **AI:** _____

"The complete **list of chemicals added to cigarettes** is too long to list here.[84] Here are some examples that will surprise you:"[90]

1. Ammonia: <u>Household cleaner</u>
2. Angelica root extract: Known to <u>cause cancer</u> in animals
3. Arsenic: Used in <u>rat poisons</u>
4. Benzene: Linked to <u>leukemia</u>

---

83  Which I have.

84  The list of 599, out of over 5,000, ingredients is in *Transforming from Consumer to Producer in 90 Days Tutorial Workbook*. A list of chewing tobacco ingredients is also in the tutorial workbook.

5. Benzene: Used in making <u>dyes, synthetic rubber</u>
6. Butane Gas: Used in <u>lighter fluid</u>
7. Cadmium: Linked to <u>lung and prostate cancer</u>
8. Cadmium: Used in <u>batteries</u>
9. Carbon Monoxide: <u>Poisonous gas</u>
10. Common additives include yeast, wine, <u>caffeine</u>, beeswax, and chocolate
11. Cyanide: Deadly <u>poison</u>
12. DDT: A banned <u>insecticide</u>
13. Ethyl Furoate: Causes <u>liver damage</u> in animals
14. Formaldehyde: Linked to <u>lung cancer</u>
15. Formaldehyde: Used to <u>preserve dead specimens</u>
16. Fungicides and pesticides: Cause many types of <u>cancers and birth defects</u>
17. Lead: <u>Poisonous</u> in high doses
18. Maltitol: <u>Sweetener</u> for diabetics
19. Methoprene: <u>Insecticide</u>
20. Methyl Isocyanate: Its accidental release <u>killed 2,000 people in Bhopal</u>, India in 1984
21. Napthalene: Ingredient in <u>mothballs</u>
22. Nickel: Causes increased susceptibility to <u>lung infections</u>
23. Polonium: Cancer-causing <u>radioactive</u> element

**Cigars** and **pipes** have numerous negative health consequences too. The Surgeon General's report concluded that cigar and pipe smokers have a 2 to 4.3 times greater risk of lung cancer than nonsmokers. These smokers' risks include heart disease, chronic lung disease, and cancer of the lip, tongue, and throat, so STOP!

❏ **AI:** _____

## Smokeless Tobacco

**"Don't be a dip sh\*t."** Men, STOP chewing tobacco! This is insane! There are a growing number of dippers in the military and high school, due to the growing bans on cigarette smoking in public and private areas. We need to reverse this nasty smokeless tobacco trend. Peer support is critical, but we also need leadership from commanding officers, parents, teachers, and Major League baseball players. High school and college coaches have a lot of influence over young adults and also have a responsibility to address this issue. Don't get fooled by the "Smokeless Tobacco" campaign trying to sell another <u>dangerous</u> product.

❑ **AI:** _____

"The Centers for Disease Control and Prevention (CDC) reports these **smokeless tobacco health risks**:"[91]

1. Contains <u>twenty-eight cancer-causing agents</u> (carcinogens).
2. Is a known cause of human cancer; it increases the risk of developing <u>cancer of the oral cavity</u> and <u>pancreas</u>.
3. Is also strongly associated with <u>leukoplakia</u>, a precancerous lesion of the soft tissue in the mouth that consists of a white patch or plaque that cannot be scraped off.
4. Is associated with <u>recession of the gums</u>, <u>gum disease</u>, and <u>tooth decay</u>.
5. Use during pregnancy increases the risks for <u>preeclampsia</u> (a condition that may include high blood pressure, fluid retention, and swelling), <u>premature birth</u>, and <u>low birth weight</u>.
6. Use by men causes <u>reduced sperm count</u> and <u>abnormal sperm cells</u>.
7. Use can lead to <u>nicotine addiction</u> and <u>dependence</u>.
8. Adolescents are <u>more likely to become cigarette smokers</u>.

For more information, consult Delta Dental Plans Association, "Spitting into the Wind: The Facts About Dip and Chew" at: <u>www.oralhealth.deltadental.com/22,DD49</u>.

## Quit Smoking Support Resources

**The EX**® is a whole new way to think about quitting smoking. They can help you learn how to do everything you currently do with a cigarette, only <u>without</u> one. The EX plan teaches smokers how to relearn life without cigarettes in three steps: 1) relearn habit, 2) addition, and 3) support. Whether this is your first try or your tenth, this plan can help you quit smoking. For the EX Smoker program, go to *www.BecomeAnEx. org*.

❏  **AI:** _____

**The Truth**: Have you seen these advertisements on TV telling "the truth" regarding the health risks and issues of smoking? These are progressive ads that purports that toughness is needed in this case to save lives. To learn the truth about the negative effects of smoking, go to *www.TheTruth.com* and share with a friend.

❏  **AI:** _____

Another resource is the Office of the Surgeon General Tobacco Cessation: You Can Quit Smoking Now! *Treating Tobacco Use and Dependence: 2008 Update* at *www.SurgeonGeneral.gov/tobacco*. Get tobacco health risks and ways to quit from the Centers for Disease Control and Prevention at *www.CDC.gov/tobacco*. Lastly, for more ideas to stop smoking, refer to Kevin Arthur Smith, *Quit Smoking While You're Smoking: An Easy and Practical Approach to Quitting* or *www. QuitSmokingWhileSmoking.com*.

## Your Family and Relationships

### Growing Yourself First

"The place to begin building any relationship is inside ourselves, inside our circle of influence, our own character. Treat everybody with the same set of principles."[92] You need to put yourself first. Of course, there are special circumstances where family and close friends come first, but we need to stop always putting our spouse and kids before us. If you lead and ultimately take care of yourself in retirement, they will understand. This means you are focused, not selfish. Stop putting off your retirement goals for your child's wants and future! Challenge your children to contribute to their own savings and college funds.

Should you really pay $30,000 or more for their wedding, a one-day event? That should never come up if your son or daughter understands what you are sacrificing at the turning point of your life. This expectation will disappear over generations with open communication. Your kids will follow your lead, especially if you lead by solid principles and strong character. I am teaching you how to grow beyond others' expectations. No more saying, "They do as I say, not as I do."

**"The results are in! You are the father!"** Pay for your children's medical expenses, educational needs, and child support, or I'll sic Judge Judy on you! If you are paying child support, you are still responsible for assisting in sending them to college, trade, or vocational school. This is your first priority. Don't be a deadbeat parent and look for excuses not to pay. Your children eat and get new clothes before you.

☝ Men, for parenting support, go to National Fatherhood Initiative™ at *www.Fatherhood.org*. Their mission is to improve the wellbeing of children by increasing the proportion of children growing up with involved, responsible, and committed fathers as role models.

Happily meet your obligations ahead of schedule. To reinforce what was previous stated, pay <u>your</u> child support, mortgages, loans, bills, taxes, and other commitments. You will be doing yourself a favor by keeping blemishes off of your credit report. We all make mistakes and unforeseen situations arise. Just admit them, ask for help, correct them, and move forward.

❑ **AI:** _____

## Creating Strong Relationships

**"Excuse my recent crankiness."** Don't project your problems on to others. "When we develop the confidence to be with people and know how to be involved with each other appropriately and evolve with our chosen partners, and never at the expense of filling a void through another person. We will keep the family together that you started when you met the right person. Come from empowerment instead of control. When couples as well as teams stay together, greater productions are the outcome."[93] Let go of controlling other people and every situation.

## BM: Before Marriage

You need to connect with other people in a deep and meaningful way. Work toward a more powerful and long-term supportive experience with people. This may be challenging to assist people experiencing difficulties but is worth the reward.

"Hey, every cheap bastard needs love. And while it's true that introducing yourself as a cheap bastard may not be the most successful way to get a date, being a cheap bastard shouldn't get in the way of having a great time. In fact, you might even score points by coming up with some original ideas for romantic liaisons."[94] Being cheap has worked for me because the money saved was wisely invested in my retirement plan, real estate, and giving back to the community. If people see you have a planned method to the madness, your loved ones will willingly help you implement it.

👍 Let's remove dating restrictions like height, skin, hair, eye color, impairment, etc. This will open up more opportunities to you, as well as more cultures and life experiences. Getting access to as many dates as possible will increase the odds of you meeting your perfect match. There are no ugly people on the outside, only on the inside.

**Beware of Fake People:** People with bad debt typically attract people that also have bad debt. They may also play the victim card and want to be saved, but at what cost to you? Don't be an enabler. This is also the case for short-sighted material items and fancy dinners with no real quantity of food. We should be analyzing that person's integrity, honesty, openness, values, love of family, love for others, and finances before swapping spit later that evening. How does he treat his mother? What is her relationship with her father? It really is significant. "Good manners make any man a pleasure to be with. Ask any woman," said Peter Mayle.

Address any money or trust issues before you get married. It can be that simple to judge people if you ask the right questions. Does s/he like to spend, save, or invest? How can you build a future on a false premise and lack of a solid foundation?

**Being Green is HOT:** It is vital to be environmentally conscious. Only date people that recycle, donate to charities, and give blood (if able). Be cautious of a person that does not enjoy walking, exercising, nature, and people.

👍 In general, do not date messy, sloppy, or totally disorganized people. Organized and productive people tend to be take pride in themselves and possessions. This may require changing your current partner. Do not move too fast, but start to have the internal conversation and then seek couples counseling. It is a turn-off for me when a woman's place is a mess. How about you? Also check out her or his auto. Do you want your kids to be messy and in disarray or productive and structured? People should treat their home as the ideal place to live and treat other people's homes with respect.

👍 Date and marry a person that can cook for themselves, neatly dress self, financially support self, and manage their household. Trust me, most guys can cook—even so-called mama's boys. If they can't, then reevaluate the relationship. Cooking or learning to cook a few dishes is not that difficult, and it is a vital part of being self-sufficient and cheap. At least make sure they have a few cookbooks so they can improve their culinary skills. This is a partnership where everybody contributes to household chores.

**55/45 Percent Dating Rule**: This is my dating rule for the relative percentage of amount to spend on each other (him/her):

- We start even at                                          50/50
- As a friend, it goes to                                   51/49
- As a male, it goes to                                     52/48
- If she makes more money, it stays at                      52/48
- If he makes more money, it goes to                        53/47
- Women spend more time getting ready,
  so it goes to                                             54/46
- Women's health issues of bearing
  children goes to                                          55/45

This percentage is measured on effort and in kind, not just the proportion of money. For example of measurements, cooking dinner is the same as taking someone out to a restaurant, and buying a shirt at a discount store is the same as buying a shirt at an expensive boutique. It's the thought that counts, right? I am happier eating at a Chinese kitchen, homeless shelter (after volunteering), or at home than at a fancy restaurant with a bunch of utensils and glasses that I have no idea in what order to use them. Do not use money as power to control the other person. Money does not have to get in the way of happiness and love.

Stay focused on that special person. There is no need for a prequel to having kids or marriage by getting a dog or another cat together. Long-term, this may complicate the household. You can bond without this aid, and having a pet is not real practice of how to care for children. Why not train a guide dog for an organization like Guiding Eyes for the Blind (_www.GuidingEyes.org_) or The Seeing Eye (_www.SeeingEye. org_)? How about volunteering as a Big Brother or Big Sister together (_www.BBBS.org_)? This is what producers do.

❏  **AI:** _____

## ES: Engagement Stage

**"Women, size is not everything."** A smaller wedding ring can be of higher quality and cheaper than one with many more carats. It can be elegant and unique without having to be expensive. How about buying an engagement ring at a pawn shop? Just make sure it can be returned if she says, "No" or changes her mind. Also make sure the original shop or another store can resize the ring. Better yet, if it's available, reset your mom's or grandmother's ring.

☝ Disregard the rule that the price of the engagement ring is equal to two or three months of the groom's pay, or at least make it one month's _net pay_ after retirement plan contributions, taxes, insurance, and other payroll deductions. Going further is to use the measurement of net income from the person making the least. How about changing the measurement of a month to a paycheck which is a huge saving since most people are paid bi-weekly or weekly. Buying stuff does not mean you love her, and the bigger the rock does not mean the bigger the commitment. Saying, "I love you" and showing it with actions are cheaper than expressing it with money. Money comes and goes, but love is forever. [Did I just say that? It's corny but true!]

👍 Ladies, if a man gives you an expensive ring, you do not have to accept it. You can say, "Yes, I will marry you, but this ring is too expensive, and our future will be built on love not extravagant items." Then you both go back to the store together to get a reasonably priced ring and invest the savings into your future, like a home, college degree, or retirement fund.

**"Why two rings?"** Are both an engagement and wedding ring really necessary? "Two rings" is a want! Isn't <u>one</u> enough? If not, why not four or five rings? For the sake of shaking things up, offer her one ring and not two and see what happens. Most of the world goes with the one or no ring. Why is the United States so different?

If this is not her first marriage, you do not have to outdo her last husband with a bigger diamond ring and wedding ceremony. That has no bearing on you. She's been looking for a better man, not a better ring. Stick with the plan to invest in your future together.

Even after wearing a huge ring for years, you can downgrade it now and invest the money earned back. If you have both an engagement and wedding ring, consider selling one.

❑ **AI:** _____

👍 Here is my marriage proposal plan: My bride-to-be will not get a

huge diamond to show our love, but a $10,000 mutual fund account.[85] This is a good idea, right! It will be presented by a HUGE check like when somebody wins a race, tournament, or the lottery.

Margaret and James Jones, Georgia Lottery

---

[85] Of course, there will be a written contract that the monies will be held in escrow until we are wed.

If you are divorced, sell the ring(s)! Invest this money. This goes for both men and women. It's never too late to do this.

❏ **AI:** _____

## D-Day: Affordable Wedding

As a couple, stay "engaged" on all of the expenses of the wedding. Don't let friends and family distract from your long-term investment goals by dividing and conquering one another to overspending on what others' perceive as necessary. No more guilt trips for the extra ten guests or elaborate flowers just because the parents will pay for it or the unplanned expense can be charged to a credit card.

🖐 Again, parents are not responsible to pay for their children's weddings. If the groom cannot afford it, maybe he is not ready to raise a family, and she needs to reconsider the cost of the wedding or the marriage altogether. Give the bride and groom money for their retirement plan, college fund, paying off debt, to start a business, improve a business, or for their first home. Men, the best WIN/WIN partnership is 55/45, and your bride is also proportionally responsible for paying for the wedding with cash and in kind effort, which will keep the expenses low. If you keep this responsibility even, you will have a nice, affordable wedding.

For more tips on how to saving on weddings, go to *Part III – Generating Savings, Chapter 8: Saving Your Energy, Focusing, Less on the Wedding.*

## AM: After Getting Married

Women are the strength of society and backbone of the family circle and shall be treated as such. Women (really all people) shall be treated as equal partners. If you see any injustice, you need to stand up and do something to correct it immediately.

Converting your spouse to being cheap is a necessary objective. Genuine change results from an inner willingness, and you cannot just impose your will on others. If a change runs completely against someone's character, the best you can hope for is a small degree of behavior modification:

- ❑ Establish joint financial goals that benefit all and provide motivation to change. At first require minor changes and later request major changes.
- ❑ Be in the lead by gathering evidence and facts to support your case. Create a budget illustrating income, necessities, expenses, and discretionary spending.
- 👍 When you discuss the issue, stick with the facts and do not get emotional. Show you care without labeling, accusing, blaming, or raising your voice to your significant other.
- 👍 This may take time, so be patient. Pushing too hard for change may cause your partner to reject your plans. Sometimes they will need to accept change by themselves without extra pressure and at a slower pace than you wish.

It is actually fun to watch their transformation. Even if there is only a minor change, it is still a change nevertheless. Leave a copy of my book lying around or buy your partner their own copy to complete their checklists and plans.

❑ **AI:** _____

## Running a Productive and Caring Home

You will need to take the initiative and drive many issues unless your family bought this book for you and they are all 100 percent committed to transforming. Do not use other people as an excuse for your indecisions or make flaccid agreements with other people's decisions. Rather than blame your spouse or kids, find alternate solutions that will benefit everybody.

"If I truly love another, I will obviously order my behavior in such a way as to contribute the utmost to his or her spiritual growth"[95] as well as economic, personal, and religious growth. "To a child, his or her parents are everything; they represent the world. They assume that the way his/her parents do things is the way things are done."[96]

## Managing the Finances

"When your spouse gets the raise you are expecting, don't raise your lifestyle with it. Save more! Invest more!"[97] Plan in advance where to <u>invest</u> raises and bonuses, but do not spend them. Remember that investing in stocks and mutual funds makes you a producer because you are investing in companies as a shareholder.

❑  **AI:** _____

👍 "Show your love frequently instead of something big once in a while. Culture has taught us that big gifts on certain occasions are the way to go, but those gifts are often put up on a pedestal, far out of proportion as a symbol of love. Instead of focusing on diamond earrings or an absurdly expensive set of golf clubs once every few years, look for smaller things that you can do more often to show your partner that you love them."[98]

👍 Take ownership and responsibility for the out-of-control spending you allow your kids to take part in and don't let them get credit cards. Getting good grades or going to college is not a free pass to go on spending sprees, even if there is a college fund with money in it. Use a debit card for computers, books, supplies, and food. This will provide records and give everybody visibility to the expenses.

**Monitor Your Money:** Review the balance in your checking account(s) weekly. This is to ensure that you do not run a negative balance so you can avoid fees. For many free accounts, there will be a minimum balance that must be maintained or a minimum number of transactions per month. You can be charged fees for being under a specific dollar amount like $1,000 or $7,500.

Both partners will be equally engaged in the family finances. Both will have access to savings and checking accounts, and be responsible for the balance or the lack thereof. Again, have weekly bill update meetings to see what is owed and how the money was spent, and have bi-weekly planning discussions of overall finances and progress of long-term investment goals. This is money management on <u>steroids</u>! Have discipline and set the same day and time (for example, Saturday at 8:00 a.m.) to have these talks, and that will eliminate the random emotionally charged money fights. This discipline will absolutely affect all parts of your life. You will look forward to opening up mail because there will be retirement plan statements and rent checks.

❑ **AI:** _____

## Managing the Family

"Make sure you're both on the same page when it comes to children. Address the question of whether to have children openly and deeply, and only commit to having children if you're both ready and committed. Children can be incredibly expensive and also incredibly demanding of your time, but the emotional and personal rewards of parenthood are many. Even knowing this, it's not a trade-off that some people want to make, and others may hide their reluctance in an effort to please their spouse. Carefully consider the child question, be open about it, and listen to what your partner has to say."[99] Add to the discussion the maximum number of children, including those from previous marriages and the cost to raise them <u>through</u> college. Also discuss limiting the number, or eliminating, pets. If you have not yet discussed these issues, now is the time.

❑ **AI:** _____

Sometimes you have to say to your kids, **"You'll get nothing and like it"** in a loving way and explain why. They cannot get everything they want. Be caring and firm at the same time. Teach your kids the value of money and that everything comes at a cost. Do not leave it up to others to teach them micro-economics. It is your responsibility to pass that lesson along.

Stop saying, "I want my kids to have everything I didn't have growing up." What message is this sending them?

- Does this mean they get designer label jeans at age ten?
- Do they get a new Beamer at sixteen?
- Do you allow them summers off to travel around Europe and not work?
- Do they get to drink or take drugs like E[86] at all-night parties with no consequences?

---

[86]  *Ecstasy*: an illicit psychoactive drug often associated with rave parties.

I think not!

You don't want to spoil them or have them believing they can have whatever they desire without any sweat. Beware of putting too much pressure on your children and living through their undertakings. Absolutely, they should get an education, but the future should be just as bright for you too. You have an opportunity to improve your situation now and accomplish your dreams too.

Treat your family as adults with needs and not children with wants. Provide the following support system (all may not apply):

- ❑ Contributing to their mental wellness and
  physical fitness                                        __/__/__
- ❑ Helping them through college, vocational,
  trade school, etc.                                      __/__/__
- ❑ Participating in family volunteering outings          __/__/__
- ❑ Paying child support on time                          __/__/__
- ❑ Exposing them to diverse communities                  __/__/__
- ❑ _____                      __/__/__
- ❑ _____                      __/__/__

"Oh yeah . . . co-signing is stupid,"[100] especially for family members and friends. There is a reason why somebody needs a co-signer: lousy credit or no credit history. They are responsible to build up their credit score to support their financial goals, not you.

**Private vs. Public Grade School:** Try to live in a community that has a good school district versus paying for private grade schools. This can save $20,000 per year per child.[87] Also factor in transportation to school, dress uniforms, and books. There may be cost associated if you need to move to a better school district. If you multiply this savings by four, eight, or twelve years per child, you will see a significant amount. This money can be applied toward higher education plans and your retirement fund. With the dramatic increase in college tuition and the

---

[87]   In 2010, the median national tuition cost is $16,970 a year, according to the National Association of Independent Schools. This cost is going up more than inflation, and does not include room and board.

lack of available credit, state colleges and universities are becoming a more affordable option over private institutions.

❑ **AI:** _____

Have children off-load the parents' tasks by taking on more ownership for their chores and family household chores: cutting the lawn, gardening, cooking, and cleaning the home, including dusting. Have your children prepare their own healthy lunches and yours too. Have them clean their rooms, make their beds, and teach them to wash their own clothes and dishes. This will free up the parents to create more income.

❑ **AI:** _____

Join moms, dads, and/or single parent online groups for finding frugal pampering nights, church barn swing dances, babysitting swaps, sleepovers for young adults, and play dates. This will provide you support beyond your existing network. Thoroughly research these events and people before participating.

❑ **AI:** _____

## Managing the Home

**Install a home security system** to protect you and your family. Secure your home possessions, business assets, and family safety with an alarm system. This is valuable for houses, condos, apartments, boats, and mobile homes. If you own your home, this will increase the value of it. If you are renting, I suggest that you still investigate getting a security system. First, request that the owner buy it. A compromise is that you both split the cost and leave it behind when you move, but the owner needs to pay for the installation. If not, get a security unit yourself that is not permanent and easy to uninstall to take with you when you move. Confirm with your landlord that this is acceptable, and get it in writing.

❑ **AI:** _____

Place a thin trim or molding over the top of the sliding glass door. This will prevent a burglar from lifting the door off the tracks. Of course, have a bar or rod at the bottom track or midway point which is standard on new doors. All other doors require deadbolts.

❑ **AI:** _____

## Teaching Your Family to Build for Their Future

**Teamwork:** Train others to support your ideas. Invite people that deserve your investment to be a part of your network to build a business. This is a lot easier than it appears. Spouses, children, parents, siblings, boyfriends, girlfriends, and best friends are perfect partners in this new lifestyle. Why? Because they will benefit from your money earned from saving money, energy, and time. We all have our strengths and weaknesses. Have your spouse, partner, or children contribute their competent experiences and complementary skills such as writing, crafts, handyperson, marketing, clerical, promotional, financial, sales, and public speaking. Take this as an opportunity to grow together and build a strong interdependent relationship that is not manufactured on material possessions.

**"Monkey see, monkey do."** Children tend to follow their parents' behavior. They learn our spending habits. Lead by example and cut expenses, reduce the material drive, and invest in growth opportunities. If you do, your children will do the same. Go green, reduce your footprint, live a simple (not simplistic) but long and meaningful life, and build for a prosperous future. For example:

- Reduce, reuse, sell, donate, and recycle.
- Reduce expenses and sell wants to pay off debt.
- Trade in your large gas-guzzling SUV for an eco-friendly smaller car with excellent fuel mileage.
- Spend less time watching sitcoms and game shows and more time reading personal growth and business development books.
- Invest the savings in:
  - Charities and volunteering
  - Growing mentally and physically
  - Growing your income and retirement plans
  - Retirement and college funds
  - Real estate and business

At birth (day one), open up a savings account for each baby. Open up a checking account for teenagers. Give them access to the accounts when they are accountable enough to balance it. Wait until they are a responsible teenager before linking a debit card to their checking account. Have them go online to check the balance and recent transaction history of both accounts. Parent and child are both responsible for growing the child's savings account.

❑  **AI:** _____

Help kids value money have good work ethics by getting them a job early in life. They can work jobs after-school, weekends, seasonal, and/ or at special events. This could be cutting lawns, delivering newspapers, painting houses, cleaning houses, babysitting, house sitting, selling crafts, cooking, serving food, working as a farmhand, or working at a market. Furthermore, help them set up Roth 401(k) retirement plans for their earned income reported to the IRS.

❑  **AI:** _____

## Building for Your Kids' Future

"Start talking to children early about the cost of college and the reality of your savings. How much can you contribute toward their education, and how much do you expect them to pay? Most teenagers don't know the price tag of college in dollars and cents."[101]

### Planning for Their College

"It's smart to save for your children's college educations. The earlier you start, the more money you'll accumulate. 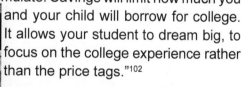 Savings will limit how much you and your child will borrow for college. It allows your student to dream big, to focus on the college experience rather than the price tags."[102]

NYIT, Old Westbury Campus

*Charles Schwab On Investing* stated, "About 60 percent of college students graduate with debt loads of more than $20,000."[103] My belief is that parents should pay for most of their children's higher education. The proportion should be discussed at an early age, and the balance can be adjusted according to each family's situation. Remember, they are not considered adults until they are eighteen years old. We are legally and morally responsible for them. In most states, they cannot start earning real significant income until they are fifteen or sixteen years old. Parents need to focus on funding each child's education starting at day one and not a lot of senseless cute clutter. You need to commit to their success before they are conceived. If they are already born, the commitment intensifies now. If you have not started a college fund yet, do it today.

❏  **AI:** _____

New York Life Insurance suggests these "**8 Strategies to Starting a College Fund**:"[104]

1.  Section 529 College Savings Plans
2.  Coverdell Education Savings Accounts
3.  The Uniform Transfers to Minors Act and the Uniform Gift to Minors Act
4.  Loans
5.  Investments
6.  Grants
7.  Tax Credits
8.  Financial Aid

**Fund 529 College Savings Plan** is a state-qualified tuition program that is offered in almost all fifty states. Most people will qualify for this plan, but there are income and possibly residential limitations. "If for some reason your child doesn't need the money to go to college, the account can always be transferred to another child or even toward your continuing education."[105]

"Like the 529 Plans, the **Coverdell Educational Savings Account (ESA)** is a tax-advantaged college savings plan. Once known as the Education IRA, the Coverdell ESA works very much like the Roth IRA: Your contributions to an investment account are non-deductible, but your earnings grow tax-free. Withdrawals are also tax-free when used for qualified higher education expenses."[106]

"**529** College Savings Plan offers **more flexibility** than an **ESA**" by Cash Money Life:[107]

•  Contribution limits per year:

- 529 Plan is $13,000 per person
- ESA is only $2,000 total
- In Cash Money Life's opinion, the 529 Plan is a more versatile plan, especially if you will have other people contributing money toward your child's education. The $2,000 limit for ESA contributions is more difficult to track when there are multiple people contributing.
- The Coverdell ESA does have several advantages, including the ability to use the funds for kindergarten through high school (through 2010 unless extended), make unlimited changes to asset allocation, and ESAs may have better investment options, depending on the state in which you open your 529 College Savings Plan.
- The good news is that you can have both plans for your children and you can roll an ESA into a 529 College Savings Plan. These plans have a lot of small print and conditions, so read the details before opening an account and making contributions.[88]

❏ **AI:** _____

For more details on both 529 Plan and ESA, refer to *Transforming from Consumer to Producer in 90 Days Tutorial Workbook*.

Amie Ha and friends at CU Boulder campus graduation, University of Colorado, Glenn J. Asakawa

Verify if your company provides tuition reimbursement programs for their employees and children.

❏ **AI:** _____

Make sure you are also taking advantage of all of the tax credits to which you are entitled. The college fund may be a tax credit, but so can childcare, elderly care, people with disabilities, and adoption. You can go back years to file for unclaimed tax breaks and credits. For more

---

[88] Some states have in-state tax breaks or attendance requirements.

details, go to Publication 970 (2010), "Tax Benefits for Education" at *www.IRS.gov/publications/p970*.

❏ **AI:** _____

## Career Options

👍 Discuss college, vocational, trade, and other school opportunities with your children. Explore everything from cosmetology, stylist, office manager, web design, automotive, acting, nursing, security, culinary careers, farming, to trucking, and so on.

Be open to apply for academies like police, firefighter, emergency, federal (like the FBI and Homeland Security), data networking (like Cisco Networking Academy and Microsoft Certification Program), West Point Naval, Air Force, etc. Look at opportunities to enroll in executive and management leadership programs as well as carpentry, electrician, plumber, political aide, and fashion designer apprenticeships. Explore internship opportunities at *www.internshipprograms.com* and *www.internships.com*.

❏ **AI:** _____

👍 Also be open to a discussion of U.S. Armed Forces: Military, National Guard, and Reserves. Other great opportunities are: Job Corps (*www.JobCorps.gov*), AmeriCorps (*www.AmeriCorps.gov*), and Peace Corps (*www.PeaceCorps.gov*).

## "Will"ful Planning

If you do not have a **Will** for your estate or guardianship of your children, create it now. This is not as complicated as it might seem. It "will" make it clear to your loved ones how your belongings and assets shall be divided, as per your wishes. A *Will*, or Last Will and Testament, is a legal document that will manage your estate assets when you pass away. If you already have a Will, that is great, but check to see if it needs to be revised. Update your Will whenever there are major changes in your life or at least every year.

❏ **AI:** _____

"Published in 2007, Harris Interactive® for Martindale-Hubbell® conducted a research study finding that for the last three years, 55 percent of all adult

Americans do not have a Will. Only one in three African-American adults (32 percent) and one in four Hispanic American adults (26 percent) have Wills, compared to more than half (52 percent) of Caucasian American adults."[108]

For simple estate or just to get one started now, use estate-planning software like Quicken WillMaker Plus. It only takes forty-five minutes to create the first draft, which is easy to update. This estate planner will also guide you in creating other documents like living trusts, promissory notes, childcare and elderly care agreements, power of attorney, executor's checklist, healthcare directives, and bill of sale.

❏ **AI:** _____

Verify if your employer offers legal services that include the creation of a Will at no charge or at a substantial discount.

❏ **AI:** _____

Wills can be contested. A probate-exempt living or revocable trust may prevent your estate from going into lengthy and costly probate proceedings. *Probate* is the legal process used to evaluate the value of your estate, pay taxes, settle debts, and distribute assets to your heirs. If your assets are over a certain amount (for example $100,000 in California, Utah, and Washington), the estate may go to probate court to be settled. To learn more about probate, refer to Julia Nissley's *How to Probate an Estate in California,* Nolo, 2008.[89] The probate process can drag on for years without proper planning.

❏ **AI:** _____

Along with the Will, establish the following to protect your estate:

- ❏ Durable power of attorney and
  health-care proxy                                  __/__/__
- ❏ Beneficiary designations of life insurance
  and retirement plans                               __/__/__
- ❏ Final letter of instructions                     __/__/__

---

[89] This is a good reference for probate in California, but if the estate is outside of California, you need to get another resource specific to that state's laws.

☝ For complex estates, seek competent legal consultation. Also discuss your charitable distributions and long-term funding of trusts.

## Your Kids Building for Their Future

**"You keep what you kill."** Involve your kids at a very early age to start to take responsible for their future. Every dollar (100 percent) the child saves and earns is kept for his/her future. These savings will be invested in CDs, savings bonds, Roth 401(k), college fund, and to pay off credit cards for their past expenses. They should benefit from their cooperation and contributions.

"Here are some great ideas for **your children to build for their own future**" by Dave Ramsey:[109]

❑ Work the buddy system and help each other monitor your spending habits. Your spending partner is now your saving partner. It will take teamwork. Saving for college ensures that a legacy of debt is not passed down your family tree.

☝ If you already have student loans or don't want to get a loan in the first place, look into the "underserved areas" programs. The government will pay for school or pay off your loans if you will go to work in an underserved area. These areas are typically rural or inner-city areas. Most of these programs are for law and medicine.

**Roth IRA** offers a great opportunity for growth because the contributed and earned money grows tax-free. These are after-tax contributions, unlike a traditional IRA, which is pre-tax money. There are income limitations on contributing to Roth IRAs, while traditional IRAs have no income limitation. However, traditional IRAs have age rules when money can be withdrawn without penalty. You can withdraw contributed money from a Roth IRA without penalty, but there are time requirements on earned income.

If you're the parent, grandparent, uncle, or aunt of a teenager, there's probably an XBOX/PS3, iPod, or smartphone on that gift list of theirs, but for the next birthday, holiday, or graduation, why not give them something they'll really appreciate long-term, like a Roth IRA? Learn how to "**Start Your Kids on the Roth Road**" by Bankrate.com:[110]

- Earned income is the key in qualifying for a Roth. There is no age limit for an IRA, but not too many preteens have jobs. Household chores don't count. Generally, a child would have to be working part-time for an employer who collected taxes and reported the earnings to the IRS. A child who, for all intents and purposes, is self-employed every weekend mowing lawns, shoveling snow, or babysitting may qualify if receipts and records are maintained.

- When it comes to retirement funds, a Roth IRA offers the greatest opportunity for growth because the money grows tax-free. Kids don't need the deferred taxes feature of a traditional IRA because they're probably not paying taxes. If a child socks away $10,000 between the ages of fifteen and twenty and then never adds another penny, that $10,000 (assuming a very reasonable 8 percent return per year) will balloon to more than $217,000 by age sixty.

- Be sure your teenager understands and is willing to let the money grow until age fifty-nine and a half. The gains will be taxed, and the IRS will impose a 10 percent penalty for early withdrawal. Contributions to a Roth can always be withdrawn penalty-free, and there are penalty-free provisions for withdrawing Roth earnings for education or a first-time home purchase. That is, money can be taken out penalty-free for education, but the gains are taxed. With a first-time home buyer, the earnings are tax-free.

- Investing in a few of the better companies that make the products kids buy can make investing more interesting for a teenager. Take time to explain the monthly or quarterly statements, and you'll give your child a hands-on understanding of how investing works.

❏ **AI:** _____

One summer or spring break, send your teenagers to a financial literacy and money management school. These classes can be found at the local community colleges and online. This could be a graduation or birthday present. Pool the money together, if necessary, to send children to these courses rather than giving individual doodads as gifts.

❑ **AI:** _____

## Growing and Having Fun Together

**Wreck It**: Recreational centers are an inexpensive place to work out, play sports, and spend time with the family. "Some of these facilities may not be state-of-the-art, but they do have much of the same equipment than you'd find at the high-price gyms. Some also offer a full schedule of exercise classes (aerobic, yoga, tai chi, boxing, and more), and some have pools. Many of the centers also have extensive programs for children and seniors plus after-school programs for kids and teenagers. The computer resource facilities at some centers offer classes and instructions on how to use the Internet and computer programs. Some of the adult classes charge a small fee in addition to the membership."[111] Religious and cultural centers are also inexpensive places to bond and grow as a family.

"**Read together as a family.** Encourage the love of reading with your children. Plan a family reading an hour each day. Then, once every few weeks, go to the library together and have everybody pick a few books to read during that period."[112] Also block out time to do class homework and after-school projects together. Plan dates and family events that will be fun, cheap, and productive. Build a strong relationship while watching each other grow together, not just physically but mentally and emotionally as well.

❑ **AI:** _____

*"When the student is ready, the teacher will appear."*
*~ Buddhist Proverb*

# CHAPTER 17: INVESTING IN YOUR COMMUNITY

*"Power is the ability to do good things for others." ~ Brooke Astor*

## Social Responsibility

It is your responsibility to create more than your take. If you have kids or a lot of material possessions, you have to give more back to make up for the resources consumed. It is not about what you have, but what you share and how you support others. How about starting a nonprofit foundation or chairing a charity ball? Be more compassionate to people going through a rough time, by volunteering and donating more. Proactively be kind to people and animals with meaningful actions!

If people do not take the responsibility to pick up after themselves or recycle, maybe we should recycle them. If they do not pick up their trash, then they are trash! Harsh words, but I expect everybody to follow through on service and social responsibilities. The few who do not carry their own weight burden the rest of society at the time when we need to be advancing ourselves and our communities. We need to spread these responsibilities evenly so more can be accomplished globally.

## Volunteerism

### Volunteering Benefits All

**"The needs of the many outweigh the needs of the one."** Share your talents, gifts, and skills with others through volunteering or working

 at a nonprofit charitable organization. This benefits the community and offers special emotional rewards as well.

HandsOn Bay Area

"**Volunteering** has a meaningful, positive impact on your community. But did you know that it can have many **benefits** for you too? Here are some reasons to volunteer given" by World Volunteer Web at *www. WorldVolunteerWeb.org*:[113]

❑ <u>Learn or develop a new skill</u>: Volunteering is the perfect vehicle to discover something you are really good at and develop a new skill. As Mahatma Gandhi said, "Live as if you were to die tomorrow. Learn as if you were to live forever." Planning and implementing a major fundraising event can develop goal setting, planning, and budgeting skills. Supervising and training other volunteers helps to develop supervisory and training skills.

👍 <u>Meeting a diverse range of people</u>: Volunteering brings together a diverse range of people from all backgrounds and walks of life. Volunteering also offers an incredible networking opportunity. Not only will you develop lasting personal and professional relationships, but it is also a great way to learn about people from all walks of life, different environments, and new industries.

👍 <u>Send a signal to your employer, teachers, friends, and family</u>: People pay attention to your life outside the environment in which they have direct contact with you. For example, your employer would be interested in the activities that give you a good work-life balance, just as academic institutions are interested in your extracurricular activities.

• <u>Be part of your community</u>: Communities are suffering due to the growth of secular societies, but at the same time, we can really bridge that expanding gap through volunteering. Volunteering is ultimately about helping others and having an impact on people's wellbeing.

• <u>Motivation and sense of achievement</u>: Volunteers predominantly express a sense of achievement and motivation, and this is ultimately generated from your desire and enthusiasm to help. It may be true that no one person can solve all the world's problems, but what you can do is make that little corner of the world where you live just a little bit better.

• <u>New interests and hobbies</u>: Sometimes we do get locked into the rat race of life, and volunteering can give that escape from everyday routines and create a balance in our lives.

Finding new interests and hobbies through volunteering can be fun, relaxing, and energizing. Sometimes a volunteer experience can lead you to something you never even thought about or help you discover a hobby or interest of which you were unaware, maybe even a "love interest!" Volunteering is a brilliant way to get life experience through hands-on work.

👍 There are many other benefits of going to volunteer events. You may be able to get tax deductions for mileage to and from the site, network with people to promote your business, enjoy music at a concert, food at a shelter, complimentary tickets, or hand-outs. Another example, if you give blood, you may be able to take advantage of special promotions and practical gifts. Plus there are therapeutic advantages in the value of compassion and being warm to people.

Have your spouse/partner and kids choose the event at which to volunteer at and the charity to which to donate. This will be fun working as a team! You should bring a date along to these charitable events. My highest score bowling was while volunteering with a group of children we took on a Saturday morning so their parents could work or run errands.

❑ **AI:** _____

## Some Organizations to Volunteer For

👍 If you are more of a people person and have some spare time, donate your time to a charitable organization, church, temple, or mosque instead of donating money. This is especially effective when you include your family, your better half, and/or your friends.[90] Use the money saved from not donating to devote into your investments while using the volunteer time to meet potential clients. For volunteer opportunities, join or affiliate with local charities and get on their mailing lists.

---

[90] Partnering can be very effective for programs like Habitat for Humanity, having one requirement: a home candidate needs to put 500 hours of sweat equity into building their home before it is finished. Others can benefit, too, totaling charitable fundraising efforts or accumulating court-mandated hours.

☝ Volunteering is a great way to get exercise, get free entry into events, enjoy something new, and eat free meals. In San Francisco, I am a project leader with HandsOn Bay Area (HOBA *www.HandsOnBayArea.org*). Here are just a few of the projects I've enjoyed as a HOBA volunteer, reaping benefits while making an impact in people's lives and the environment:

- Free meals while volunteering is a bonus, like at Project Open Hand (*www.OpenHand.org*), Ronald McDonald House (*www. RonaldsHouse.com*),[91] and Glide Memorial Church (*www.Glide. org*).
- Learn skills like planting and caring for trees at Friends of the Urban Forest (*www.FUF.net*) and Conservatory of Flowers (*www. ConservatoryofFlowers.org*).
- Exercise at Special Olympics track and field (*www. SpecialOlympics.org*).
- Free entry into the zoo,[92] botanical gardens, concerts, bowling, and amusement parks.

"Over one billion people do not have enough food to eat, and 25,000 people die every year from hunger and related causes."[114] There are many organizations that are actively working to address this devastating crisis and they need volunteers:

- Meals on Wheels (*www.mowaa.org*) feeds thousands daily.
- Feeding American (*www.FeedingAmerica.org*) is the nation's largest domestic hunger-relief charity supplying food to more than twenty-five million Americans each year.
- World Food Programme (*www.WFP.org*) is the world's largest humanitarian agency fighting hunger worldwide.

---

[91]   We provide the food and cook it. The joy of sitting and speaking with the families over a home-cooked meal is overwhelming. One time I received free tickets to Raiders vs. 49ers football game.

[92]   Attend zoos that have enough room for animals to roam freely without having to pace back and forth. Also do not attend traveling circuses that have animals that have to be caged between performances.

**"Little Baby Gorilla"**: Did you know there are amazing ways to volunteer in your community at your fingertips? Check out your local

paper or go online to Volunteer Match at *www.VolunteerMatch.org*.

❏ **AI:** _____

Artie Lange "Little Baby Gorilla" comedy performance in Afghanistan 2008, Hoboken411.com

**Bruh'man**: During a long, fulfilling morning of volunteering, the Hands On Denver organization provided lunch at the old Stapleton Airport, that has been replaced with Denver International Airport. After finishing, we gathered at the end of an inactive runway, where I was able to race my Mitsubishi 3000 GT (licensing plate "BROMAN") to "possibly" well over 125 MPH. What a rush! You just never know what new experiences you will enjoy while volunteering.

Take a leadership role on nonprofit boards. You can go to *www. VolunteerMatch.org*, *www.HelpNow.org/boardlink_npos.php*, or do a web browser search. There are so many places where you can volunteer and contribute. For a list of other nonprofit organizations where you can volunteer, go to *Part VII – Your Support Structure and Resources, Appendix H: Honorably Mentioned Charitable Organizations*.

❏ **AI:** _____

## Pay It Forward

### Giving

**"Spread the wealth, that's what I always say."** Create a yearly percentage goal like 1 percent, 2 percent, 5 percent, or 10 percent of income to give to charity. Yes, you need to have a monthly budget item for charity and/or church tax-deductible contributions. This will be a monthly dollar amount budgeted like $25, $50, $125, or $250. Donate to charities, schools, shelters, food banks, Lions Club, Boys & Girls Clubs, the Scouts, city zoos, churches, temples, mosques, etc. You can also donate to first responders that are killed in the line-of-duty children's college funds like local law enforcement assistance and firefighters' toy programs.

❑ **AI:** _____

**No Postage Necessary :** I prefer to give annual donations by becoming a member instead of responding to special fundraiser mailings. Beware that once you get on their mailing list, you will get mailed special campaigns and petitions throughout the year. This is why I recommend being a member with annual dues so that when you get an annual membership dues reminder, you know it is time to donate and disregard other solicitations. Even if the application form or envelope says twenty-five dollars, you can donate less and still be a member with the same benefits. You might give twice a year if you receive bonus or an income tax return refund.

☝ Do not give donations to telephone solicitors. In fact, ask to be removed from their phone list, but not the mailing list. Also do not get suckered in when you get little gifts and mailing labels soliciting donations. One is never under any obligation from unsolicited mail. Use this stuff or give it to charity. Donate first to those that send a nice gift in return like a t-shirt, backpack, water bottle, or picnic basket. Then I prefer to give, but not exclusively, when the return envelope postage is paid ("NO POSTAGE NECESSARY IF MAILED IN THE UNITED STATES"). Be prepared to say, "I gave at the office" or "I'm all tapped out this month" to children selling things at your doorstep or in front of stores when you leave. For some reason, I always give a dollar to the Salvation Army workers ringing the bell in front of a store. It always put me in the holiday spirit.

There are always goodies and coins to be found in unsolicited junk mail. Never buy a birthday, holiday, or greeting card again. These free greeting cards from charity organizations can be used for many occasions. So what if their name and address are on the back of the cards? Maybe that will just inspire your loved ones to give to that charity as well. Give what you do not use to young children for class art projects or to charities as donations.

❑ **AI:** _____

It is very important that you give to others, no matter what your situation is. It does not have to be a lot of money. Giving five dollars a month of your hard-earned money would be greatly appreciated by others, and it feels heartwarming. In my opinion, not giving anything is really not an option. Once you select your cause(s), it is hard not to give.

☝ However, charity starts at home! Follow my suggestion that your future and family priorities come first. If your situation requires that you need to temporarily cut back on your charitable contributions, do so immediately. But first, see if you can reduce the amount and/or the frequency before stopping all contributions. It is good to stay in the habit of giving when you can. It can also be donating services, material, or love versus money. If you are extremely busy working to pay off your massive debt or running a business, encourage your children to volunteer on your behalf.

Donating time is equally as important, sometimes more, as monitory contributions. Many companies and government employers will contribute money to a nonprofit organization for the hours that you volunteered. The more hours you volunteer, the more money the charity will receive. There is usually an online system managed by your employer where you can log hours to an organization that your employer recognizes. You may need to submit a request to get your favorite charities added to the approved list. They may also provide paid time off for company-sponsored charity events. Some professional organizations, colleges, and schools provide units or credits for volunteering.

❏ **AI:** _____

Give specific products like diapers, baby formula, a child car seat, a wheelchair, and of course food and clothing. Items may be used (not the diapers), as long as they are in good condition.

❏ **AI:** _____

Bill Gates and Warren Buffet donate a vast portion of their fortunes. The New York Times stated, "In 2006, Mr. Buffett gave away 85 percent of his fortune, or about $37.4 billion. Of that amount, he will channel the greatest share, about thirty-one billion dollars, into Bill & Melinda Gates Foundation (*www.GatesFoundation.org*). The Gates Foundation, dedicated to improving health and education, especially in poor nations, is already the United States' largest grant-making foundation."[115] This is one of my favorite charities!

Bill Gates and Warren Buffett have organized dinners inviting the wealthiest billionaires in America to pledge at least half their net worth to charity, in their lifetimes or at death. The Giving Pledge stated, "By early 2011, at least fifty-five generous people have committed to this extraordinary unselfish contribution to society."[116] We can drive for this type of commitment to help others too, no matter how much money we have! Warren Buffet has pledged ninety-nine percent of his fortune. **How much will you pledge?**

- ❏ Lifetime charitable donation pledge:
  $ _____ or _____%
- ❏ Upon death charitable donation pledge:
  $ _____ or _____%

## Tax Benefits of Giving

Note that not every charity or not-for-profit organization will be tax deductible. With 501(c)(3) classification it should read, "tax-deductible gift" or "donation is tax deductible." Sometimes the donation or event is not 100 percent tax deductible, so read the fine print. If it says 50 percent, that is all you can write off on your taxes.

👍 Donate to support nonprofit organizations including Girl Scotts, 4-H, PTA, Breast Cancer Fund, American Diabetes Association, wildlife funds, animal rescues, etc. Other tax deductible charities can be foundations, schools, colleges, clubs, or pace of worship, but do your research. Political campaigns, political action committees (PACs), working to influence laws and policies, other political organizations, and for-profit companies are not tax-deductible. Ask for and keep receipts for all donations, especially for cash donations of fifty dollars or more, in kind services, material items, and events. I like to keep all receipts for at least five years, it is better to be safe than sorry. For tips from the IRS of deducting charitable contributions refer to *Transforming from Consumer to Producer in 90 Days Tutorial Workbook*.

Donate to whatever your past educational institutions, heritage, background, or heart desires. I appreciate my college education and donate annually to my alma mater engineering departments at NYIT and CU. Furthermore, I support organizations like the American Indian Education Foundation, National Society of Black Engineers, and United Negro College Fund that are all tax write-offs. For a list of other nonprofit organizations to donate which I am familiar with, go to *Part VII – Your Support Structure and Resources, Appendix H: Honorably Mentioned Charitable Organizations*.

❏ **AI:** _____

👍 Remember to verify these are 501(3)(c) or tax-exempt organizations, and write "*100 percent Tax-Deductible Donation*" in the check memo field. To be clear, add "*Foundation*" to the charity name and "*Educational Purposes Only*" in the memo field so the receiving organization knows how you want the donating spent.

# Go Green to Benefit the Environment and Yourself

## Going Green to Save Money

We all need to reduce the footprint we are leaving on Earth, the planet we all call home. Being eco-friendly and living green can save money while enabling you to live healthier simplifier life. Help Mother Earth by reducing energy consumption and pollution while putting savings into your investments by cutting utility bills.

"Paper bags aren't the answer to not using plastic bags. Producing paper bags from virgin timber requires even more energy and water than making plastics ones and creates more greenhouse gases, solid, and waterborne waste. Oh, and did we mention that fourteen million trees are sacrificed each year to make paper bags?"[117] Remember to bring your own **canvas** and **nylon bags** to the store, or at least reuse the paper and plastic bags you already have.

I hate to go there, but we should have economical **green funerals** are usually much cheaper than traditional services. Certainly, we need to honor and respect people that have passed on. Green, natural, and eco-friendly caskets are 100 percent biodegradable and less expensive than traditional hardwood, copper/bronze, and metal caskets. If your beliefs support it, you should consider cremation as a more eco-friendly and less expensive alternative to a casket burial. The event can just be all in one day and not spread over several days with a wake or viewing. Save on not having a limousine by carpooling. Have the memorial gathering at a home. You can even make it a potluck.

TreeHugger™ states, "Traditional burial and cremation practices can have significant negative environmental impact, but green funerals and eco-burials are one way to lessen the impact. While death can be a difficult subject, it is still important to keep ethical beliefs and environmental convictions in mind while tending to end-of-life arrangements. After all, if you gotta go, why not go green?"[118] To learn about green funerals and burials, go to TreeHugger at *www.treehugger.com/files/2008/03/how-to-go-green-funerals.php*.

## Green is Fun and Sexy!

Let's have fun being green. It may be a minor lifestyle change. Take one step at a time, like barbequing and dressing green.

BBQ in the park with friends and family. This community sharing will  save in cooking costs while also affording you the opportunity to bond with potential business partners and new friends. Cook extra food to bring home for another meal or two.

flickr from Yahoo!, woodleywonderworks

👍 **Top Ten Ways to have a Green Barbeque:**

1. Provide alternate transportation methods on the invitation to encourage people to bike, carpool, or take mass transit.
2. Fill up pitchers or reused gallon jugs of ice water, homemade lemonade, or sweet iced tea instead of buying personal-sized beverages.

3. Use reusable or biodegradable plates, cups, and utensils, and buy in bulk to reduce the amount of packaging. Provide markers so people can write their names on their cups and plates to keep from using new ones for each serving.

4. Set up three different containers to separate the trash, reusable, and recyclable items.

5. Serving less meat is the biggest way to mitigate the environmental impact of your BBQ.[93] For the meat you do serve, choose organic and grass- or grain-fed selections.

6. Offer more vegetarian dishes, and grill veggies that are grown locally. Remember, locally produced food typically have fewer chemicals applied to grow and preserve them, and less energy is consumed in transporting them.

7. Gas grills are better than charcoal grills because natural gas and propane burn cleaner and leave behind less waste. If you do use coal, choose all-natural lump varieties, which eliminates additives like lighter fluid contained in briquettes.

8. Grilling with the hood of the barbeque down not only helps maintain energy efficiency, but also ensures that heat will be distributed more evenly throughout the grill and keeps the moisture in. If cooking on an open grill, use aluminum foil or a foil tray as an ad-hoc lid.

9. Bring reusable plastic containers in which to pack leftovers.

10. Require guests to bring organic and local brews. Serving beer from a half keg, pony keg, or growler also cuts down on excess packaging. Also get wine with organically grown grapes bottled in eco-friend paper cartons, or brings wines that are in a box or jug.

Found at THREADshow.com: CalNaturale from Paso Robles, California is packaged in Terra Pak paper cartons that require half the energy consumed in producing traditional glass bottles.

---

[93] Here's why: It takes 1,916 gallons of water to produce one pound of beef, and cattle produce enormous amounts of methane, a greenhouse gas that's almost 20 times more harmful than carbon dioxide.

👍 Using an artificial **Christmas tree** is better for the environment (and your wallet) than cutting down a tree every year, especially if you use the same artificial tree for at least ten years and the tree is made of recycled plastics. If you want a real tree, get one from a company that has a program to replace that tree (like buy one tree, and they plant three). Also consider getting a live potted tree, and the organization will plant the tree for you after Christmas. Many cities, like San Francisco, have programs like this.[94] It will cost a little more than a cut tree, but it will live on a city block near you for many years. For a nationwide program to rent a potted Christmas tree from $45 to $125, go to Rent a Living Christmas Tree at *www.rentxmastree.com*.

**Stylish, Green, and Within Your Means:** "Green fashion is blowing up, but before you assume you have to buy something new to be green, consider buying used items (what eco fashionista Karla calls Found Fashion at *www.karlasbonanza.com/?p=84*. It is one of the easiest ways to achieve true Earth-friendly style. Karla will show how you can put together a 'fabulous' wardrobe (or home) on a tiny budget, while reducing your dependence on new items that are often cheaply and unethically made. For inexpensive style advice and practical tips, go to *www.KarlasBonanza.com/?p=33*."[119]

👍 Here are Karla's **"Top 10 Tips for Thrift Store Scoring**."[120] These would actually apply in any shopping situation:

1. Wear comfortable clothes that are easy to get in and out of, slip-on shoes, and a cross-body purse so you have both hands free. Always take a cart if one is available.
2. If you're a novice and still squeamish about thrift store cooties, start with accessories: handbags, scarves, and belts are a safe bet.
3. Don't count on finding *exactly* what you want, but do carry a list of items so you can keep an eye out for them.

---

[94] In 2010, Friends of the Urban Forest and SF Environment offered San Francisco residents a chance to order a living, potted Christmas tree (not a tradition fir tree) for only eighty dollars. For details, go to: *www.fuf.net* or *www.sfenvironment.com/greenchristmas*.

4. Learn to shop quickly and make fast decisions or it'll take forever: Work your way across the store, methodically running one hand along the clothing racks. Stop only when your hand lands on quality fabric in a color that excites you. Take a quick look. If the piece suits you and is the right size, add it to your pile to try on.

5. Try EVERYTHING on. Make sure it fits and flatters, and doesn't have any imperfections.

6. Check the go-back rack near the dressing room and the racks near the mirrors on the store floor.

7. Hit stores in affluent suburbs. They're likely to be less picked over and will have better quality clothes. Read store reviews online before you go, like Yelp at *www.Yelp.com*.

8. Shop often and during off times if you can. Evenings are a good time because that is typically when new stock is put out for the next day.

9. Familiarize yourself with sale days. You can sometimes sign up for e-mail alerts.

10. Thrift store karma = amazing finds. Be kind to the people working in [all] stores. Put your discarded items back on the hanger after trying them on, and pick up anything you knock off the racks.

## Building Green

✍ Homes in the U.S. typically use one and a half to two times the energy required to achieve the homeowner's desired level of comfort. "Would you ever guess that homes produce twice as much greenhouse gas emissions as passenger cars? Twenty-one percent of U.S. carbon footprint come from existing homes. Home performance retrofitting[95] represents some of the most achievable deep reductions in the country's environmental impact. Retrofitting your home will not only cut down on your environmental impact, but it will also reduce your bills and your family's symptoms of allergies or asthma while improving comfort in your home. Recent studies have also shown that certified energy

---

[95] Retrofitting is adding new technology, material, or features to improve older systems.

efficient homes sell faster and are valued higher than comparable non-certified homes."[121]

CalRecycle's "**Green Building Basics**:"[122]

- A *green building* (a.k.a., sustainable building) is a structure that is designed, built, renovated, operated, or reused in an ecological and resource-efficient manner. Green buildings are designed to meet certain objectives such as protecting occupant health; improving employee productivity; using energy, water, and other resources more efficiently; and reducing the overall impact to the environment.
- A green building may cost more up front but saves through lower operating costs over the building's life.

"Some other **green building benefits**, such as improving occupant health, comfort, productivity, and reducing pollution and landfill waste are not easily quantified. Thus, they are not adequately considered in cost analysis. Even with a tight budget, many green building measures can be incorporated with minimal or zero increased up-front costs and they can yield enormous savings."[123]

Investing in green properties, businesses, or mutual funds can make you money. The property market value is increased for certified green buildings and homes. Consider converting your house, condo, or apartment building to be a green living space to reduce operating costs, increase the resell value, and improve your quality of life.

❏ **AI:** _____

For more detail on green building certification refer to *Transforming from Consumer to Producer in 90 Days Tutorial Workbook*.

*"The price of greatness is responsibility."* ~ *Sir Winston Churchill*

# Part IV: Your Investing Strategy Endnotes

[1] Dave Ramsey, *The Total Money Makeover: A Proven Plan for Financial Fitness*, Thomas Nelson Publishing, 2003, pp. 4, 14.

[2] Ramsey, p. 33.

[3] Ibid, p. 101.

[4] Ibid, p. 62.

[5] Dave Ramsey at *www.DaveRamsey.com*.

[6] Dave and Tom Gardner, *You Have More Money Than You Think*, Simon & Schuster, 1998, pp. 32-33, 35.

[7] Ramsey, p. 261.

[8] Ibid, pp. 104, 145, 146, 104, 136, 134, 140.

[9] Trent Hamm, *365 Ways to Live Cheap: Your Everyday Guide to Saving Money*, Adams Media, 2009, p. 37.

[10] Chris Farrell, *The New Frugality: How to Consume Less, Save More, and Live Better,* Bloomsbury Press, 2010, p. 43.

[11] Hamm, pp. 31, 206-207.

[12] Ibid, pp. 76-77.

[13] Wikipedia at *www.en.wikipedia.org/wiki/FICO* (April 30, 2011).

[14] Rande Spiegelman, "Boost Your Credit Score: Five Ways to Improve Your Credit", *Charles Schwab On Investing*, Fall 2009.

[15] Data from U.S. Department of Health and Human Services.

[16] Judge Greg Mathis, *Judge Mathis*, Warner Brothers, 2010, at *www.askjudgemathis.com*.

[17] Ramsey, p. 152.

[18] Hamm, p. 105.

[19] Timothy J. Mayclin, CPA, *Tax and Business Services Newsletter*, November 2009, at *www.taxbizservices.com*.

[20] Farrell, p. 141.

[21] Laura Bruce, "Start your kids on the Roth road," Bankrate.com, March 11, 2008, at *www.bankrate.com/brm/itax/news/taxguide/20060127a1.asp* (April 30, 2011).

[22] Benjamin Graham updated commentary by Jason Zweig, *The Intelligent Investor: The Definitive Book on Value Investing*, HarperCollins Publishers, 2003, pp. 529, 535.

[23] Mayclin.

[24] Carrie Schwab-Pomerantz, "What Should I Do about my Credit Card Debt?" *Charles Schwab On Investing*, Summer 2009.

25    Benjamin Graham updated commentary by Jason Zweig, *The Intelligent Investor: The Definitive Book on Value Investing*, HarperCollins Publishers, 2003, pp. 528, 18.

26    Janus, "Keeping Your Eyes On the Horizon", *Janus Report*, Summer 2009.

27    Sarah Caron, "Thought you couldn't start a company during a recession? These enterprises made it big by doing just that", November 11, 2008.

28    Dave Ramsey, *Dave Ramsey Show*, FOX Business Network, 2009.

29    Mayclin.

30    Startup Nation's "Ten Steps to Start a Business" at *www.startupnation.com/steps/55/10-steps-open-start-business.htm* (April 30, 2011).

31    U.S. Small Business Administration, "Starting a Business", at *www.sba.gov/category/navigation-structure/starting-managing-business/starting-business* (May 19, 2011).

32    U.S. Small Business Administration, "Developing a Marketing Plan", at *www.sba.gov/content/developing-marketing-plan* (May 19, 2011).

33    U.S. Small Business Administration, "Protecting Your Ideas", at *www.sba.gov/smallbusinessplanner/start/protectyourideas/SERV_SBP_PRTIDEAS.html* (June 25, 2011).

34    Ibid.

35    Wikipedia at *www.en.wikipedia.org/wiki/Patent* (April 30, 2011).

36    U.S. Patent and Trademark Office, "Patent", at *www.uspto.gov/patents/index.jsp* (May 1, 2011).

37    Ibid.

38    Ibid.

39    U.S. Copyright Office at *www.copyright.gov/help/faq/faq-protect.html* (May 1, 2011).

40    Mark J. Kohler, *Lawyers Are Liars: The truth About Protecting Our Assets!*, Life's Plan Publishing, 2007, pp. xvii, 152-153.

41    Ibid, p. 6.

42    Ibid, p. 146.

43    Moneychimp, "Federal Tax Brackets", at *www.moneychimp.com/features/tax_brackets.htm* (May 1, 2011).

44    Mayclin.

45    Kohler, p. 127.

46    Ibid.

47    Ibid, pp. 154-155, 162.

48    Apple at *www.support.apple.com* (May 1, 2011).

49   John Dessauer, *Real Estate H²O: Quenching Your Financial Thirst in a Parched Economy*, Dessauer Publishing, 2008, p. 180.

50   Ibid, pp. 180-181.

51   Ibid, p. 182.

52   Ibid, pp. 182-184.

53   Lynn Alder, "U.S. 2009 Foreclosures Shatter Record Despite Aid", Reuter, January 14, 2010, at *www.reuters.com/article/idUSTRE60D0LZ20100114* (May 1, 2011).

54   Diana Olick, "The Foreclosure Dump", CNBC, January 13, 2011, at *www.cnbc.com/id/41059824/The_Foreclosure_Dump* (May 14, 2001).

55   Janna Herron, "Foreclosures in 2011 to top 2010's record", Associated Press, January 14, 2011.

56   Billeater.com, "Property Tax Appeal - Challenge your property tax appraisal and save", at *www.billeater.com/tips/property-tax-appeal-challenge-your-property-tax-appraisal-and-save* (May 1, 2011).

57   Fulton County Board of Assessors, "New Atlanta Homestead Law", March 9, 2009.

58   Stephen R. Covey, *The 7 Habits of Highly Effective People*, Simon and Schuster, 1989, p. 11.

59   Ibid, pp. 303, 19, 34, 42-43, 49, 51.

60   David J. Schwartz, PhD., *The Magic of Thinking Big: Acquire the Secrets of Success...Achieve Everything You've Always Wanted*, Simon & Schuster, 1987, p. 103.

61   His Holiness, the Dalai Lama and Howard C. Cutler, MD, *The Art of Happiness: A Handbook for Living*, permission of Riverhead Books, imprint of Penguin Group (USA) Inc., 1998, p. 13.

62   Adrian Flores, *Transforming Your Community Through Dance: 13 Steps to a Great Dance Team*, Mitchell Levy, 2009, p. 11.

63   Mahatma Gandhi, "Seven Deadly Sins", 1929.

64   Flores, pp. 16-17.

65   Dalai Lama and Cutler, pp. 190-191.

66   National Alliance of Mental Illness, "What is Mental Illness: Mental Illness Facts", at *www.nami.org/Content/NavigationMenu/Inform_Yourself/About_Mental_Illness/About_Mental_Illness.htm* (May 1, 2011).

67   NAMI, *Mental Illness: Facts and Numbers sheet*, October 2007.

68   SAMHSA, "Getting Through Tough Economic Times", at *www.samhsa.gov/economy* (May 1, 2011).

69   Ramsey, p. 182.

[70]    Military.com, "The GI Bill", at *www.military.com/benefits/gi-bill* (May 1, 2011).

[71]    Covey, p. 292.

[72]    United HealthCare at *www.UHC.com*.

[73]    Jeff Davidson, *The Joy of Simple Living: Over 1,500 Simple Ways to Make Your Life Easy and Content*, Rodale Press, 1999, p. 44.

[74]    Dr. Christina Scott-Moncrieff, *Detox: Cleanse and Recharge Your Mind, Body, and Soul*, Collins & Brown, 2001, pp. 90, 92, 100.

[75]    Davidson, p. 311.

[76]    United HealthCare at *www.UHC.com*.

[77]    American Heart Association, "Cooking for Lower Cholesterol", at *www.heart.org/HEARTORG/Conditions/Cholesterol/PreventionTreatmentofHighCholesterol/Cooking-for-Lower-Cholesterol_UCM_305630_Article.jsp* (May 1, 2011).

[78]    American Heart Association, "Saturated Fats", at *www.heart.org/HEARTORG/GettingHealthy/FatsAndOils/Fats101/Saturated-Fats_UCM_301110_Article.jsp* (May 1, 2011).

[79]    Scott-Moncrieff, p. 76.

[80]    Ibid, p. 29.

[81]    Ibid, p. 35.

[82]    Autumn Conley Bittick, "Coffee and Weight Loss - Does it Really Play a Role?", May 31, 2006, at *www.associatedcontent.com/article/34734/coffee_and_weight_loss_does_it_really.html?cat=51* (May 1, 2011).

[83]    Scott-Moncrieff, pp. 39, 116.

[84]    QuitSmokingSupport.com, "A List of 599 Ingredients Found in Cigarettes", at *www.quitsmokingsupport.com/ingredients.htm* (May 1, 2011).

[85]    Scott-Moncrieff, p. 42.

[86]    U.S. Department of Health and Human Services Centers for Disease Control and Prevention, "Health Effects of Cigarette Smoking", at *www.cdc.gov/tobacco/data_statistics/fact_sheets/health_effects/effects_cig_smoking* (May 1, 2011).

[87]    California Department of Public Health's TobaccoFreeCA.com program, "TV ADS", at *www.tobaccofreeca.com/ads_tv.html* ("Deadliest" - May 1, 2011).

[88]    California Department of Public Health's TobaccoFreeCA.com program, "Secondhand Smoke", at *www.tobaccofreeca.com/resources.html* (May 1, 2011).

[89]    Scott-Moncrieff, p. 42.

90   QuitSmokingSupport.com, "List of 599 Ingredients Found in Cigarettes", at *www.quitsmokingsupport.com/ingredients.htm* (May 1, 2011).

91   U.S. Department of Health and Human Services Centers for Disease Control and Prevention, "Smoking & Tobacco Use", at *www.CDC.gov/tobacco* (May 1, 2011).

92   Covey, pp. 187, 196.

93   Flores, pp. xxiv, xviii.

94   Rob Grader, *The Cheap Bastard's Guide to New York City*, Global Pequot Press, 2008, p. 265.

95   M. Scott Peck, MD, *The Road Less Traveled: A New Psychology of Love, Traditional Values and Spiritual Growth*, Simon and Schuster, 1978, p. 155.

96   Ibid, p. 48.

97   Ramsey, p. 189.

98   Ibid, p. 176.

99   Hamm, p. 177.

100  Dave Ramsey, "The David Ramsey Show", *Fox Business Network*, 2009.

101  Farrell, p. 194.

102  Ibid, p. 193.

103  Michael Townsend and Rande Spiegelman, "What President Obama's 2010 Budget Could Mean for You", *Charles Schwab On Investing*, Summer 2009.

104  New York Life Insurance Company, "Start a College Fund: 8 Strategies", at *www.NewYorkLife.com/cda/0,3254,11796,00.html* (May 1, 2011).

105  Farrell, p. 195.

106  Financial Aid Finder, "Coverdell Educational Savings Account", at *www.financialaidfinder.com/financial-aid/financial-aid-programs/coverdell-educational-savings-account* (May 1, 2011).

107  Ryan Guina, "College Savings Plans: 529 vs. Coverdell ESA", Cash Money Life, at *www.cashmoneylife.com/2009/03/11/college-savings-plans-529-vs-coverdell-esa* (May 1, 2011).

108  WikiAnswer® at *www.wiki.answers.com/Q/What_percentage_of_people_in_the_US_die_without_a_Will* (May 1, 2011).

109  Ramsey, pp. 232, 177, 181-182.

110  Laura Bruce, "Start your kids on the Roth road", Bankrate.com, March 11, 2008, at *www.bankrate.com/brm/itax/news/taxguide/20060127a1.asp* (May 1, 2011).

[111]　Grader, pp. 175, 176.

[112]　Hamm, p. 47.

[113]　World Volunteer Web, "Benefit of Volunteering", at *www.worldvolunteerweb. org/resources/how-to-guides/volunteer/doc/benefits-of-volunteering. html* (May 1, 2011).

[114]　World Food Program, "Hunger Stats", at *www.wfp.org/hunger/stats* (May 1, 2011).

[115]　Timothy L. O'Brien and Stephanie Saul, "Buffett to Give Bulk of His Fortune to Gates Charity", *The New York Times*, June 26, 2006.

[116]　The Giving Pledge at *www.GivingPledge.org*.

[117]　GreenZebra at *www.theGreenZebra.org*.

[118]　TreeHugger, "How to Go Green: Funerals", at *www.treehugger.com/ files/2008/03/how-to-go-green-funerals.php* (May 1, 2011).

[119]　Karl's Bonanza, "All Time Greatest Tips", at *www.KarlasBonanza. com/?p=33* (May 1, 2011).

[120]　Ibid.

[121]　Recurve (formally Sustainable Spaces) at *www.recurve.com*.

[122]　CalRecycle at, "Green Building", *www.calrecycle.ca.gov/epp/ procurement/GreenGuide/Building.htm* (May 1, 2011).

[123]　Ibid.

# PART V – THE PLAN OF ATTACK

*"If your ship doesn't come in, swim out to it!" ~ Jonathan Winters*

## CHAPTER 18: NEW RELATIONSHIP BETWEEN SAVING AND INVESTING

### Confronting Old Behaviors and Mindsets

You need to love money and what it provides. Money is not bad but a necessity in order to thrive in today's society. It's what people do with their money that counts. Do not make a big deal about money. Keep this relationship with money simple. Money is a means to an end that you define. In this society, it is necessary to buy goods and services, but also to give to others. Do you *deserve* to receive money? I sure do! If you do, too, say it out loud:

- "I deserve to receive money!"
- "I add value and deserve to receive a raise!"
- "I am a valuable customer and deserve a discount!"
- "I am working hard to save money and deserve to invest in my Inner Economy!"

❏  **AI:** _____

### Valuing People

Being rich does not make you classy; being classy is about respecting yourself and ALL people with integrity, equality, dignity, and honor. We are all human beings on this beautiful and bountiful Earth. We are all born with a brain, heart, and soul, so let's treat all life as equal and all creatures with admiration.

Photo by Angyl Nihthasu

Rather than say a category of people are *lower-class* or *middle-class*, use *lower-income* or *middle-income*. Also, do not use *working-class* or *blue-collar*. How about just *work force* or *employees*? There is no more class warfare. I classify myself as *"purple-collar"* with is mix of blue- and white-collar with a funky twist!

Let's also value our diversity. We all have different cultural and geographical backgrounds and ways of life that shall be honored. It is cool to hear other people speak in a different language, so don't be jealous. Cultural problems were created to divide us so we are easy to manage. We have no right to categorize people based on how they look. You do not know them. It is better to focus on feeling impressed about yourself and treating other people <u>with</u> class. It is not about money and material possessions, but what you do with them that affect other people besides just yourself.

Late on a windy spring afternoon, I got lost driving from DFW airport to a hotel in Dallas, so I pulled into a gas station off of the highway. This big Texan wearing a cowboy hat and driving a pickup truck asked where I was heading. He was a nice man and gave me directions, along with his map. I will never trash talk Texas again! Another night, I was lost in the deep suburbs in Highlands Ranch, Colorado, heading to a friend's birthday party. As in many suburbs, the men were hanging out in their garages with the doors open. I walked up to one house from my car and asked for directions. The gentlemen gave me directions and their map too. Life is good!

👍 Respect others' culture and heritage as well as their lifestyles. Look through people's facial features, body appearance, and other physical attributes, directly into their eyes and soul. Color and beauty are truly only skin deep.

When I was growing up in Jersey, there was a lot of discrimination. Everybody was getting sh*t, and we had to define ourselves. There was a pecking order after a while. This was bad because to get passage to join the clique, you had to pick on another group. First, it was the Blacks, then Puerto Ricans, Jews, Italians, people with disabilities, low-income, looks, weight, sexual orientation, and so on—whatever anyone could find to divide and conquer.

My family had a monthly family food shopping spree. One month, we filled two carts full of food and went to wait in the checkout line. At the next register, a three-year-old boy pointed to my mother's face and said to his mother, "Mommy, what is *that*?" The child's mother was very embarrassed and apologized. It was obvious this was the first time the child had seen a Black woman. Don't let this happen to your children! Teach them the strength derived from diversity and respect for ALL mankind.

It is the proverbial slippery slope, and like it or not, we will all eventually be classified somehow. The only way to stop it is to just be strong and refuse to support these bad actions of social injustice. At this point in U.S. history, it is up to each individual to change this behavior, not the government. There are different levels of prejudice, but do not fool yourself, for it is still discrimination. Break the first level and do not go any lower, and that will stop the cycle.

*"They came first for the Communists, and I didn't speak up because I wasn't a Communist. Then they came for the trade unionists, and I didn't speak up because I wasn't a trade unionist. Then they came for the Jews, and I didn't speak up because I wasn't a Jew. Then they came for me, and by that time no one was left to speak up."*
*~ Pastor Martin Niemöller*

## Valuing Money

Ask yourself, "How much stuff do I need? Is it that important to me?" Really, it is not like you made it. Sometimes we just need to release and let things go. In the long term, material items you have will eventually be forgotten, but relationships and happiness are forever.

We are not perfect, and as the old adage says, "We can't judge a book by its cover"—and we shouldn't try to. You may need to ask to be forgiven so you can accept past mistakes and move on today. This will increase your self-esteem and value of yourself. Do not burden your progress anymore. Do you want to fund an elementary school trip to DC, sponsor a student in college, or donate to a hospital's cancer wing? Maybe you can create a foundation in memory of someone special so their legacy lives on in the lives of others. Release your baggage by forgiving yourself and others in order to lighten the load.

Retrain your mind to focus on complex producer behavior, and the wants will become simpler. I remember simple, fun moments that were cheap and meaningful:

- Attending a rally against Hugo Chavez presidential run in Caracas.
- Dutch women buying the first drink in Amsterdam.
- Enjoying a one-dollar museum in Taipei.
- Going to the Jewish Ghetto Holocaust Museum in Warsaw.
- Hiking in Red Rocks, hiking in the Des Moines foothills followed by a powwow, and rock climbing in Boulder.
- Jogging in Sidney's botanical gardens, to the World Trade Center and back, around a lake in Alabama, on Mississippi levees, and on New Orleans railroad tracks.
- Listening to five-o'clock prayers in Malaysia.
- Listening to Neil Diamond in a Earl's Court London pub that

played nothing by him.
- Snow shoeing alone in Banff Alberta Rocky Mountains.
- Lying on the rocks in New York City Central Park.

Wikimedia Commons, Benutzer

What are the **simple adventures** and **moments** that made the hair on the back of your neck stand up, those experiences with wonderful value that cost hardly any money, the ones you are always telling people about? Record them here so you'll never forget and continue these inexpensive activities in the future:

_____

_____

_____

❏ **AI:** _____

## Investing Is Good!

Please give yourself frequent rewards for significant contributions to your investments. It can be big investments like buying an investment property and starting a business. Just as important is starting a college fund, releasing weight, increasing contributions to 401(k) or other retirement plans, and increasing monthly amounts to pay off credit card balances. Reward and gift children with money in their Roth 401(k) or college fund, not a present or promise of a car at graduation. Treat yourself and your family to low-cost meals with coupons or discount cards. Another treat is a free day at the museum with a picnic in the park or walk on the beach. The quality of time is more important than the amount of money spent. Results are the best reward, no matter how big or small. Celebrate the little and big successes—you deserve it!

❑  **AI:** _____

**"The WINNER is?"** Create a weekly cheapest idea and best savings contest. Make a friendly game among couples, families, neighbors, or coworkers. Have a jar in which everybody puts a dollar. Vote on the best idea and saving experience. The winner takes all and will invest the winnings.

❑  **AI:** _____

Remember to set up monthly automatic withdrawals from banking your account or paycheck to directly finance pre-tax retirement plan, after-tax mutual fund, college fund, and emergency fund, plus payoff mortgage and car loans. This will make investing as simple and automated as possible. It feels great!

❑  **Automatic Investment Program: <u>On</u>**

Cheap is not just about saving moving, but also about investing it.

*"We cannot solve our problems with the same thinking we used when we created them." ~ Albert Einstein*

# CHAPTER 19: GIVING THINGS UP AND LETTING GO

*"When I let go of what I am, I become what I might be." ~ Lao Tzu*

## Less Is Better

Less can be more impactful and powerful. Refer to the biblical tale of David and Goliath. Which of the following would you rather be: overburdened with heavy debt and no savings, or lean 'n mean with positive cash-flowing investment properties and a fully funded retirement plan? I don't know about you, but I'd choose David!

Many "successful" cultures practice achieving meaningful dreams simply by focusing. You do not have to have everything you see. Luxurious items, pleasures, and habits will be scaled back to make room for your dreams and goals. You will have to give some things up and other things back. This is the harsh reality of adding a new aspect to your life. You can't miss something you've never had.

## It Will Take Sacrifice

Hope is alive and well, but hope needs to be combined with personal effort and sacrifice. You deserve nice, reliable, quality items. Don't sacrifice value for price, but there are limits. You can still acquire most of what you need by being cheap. This is not necessarily a contradiction. Focus on goals and not perishables. Accomplishing your goals will bring you true joy and fulfillment, and as a result, your effectiveness will increase.

**"Why you such a fake?"** Get over your urge to try to live like the Joneses. "Forget the traditional symbols of success. Attempting to keep up with the Joneses is inherently complex. At its worst, it means always having the latest-model car, the fastest computer, the largest house, and most chic vacation home. It means maintaining an extravagate wardrobe, sending your children to exclusive schools, joining the right clubs, and making appearances. Chasing after such symbols of achievement can be an all-consuming hollow existence. Let go of the trappings of social status. Instead, focus on the things in life that are the most comfortable, rewarding, or enjoyable to you."[1]

Do material items and their debt control you? No more fake smiles and building a house of cards on credit. Stop allowing others to blindly endorse your frivolous lifestyle, out-of-control spending habits, or other addictive and counterproductive behaviors. Also do not be a yes-man to everything people do. You need to be open to provide candid input and receive others' constructive feedback. Sacrifice will be required to regain more control of your destination, and your lifestyle will change to have a better future.

You need to commit to let go. The transformation process to create more money to invest comes at a price:

- What are you willing to give up to achieve your dreams?
- What will you sacrifice for your health?
- What will you sacrifice for your long-term happiness?
- What will you sacrifice to create a better life for your children and help your parents retire with dignity?

**Give Up a Vice Now:** Just give one up now—right now! This will not be easy at first. You may need to sacrifice two or three vices to start with so you can move forward to implement your 90-day transformation plan. Then, give up at least one vice a year, more often if necessary. Giving up a vice may also be a reduction or doing less of something. Here are some vice examples (add the specifics, for all may not apply to you):

❑ Buying expensive luxury or sport vehicles     __/__/__
❑ Compulsive shopping for items like clothes and crafts     __/__/__
❑ Excessive shopping for items like shoes and jewelry     __/__/__
❑ Shopping at exclusive stores     __/__/__
❑ Smoking tobacco     __/__/__
❑ Drinking alcohol     __/__/__

- ❏  Drinking coffee and soda                          __/__/__
- ❏  Eating fast and junk food                         __/__/__
- ❏  Watching games and reality TV shows               __/__/__
- ❏  Watching sporting events and news                 __/__/__

                                         ❏  **AI:** _____

_____**'s Vices to Give Up List**          __/__/__

- ❏  _____                  __/__/__
- ❏  _____                  __/__/__
- ❏  _____                  __/__/__
- ❏  _____                  __/__/__
- ❏  _____                  __/__/__
- ❏  _____                  __/__/__
- ❏  _____                  __/__/__
- ❏  _____                  __/__/__
- ❏  _____                  __/__/__
- ❏  _____                  __/__/__

                                         ❏  **AI:** _____

## Trading Down

Reduce your living space and start the downsize or "right size" process by emptying a room or closet once a year until you can move into a more efficient and low-maintenance home. Reducing the clutter in your home will reduce the time and energy that clutters your mind. Also consider moving to a less expensive but safe community with good schools, lower property values, and lower property and sales taxes.

                                         ❏  **AI:** _____

I once moved from an Old Victorian house to a smaller ranch-style bungalow and sold two rooms' worth of belongings I was not utilizing. When I moved from my bungalow in Denver to a loft in San Francisco, I had a basement full of things I had to leave behind. This included selling a leg press hip sled with 100-pound plates. I've been able to replace the hip sled exercises with dumbbell lunges. I also had to give away my bunny rabbit (Nummy Muffin Coocol Butter),[96] but she has more room to play now. Sometimes to quickly get ahead in life, you have to leave a few things behind to lighten the load . . . because sometimes less really is more!

👍 Sell recreational vehicles that do not generate income like monster trucks, all-terrain vehicles, snowmobiles, and jet skis. Trading in does not necessarily mean downgrading your lifestyle.

**Trading-Down Wants List Example** (all may not apply to you):

- ❏  30 minutes of TV to 30 minutes of reading    __/__/__
- ❏  5-bedroom to 4- or 3-bedroom home    __/__/__
- ❏  70" to 50" TV    __/__/__
- ❏  Coffee to juice    __/__/__
- ❏  Dating a high- to low-maintenance person    __/__/__
- ❏  Diet soft drink to water    __/__/__
- ❏  Elevator to taking the stairs    __/__/__
- ❏  Home cleaning service every two weeks to once a month    __/__/__
- ❏  Imported beer to domestic light beer    __/__/__
- ❏  Large SUV to electric mid-sized sedan    __/__/__
- ❏  Lying on couch to jogging around the lake    __/__/__
- ❏  Leading brands to generic brands    __/__/__
- ❏  Leasing latest-model car to buying a reliable used car    __/__/__
- ❏  Marriott Suites to Marriott Court Yard    __/__/__
- ❏  Nice bottle of wine to decent carton of wine    __/__/__
- ❏  Nordstrom to Nordstrom Rack    __/__/__
- ❏  Private school to good public school    __/__/__
- ❏  Pro-sports to shared college season tickets    __/__/__
- ❏  **AI:** _____

---

[96]  MST3K "Nummy Muffin Coocol Butter" song by Frank on YouTube at: *www.youtube.com/watch?v=nwMPZmtpWIE* (April 29, 2011)

_____'s Trading-Down Wants List    ___/___/___

❑ _____ to _____    ___/___/___
❑ _____ to _____    ___/___/___
❑ _____ to _____    ___/___/___
❑ _____ to _____    ___/___/___
❑ _____ to _____    ___/___/___
❑ _____ to _____    ___/___/___
❑ _____ to _____    ___/___/___
❑ _____ to _____    ___/___/___
❑ _____ to _____    ___/___/___
❑ _____ to _____    ___/___/___
                                    ❑ AI: _____

*"As you become more clear about who you really are, you'll be better able to decide what is best for you—the first time around."*
*~ Oprah Winfrey*

# CHAPTER 20: REQUIRED CHANGES

*"You cannot change your destination overnight, but you can change your direction overnight." ~ Jim Rohn*

## The Path to Change

Making a major change in your life and behavior will not be easy or pleasant. It will be a hard and challenging process. I have pushed at times and did my best to make it interesting while making continuous progress. Please set new boundaries and comfort levels. With your commitment and strength, the only option is success! I have provided many different money-saving and money-making strategies for you to choose from within the pages of this book, but it is up to you to implement them.

"Real change comes from the inside out. It doesn't come from hacking at the leaves of attitude and behavior with quick-fit personality ethic techniques. It comes from striking at the root—the fabric of our thought, the fundamental, essential paradigms, which give definition to our character and create the lens through which we see the world."[2]

👍 "When embarking on the path to change, it is important to set reasonable expectations. If our expectations are too high, we're setting ourselves up for disappointment. If they are too low, it extinguishes our willingness to challenge our limitations and achieve our true potential."[3]

The gradual process of learning new behaviors, habits, and skills will take time. In some areas, you will be retraining your thought patterns and body actions. This is the time to make pivotal, smart decisions. With new knowledge, education, and drive, you will make major positive changes in your life direction.

## Incremental Steps to Bring About Change

"Success is not going to come quick or easy. Take the success in increments because you will feel better about yourself every increment.

Don't look so much at the big picture until you aspire to it. You should feel successful every step of the way that way you continue. Because if every three months, six months, or one year you achieve one goal or another, that's how often you will feel successful. If you feel successful all the time, there is no room for giving up. So find increments of successful so you do not fall back to bad patterns, habits, and behavior."[4]

❑ **AI:** _____

"Yes, but in discussing an approach to bringing about positive changes within oneself, learning is only the first step. There are other factors as well: conviction, determination, action, and effort:"[5]

[1.] *So the next step is developing* <u>*conviction*</u>. Learning and education are important because they help one develop conviction of the need to change and help increase one's commitment.

[2.] *This conviction to change then develops into* <u>*determination*</u>.

[3.] *Next, one transforms determination into* <u>*action*</u>—the strong determination to change enables one to make a sustained effort to implement the actual changes.

[4.] *This final factor of* <u>*effort*</u> *is critical.*

"Now, no matter what behavior you are seeking to change, no matter what particular goal or action you are directing your efforts toward, you need to start by developing a strong willingness or wish to do it. You need to generate great enthusiasm. *And, here, a sense of urgency is a key factor.* This sense of urgency is a powerful factor in helping you overcome problems."[6] Overcoming these challenges will enable you to focus on your goals. I applaud you for taking this first two steps and starting to implement the last two steps.

## Change Is Action in Motion

**"Drop and give me twenty!"** Do not let fear slow you down or stop you anymore. Fear is a manifestation in our minds. No more will we be deterred. Action cures fears and stagnation. Get the blood moving to your brain, muscles, and nervous system. Little steps will soon become big steps. What little actions do you need to take now to breakthrough to the next big steps?

❑ _____ __/__/__
❑ _____ __/__/__
❑ _____ __/__/__
　　　　　　　　　　　　　　　❑ **AI:** _____

👍 Take action to join a club that will teach you the skills what will be required in your next profession. In my teens, I was a Police Explorer. It was an exceptional experience that taught me to respect law enforcement and the justice system. There are many types of these cadet and training programs that enable people to learn about certain professions such as military, medical, business, politics, and civil service. To make it easy to participate and grow, these different service trades have structured local, regional, and national chapters. They build teamwork, leadership, and practical trade skills for their desired profession while keeping teens out of trouble during those impressionable high school years.

Our squad was competing at a week-long junior police academy at Fort Monmouth Army Base. One night, we stayed up past lights-out to study for a domestic violence scenario test. The next morning at revelry, we were busted, so we had the courage to step out of line to admit to over 250 other candidates, soldiers, and police officers that we had broken curfew. I was so nervous my legs were shaking uncontrollably, and you could hear my knees knocking. The drill sergeant said, "Do you want to drop to the ground and give to twenty push-ups, maggot?" (Okay, so I threw in "maggot.") I replied, "Yes, Drill Sergeant!" So I dropped to the ground did twenty push-ups. When I got up, my legs were not shaking anymore.

👍 Yes, we would have done it again—and did the next night without getting caught. This action of doing push-ups built confidence, and later that day, we did an outstanding job in the domestic dispute test. We defused the situation, and nobody was harmed. The moral of the story is that doing a physical action cleared the mind so we could continue practicing to eventually pass another life test.

Mom and Darryl (What waist size was this, like 24 inches?)

Focus your passion to gain control of when and how you reach your destination. Use this power to change your results, which will change your life. Failures are temporary and are lessons learned that will strengthen new experiences. Change can be painful and make you cry or get angry. You may also laugh and rejoice. You reached a major milestone by just wanting to learn about change from this book—CONGRATS!

❑   Say aloud, "I will take action today to make the required changes that will improve my situation to reach my goals."

*"The entrepreneur always searches for change, responds to it, and exploits it as an opportunity." ~ Peter F. Drucker*

# CHAPTER 21: GOAL SETTING

*"Goals are dreams with deadlines." ~ Diana Scharf Hunt*

## A Fresh New Process of Setting Goals

**Think Really BIG:** The sky is the limit. Do not censor your abilities by aiming too low. A BIG goal may be made up of little ones. "Think success, not failure. Think I can. It is possible."[7] You need to take extreme measures to reach these goals, like being increasingly more cheap, consciously acquiring less things, and aggressively expanding your investment portfolio.

Develop a well-thought-out and effective plan of action. There will be immediate-term (days), short-term (weeks), mid-term (months), and long-term (years) goals, objectives, and tasks. They will guide you to a happier place where you can be fulfilled without all of the empty calories, noise, and wants. This is an inclusive approach to goal setting by covering all aspects of your life. These goal-oriented action plans, in the form of checklists, are provided in this and later chapters for you to complete.

**InFocus®:** Focus, focus, focus like a laser beam on your goals. Do not let other people distract you, especially family members or your significant other. Choose to eliminate distractions like cable or satellite channels that you can get sucked into or can get the information another way. For example, look to eliminate talk shows, late-night shows, reality, celebrity, and sports channels. You can block the channels from yourself by using the parental control feature. Stop ordering pay-per-view concerts and sporting events,[97] and on demand movies and adult films. Migrate to listening to music or watching nature shows with the sound off. This will now be time saved that can be more effectively used to achieve your goals.

❏ **AI:** _____

---

[97] If you simply cannot miss a pay-per-view event, go to a friend's home to watch it and split the cost among everyone. Try to only pay five dollars.

## Gooooooooooal!!!!!! [98]

Goals are critical to motivate people to work harder and longer at something that is a little agonizing and may be new to us. You must strive for action and positive change. Goals should be quantitative, clear, obtainable, and time sensitive.

There are two types of goals:

1. <u>Firm or committed goals</u>, which you are confident you can achieve on time.
2. <u>Stretch goals</u>, which have a higher return or earlier due date that push you harder to accomplish them.

One firm goal may be to retire early—perhaps by the age of fifty-five, and in style. A stretch goal may be for you to become financially free and accomplish your goals while giving back to society by the age of fifty.

Wikimedia Commons, Shalom Jacobovitz

You have graciously allowed me to push the envelope and be myself by sharing my experiences with you. One of my greatest accomplishments was going from a stuttering teenager to recently standing in the front of a classroom giving lectures to hundreds of students. One goal of this book is to provide insight into many different concepts that will best support your quest for fulfillment and prosperity. My firm goal is to positively change 250,000 lives. Influencing over one million people is my stretch goal. I am passionate about enhancing as many lives as possible.

**"Oh, no! Turn left!"** Anytime is right for an early-, mid-, or late-course correction. There is no time like the present to revamp, modify, or totally change your decision processes and direction in life. This book assists

---

[98]    Dizzy Dean, a soccer announcer.

you in the discovery process and provides a clear direction to self actualization and fulfillment. We WILL win the game, tournament, and championship. SCORE!

## Putting Yourself First

**"BUFU!"** You deserve people to buy your products and services. Help yourself first, and then help somebody else by being a producer. You need to take care of yourself first to be in the position to assist others. There is a reason the flight attendant instructs you to, "Put on your oxygen mask first, before assisting other people in need."

👍 If you need to, feel free to use my name as an excuse to make your required changes for the desired results. Chalk it up to Wortham Logic! Remember, though, that it may not be wise to continually invoke *my* name to your partner or friends. Too many, "Darryl says" might be a bad thing that turns them off to **\$ET=M² to INVEST** action plan; it's a judgment call.

If you want to help your partner, relative, or friend along the way, give them their own copy of this book. See what s/he will gain from it independently of you. After a couple weeks, check in with each other on their progress. If this does not create the required changes, you may need to take the lead as their accountability partner.

❏ **AI:** _____

## Keep It Simple, Stupid

**"It's so easy even a caveman can do it."** This book is governed on the principle of *K.I.S.S.* = Keep It Simple, Stupid! I have tried to present ideas, strategies, and philosophies in a skillful, clear, and implementable approach. Simple tasks will be easy to integrate into the larger, more complex objectives. Start with straightforward tasks that require little decision and then migrate to multipart undertakings that require more effort.

👍 Start with the easiest items first, the "low-hanging fruit." Pick them fast and then quickly reach for the next goal. When you achieve one goal, it becomes easier to focus on the next goal because there are fewer from which to choose.

Take many small steps to get started, then take larger ones and risks, followed by more frequent steps. Taking little steps more frequently will get you there in good time and at a healthy, productive pace. Just like  the *World's Strongest Man*™ truck-pull competition, the resulting momentum will press you forward at a faster pace.

Mariusz Pudzianowski, Wikimedia Commons, Artur Andrzej

**Get It Over With:** Another alternative is "any time the order in which you tackle tasks or components of a task is at your discretion, opt for the seemingly unpleasant one first. Achieving simplicity in your life starts with the simple notion that you are in control."[8]

## Creating and Documenting Your Goals

"A Personal Mission Statement is so important when you have a deep understanding of your core and purpose. Here is an example, 'My money will be a servant, not my master. I will seek financial independence over time. My wants will be subject to my needs and my means. Except for long-term home and car loans, I will seek to keep myself free from consumer debt. I will spend less than I earn and regularly save or invest part of my income.'"[9]

**My Mission is to** _____

_____

_____

_____

❏ **AI:** _____

"Believe big and grow big. The size of your success is determined by the size of your belief. Think little goals and expect little achievements. Think big goals and win big success."[10] Set goals high and target completion dates that are obtainable. Write them down and post them. Document major past achievements, check them off, and note the estimated completion date. This will illustrate that they <u>can</u> be achieved and bring a smile to your face. "It is fun to feel yourself growing more confident, more effective, more successful day by day, month by month. Nothing—absolutely nothing—in this life gives you more satisfaction than knowing you're on the road to success and achievement."[11]

Set your goals with realistic target dates for **<u>not</u> living paycheck to paycheck** by accumulating cash reserves and liquid assets:

| Reserve Goals | Target Date | Completed Date |
|---|---|---|
| ❑ Living paycheck to every other paycheck | __/__/__ | __/__/__ |
| ❑ Living paycheck to every fourth paycheck | __/__/__ | __/__/__ |
| ❑ Living without a paycheck for six months | __/__/__ | __/__/__ |
| ❑ Living without a paycheck for one year | __/__/__ | __/__/__ |
| ❑ Living without a paycheck for _____ | __/__/__ | __/__/__ |
| ❑ Al: _____ | | |

👍 These reserves include assets that can be easily liquidated with no major financial penalties to withdraw the funds or sell the investments. Many accounts are linked to money markets, which have higher interest rates than traditional savings accounts. Saving cash is good, but we also want to be investing your savings to create passive income.

Proudly advertise your goals on your refrigerator door or most visited place in the home that others can see. You probably spend more time in the kitchen or home office than the bathroom. Your friends and family will be the support system and will test your progress as your accountability partners. Work together as a team. However, even if others don't back you 100 percent at first, you need to find the internal courage to move forward. They will follow, be left behind, or be pushed aside, and that role will be up to them.

❑ **AI:** _____

"If you're single, identify a 'money buddy' whom you can be open with about recent financial successes and failures. Plan goals together and actively support each other in making good spending and financial choices while offering advice in difficult situations."[12]

❑ **AI:** _____

## My Needs and Wants

**Needful Things**: Not all "needs" are equal, and their priorities may be different. Many "wants" you interpret to be "needs" but are not. Resolve this conflict of your desire to make non-essential items as a requirement to live a productive life. You need to forego instant gratification and pleasures for the sake of long-term goals and meaningful results. Do not lose focus and spend your successes away.

Create a "needs" and "wants/doodads" lists with dollar amounts required to obtain an item and the desired date. List them in priority order and check off items when completed. Each family member should have one. Replace the pictures on the refrigerator with these lists.

Here are examples of "**Needs List**" (all may not apply to you):

❑ Lose 15 lbs. (Oct 2011)     __/__/__
❑ Quit smoking (March 2012)     __/__/__
❑ Run in half marathon or 10K (2013)     __/__/__
❑ Create/Update Will     __/__/__
❑ File cabinet for office     __/__/__
❑ Home office wireless broadband router     __/__/__
❑ Business briefcase     __/__/__
❑ Install energy efficient blinds     __/__/__
❑ Replace light bulbs with CFL bulbs     __/__/__

❑ **AI:** _____

**_____'s Needs List \_\_\_/\_\_\_/\_\_\_**

- ❑ _____    \_\_/\_\_/\_\_
- ❑ _____    \_\_/\_\_/\_\_
- ❑ _____    \_\_/\_\_/\_\_
- ❑ _____    \_\_/\_\_/\_\_
- ❑ _____    \_\_/\_\_/\_\_
- ❑ _____    \_\_/\_\_/\_\_
- ❑ _____    \_\_/\_\_/\_\_
- ❑ _____    \_\_/\_\_/\_\_
- ❑ _____    \_\_/\_\_/\_\_
- ❑ _____    \_\_/\_\_/\_\_

❑ **AI:** _____

Here are examples of "**Wants/Doodads List**" (all may not apply):

- ❑ Remodel kitchen[99]                              \_\_/\_\_/\_\_
- ❑ Large artwork piece                             \_\_/\_\_/\_\_
- ❑ All premium channel cable/satellite package    \_\_/\_\_/\_\_
- ❑ XBOX 360, Wii, or PS3                           \_\_/\_\_/\_\_
- ❑ Disney World/Land                               \_\_/\_\_/\_\_
- ❑ Luxury SUV                                      \_\_/\_\_/\_\_
- ❑ Designer jeans                                  \_\_/\_\_/\_\_
- ❑ Diamond earrings                                \_\_/\_\_/\_\_
- ❑ 30 or more pairs of shoes, boots, sneakers      \_\_/\_\_/\_\_
- ✓ Platform shoes with fish in them     ***$50***   **12/01/10**

❑ **AI:** _____

Yes, that is a fish in the heel!

---

[99]    May also be a "need" if remodeling adds more resell market value to your home that you spent. First investigate only upgrading the kitchen.

**_____'s Wants/Doodads List ___/___/___**

- ☐ _____ ___/___/___
- ☐ _____ ___/___/___
- ☐ _____ ___/___/___
- ☐ _____ ___/___/___
- ☐ _____ ___/___/___
- ☐ _____ ___/___/___
- ☐ _____ ___/___/___
- ☐ _____ ___/___/___
- ☐ _____ ___/___/___
- ☐ _____ ___/___/___

☐ **AI:** _____

☝ Evaluate moving some "needs" to the "Wants/Doodads List." Your goal is to get the number of items and their cost on the "Wants/Doodads List" to be less than the "Needs List." At the same time, reduce the overall item number and cost of items appearing on these lists.

## My Career and Financial Goals

Create a list of your career and financial goals with desired dollar amounts or required amounts and desired date to accomplish your goal. List them in priority order and check off items when completed. Post the list where you will see it several times a day.

Here are examples of "**Career and Financial Goals List**" (all may not apply to you):

- ☐ Get promotion and salary increase ___/___/___
- ☐ Get second or part-time job ___/___/___
- ☐ Work extra time for overtime pay ___/___/___
- ☐ Build up $___,000 Emergency Fund ___/___/___
- ☐ Pay off department store card _____ ___/___/___
- ☐ Pay off Credit Card _____ ___/___/___
- ☐ Add extra $100/month principal on home ___/___/___
- ☐ Start home-based business ___/___/___
- ☐ Amass real estate portfolio (___ properties) ___/___/___

❑  Fully fund 401(k), 403(b), 457, IRA, TSP, ___    __/__/__
❑  Fully fund 529 college savings fund              __/__/__
❑  Retire by age sixty (or earlier ___)             __/__/__
                                    ❑  AI: _____

_____'s Career and Financial Goals List __/__/__

❑  _____        __/__/__
❑  _____        __/__/__
❑  _____        __/__/__
❑  _____        __/__/__
❑  _____        __/__/__
❑  _____        __/__/__
❑  _____        __/__/__
❑  _____        __/__/__
❑  _____        __/__/__
❑  _____        __/__/__
                                    ❑  AI: _____

## My Life and Personal Goals

Create a list of your life and personal goals with dollar amounts required to and desired date accomplish your goal. List them in priority order and check off items when completed. As a reminder, post the list where you will see it several times a day.

Here are examples of "**Life and Personal Goals List**" (all may not apply to you):

❑  Be a teacher, mentor, or coach                __/__/__
❑  Get professional license or certification     __/__/__
❑  Helping others by volunteering weekly         __/__/__
❑  Get bachelor's degree                         __/__/__
❑  Get master's degree                           __/__/__
❑  Be an inventor and patent my ideas            __/__/__
❑  Enroll children in college                    __/__/__
❑  Business owner who employs others             __/__/__
❑  Fund charities to $___,000 a year             __/__/__

- ❑ Start a nonprofit foundation          __/__/__
- ❑ Take care of parents          __/__/__
- ❑ Journey to Mecca, Vatican, Mount Kailash          __/__/__
  - ❑ **AI:** _____

_____**'s Life and Personal Goals List ___/___/___**

- ❑ _____          __/__/__
- ❑ _____          __/__/__
- ❑ _____          __/__/__
- ❑ _____          __/__/__
- ❑ _____          __/__/__
- ❑ _____          __/__/__
- ❑ _____          __/__/__
- ❑ _____          __/__/__
- ❑ _____          __/__/__
- ❑ _____          __/__/__
  - ❑ **AI:** _____

Career and financial goals list and life and personal goals list are where the investments go! Special kind words of admiration and respect spoken about you because you earned it as a producer providing a significant contribution to your family and community.

*"When you are interested, you will do what is convenient. When you are committed, you will do whatever it takes to accomplish your goals." ~ Don Staley*

# CHAPTER 22: THE TRANSFORMATION FROM CONSUMER TO PRODUCER

*"Leadership is the capacity to translate vision into reality."*
*~ Warren G. Bennis*

## Time to Choose: Consume or Produce?

Look at these key words to choose the side you want to be on.

The definition of "**to consume**:"[13]
1. to do **away with completely**: <u>DESTROY</u>
2. to **spend wastefully**: <u>SQUANDER</u> or <u>USE UP</u>
3. to **eat or drink especially in great quantity**
4. to **waste** or **burn away**: <u>PERISH</u>

The definition of "**to produce**:"[14]
1. to **offer to view or notice**
2. to give birth or **rise to**: <u>YIELD</u>
3. to **make available for public exhibition or dissemination**
4. to **provide funding for**
5. to cause to have existence or to **happen**: <u>BRING ABOUT</u>
6. to **give being, form, or shape to**: <u>MAKE</u> or <u>MANUFACTURE</u>
7. to **compose, create, or bring out by intellectual or physical effort**

Watch the local news and how they negatively portray consumers, people who appear to be waiting in line in shopping malls and have unhealthy eating habits. Then watch business news and notice how they positively portray producers, who tend to be executives and business owners that look fit.

❑ It's time to choose one: **Consumer** _____ or **Producer** _____

## Making the Move to Producing

👍 Reduce the time, money, and energy spent on consumer activities, spend it more wisely. To reinforce the point, replace material possessions with mental wellness, physical fitness, and fulfillment. Don't invest your savings in team sports outfits or apparel. It's fine if you want a hat and shirt, but stay away from collecting all of their stuff. It will not generate income or earn interest and will only collect dust. You are not responsible to buy everything teams sell. If the team changes their uniform or logo, that is their problem. This is by financial design, for they know there will be a continuous flow of revenue if they can turn fans' items into perishables. Do not fall into their trap. Why are you supporting multi-millionaire players and the billionaire owners? Support your investments, your parents, your children, and people in need. Be the company that others pay for services, applications, or products.

You are also not responsible to buy furniture for and decorate somebody else's home. They can buy that themselves. Give them a book or DVD of knowledge that can help them grow, without being too obvious. Give a gift that will generate income for somebody or bring them peace of mind and happiness.

👍 Do not send texts to vote for sports, dance, and talent TV contests and news poll. What a waste of money and energy! Do you really think you make a difference? Stop playing impractical contests with little return. Just pass on them and replace them with revenue-generating activities. Use the time to trade stocks and monitor your mutual funds performance.

**Increase Social Capital:** Walk Score™ states, "Walking promotes interaction among neighbors and potential clients. Each ten-minute decrease in daily car commute time translates to 10 percent more time spent in community activities and networking."[15] Walk around expecting to meet people every time you go out. Be prepared to give them your "thirty-second evaluator pitch" and a promotional flyer. To find walkable neighborhoods, go to *www.WalkScore.com*.

❑ **AI:** _____

Being a producer is not just about selling goods and services, but it is also about ownership. You might already be closer than you realize. As stated, owning stocks is direct ownership in a company as a shareholder. Most mutual funds are a mix of shares in public-traded companies. This is ownership as well, just not as direct and typically with less risk.

*"At first dreams seem impossible, then improbable, then inevitable."*
*~ Christopher Reeve*

# CHAPTER 23: THE TRANSFORMATION PLAN

*"It is more blessed to give than to receive." ~ Acts 20:35*

Now, are you ready to create your transformation plan? This is synergizing everything together. Here is an asset allocation model at Day 0 (today). Your situation may be different. The key is for your consumer wants and needs to decrease as your producer investments grow. These percentages are not as important as the changes in proportion. Increasing your income can also change these percentages by directing these new funds toward producer investments over needs and wants. There will be a new model after each transformation plan is implemented.

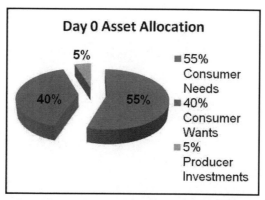

Example of a present situation asset allocation model.

To make this manageable, the **transformation plan** is divided into smaller time intervals:

1. **90-Day Plan**
2. **6-Month Plan**
3. **1-Year Plan**
4. **3-Year Plan**
5. **5-Year Plan**
6. **Rolling 5-Year Plan**

Migrate from one plan to the next. Fill in a plan on the start day and check off items when completed. At the end of the period, carry over uncompleted items to the next plan and add in new items.

## Transforming to a Producer in Ninety Days

| 90-Day Transformation Plan | |
|---|---|
| **Saving Money** | |
| ❏ | ❏ |
| ❏ | ❏ |
| **Saving Energy and Time** | |
| ❏ | ❏ |
| ❏ | ❏ |
| **Investing in Yourself** | |
| ❏ | ❏ |
| ❏ | ❏ |
| **Investing in Debt Reduction While Increasing Your Savings** | |
| ❏ | ❏ |
| ❏ | ❏ |
| **Investing in Your Career, Job, and Generating Income** | |
| ❏ | ❏ |
| ❏ | ❏ |
| **Investing in Your Retirement Plan** | |
| ❏ | ❏ |
| ❏ | ❏ |
| **Investing in Your Business** | |
| ❏ | ❏ |
| ❏ | ❏ |
| **Investing in Real Estate** | |
| ❏ | ❏ |
| ❏ | ❏ |
| **Investing in Your Community** | |
| ❏ | ❏ |
| ❏ | ❏ |

Note: Carry over uncompleted ideas and strategies to the "6-Month Transformation Plan" sheet.

❏  **AI:** _____

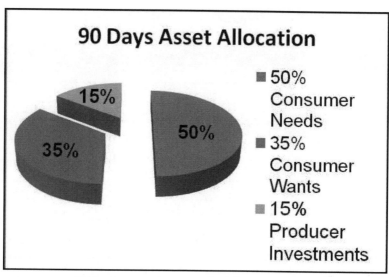

## 90 Days Asset Allocation

- 50% Consumer Needs
- 35% Consumer Wants
- 15% Producer Investments

Target goal changes in 90-day model.

Notes:

_____

_____

_____

_____

_____

_____

_____

_____

_____

_____

_____

_____

_____

_____

# Transforming to a Producer in Six Months

| 6-Month Transformation Plan | |
|---|---|
| **Saving Money** | |
| ❏ | ❏ |
| ❏ | ❏ |
| **Saving Energy and Time** | |
| ❏ | ❏ |
| ❏ | ❏ |
| **Investing in Yourself** | |
| ❏ | ❏ |
| ❏ | ❏ |
| **Investing in Debt Reduction While Increasing Your Savings** | |
| ❏ | ❏ |
| ❏ | ❏ |
| **Investing in Your Career, Job, and Generating Income** | |
| ❏ | ❏ |
| ❏ | ❏ |
| **Investing in Your Retirement Plan** | |
| ❏ | ❏ |
| ❏ | ❏ |
| **Investing in Your Business** | |
| ❏ | ❏ |
| ❏ | ❏ |
| **Investing in Real Estate** | |
| ❏ | ❏ |
| ❏ | ❏ |
| **Investing in Your Community** | |
| ❏ | ❏ |
| ❏ | ❏ |

Note: Carry over uncompleted ideas and strategies to the "1-Year Transformation Plan" sheet.

❏  **AI:** _____

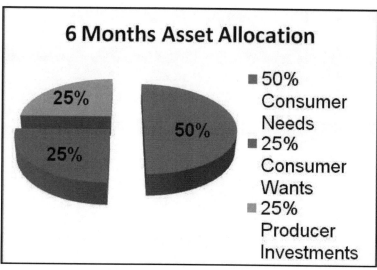

## 6 Months Asset Allocation

25%

25%

50%

- 50% Consumer Needs
- 25% Consumer Wants
- 25% Producer Investments

Target goal changes in six-month model.

Notes:

_____

_____

_____

_____

_____

_____

_____

_____

_____

_____

_____

_____

_____

_____

# Transforming to a Producer in One Year

| 1-Year Transformation Plan | |
| --- | --- |
| **Saving Money** | |
| ❑ | ❑ |
| ❑ | ❑ |
| **Saving Energy and Time** | |
| ❑ | ❑ |
| ❑ | ❑ |
| **Investing in Yourself** | |
| ❑ | ❑ |
| ❑ | ❑ |
| **Investing in Debt Reduction While Increasing Your Savings** | |
| ❑ | ❑ |
| ❑ | ❑ |
| **Investing in Your Career, Job, and Generating Income** | |
| ❑ | ❑ |
| ❑ | ❑ |
| **Investing in Your Retirement Plan** | |
| ❑ | ❑ |
| ❑ | ❑ |
| **Investing in Your Business** | |
| ❑ | ❑ |
| ❑ | ❑ |
| **Investing in Real Estate** | |
| ❑ | ❑ |
| ❑ | ❑ |
| **Investing in Your Community** | |
| ❑ | ❑ |
| ❑ | ❑ |

Note: Carry over uncompleted ideas and strategies to the "3-Years Transformation Plan" sheet.

❑ **AI:** _____

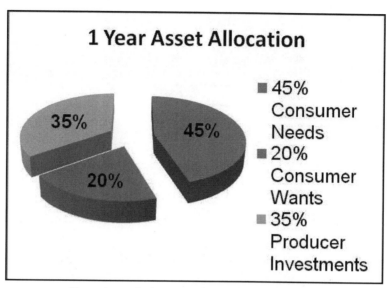

# 1 Year Asset Allocation

- 45% Consumer Needs
- 20% Consumer Wants
- 35% Producer Investments

Target goal changes in one-year model.

Notes:

_____

_____

_____

_____

_____

_____

_____

_____

_____

_____

_____

_____

_____

_____

# Transforming to a Producer in Three Years

| 3-Year Transformation Plan | |
|---|---|
| **Saving Money** | |
| ❑ | ❑ |
| ❑ | ❑ |
| **Saving Energy and Time** | |
| ❑ | ❑ |
| ❑ | ❑ |
| **Investing in Yourself** | |
| ❑ | ❑ |
| ❑ | ❑ |
| **Investing in Debt Reduction While Increasing Your Savings** | |
| ❑ | ❑ |
| ❑ | ❑ |
| **Investing in Your Career, Job, and Generating Income** | |
| ❑ | ❑ |
| ❑ | ❑ |
| **Investing in Your Retirement Plan** | |
| ❑ | ❑ |
| ❑ | ❑ |
| **Investing in Your Business** | |
| ❑ | ❑ |
| ❑ | ❑ |
| **Investing in Real Estate** | |
| ❑ | ❑ |
| ❑ | ❑ |
| **Investing in Your Community** | |
| ❑ | ❑ |
| ❑ | ❑ |

Note: You can also track more frequently, maybe every year. Carry over uncompleted ideas and strategies to the "5-Year Transformation Plan" blank sheet.

❑ **AI:** _____

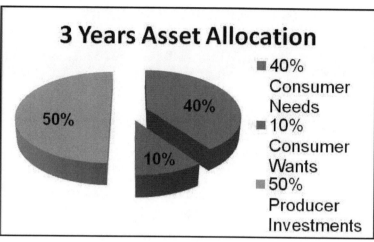

**3 Years Asset Allocation**

- 40% Consumer Needs
- 10% Consumer Wants
- 50% Producer Investments

Target goal changes in three-year model.

Notes:

_____

_____

_____

_____

_____

_____

_____

_____

_____

_____

_____

_____

_____

# Transforming to a Producer in Five Years

| 5-Year Transformation Plan | |
|---|---|
| **Saving Money** | |
| ❑ | ❑ |
| ❑ | ❑ |
| **Saving Energy and Time** | |
| ❑ | ❑ |
| ❑ | ❑ |
| **Investing in Yourself** | |
| ❑ | ❑ |
| ❑ | ❑ |
| **Investing in Debt Reduction While Increasing Your Savings** | |
| ❑ | ❑ |
| ❑ | ❑ |
| **Investing in Your Career, Job, and Generating Income** | |
| ❑ | ❑ |
| ❑ | ❑ |
| **Investing in Your Retirement Plan** | |
| ❑ | ❑ |
| ❑ | ❑ |
| **Investing in Your Business** | |
| ❑ | ❑ |
| ❑ | ❑ |
| **Investing in Real Estate** | |
| ❑ | ❑ |
| ❑ | ❑ |
| **Investing in Your Community** | |
| ❑ | ❑ |
| ❑ | ❑ |

Note: You can also track more frequently, maybe every year. Carry over uncompleted ideas and strategies to the "Rolling 5-Year Transformation Plan" blank sheet.

❑ **AI:** _____

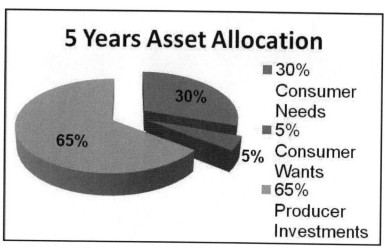

## 5 Years Asset Allocation

- ■ 30% Consumer Needs
- ■ 5% Consumer Wants
- ■ 65% Producer Investments

30%

5%

65%

Target goal changes in five-year model.

Notes:

_____

_____

_____

_____

_____

_____

_____

_____

_____

_____

_____

_____

_____

_____

## Transforming to a Producer in Ten-Plus Years

| Rolling 5-Year Transformation Plan | |
|---|---|
| **Saving Money** | |
| ❑ | ❑ |
| ❑ | ❑ |
| **Saving Energy and Time** | |
| ❑ | ❑ |
| ❑ | ❑ |
| **Investing in Yourself** | |
| ❑ | ❑ |
| ❑ | ❑ |
| **Investing in Debt Reduction While Increasing Your Savings** | |
| ❑ | ❑ |
| ❑ | ❑ |
| **Investing in Your Career, Job, and Generating Income** | |
| ❑ | ❑ |
| ❑ | ❑ |
| **Investing in Your Retirement Plan** | |
| ❑ | ❑ |
| ❑ | ❑ |
| **Investing in Your Business** | |
| ❑ | ❑ |
| ❑ | ❑ |
| **Investing in Real Estate** | |
| ❑ | ❑ |
| ❑ | ❑ |
| **Investing in Your Community** | |
| ❑ | ❑ |
| ❑ | ❑ |

Note: Carry over uncompleted ideas and strategies to the next "Rolling 5-Year Transformation Plan" sheet.

❑  **AI:** _____

*"Courage is grace under pressure."* ~ *Ernest Hemingway*

# Part V: The Plan of Attack Endnotes

[1]  Jeff Davidson, *The Joy of Simple Living: Over 1,500 Simple Ways to Make Your Life Easy and Content*, Rodale Press, pp. 13, 19.

[2]  Stephen R. Covey, *The 7 Habits of Highly Effective People*, Simon and Schuster, 1989, p. 317.

[3]  His Holiness, the Dalai Lama and Howard C. Cutler, MD, *The Art of Happiness: A Handbook for Living*, permission of Riverhead Books, imprint of Penguin Group (USA) Inc., 1998, pp. 231-232.

[4]  Judge Greg Mathis, *Judge Mathis*, Warner Brothers, 2010, at *www.askjudgemathis.com*.

[5]  Dalai Lama and Cutler, p. 220.

[6]  Ibid, pp. 220-221.

[7]  David J. Schwartz, PhD., *The Magic of Thinking Big: Acquire the Secrets of Success...Achieve Everything You've Always Wanted*, Simon & Schuster, 1987, p. 26.

[8]  Davidson, pp. 344, 2.

[9]  Covey, pp. 294, 107.

[10]  Schwartz, p. 26.

[11]  Ibid, p. 62.

[12]  Trent Hamm, *365 Ways to Live Cheap: Your Everyday Guide to Saving Money*, Adams Media, 2009, pp. 6-7.

[13]  Merriam Webster at *www.merriam-webster.com/dictionary/consume* (May 1, 2011).

[14]  Merriam Webster at *www.merriam-webster.com/dictionary/produce* (May 1, 2011).

[15]  Work Score, "Walkable Neighborhoods", at *www.walkscore.com/walking-matters.shtml* (May 1, 2011).

# PART VI – BEYOND THE SPEED OF LIGHT INTO THE FUTURE

*"We are all made up of stars"* ~ *National Geographic Channel*

"Somewhere, something incredible is waiting to be known," said Carl Sagan. Eagle Nebula M16 from the Hubble Telescope, NASA[100]

## CHAPTER 24: MOVE FORWARD WITH CONFIDENCE AND SPEED

## Do It Now with Confidence

**Sooner Rather Than Later:** Action beats inaction. It is not always best to wait until everything is perfect to act. Defeat is only a moment in time. Take a fresh perspective and start again. Take massive action NOW!

"Certainty brings stability to our lives. Those things we are certain about are things we can count on, both in times of accomplishment and in times of need. Otherwise, we become complacent. Even if we are on the right track, if we are not moving, eventually we are going to get run over."[1]

👍 Do not feel overwhelmed. Take several deep breaths and exhale slowly. Release . . . You can and will do it! This is not a race but a memorable journey. Progress may appear slow, but that is relative.

---

[100] M16, the Eagle Nebula is a giant cloud of interstellar gas and dust that has already created a considerable cluster of young stars. Within M16 are several complex active star forming regions referred to as the "Pillars of Creation" that are more than six light years from end to end. The image can be downloaded at *www.nasa.gov/externalflash/Hubble20*.

Nevertheless, be positive, it is still progress. To loosen up a little, think of a car side mirror: *"Objects may appear smaller than they are"*—but they are not. You are <u>not</u> your own worst critic but your biggest fan! You have to love and believe in yourself to make this work.

"When life becomes too complicated and we feel overwhelmed, it's often useful just to stand back and remind ourselves of our overall purpose, our overall goal. When faced with a feeling of stagnation and confusion, it may be helpful to take an hour, an afternoon, or even several days to simply reflect on what it is that will truly bring us happiness, and then reset our priorities on the basis of that. This can put our life back in proper context, allow a fresh perspective, and enable us to see which direction to take."[2]

❑ **AI:** _____

These are some of the distractions that can occur, according to "**The Secret to Successful Writing**" by Deanna Mascle that can be applied in other life experiences:[3]

- Suddenly numerous opportunities in what seem like "better" directions will pop up all at once.
- Something isn't working the way you thought it would.
- It's going "slower" than you had hoped.
- Someone you trust questions what you're doing.

👍 "Use distractions to your advantage. The distraction showed up for a reason. Don't simply discard it or push it away. Use this as a time to revisit your vision, goal, purpose, or desire. More than likely, the distraction is a synchronistic event that will help you to fine-tune your vision. Think about different times when you seemed headed down a particular path toward something you wanted and you chose to leave that path—out of fear, doubt, insecurity, or because the grass was greener elsewhere."[4]

Start by completing and periodically updating these **worksheets**:

- ❑ Financial and Investment Strategies List     __/__/__
- ❑ Passion List                                 __/__/__
- ❑ Motivational Questions Lists                 __/__/__
- ❑ Behaviors, Habits, Savings to Repeat List    __/__/__
- ❑ Behaviors, Habits, Expenses to Discontinue List   __/__/__
- ❑ Delegation List                              __/__/__
- ❑ Smartphone Application Lists                 __/__/__
- ❑ Educational/Knowledge Requirements List      __/__/__
- ❑ Debts List                                   __/__/__
- ❑ Specialties, Strengths, Weaknesses List      __/__/__
- ❑ Retirement Plans List                        __/__/__
- ❑ Ten Steps to Start a Business                __/__/__
- ❑ Financial Checklist for Starting a Business  __/__/__
- ❑ Vices to Give Up List                        __/__/__
- ❑ Trading-Down Wants List                      __/__/__
- ❑ Living Paycheck to Paycheck                  __/__/__
- ❑ Needs List                                   __/__/__
- ❑ Wants/Doodads List                           __/__/__
- ❑ Career and Financial Goals List              __/__/__
- ❑ Life and Personal Goals List                 __/__/__
- ❑ 90-Day Transformation Plan                   __/__/__

❑ **AI:** _____

**"It smells like, Victory."** You need to decide and set your mind to move forward with this plan. Track the advancement of your individual development and investment plans. A little growth is still a step forward. Do not allow others' envy and jealousy or your own negative thinking force you to believe it's not progress, because it is. Don't let them tell you otherwise! You are so close to crossing the finish line and winning the first of many victories.

Make progress on different fronts just like a General on the field of battle. Yes, you will be fighting many battles and may have a setback that requires readjusting the plan of attack, but in the end, you will win

the war to achieve your personal and financial goals!

World War II 60th Anniversary Victory Day Parade 2005, Wikimedia Commons, President of the Russian Federation

Use your knowledge and confidence in your new role as a producer. The rental properties and business cash flow will be directed into the emergency funds, paying down the mortgages, contributing to a retirement plan, and funding future investments. This will create real wealth. Get ready for big wins! Don't be surprised what you get after a few quick successes like cutting household expenses dramatically and having stocks grow rapidly in a quarter. Soon you will be in the **top 2** then **1 percent** of the income earners in the world.[101]

## Do It Faster with Even More Confidence

"Although there are no easy solutions to avoiding these destructive pleasures, fortunately we have a place to begin: the simple reminder that what we are seeking in life is happiness. As the Dalai Lama points out, that is an unmistakable fact. If we approach our choices in life keeping that in mind, it is easier to give up the things that are ultimately harmful to us, even if those things bring us momentary pleasure. The reason why it is usually so difficult to 'Just say no!' is found in the word 'no'; that approach is associated with a sense of rejecting something, of giving something up, or of denying ourselves . . ."[5]

"But there is a better approach: framing any decision we face by asking ourselves, 'Will it bring me happiness?' That simple question can be

---

[101] "The top 2 percent household income in the United States is about $210,000 and up, the top 1 percent is 365,000 and up." (Wikipedia, _www.en.wikipedia.org/wiki/Household_income_in_the_United_States_, April 29, 2011) My firm goal is to be in the top 1 percent! What is yours? ___%

a powerful tool in helping us skillfully conduct all areas of our lives, not just in the decision whether to indulge in drugs or that third piece of banana cream pie. It puts a new slant on things. Approaching our daily decisions and choices with this question in mind shifts the focus from what we are denying ourselves to what we are seeking—ultimate happiness, a kind of happiness, as defined by the Dalai Lama, that is stable and persistent. We are searching for a state of happiness that remains despite life's ups and downs and normal fluctuations of mood, one that is part of the very matrix of our being. With this perspective, it's easier to make the 'right decision' because we are acting to give ourselves something, not denying or withholding something from ourselves—an attitude of moving toward rather than moving away, an attitude of embracing life rather than rejecting it. This underlying sense of moving toward happiness can have a very profound effect, it makes us more receptive, more open, to the joy of living."[6]

You have to keep trying when you fall short on a task, objective, or goal. Mistakes will happen, but at least there will be no regrets. Make an honest attempt to solve the problem and move forward with your master plan.

**Full Throttle!** Go full speed like you are racing a NASCAR stock car,[102] so you can get things finished quicker. Put the pedal to the metal to get up to full speed as quickly as possible. This is perfect for everyday jobs like taking showers, washing dishes, mowing the lawn, walking,

 shopping, and making love (just kidding). Refrain from applying the brakes. Power through tasks with <u>momentum</u> to complete the next task quickly.

❑ **AI:** _____

Wikimedia Commons, U.S. Army

---

[102] In 2011, NASCAR is getting greener by using 15 percent ethanol (E15) fuel mix that is in all three of its racing series. Go Kyle Busch (#18), go!!!

Drafting as a pair allow these stock cars to drive 20 mph faster at over 215 mph than racing against each other. Wikimedia Commons, Dave Hogg

As you progress in your transformation, complete the following **worksheets**:

- ❏ 6-Month Transformation Plan          __/__/__
- ❏ 1-Year Transformation Plan           __/__/__
- ❏ 3-Year Transformation Plan           __/__/__
- ❏ 5-Year Transformation Plan           __/__/__
- ❏ 10-Year Transformation Plan          __/__/__
- ❏ Rolling 5-Year Transformation Plan   __/__/__

The rolling transformation plan will be for fifteen, twenty years, and so on. You can also track more frequently, perhaps every year.

Stay with this process and these strategies. You should see real results in days, weeks, months, years, and in the long-term growth of your retirement plan and personal life satisfaction. Acknowledge the positive results and drive forward to the next goal. Keep challenging yourself further to pass beyond your own expectations. Continue the migration from emergency fund to debt reduction to retirement plan to business ownership to real estate ownership to paying it forward and finally to retirement!

"To 'stay the course' doesn't mean staying on the path that doesn't work. It means that you want to continue revisiting your vision, fine-tuning that vision, and taking action toward that vision. Sometimes you'll feel like you're altering course 180 degrees. You might. But, it only shows that you have been headed in the wrong direction in the first place."[7]

*"If we are facing in the right direction, all we have to do is keep on walking." ~ Buddhist Proverb*

# CHAPTER 25: CELEBRATING SUCCESS—LET THE PARTY BEGIN

*"Maturity is achieved when a person postpones immediate pleasures for long-term values." ~ Joshua L. Liebman*

Wow, how much fun was this?!?!? How does it feel to be a producer, or to at least start the transformation? What an epic journey we took together. Now we need to have a quick celebration and get ready for tremendous success. You are on the correct path to a continuous party of happiness and fulfillment. You are seeing yourself transition to contributing to your Inner Economy and the macro-economy on the producer side as an investor and employer, not as a consumer buying perishable items. Consumers will be buying your products and services. That is a reason to celebrate!

There are many opportunities to save and invest all at once. Your savings of money, energy, and time will be multiplied and shrewdly invested (**$ET = M² to INVEST**). Now there is little need for consumer wants. You will feel strong and confident in the decisions you make for you and your family's futures.

**Until We Next Meet:** Let's go further together. I look forward to meeting you at a book signing, on my nationwide speaking tour, via social media, the next time you are in San Francisco, or as your coach. Heck, I could be sitting next to you on the airplane, train, or bus, so look out for me. The first happy hour drink is on me . . . .

Visit my website to exchange new ideas, feedback, and your own success story at *www.TransformingToProducer.com*. Please share any other creative and innovative ways of a productive life and cheap tips. Let's network and become friends! Add me (darrylwortham) on Facebook, LinkedIn, MySpace, or Twitter.

❑ **AI:** _____

Many complex saving and investing strategies have been communicated here. You may need assistance to incorporate these principles and ideas into your lifestyle. For **one-on-one coaching** to quickly implement $ET = M^2$ to INVEST™ strategies, obtain my transformation consulting services. For coaching session details and to schedule an appointment, go to _www.TransformingToProducer.com/Transformation_Services_ or send an e-mail to _darrylwortham@gmail.com_.

❏ **AI:** _____

The immediate follow up to this book will be a full sized **workbook** providing additional blank list sheets and plans in a larger format, detailed instructions, numerous resources, interesting pictures, and many more references. The coaching will be synchronized with completing the workbook but not required to complete it. For additional guidance and a perfect aid, the _Transforming from Consumer to Producer in 90 Days Tutorial Workbook_ will be released November 2011.

❏ **AI:** _____

Here's to your success as a producer! Bless you and those all around you!!!

Photo by Alan Blaustein

_"Be the change you want to see in the world."_ ~ Mahatma Gandhi

# Part VI: Beyond the Speed of Light into the Future Endnotes

[1] Chris J. Snook with Chet Snook, *Wealth Matters: Abundance is Your Birthright!*, LifeSuccess Publishing, 2007, p. 60.

[2] His Holiness, the Dalai Lama and Howard C. Cutler, MD, *The Art of Happiness: A Handbook for Living*, permission of Riverhead Books, imprint of Penguin Group (USA) Inc., 1998, p. 62.

[3] Deanna Mascle, "The Secret to Successful Writing," Business Wordsmith, 2007, p. 42.

[4] Ibid.

[5] Dalai Lama and Cutler, p. 36.

[6] Ibid.

[7] Mascle, p. 43.

# PART VII – YOUR SUPPORT STRUCTURE AND RESOURCES

*"Don't just read the easy stuff. You may be entertained by it, but you will never grow from it." ~ Jim Rohn*

## Appendix A: Cited and Recommended Readings

Ashby, Muata Abhaya, *Egyptian Proverbs: Mystical Wisdom Teachings and Meditations*, Cruzian Mystic Books, 1996.

Bach, David, *Go Green, Live Rich: 50 Simple Ways to Save the Earth (and Get Rich Trying)*, Broadway Books, 2008.

Carrico, Mara, *The Wisdom of the Yoga Journal's Yoga Basics: The Essential Beginner's Guide to Yoga for a Lifetime of Health and Fitness*, Henry Holt and Company, 1997.

Covey, Stephen R., *The 7 Habits of Highly Effective People*, Simon and Schuster, 1989.

Dacyczyn, Amy, *The Complete Tightwad Gazette: Promoting Thrift as a Viable Alternative Lifestyle*, Random House, 1999.

Davidson, Jeff, *The Joy of Simple Living: Over 1,500 Simple Ways to Make Your Life Easy and Content*, Rodale Press, 1999.

Dessauer, John, *Real Estate H²O: Quenching Your Financial Thirst in a Parched Economy*, Dessauer Publishing, 2008.

Dominguez, Joe and Robin Vicki, *Your Money or Your Life: Transforming Your Relationship with Money and Achieving Financial Independence*, Penguin Books, 1993.

Farrell, Chris T., *The New Frugality: How to Consume Less, Save More, and Live Better*, Bloomsbury Press, 2010.

Fennimore, Chris, *America's Home Cooking: Easy Recipes for Thrifty Cooking*, WQED Multimedia, 2009.

Flores, Adrian, *Transforming Your Community Through Dance: 13 Steps to a Great Dance Team*, Mitchell Levy, 2009.

Gardner, Dave and Tom, *You Have More Money Than You Think*, Simon & Schuster, 1998.

Gladstar, Rosemary, *Herbs for Reducing Stress & Anxiety*, Storey Books, 1999.

Gladwell, Malcolm, *The Tipping Point: How Little Things Can Make a Big Difference*, Little, Brown and Company, 2000.

Grader, Rob, *The Cheap Bastard's Guide to New York City*, Global Pequot Press, 2008 (there are also series in Washington DC, Chicago, Boston, and San Francisco).

Graham, Benjamin, updated commentary by Jason Zweig, *The Intelligent Investor: The Definitive Book on Value Investing*, HarperCollins Publishers, 2003.

GreenZebra, *Local Savings for Sustainable Living*, San Francisco edition, 2010, at <u>*www.theGreenZebra.org*</u>.

Hamm, Trent *365 Ways to Live Cheap: Your Everyday Guide to Saving Money*, Adams Media, 2009.

His Holiness, the Dalai Lama and Cutler, Howard C., MD, *The Art of Happiness: A Handbook for Living*, permission of Riverhead Books, imprint of Penguin Group (USA) Inc., 1998.

Imus, Deirdre, *The Essential Green You!*, Simon & Schuster, 2009.

Kohler, Mark J., *Lawyers Are Liars: The truth About Protecting Our Assets!*, Life's Plan Publishing, 2007.

Kohler, Mark J., *What Your CPA Isn't Telling You: Life-changing Tax Strategies*, McGraw-Hill, 2011.

Levinson, Jay Conrad, James Dillehay, and Marcella Vonn Harting, *Guerrilla Multilevel Marketing: 100 Low-Cost Tactics for Growing Your Network and Advancing to the Top of You Pay Plan*, Warm Snow Publishers, 2008.

Mathis, Judge Greg, *Street Judge: A Novel*, Strebor Books, 2008.

Matthews, Caitlin and John, *Encyclopedia of Celtic Wisdom: A Celtic Shaman's Source Book*, Element Books, 1994.

Nissley, Julia, *How to Probate an Estate in California*, Nolo, 2008 (get the most recent edition).

O'Brien, Sally, *Lonely Planet Sydney: The bold and the beautiful*, Lonely Planet Publications, 2006.

Osho, *Osho on Zen: A Stream of Consciousness Reader*, Renaissance, 2001.

Peck, Scott M., MD, *The Road Less Traveled: A New Psychology of Love, Traditional Values and Spiritual Growth*, Simon and Schuster, 1978.

Pond, Jonathan D., *Grow Your Money! 101 Easy Tips to Plan, Save, and Invest?*, HarperCollins Publishers, 2008.

Pressman, David, *Patent It Yourself*, Nolo Press, 2009 (get the most recent edition).

Quadree, Tamir, PhD., *The Reclining Master Awaken: One Minute to Healthy Esteem*, More Heart Than Talent Publishing, 2006.

Rainbow Eagle, *The Universal Peace Shield of Truths: Ancient American Indian Peace Shield Teachings*, Rainbow Light & Company, 1998.

Ramsey, Dave, *Financial Peace: Restoring Financial Hope to You and Your Family*, Viking Adult, 2003.

Ramsey, Dave T., *The Total Money Makeover: A Proven Plan for Financial Fitness*, Thomas Nelson Publishing, 2003.

Ray, James Arthur, *Harmonic Wealth: The Secret of Attracting the Life you Want*, Hyperion Books, 2008.

Roth, J.D., *Your Money: The Missing Manual*, O'Reilly Media, Inc., 2010.

Schuffman, Stuart, *Broke-Ass Stuart's Guide to Living Cheaply in New York*, Falls Media, 2008.

Schuffman, Stuart, *Broke-Ass Stuart's Guide to Living Cheaply in San Francisco*, Falls Media, 2007.

Schwab, Charles, *Guide to Financial Independence: Practical Solutions for Busy People*, Three Rivers Press, 2004.

Schwartz, David J., PhD, *The Magic of Thinking Big: Acquire the Secrets of Success . . . Achieve Everything You've Always Wanted*, Simon & Schuster, 1987.

Schwarzenegger, Arnold with Bill Dobbins, *Encyclopedia of Modern Bodybuilding*, Simon & Schuster, 1985.

Scott-Moncrieff, Dr. Christina, *Detox: Cleanse and Recharge Your Mind, Body, and Soul*, Collins & Brown, 2001.

Shepard, Kathy, *The Recovering Drama Queen*, More Heart Than Talent Publishing, 2007.

Simmons, Russell with Chris Morrow, *Super Rich: A Guide to Having It All*, Gotham Books, 2011.

Smith, Kevin Arthur, *Quit Smoking While You're Smoking: An Easy and Practical Approach to Quitting*, Arthur Publishing, 2009.

Snook, Chris J., with Chet Snook, *Wealth Matters: Abundance is Your Birthright!*, LifeSuccess Publishing, 2007.

Steinfeld, Carol, *Liquid Gold: The Lore and Logic of Using Urine to Grow Plants*, Ecowaters Books, 2007.

Stim, Richard, *Patent, Copyright, and Trademark: An Intellectual Property Desk Reference*, Nolo Press, Tenth Edition, 2009 (get the most recent edition).

Toffler, Alvin, *Power Shift: Knowledge, Wealth, and Violence at the Edge of the 21st Century*, Bantan Books, 1990.

Vanzant, Iyanla, *One Day My Soul Just Opened Up: 40 Days and 40 Nights Toward Spiritual Strength and Personal Growth*, Simon & Schuster, 1998.

Vogel, Nadine O., as told by Cindy Brown, *Dive In: Springboard into the Profitability, Productivity, and Potential of the Special Needs Workforce*, Paramount Market Publishing, 2009.

Wade, Chad A., *Cracking the Producers Code*, More Heart Than Talent Publishing, 2007.

Wilhite, Phillip, *Surviving Chadwick*, iUniverse, 2009.

Wilson, Justin, *Homegrown Louisiana Cookin*, Macmillan, 1990.

Winget, Larry, *You're Broke Because You Want To Be: How to Stop Getting By and Start Getting Ahead*, Gotham Books, 2008.

# Appendix B: Reference Material, Publications, and Articles

Alder, Lynn, "U.S. 2009 Foreclosures Shatter Record Despite Aid", Reuter, January 14, 2010, at *www.reuters.com/article/idUSTRE60D0LZ20100114* (May 1, 2011).

Bruce, Laura, "Start Your Kids on the Roth Road," Bankrate, May 1, 2008, at *www.bankrate.com/brm/itax/news/taxguide/20060127a1.asp* (May 1, 2011).

California Public Utility Commission (PUC) and Pacific Gas & Power (PG&E), "A Step-by-Step California Guide to Smarter Energy Use", 2008.

CalRecycle, "Green Building Basics," at *www.CalRecycle.ca.gov/ GreenBuilding/Basics.htm* (May 1, 2011).

Claudette Pendleton, "How to Have an Inexpensive Economical Wedding," at *www.suite101.com/content/how-to-have-an-inexpensive-economical-wedding-a338965* (May 1, 2011).

Conley-Bittick, Autumn Conley, "Coffee and Weight Loss - Does It Really Play a Role?", Associated Content, May 31, 2006, at *www.associatedcontent.com/article/34734/coffee_and_weight_loss_does_it_really.html?cat=51* (May 1, 2011).

Conley-Bittick, Autumn, Conley, "Soda: The Candy We Drink: The Many Risks of Our Dependence on Soft Drinks," Associated Content, June 19, 2006, at *www.associatedcontent.com/article/38759/ soda_the_candy_we_drink_pg2.html?cat=5* (May 1, 2011).

Contractors State License Board, "What You Should Know Before Hiring a Contractor," California Department of Consumer Affairs, at *www.cslb.ca.gov/consumers/hireacontractor* (May 1, 2011).

Cook, Bob, "10 Affordable Ways to Get Your Sports Fix," at *www. nbcsports.msnbc.com/id/27209782* (May 1, 2011).

Delta Dental Plans Association, "Spitting into the Wind: The Facts About Dip and Chew," Oral Health, at *www.oralhealth.deltadental. com/22,DD49* (May 1, 2011).

Grover, Sami, "How to Go Green: Weddings," at *www.treehugger.com/ files/2007/04/how-to-go-green-weddings.php* (May 1, 2011).

Guina, Ryan, "College Savings Plans: 529 vs. Coverdell ESA," Cash Money Life, at *www.cashmoneylife.com/2009/03/11/college-savings-plans-529-vs-coverdell-esa* (May 1, 2011).

Hansen, Katharine, Ph.D., "Making Your Case for Telecommuting: How to Convince the Boss", Quintessential Careers, at *www. quintcareers.com/telecommuting_options.html* (May 1, 2011).

Hoffman, Matthew, MD, "YOGA: The Health Benefits of Yoga," WebMD®, at *www.webmd.com/balance/the-health-benefits-of-yoga* (May 1, 2011).

International Revenue Service (IRS), "Business Structures," at *www.irs. gov/businesses/small/article/0,,id=98359,00.html* (May 1 2011).

International Revenue Service (IRS), "Checklist for Starting a Business," at *www.irs.gov/businesses/small/article/0,,id=98810,00.html* (May 1, 2011).

International Revenue Service (IRS), "Operating a Business," at *www. irs.gov/businesses/small/article/0,,id=99930,00.html* (May 1, 2011).

International Revenue Service (IRS), "Publication 527 (2009), Residential Rental Property," at *www.irs.gov/publications/p527/index.html* (May 1, 2011).

International Revenue Service (IRS), "Real Estate (Taxes, Mortgage Interest, Points, Other Property Expenses)," at *www.irs.gov/faqs/content/0,,id=199901,00.html* (May 1, 2011).

International Revenue Service (IRS), "Rental Income and Expenses - Real Estate Tax Tips," at *www.irs.gov/businesses/small/industries/article/0,,id=98895,00.html* (May 1, 2011).

International Revenue Service (IRS), "Tax Benefits for Education, Publication 970 (2010)," 2009, at *www.IRS.gov/publications/p970* (May 11, 2011).

Janus Distributors Ltd., "Helping You Go Further," *Janus Report*, Winter 2010.

Janus Distributors Ltd., "Keeping Your Eyes On the Horizon," *Janus Report*, Summer 2009.

Lee, Jennifer B., "Cigarettes Top $9 a Pack in City," *The New York Times*, April 18, 2009 at *www.cityroom.blogs.nytimes.com/2009/04/01/cigarettes-top-9-a-pack-in-new-york-city* (May 1, 2011).

Mascle, Deanna, "The Secret to Successful Writing," Business Wordsmith, 2007, at *www.WriteAndPublishYourBook.com*.

Mayclin, Timothy J., *Tax and Business Services Newsletter*, November 2009, at *www.taxbizservices.com*.

McGraw, Dr. Phil, "An Action Plan for Eliminating Debt," at *http://www.drphil.com/articles/print/?ArticleID=233* (May 1, 2011).

New York Life Insurance Company, "Start a College Fund: 8 Strategies," at *www.newyorklife.com/cda/0,3254,11796,00.html* (May 1, 2011).

Pacific Gas and Electric, PG&E, "Home Energy-Saving Checklist and Energy Efficiency Tips," at *www.pge.com/myhome/saveenergymoney* (May 1, 2011).

Pacific Power, "Bright Ideas: A Helpful Guide to Managing Energy Use in Your Home," July 2008, at *www.pacificpower.net/brightideas* (May 1, 2011).

Pratt, Rebecca, "Wake Up to the Importance of Exercise: Working Out Improves Sleep Patterns," SparkPeople, at *www.sparkpeople. com/resource/fitness_articles.asp?id=373* (May 1, 2011).

Quit Smoking Online, "Damaged Lung Photos", at *www.quitsmokinghelp. net/smokers_lungs.html* (May 1, 2011).

Rayment, Will J., "Health Benefits of Spices and Herbs," In-Depth Info. com, at *www.indepthinfo.com/spices* (May 1, 2011).

Silver, Rebecca, "How to Go Green: Barbeques," Green Planet™, at          *www.treehugger.com/files/2007/02/how-to-go-green-barbecues.php* (May 1, 2011).

Spiegelman, Rande, "Boost Your Credit Score: Five Ways to Improve Your Credit," *Charles Schwab On Investing*, Fall 2009.

U.S. Department of Energy, Energy Efficiency and Renewable Energy, "When to Turn Off Your Lights," at *www.energysavers.gov/ your_home/lighting_daylighting/index.cfm/mytopic=12280* (May 1, 2011).

U.S. Department of Energy, Motor Challenge, "Reducing Power Factor Cost Fact Sheet," 1996.

U.S. Department of Health and Human Services Office of the Surgeon General, Tobacco Cessation—You Can Quit Smoking Now! "Treating Tobacco Use and Dependence: 2008 Update," at *www. SurgeonGeneral.gov/tobacco* (May 1, 2011).

U.S. Green Building Council, "Green Home Guide," at *www. greenhomeguide.org* (May 1, 2011).

U.S. Patent and Trademark Office, PTO, "Patent Basics," at *www.uspto. gov/patents/resources/types/index.jsp* (May 1, 2011).

U.S. Small Business Administration, "Protect Your Ideas," at *www. sba.gov/smallbusinessplanner/start/protectyourideas/serv_ copyrtfaq.html* (May 1, 2011).

Vohwinkle, Jeremy, "How to have an Affordable Wedding," at *www.financialplan.about.com/od/planningforlifestages/a/ saveonwedding.htm* (May 1, 2011).

Warren, Michelle, "Add-ons that Don't Add Value to Your New Car," Bankrate, at *www.bankrate.com/finance/auto/add-ons-that-don-t-add-value-to-your-new-car.aspx* (May 1, 2011).

Wheeland, Matthew, "Green Computing at Google", GreenBiz. com, May 2, 2007, at *www.greenbiz.com/news/2007/05/02/ green-computing-google* (May 1, 2011).

# Appendix C: List of Key Websites

Become an Ex Smoker program at *www.BecomeAnEx.org*

Benefits of volunteering at World Volunteer Web at *www. worldvolunteerweb.org*

California Department of Public Health's TobaccoFreeCA.com program at *www.tobaccofreeca.com* or 1-800-NO BUTTS

Cheap events in San Francisco at *www.sf.funcheap.com*

CNET's monthly expense calculator 1.1 (Windows) download at *download.cnet.com/Monthly-Expense-Calculator/3000-2064_4-10896867.html*

CNN's retirement planner calculator at *cgi.money.cnn.com/tools/ retirementplanner/retirementplanner.jsp*

Evite tool at *www.Evite.com*

Federal Trade Commission (FTC) fraud complaints at *www. ftccomplaintassistant.gov*

Financial Aid Finder's free college scholarship search service at *www. financialaidfinder.com/scholarships/find-a-scholarship*

Financial Aid Finder's unclaimed college scholarships at *www. financialaidfinder.com/scholarships/unclaimed-scholarships-reality*

For review of the latest security software, go to *www.cnet.com*

Free annual credit report from the federal government at *www. AnnualCreditReport.com*

Free Wi-Fi in CA at *www.wififreespot.com/ca.html*

Frugal Village's online monthly budget table at *www.frugalvillage.com/ budget.shtml*

Future income tax bracket rates at *www.moneychimp.com/features/ tax_brackets.htm*

GI Bill and other VA benefits at *www.gibill.va.gov*

Green funerals and burials by TreeHugger at *www.treehugger.com/ files/2008/03/how-to-go-green-funerals.php*

Green Living Ideas at *www.GreenLivingIdeas.com*

Greener Computing at *www.GreenerComputing.com*

Home-Based Working Moms at *www.hbwm.com*

HUD's "Avoiding Foreclosure" at *www.HUD.gov/foreclosure*

Increased social capital at *www.WalkScore.com*

Internships opportunities at *www.internshipprograms.com* and *www. internships.com*

IRS at _www.IRS.gov_ or by calling 800-TAX-FORM (800-829-3676)

Karl's Bonanza green fashion at _www.KarlasBonanza.com_

Leadership in board positions at _www.volunteermatch.org_ and _www. helpnow.org/boardlink_npos.php_

Low-flow showerhead's installation tips at _conserve.sfwater.org_

Military.com newsletter at _www.Military.com_

Military.com, *The GI Bill*, Military Advantage, at _www.military.com/ benefits/gi-bill_

National Alliance of Mental Illness at _www.nami.org_

National Do Not Call Registry at _www.donotcall.gov_ and file a complaint at _complaints.donotcall.gov/complaint/complaintcheck.aspx?panel=2_

National Fatherhood Initiative at _www.Fatherhood.org_

National Suicide Prevention Lifeline at 1-800-273-TALK (8255) or _www. SuicidePreventionLifeline.org_

Online business cards and other prints services at _www.OvernightPrints. com_ and _www.VistaPrint.com_

Online store, restaurant, and club reviews at _www.Yelp.com_

Pandora internet radio at _www.Pandora.com_

Partnership for a Drug-Free America at _www.DrugFree.org_

Price Grabber at _www.PriceGrabber.com_

Quit Smoking Online at _www.quitsmokinghelp.net_

Rent a Living Christmas Tree at _www.rentxmastree.com_

San Francisco club join guest lists at _www.sfstation.com/clubs_

San Francisco Environment Potted Christmas Tree program at _www. sfenvironment.com/greenchristmas_

Search patents at _www.uspto.gov_

Smart Shopper at _www.SmartShopperUSA.com_

Smoking and Tobacco Use facts and ways to quit by U.S. Centers for Disease Control and Prevention at _www.CDC.gov/tobacco_

Solar oven instructions, go to _www.solar-cooking-oven.com_ or _www. SolarCooking.org/plans_

Stop smoking support at _www.QuitSmokingSupport.com_ and list of ingredients at _www.quitsmokingsupport.com/ingredients.htm_

Suze Orman's monthly expense budget calculator at _www.oprah.com/article/money/personalfinance/ pkgyourmoney/20081119_expert_suzeexpense_

The Freecycle Network at _www.Freecycle.org_

The negative effect of smoking from SteadyHealth.com at _www. steadyhealth.com/about/tag/Smoking_

The Telework Coalition's at *www.telcoa.org*
The true facts about smoking at *www.TheTruth.com*
Thrift Savings Plan (TSP) at *www.TSP.gov*
U.S. Department of Agriculture, "MyPyramid Blast-Off Game to Teach Your Children about Good Nutrition," at *www.mypyramid.gov/kids/kids_game.html*
U.S. Substance Abuse & Mental Health Services Administration at *www.samhsa.gov/economy*
U.S. Small Business Administration at *www.SBA.gov*
Weather forecast websites are *www.wunderground.com*, *www.weather.com*, and *radar.weather.gov*
Yahoo Finance at *finance.yahoo.com*
Zipcar at *www.Zipcar.com*

## Hot Links

*"Risk comes from not knowing what you are doing." ~ Warren Buffet*

Considering the fluid state of the Internet, the author realizes it is risky to permanently print web links into the text of the book. However, because the information provided at these links will prove to be exceptionally  beneficial to most readers, they were included in the book. If any link does not function properly, you are encouraged to use your web browser search engine of choice to find an updated Uniform Resource Identifier (URL).

Wikimedia Commons, Steven Depolo

This book's intent is to provide accurate information. However, in a time of rapid change, it is difficult to ensure that all of the information provided is entirely accurate and up to date. Therefore, the author and publisher accept no responsibility for any inaccuracies or omissions and especially disclaim any liability, loss, or risk, personal or otherwise, incurred as a consequence, directly or indirectly, by the use and/or applications of any of the contents of this book.

# Appendix D: Shout-Outs!!!

**"Baba Booey, Baba Booey, Baba Booey!"**[103] Real warm thanks to all of these people that have provided creative ideas for this book:

| | | | | |
|---|---|---|---|---|
| Jon C | Pierre V | Krisjon S | Terri | Chavivah |
| Tracey | Sonia A | Dawn W | Ronald W | Spencer C |
| Josie P | Jean R | Brenda | Jeannie V | Di M |
| Rachel L | Marianne C | Kimmie | Alex M | Kurt M |
| Mike R | Cark M | Elvin M | Derek W | Sue K |
| Glen G | herberkids3 | Karla Z | Russ H | Damian K |
| Sally F | Donna B | Dale S-M | Jeannie V | Amy H |
| Del H | Ginny D | Jasmey L | Bina A | Tania F |
| Mark | Rolf B | texasbluesfan | John H | Clarence J |
| Carrye M | Julian L | Mark F | Tim O | Chris S |
| Rachel S | Carolyn O | David G | Ted R | Mark H |
| Matt M | Diana F | Sharon R | Isaac R | Sharon S |
| Ruba | Mike R | Bill B | Roger W | Jillian A-P |
| Tim T | Tony RG | 7th Heaven Yoga | Carol S | Jacie T |
| Steve W | Diane G | Claudia G | Cary | Jason S |
| Rick B | Matt H | Suzanne K | Anna DM | JR R |
| Anthony N | Henny L | Marguerite L | Zsuzsi | Glynis F |

# Appendix E: Suggested Products to Research

- AB Force (4 inline passive wheels) at *www.ab-force.com*
- AB Slide (4 active wheels design with resistance)
- Billy Blanks, *Tae Bo II Get Ripped*, 2001 at *www.BillyBlanks. com*.
- Bodyrev Perfect Pushup at *www.bodyrev.com*
- Denise Austin, *Power Zone Abs Workout—The Ultimate Metabolism Boosting Workout*, Volume III, Artisan Home Entertainment, Inc., 2004.

---

[103] Gary Dell'Abate's nickname as the producer on *Howard Stern Show*. Check out his awful first pitch at New York Yankees Stadium May 9, 2009: *www.youtube.com/watch?v=wfLIyT8HExY&feature=related* (May 1, 2011).

- Evert-Fresh GreenBags at *www.EvertFresh.com*
- Helmet lock at *www.theHelmetLock.com*
- Language home study program from Rosetta Stone at *www. RosettaStone.com*
- Living Arts, *Power Yoga—The Complete Workout*, GAIAM, 2000 and *Yoga Abs for Beginners*, GAIAM, 2000 at *www.gaiam.com/ category/yoga-studio/yoga-media.do*.
- Nintendo Wii *Fit* Plus at *www.wiifit.com*
- XPS100™ at *www.xediadirect.com/dwortham* (click "Energy Conservation")
- XygenAir at *www.xediadirect.com/dwortham* (click "Clean Air")
- Yoga Zone, *Power Yoga for Strength and Endurance*, 1999.

## Appendix F: Suggested Services to Research

Beth Crittenden's Home and Office Organizing Services at *www. OrganizationCoach.net*

Bonny Lin's Mandarin Chinese and Taiwanese Interpretation and Translation Services at *www.Linterpreting.com*

Carbonite's online backup service at *www.Carbonite.com*

Carrie's Medical Transcription Training and Services at *www. MedTranscription.com*

Cathy Lara and Associates German Translation Services at *www. CathyLara.com*

Karen Diggs' Nutrition and Detox Consultant Services at *www. BeNourishedsf.info*

Recurve home energy performance services at *www.recurve.com*

# Appendix G: Suggested Self-Development, Training, and Coaching Programs to Research

- Darryl Wortham's $ET = M² to INVEST™ planning and execution transformation consulting services at _www.TransformingToProducer.com/Transformation_Services_
- Del Hargis' Speech Coach at _www.DelHargis.com_ and Life Coach at _www.mgt.me_
- Erica and Jeffrey Combs' Network Marketing and Life Coaching at _www.goldenmastermind.com/webstore/personal_coaching.html_
- Golden Mastermind Seminars Breakthrough to Success at _www.goldenmastermind.com/webstore/seminar_events.html_
- Jeffrey Combs' "The Psychology of A$king" and "The Psychology of Clo$ing" CDs at _www.goldenmastermind.com/webstore/audio_cds.html_
- John Dessauer's Multi-Family Dwelling Field Training at _www.theDessauerGroup.com_
- Renatus Real Estate on-demand education and coaching program at _www.RetireSoonerThanLater.com/Education_
- Ron White's "Memory in a Month" DVD at _www.MemoryInaMonth.com_
- StartupNation's "2011 Hot List: 26 Hot Businesses to Start Right Now!" at _www.startupnation.com/hot-business_

Jeffrey Combs and Darryl at Golden Mastermind Seminars Breakthrough to Success III.

# Appendix H: Honorably Mentioned Charitable Organizations

- Adopt-a-Greyhound at *www.Adopt-A-Greyhound.org*
- Alpine Meadows Wildlife Rehab at *www. AlpineMeadowsWildlifeRehab.com*
- Alzheimer's Association at *www.alz.org*
- American Behcet's Disease Association at *www.Behcets.com* (in memory of Barbara Wortham)
- American Diabetes Association at *www.diabetes.org*
- American Heart Association at *www.AmericanHeart.org*
- American Red Cross at *www.RedCross.org*
- Amnesty International USA at *www.Amnestyusa.org*
- Arthritis Foundation at *www.Arthritis.org* (in honor of Mrs. Delores Peterson Becker)
- ASPCA at *www.aspca.org*
- Big Brothers Big Sisters at *www.BBBS.org*
- Bill and Melinda Gates Foundation at *www.GatesFoundation. org*
- Boy & Girls Clubs of America at *www.bgca.org*
- Breast Cancer Fund at *www.BreastCancerFund.org*
- Burlington Coat Factory Coat Drive Program at *www. burlingtoncoatfactory.com/content/coat-drive*
- Conservancy of Flowers at *www.conservatoryofflowers.org*
- Defenders of Wildlife at *www.defenders.org*
- Doctors without Borders at *www.DoctorsWithoutBorders.org*
- Epilepsy Foundation at *www.epilepsyfoundation.org* (in memory of Brent Wortham)
- Englishtown/Manalapan First Aid Squad at *www.emfas.org*
- Feeding American at *www.FeedingAmerica.org*
- Friends of the Urban Forest at *www.FUF.net*
- Glide Memorial Church at *www.Glide.org*
- Goodwill at *www.GoodWill.org*
- Greyhound Pets of America at *www.GreyhoundPets.org*
- Guiding Eyes for the Blind at *www.GuidingEyes.org*
- Habitat for Humanities at *www.Habitat.org*
- HandsOn Bay Area at *www.HandsOnBayArea.org*

- Homes for Our Troops at *www.HomesForOurTroops.org* (If you in the military or work for the government you can pledge through Combined Federal Campaign #12525.)
- Kyle Busch Foundation at *www.KyleBuschFoundation.org*
- Leukemia & Lymphoma Society at *www.lls.org*
- Locks of Love at *www.LocksOfLove.org*
- Make-A-Wish Foundation at *www.wish.org*
- Marine Toys for Tots Foundation at *www.ToysForTots.org*
- McCullum Youth Court at *www.YouthCourt.org*
- Meals on Wheels at *www.mowaa.org*
- MicroGiving.com at *www.MicroGiving.com*
- Muscular Dystrophy Association at *www.MDA.org*
- National Breast Cancer Foundation at *www.NationalBreastCancer.org*
- National Marrow Donor Program at *www.Marrow.org*
- National Relief Charities at *www.nrcprograms.org*
- National Society of Black Engineers at *www.NSBE.org*
- One Brick at *www.OneBrick.org*
- One Warm Coat at *www.OneWarmCoat.org*
- Operation AC at *www.OperationAC.com*
- Operation USO Care Package at *www.USO.org/OUCP*
- PBS station at *www.PBS.org*
- People for the Ethically Treatment of Animals (PETA) at *www.PETA.org* and *www.FurIsDead.com/donate.asp*
- Project Coyote at *www.ProjectCoyote.com*
- Project Healing Waters at *www.ProjectHealingWaters.org*
- Project Open Hand at *www.OpenHand.org*
- Real Options for City Kids (ROCK) at *www.rocksf.org*
- Recording for the Blind & Dyslexic at *www.rfbd.org*
- Ronald McDonald House at *www.RonaldsHouse.com*
- San Francisco Food Bank at *www.SFFoodBank.org*
- San Francisco Zoo at *www.SFZoo.org*
- Smile Train at *www.SmileTrain.org*
- Special Olympics at *www.SpecialOlympics.org*
- The Association for the Protection of Fur-Bearing Animals at *www.FurBearerDefenders.com*
- The Elephant Sanctuary in Tennessee at *www.elephants.com*
- The Giving Pledge at *www.GivingPledge.org*

- The Humane Society of the United States at *www.humanesociety.org*
- The Nature Conservancy at *www.nature.org*
- The Seeing Eye at *www.SeeingEye.org*
- The Salvation Army at *www.SalvationArmyusa.org*
- United Negro College Fund at *www.UNCF.org*
- World Food Program at *www.WFP.org*
- World Wildlife Fund at *www.WorldWildLife.org*

# Appendix I: Disclaimer

The information contained in this book is for general guidance and is not intended as legal or specific financial advice for any individual or particular transaction. It is recommended that each individual obtains their own legal advice that particularly and specifically applies to their own set of circumstances, facts, and situation. The author is not responsible or liable for any advice that is taken and applied by readers in any situation without his direct consultation and representation specific to that individual's needs. Readers are expressly advised to seek the assistance of a competent legal, accounting, or financial professional for actual transactions.

The author may have interests in certain companies. Do not use any mention of specific stocks, bonds, or mutual funds as recommendations. These are only for illustration purposes and are not to be used as specific financial advice.

The author does not condone any investment technique or strategy that requires the use of fraud, deceit, false statement, misrepresentation, concealment, conspiracy, breach of contract, tortious act, or violation of local, state, or federal common law, statutory law, or regulatory law.

Talk with your doctor before starting any new exercise routine. Readers are strongly encouraged to consult with a physician or other healthcare professional before using any information contained in this book. No book can substitute for professional care and advice. The author and publisher do not intend to engage in rendering medical or physical services. If medical problems appear or persist, the reader should consult with a qualified physician or other healthcare professional. Accordingly, the author and publisher expressly disclaim any liability, loss, damage, or injury caused by the ideas and contents in this book.

Verify that whatever you do is legal, and be sure to follow all local, state, and federal laws and codes of conduct. The author does not condone any illegal activity whatsoever.